Legal Interaction between [illegible]
Organiz[illegible]

Europa Law Publishing, Groningen 2004

Legal Interaction between Decisions of International Organizations and European Law

Nikolaos Lavranos

Europa Law Publishing is a publishing company
specializing in European Union Law.
For further information please contact Europa Law
Publishing via email: info@europalawpublishing.com
or visit our website at: www.europalawpublishing.com.

Typeset in Scala and Scala Sans, Graphic design by
G2K Designers, Groningen/Amsterdam

NUR 828; ISBN 90-76871-19-1

British Library Cataloguing-in-Publication Data
A catalogue record for this book is available from the
British Library

To my parents,
Simone & Luca

Acknowledgements

To present the complex issues of this thesis in an understandable manner, one of the important difficulties and necessities was to be selective. Similarly, many people who have contributed in one way or another to this book could not be mentioned here, although they surely deserve it. Having said that, I nevertheless would like to thank specifically the following people.

Firstly, I am deeply indebted to my supervisor Prof. Bruno de Witte for giving me the opportunity to discover the most exciting areas of law, namely European and International law. Without his patience and guidance over the years, this book would not have been finished.

Secondly, I am also deeply indebted to my second supervisor Prof. André Nollkaemper who – while joining only at a very late stage of the process of writing – substantially improved the overall text by his critical and detailed comments.

Thirdly, I am very grateful to all the members of the examining committee who were prepared to spend their precious time in reading, commenting and judging the thesis.

However, above all, I am indebted to my parents. Without their love and support, I would not have been able to study law, let alone write a Ph.D. in law. It is solely due to their life long struggle as guest workers – an euphemism for modern slaves – that I could enjoy such a relaxed life. Accordingly, by dedicating this book to them, it is hoped that their hearts are filled with happiness and the recognition that their efforts have not been completely wasted. Similarly, this book is also dedicated to my wife Simone (and her family) whose unlimited love and support over the past decade has been absolutely essential to me. The book is also dedicated to our wonderful son Luca who shows me everyday what is *really* important in life.

Finally, special thanks are due to Jan Helmholz and Wanja Welke for accepting the heavy duty of being *'paranimfen'* (supporters) during my public defence of the thesis. Moreover, I want to thank all my friends, colleagues and all other people for their support, input and stimulating discussions over the past years and thus have helped me to bring this project to a good end.

Last but not least, I want to express my gratitude to Jacqueline Lensink of Europa Law Publishing for the high quality production of this book and to Jan Major for the excellent proof reading.

Contents

CHAPTER 1 **Introduction**

1 Research question 3

2 Structure 10

3 Definitions 11

CHAPTER 2 **The Domestic Legal Status of International Treaties**

1 International treaties within domestic law 17

1.1 Germany 17

1.2 The Netherlands 19

1.3 France 21

1.4 Summary 22

2 International treaties within the European legal order 23

2.1 Various types of international treaties 23

2.1.1 Treaties concluded by the EC alone 23

2.1.2 Treaties concluded by the EU alone 24

2.1.3 Treaties concluded by the EC together with its Member States (mixed agreements) 27

2.1.4 Treaties concluded by the EU together with its Member States (mixed EU agreements) 28

2.1.5 Treaties concluded by the Member States alone 28

2.2 The jurisdiction of the ECJ over international treaties 31

2.2.1 Treaties concluded by the EC alone 32

2.2.2 Treaties concluded by the EU alone and mixed EU agreements 32

2.2.3 Treaties concluded by the EC together with its Member States (mixed agreements) 32

2.2.4 Treaties concluded by the EU Member States alone 33

2.3 The case-law of the ECJ on the direct effect of international treaties 35

2.3.1 Clear, precise and unconditional 35

2.3.2 'Supplemental' criteria 35

2.3.3 Direct effect of GATT/WTO law 36

2.3.4 Direct effect of FTAs, Co-operation and Association Agreements 41

3 Summary 44

CHAPTER 3 **The Domestic Legal Status of Decisions of International Organizations**

1 The general position of decisions of IOs within domestic law 49

1.1 Germany 49

1.2 The Netherlands 50

1.3	France	51
1.4	Summary	52
2	The general position of decisions of IOs within the European legal order	53
3	Decisions of Regional Fisheries Organizations	53
3.1	International law level	54
3.2	European law level	55
3.3	National law level	57
3.3.1	Germany	57
3.3.2	The Netherlands	58
3.3.3	France	59
3.4	Summary	60
4	EC-Turkey Association Council Decisions	61
4.1	International law level	61
4.2	European law level	62
4.3	National law level	65
4.3.1	Germany	65
4.3.2	The Netherlands	70
4.3.3	France	73
4.4	Summary	75
5	Decisions adopted by COPs/MOPs	76
5.1	International law level	77
5.1.1	General legal structure of most MEAs	77
5.1.2	COPs/MOPs: organs of IOs?	79
5.2	European law level	81
5.3	National law level	84
5.3.1	Germany	84
5.3.2	The Netherlands	87
5.3.3	France	89
5.4	Summary	92
6	Security Council Resolutions	94
6.1	International law level	94
6.2	European law level	94
6.3	National law level	100
6.3.1	Germany	100
6.3.2	The Netherlands	104
6.3.3	France	107
6.4	Summary	110
7	Decisions of the ICAO Council	111
7.1	International law level	111
7.2	European law level	114
7.3	National law level	117
7.3.1	Germany	118

7.3.2 The Netherlands 120
7.3.3 France 124
7.4 Summary 127
8 Concluding remarks 127

CHAPTER 4 **Judicial and Quasi-judicial Binding Decisions**
1 WTO dispute settlement reports 134
1.1 International law level 134
1.2 European law level 135
1.2.1 The legal status of WTO dispute settlement reports in the EC legal order 139
1.2.2 The bindingness of WTO dispute settlement reports on European Courts 142
1.2.3 Direct effect of WTO dispute settlement reports 143
1.3 National law level 148
1.3.1 Germany 148
1.3.1.1 The legal status and effect of WTO dispute settlement reports in the German legal order 148
1.3.1.2 The effects of the ECJ case-law on the legal status and effect of WTO dispute settlement reports in the German legal order 148
1.3.2 The Netherlands 155
1.3.2.1 The legal status of WTO dispute settlement reports in the Dutch legal order 155
1.3.2.2 The effects of the ECJ case-law on the legal status and effect of WTO dispute settlement reports in the Dutch legal order 157
1.3.2.3 Mixed agreement situation 158
1.3.3 France 162
1.3.3.1 The legal status and effect of WTO dispute settlement reports within the French legal order 162
1.3.3.2 The effect of the ECJ on the legal status and effect of WTO dispute settlement reports within the French legal order 163
1.3.3.3 Mixed agreement situation 164
1.4 Summary 164
2 ECHR judgments 165
2.1 International law level 167
2.1.1 The ECrtHR as an organ of an IO 167
2.1.2 The binding effect of ECrtHR judgments 168
2.2 European law level 169
2.2.1 Interaction between the ECJ and the ECrtHR 171
2.2.2 Divergent interpretations of the ECHR 174
2.3 National law level 177

2.3.1 Germany 177
2.3.2 The Netherlands 180
2.3.3 France 182
2.4 Summary 185
3 Concluding remarks 186

CHAPTER 5 **Decisions Adopted by the EU within the II. and III. Pillars**
1 The EU as an IO when acting within the II. and III. pillars 192
2 The legal effect of II. and III. pillar decisions 194
2.1 The II. pillar decisions 194
2.1.1 Common Positions 194
2.1.2 Joint Actions 198
2.1.3 The choice between Common Position and Joint Action 202
2.2 The III. pillar decisions 203
2.2.1 Common Positions 204
2.2.2 Framework Decisions 205
2.2.3 Decisions 209
2.3 Summary 210
3 The application of Community law principles (supremacy and direct effect) to II. and III. pillar decisions 211
3.1 Reasons for developing supremacy and direct effect of Community law 211
3.1.1 Direct effect 211
3.1.2 Supremacy 212
3.2 Supremacy and direct effect applicable to II. pillar decisions? 214
3.3 Supremacy and direct effect applicable to III. pillar decisions? 218
3.3.1 Institutional aspects 218
3.3.2 Substantive aspects 222
3.4 Summary 226
4 The 'EC law influenced' legal status and effect of II. and III. pillars decisions 227
4.1 The II. pillar decisions 227
4.2 The III. pillar decisions 228
5 Concluding remarks 229

CHAPTER 6 **General Conclusions**
1 International law level 233
1.1 The definition of an organ of an IO 234
1.2 Binding decisions of IOs 234
1.3 Non-consensual decision-making process within organs of IOs 235
2 European law level 236

2.1 EC legal order 237
2.1.1 Legal status and effect of decisions of IOs in the EC legal order 237
2.1.2 Communitarization of decisions of IOs through EC legislation 238
2.1.3 Communitarization of decisions of IOs through the jurisprudence of ECJ and CFI 240
2.2 EU legal order 242
3 National law level 244
3.1 Implementation of communitarized decisions of IOs through national legislation 245
3.2 Application of communitarized decisions of IOs by national courts 245
4 Conclusion and outlook 247

Bibliography 251

Table of Cases 281

Abbreviations 291

Index 295

Samenvatting 299

Curriculum Vitae 307

CHAPTER I

Introduction

1 Research question

Developments such as globalisation, economic and political interdependency, transboundary environmental problems, international organized crime, to name but a few, have changed the understanding of the role and function of public international law in general and International Organizations (IOs) in particular.[1] Nation states increasingly seek the co-operation of other states in order to find common solutions. Over the years the conclusion of international treaties has exploded to the extent that practically every policy area is now covered by international law.[2] In addition, nation states have established numerous IOs to solve common problems. One could describe this development as 'institutionalized cooperation' between sovereign nation states.[3]

As Tomuschat rightly remarks:

> '[...] the individual State forego its absolute sovereign rights when joining an IO based on majority voting. As a compensation for sovereign power lost, it gains, in particular, the right to participate in the decision-making process of the organization, as well as the certainty that the task entrusted to the IO, which it could not discharge in isolation, will be tackled in a more competent and effective way [...]'[4]

Moreover, even if the decision-making process within an IO is not based on majority but on unanimity voting, the decisions of the IO affect, in one or another way, the domestic legal order of the state from the moment they become binding. Consequently, the sovereignty of the state can be substantially limited by the law-making activities of IOs.[5] However, while the increasing impact of public international law, more specifically of decisions of IOs, on the national legal system is irrefutable, it must at the same time be emphasized that it is the national legal system of each state that determines on which conditions sources of public international law interact with the domestic legal system. Hence, in order to be fully effective, decisions of IOs depend to a large extent on their proper implementation on the national law level. Thus, an interaction between the international and national law level takes place whereby decisions of IOs impose certain obligations on the states, while the individual state determines how it implements them. This type of interaction between decisions of IOs and national law is referred here as the *classic legal situation*.

---

1 See: Schreuer (1993); Tietje (1999).

2 Buergenthal (1992) at 313.

3 See generally: Uerpmann (2001); Ruffert (2000); Delbrück (2002).

4 Tomuschat (1993) at 328.

5 See generally: Stein (2001); Delbrück (2002).

Most of the constitutions of the EU Member States are simply silent, or at the very best vague, concerning the legal effect of decisions of IOs. One can distinguish five groups of constitutions.[6] The first group comprises states that do not have a written constitution and thus no provisions regarding IOs or the legal effect of their decisions exist (United Kingdom). The second group refers to states that mention only international obligations (Finland) or international treaties in their constitutions (Ireland and Italy) without specifying their legal status. The third group encompasses constitutions that mention in very general terms the possibility of participating in IOs, while remaining silent on the internal legal status of decisions of IOs. This is the case in the constitutions of Germany, Austria, Belgium, Luxembourg, Denmark, Spain and Sweden. The fourth group mentions the legal status of international treaties but is silent on the status of decisions of IOs, as is the case in France and Greece. The fifth group, composed of the Netherlands and Portugal, contains constitutions that explicitly deal with both the status of international treaties and of decisions of IOs. Thus, the majority of the EU Member States' constitutions do not explicitly deal with the question of how binding decisions of IOs should be treated in their domestic legal order, despite the fact that all nation states have to deal in one way or another with the increasing flux of decisions of IOs.

However, for the EU Member States, the classic relationship between national law and law of IOs is modified since EU membership has added a new distinct layer of law between the international and national legal orders, thereby affecting the classic legal situation.[7] The main reason for this is the fact that the EU has over time obtained extensive competences to legislate in many policy areas that have created parallel external competences.[8] Accordingly, the EU has become a member of many IOs – either alone or beside its Member States – which have the capacity to adopt binding decisions. Hence, in many cases the EU is obliged to implement those decisions of IOs – either fully or to the extent covered by its competence.[9] In addition, by virtue of its internal competences to legislate in certain policy areas, the EU sometimes implements binding decisions of IOs even without being a member of that IO when some or all EU Member States are members of that IO.

As the case-law of the European Court of Justice (ECJ) indicates, international treaties which have been concluded by the EC are an integral part of the Community legal order from the moment they enter into force.[10] The same applies to decisions of organs IOs that have been established by treaties that

---

6 See: Martin Martinez (1996); Roucounas (1996).

7 See for an excellent analysis of this point: Bethlehem (1998).

8 Case 22/70 *AETR* [1971] ECR 263.

9 See: Sack (2001).

10 Case 181/73 *Haegeman* [1974] ECR 449; Case 104/81 *Kupferberg* [1982] ECR 3641.

have been concluded by the EC.[11] In this way, from the point of view of the EU Member States, the decisions of IOs are partially transformed from being a source of public international law into Community law measures in as far as they become an integral part of EC law. Consequently, EU membership results in a modification of the legal nature of binding decisions of IOs by attaching Community law characteristics such as supremacy over all national law and possible direct effect to them – features that they previously did not necessarily possess. In other words, decisions of IOs are partially 'communitarized' from the moment they become legally binding on the EC and thereby enter the Community legal order. Thus, it is no longer exclusively the EU Member States' national legal systems that determine how the decisions of IOs are implemented and which legal rank they have in their domestic legal order, but rather it is the European legal order which supersedes and thus replaces this function of the national legal orders. Accordingly, the previously existing classic legal situation is modified into an *'EC law transformed' legal relationship* 'law of IOs–European law–national law'.

A different but, to a certain extent, comparable development can be observed in the case of the EU acting within the II. and III. pillars (Common Foreign and Security Policy and Justice and Home Affairs) as an IO vis-à-vis its Member States. At first sight the relationship between the EU and its Member States in the II. and III. pillars appears to be a classic one (EU law–national law). The EU adopts binding decisions that impose legal obligations on the EU Member States, while, to a large extent, leaving it to them in which manner they implement those decisions. However, due to the close legal and functional relationship between, on the one hand, the I. Pillar and, on the other hand, the II. and III. pillars, Community law characteristics of the I. pillar (supremacy and possible direct effect) can have a significant influence also in the II. and III. pillars. Accordingly, it is conceivable that the classic legal situation is influenced by Community law features such as supremacy and possible direct effect that can modify the classic legal situation into an 'EC law influenced EU law–national law' legal situation that is to a certain extent comparable to the 'EC law transformed' legal situation. A good example of this is the implementation of UN Security Council Resolutions that first require an EU act and then an EC act before they are implemented in the domestic legal order of the EU Member States.[12]

The influence of European law on the legal status and effect of decisions of IOs can be explained by using the following metaphor. One can consider the classic legal relationship as an electric circuit in which decisions of IOs have a current of 12 Volt, while a transformer at the national law level determines with which voltage the current enters the domestic circuit. The voltage is determined

---

11 Opinion AG Alber in Case C-93/02 P *Biret* of 15.5.2003; Case C-192/89 *Sevince* [1990] ECR I-3461.

12 See Chapter 3 on Security Council Resolutions.

by the respective constitutional system of each state, i.e. the voltage can range from 110 Volt for more monistic systems to 1,5 Volt for more dualist systems.

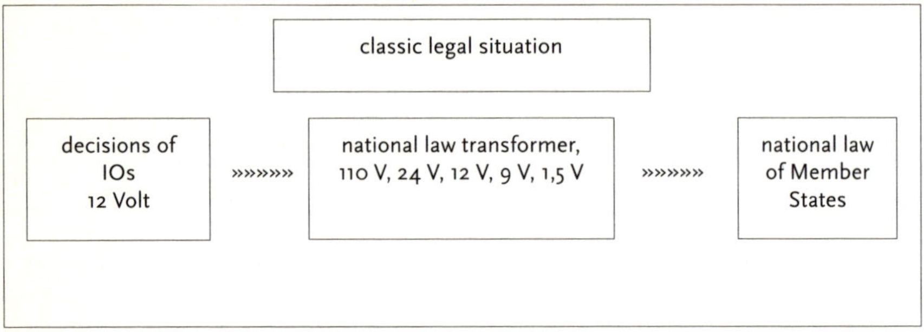

This classic legal relationship is modified through the 'EC law transformer' that is placed between the decisions of IOs and national law. Due to the Community law features of supremacy and possible direct effect, the current of 12 Volt of decisions of IOs is transformed into a current of 220 Volt, while at the same time the national law transformer has lost its function – at least as far as decisions of IOs are concerned that fall within the competence of the EC.

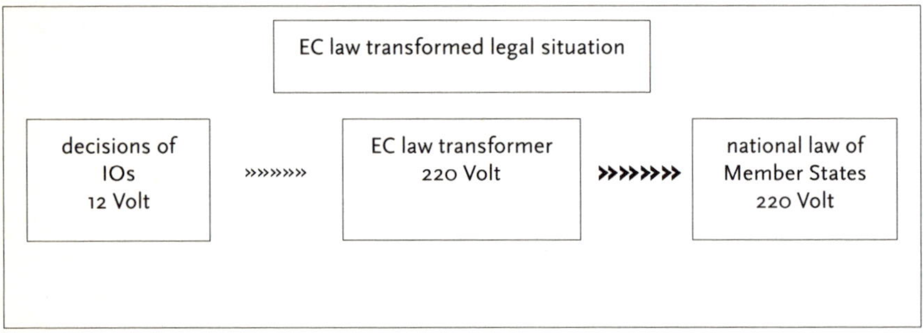

Finally, as regards the 'EC law influenced EU law–national law' legal relationship concerning II. and III. pillar decisions, the above graphic is modified as EC law is merely influencing but not transforming the legal status and effect of II. and III. pillar decisions. Nevertheless, this could still result into an amplification of the legal status and effect of II. and III. pillar decisions in particular through the impact of supremacy.

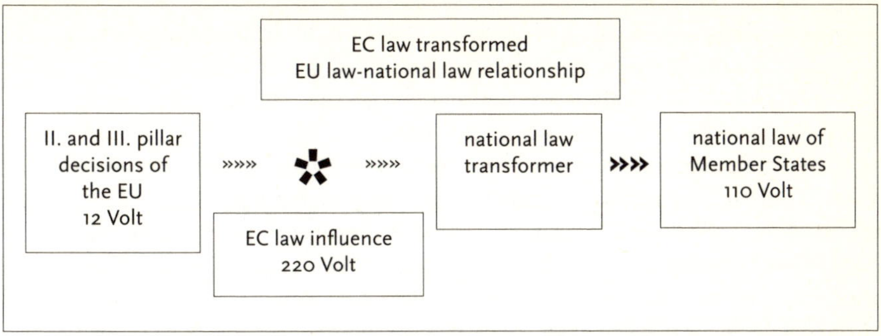

Hence, the central research question of this contribution is to analyse how the influence of Community law affects the legal status and application of binding decisions of IOs in selected EU Member States. In other words, whether and to what extent the transformation of the classic legal situation into the 'EC law transformed' legal situation can be traced in the legal practice of the selected EU Member States.

For the purpose of defining the scope of this research more closely, it seems helpful to shortly review the existing literature on this subject.

Despite the proliferation of IOs with decision-making powers,[13] so far, little attention has been paid to their legal status and effect in the domestic legal order of states.[14]

General textbooks on public international law restrict themselves to recognizing that indeed a few IOs exist that can adopt binding decisions and mention a few examples. For example, Brownlie spends one paragraph on the law-making power of IOs. He refers in particular to the EC, the World Health Assembly of WHO and the Council of the ICAO.[15] Shaw discusses the question whether and to what extent IOs have the competence to act bindingly. Referring to the ICJ Reparation case, he concludes that IOs can act even on the basis of implied powers to fulfil their tasks.[16] Hence, Brownlie and Shaw at least recognize the existence of decisions of IOs without, however, discussing their legal status and effect in the international or domestic legal orders. Seidl-Hohenveldern/Stein discusses the consequences of decisions adopted by IOs within the context of sovereignty and democratic control. In particular, they fear that binding decisions adopted on the basis of majority voting procedures undermine the possibilities of the national parliaments exerting any democratic control.[17] In this context, they refer to the EC as one of the most extreme

[13] See the contributions in: Blokker/Schermers (2001).

[14] See for an early attempt to shed light on various issues concerning the activities of IOs the contributions in: Schätzel/Schlochauer (1956).

[15] Brownlie (4th ed., 1990), at 700-701. It should be noted that in the 5th edition the paragraph on law-making powers of IOs has been deleted.

[16] Shaw (1997) at 916-917.

[17] Seidl-Hohenveldern/Stein (2000) at 96-97.

examples of far-reaching majority voting decisions. Thus, the general textbooks on public international law only mention the existence of a few IOs having the power to adopt binding decisions without discussing the classic legal interaction between decisions of IOs and national law.

Within the more specialized literature on IOs, *'International Institutional Law'* by Schermers/Blokker is probably the most comprehensive study on the institutional aspects of IOs. It mentions several examples of IOs having the competence to adopt binding decisions, such as the Security Council, the OAS, the WEU, NATO, OEEC/OECD, UPU and the EC.[18] Also, Ameransinghe's *'Principles of the institutional law of International Organizations'* discusses a number of examples of IOs, such as the Security Council under Chapter VII, WHO, WMO, ICAO Council, IMF and the UN General Assembly in certain limited cases.[19] In their book *'Das Recht der Internationalen Organisationen'*, Seidl-Hohenveldern/Loibl start their analysis by accepting that IOs can, for the purpose of fulfilling their tasks, adopt decisions that affect the domestic legal order of the member states. As regards binding decisions of IOs, they refer to ICAO recommendations with opting-out possibility, OEEC/OECD decisions and secondary Community law decisions.[20] In addition, Tammes and Sørensen should be mentioned as they recognized decisions of IOs as a special source of international law.[21] However, none of these sources specifically discuss the interaction between decisions of IOs and the national legal order.

Schreuer's book *'Decisions of International Institutions before domestic courts'* particularly deals with the interaction of decisions of IOs and national law.[22] Schreuer starts his analysis by distinguishing between non-binding recommendations and binding prescriptions. Prescriptions are roughly categorized in three different types: (i) amendments to treaties, (ii) official interpretations of treaties and (iii) regulations issued in addition to treaties.[23] Under the heading 'Regulations', Schreuer refers to several examples such as regulations adopted by international river commissions, Annexes adopted by the ICAO Council, decisions adopted by the WHO and regional organizations such as the OECD Council and, as the most far reaching example, the decisions and regulations adopted within Community law.[24] On that basis, he examines how domestic courts deal with various international decisions. Since, as mentioned above, the respective national legal systems of each state determine how to deal with international law sources, the domestic courts have to work within that frame-

---

18 Schermers/Blokker (2004) at 824-832.

19 Ameransinghe (1996) at 200-203.

20 Seidl-Hohenveldern/Loibl (2000) at 229-244.

21 Tammes (1958); Sørensen (1983).

22 Schreuer (1981).

23 *Ibid.*, at 65.

24 *Ibid.*, at 70-73.

work. Consequently, Schreuer describes the many existing facets of monist, dualist and in-between domestic legal systems. Essentially, he comes to the conclusion that domestic courts generally try to give as much as possible effect to the decisions of IOs within the framework of their respective constitutional systems. However, Schreuer's book is confined to the examination of the classic legal interaction between decisions of IOs and domestic courts without dealing with the possible effects of EU membership on the implementation of decisions of IOs.

As far as I am aware, Bethlehem is the only author who discusses in a conceptual way the interaction between decisions of IOs, European law and domestic law of EU Member States.[25] In a recent contribution, Bethlehem develops this concept by discussing the implementation of UN Security Council Resolutions by the EU and its Member States.[26]

Bethlehem starts his analysis with a description of the usual dichotomy of monism and dualism and the different methods applied to implement various sources of public international law into the domestic legal order. He then remarks:

> 'Intruding into this arena and debate more recently is European Community law. With its doctrines of direct effect and the supremacy of Community law over national law, Community law has, at one level, fundamentally reconceived the relationship between national law and "inter"-national law, at least for the Member States of the EC. At another level, interposing itself, in many areas, between municipal and traditional international law, Community law has become a conduit for the incorporation and application of international law in the municipal sphere. At yet another level, Community law is in the process of fundamentally reshaping the traditional boundaries of state competence with the result that, for the Member States of the EC, the traditional interaction between international law and municipal law at the level of policy formulation has been caught up in the often bewildering dynamic of competence, that of the Community versus that of the Member States.'[27]

On that basis, he describes the dynamic development of Community law, noting in particular that:

> 'The thesis of Community law as process, which is not in itself particularly novel, is, in the view of the present writer, essential to an appreciation of the evolving relationship not only between international law and Community law, on the one hand, and Community law and national law, on the other, but also between inter-

[25] Bethlehem (1998).

[26] Bethlehem (2001).

[27] Bethlehem (1998) at 172.

> national law and municipal law, to the extent that the evolutionary character of the Community legal order, often standing between international law and municipal law, has also influenced that wider relationship. Most important perhaps is that, over time, with the accretion of treaty provisions, secondary legislation and case law, the Community legal order has given rise to a fundamental alteration in the traditional boundaries of state competence and, in consequence, in the relations between the Member States, and between the Member States and the Community, when seen from the perspective of international law.'[28]

After having discussed in particular the example of the implementation of UN Security Council sanctions, Bethlehem concludes:

> 'Just as a web, or net, is made up of numerous strands criss-crossing at various points while, at the same time, going in different directions, so is the relationship between international law, Community law and national law; interacting constantly even though the focus may be slightly different.'[29]

Bethlehem emphasizes the point that the legal and political interaction of the EU Member States on the international law level is increasingly influenced by the EU and the specific characteristics of the European legal order. Thus, the contribution of Bethlehem undoubtedly must be recognized as path breaking in the sense that he exposed the existence and fundamental importance of European law for the interaction between the three legal orders.

The research question of this study is to assess the impact of Community law on the transformation of the legal status and effect of decisions of IOs in the domestic legal orders of the selected EU Member States.

2 Structure

The structure of the study is as follows. First, due to the fact that practically all IOs are established by an international treaty, the decisions of the IOs are adopted on the basis of that founding treaty. Consequently, the decisions of IOs are closely linked to their founding treaties. Indeed, as will be discussed below, the close relationship between international agreements and decisions of IOs is also reflected by their almost similar treatment by the constitutions and courts of the selected EU Member States. For that reason, in Chapter 2, the legal status of international treaties in the domestic legal order of the selected EU Member States as well as in the European legal order will be analysed before examining the main research question.

---

[28] *Ibid.*, at 181.

[29] *Ibid.*, at 195.

Second, since it is impossible to analyse the legal effect of all relevant IOs and their decisions, a selection of a number of IOs had to be made. This selection represents a variety in terms of membership (either the EC is alone member, or the EC and its Member States are both members or only the Member States are members) as well as in terms of competence, i.e. exclusive competence of the EC, concurrent competence of the EC and the Member States and exclusive competence of the Member States. In addition, the selection of the various IOs covers many different subject matters. In this way, it is possible to cover a broad range of different decisions of IOs that allows for the analysis of various facets of the legal issues involved.

Accordingly, the first example in Chapter 3 (decisions of regional fisheries organizations) covers a subject matter that falls within the exclusive competence of the EC and the EC is a lone member in the various fisheries organizations. The following two examples in Chapter 3 (decisions of the Association Council EC-Turkey and decisions adopted within Conferences or Meetings of Parties (COPs/MOPs) established by Multilateral Environmental Agreements (MEAs) cover organs of IOs to which the EC and its Member States are members. The next two examples in Chapter 3 (Security Council Decisions and ICAO Decisions) cover IOs to which the EC is not a member but nevertheless implements many of their binding decisions. Chapter 4 covers WTO dispute settlement reports as quasi-judicial decisions and judgments of the European Court of Human Rights (ECrtHR) as judicial decisions. Chapter 5 focuses specifically on the decisions adopted by the EU within the II. and III. pillar policy areas and their implementation by the EU Member States. Finally, Chapter 6 presents the main conclusions of this study.

3 Definitions

The research question is tackled on the basis of the following definitions and concepts.

As a starting point for the definition of the term 'International Organization', reference is made to the definition proposed by Schermers/Blokker:

> 'forms of co-operation founded on an international agreement usually creating a new legal person having at least one organ with a will of its own, established under international law'.[30]

A broader definition of the term 'International Organization' has been recently proposed by Special Rapporteur Gaja in his First Report on Responsibility of International Organizations. His definition reads as follows:

---

30 Schermers/Blokker (2004) at 26.

> 'For the purposes of the present draft articles, the term "international organization" refers to an organization which includes States among its members insofar as it exercises in its own capacity certain governmental functions.'[31]

This definition is somewhat different insofar as it explicitly recognizes the fact that other subjects of public international law such as International Organization can also be members of an IO. This refers, for instance, to the EC which is a member of a many IOs. Moreover, the term 'certain governmental functions' covers 'certain normative, executive or judicial functions' which explicitly recognizes the existing variety of governmental functions that are exercized by the various IOs.[32] Besides, this definition does not explicitly require that the IO is established by an international agreement. That reflects the situation of some IOs which have not been formally established by an international treaty but nevertheless are accepted to be an IO and operate as such.

However, the International Law Commission (ILC) did not fully adopt the definition proposed by Gaja. The text of the draft articles on responsibility of International Organizations provisionally adopted so far by the ILC reads as follows:

> 'For the purposes of the present draft articles, the term "international organization" refers to an organization established by a treaty or other instrument governed by international law and possessing its own international legal personality. International organizations may include as members, in addition to States, other entities.'[33]

The definition of the ILC appears to be a combination of the definitions of Schemers/Blokker and Gaja. In order to emphasize that only organizations governed by public international law are covered by this draft article, the ILC adds the requirement that the IO is established by a treaty or other instrument of international law. By including the term 'other instruments' , the ILC indicates that a treaty is not necessarily required for the establishment of an IO, but that also other instruments such as Resolutions by the UN General Assembly are sufficient.[34] Besides, the ILC added the requirement of international legal personality in its definition which is neither included in the definition of Schermers/Blokker nor in the one of Gaja. With the inclusion of this requirement, the ILC wishes to underline the point that the legal personality of the IO needs to be distinct from that of its member states in order to give rise to the international responsibility of the IO.[35] However, the ILC emphasizes that it

---

[31] Gaja (2003) at 18.

[32] *Ibid.*, at 15.

[33] Reports of the ILC, 55th session (A/58/10) (2003) at 33.

[34] *Ibid.*, at 40.

[35] *Ibid.*, at 43.

does not require that the legal personality is explicitly stated in the instrument that establishes the IO but rather adopts the more liberal view which accepts the existence of a legal personality by virtue of the implied powers theory.[36]

For the purpose of this research the term 'International Organization' is understood as encompassing forms of co-operation founded on an international agreement or other instrument governed by public international law creating at least one organ which exercizes in its own capacity governmental functions and which may include other entities than states. Hence, only Inter-Governmental Organizations (IGOs) that are established by states and other entities under public international law will be examined, thereby excluding other forms of international organizations such as non-governmental organizations (NGOs) and multi-national corporations.

Decisions of IOs can be divided into several categories. In the first place, a distinction can be made between decisions concerning internal rules or decisions intended to have external effect, that is, either addressed to the member states or other subjects of public international law. Although a clear-cut distinction is not always possible,[37] in this contribution only decisions intended to have external effect will be examined. In the second place, decisions can be distinguished between legally binding and non-binding ones. The terminology used by the various IOs for their decisions is not consistent, and therefore the title assigned to a decision does not necessarily correspond to its legal effect. Accordingly, the binding effect of the specific decision is determined by the text of the treaty establishing the IO and/or the text of the decision itself.[38]

The term 'decision of an IO' is understood as referring to a law-making decision which is binding on its addressees and which lays down general and abstractly formulated rules of conduct.[39] The term 'decision of an IO' used in this research also encompasses final and binding decisions of (quasi)judicial bodies and courts resolving a specific dispute. While there are differences between executive and judicial and quasi-judicial decisions, they are, regarding the 'EC law transformed' legal situation, to a large extent comparable with each other and thus included in this research. Moreover, it should be noted that there is also a difference with regard to the mode of adoption of binding decisions in the various organs of IOs. This study encompasses both decisions that are adopted on the basis of consensus and some sort of majority voting, i.e. on a non-consensual basis.

Hence, the term 'decision of an IO' is thus defined as a binding and final decision of the competent organ established by the founding treaty imposing

---

36 *Ibid.*, at 41-42.

37 Schermers/Blokker (2004) at 754.

38 See: Skubiszewski (1968) at 509.

39 *Ibid.*

legal obligations either on all or most members or on the members involved in a specific dispute.

Finally, several disclaimers must be made. As to the selection of the EU Member States, Germany, the Netherlands and France were selected because they differ in the treatment of international sources in their respective domestic legal orders and also because sufficient resources were available. As to the selected case-law, it was not possible to examine the complete jurisprudence in all three selected EU Member States as regards all selected IOs. However, an attempt has been made to collect and analyse the leading cases – very often rendered by the highest courts – concerning the respective issues. Accordingly, the case-law covered in this research reflects – as much as possible – the general approach of the courts regarding the decisions of IOs covered in this book. Finally, it must be emphasized that this research does not cover the issues of parliamentary and judicial control of decisions of IOs, but rather confines itself in analyzing the legal interaction between decisions of IOs, European law and domestic law of the selected EU Member States.

CHAPTER 2

The Domestic Legal Status of International Treaties

Decisions of IOs as defined in this book emanate from the competent organs that usually are established by a founding treaty. The contracting parties which ratify the founding treaty accept in principle all future binding decisions of the competent organ – without being able to fully anticipate at the moment of ratification the contents and legal effects of those decisions. One of the main differences between the founding treaty and the binding decision is that binding decisions of the organs do not require ratification by the member state. In fact, in some cases, the member state has to accept a binding decision even against its will. Since the organs that adopt the decisions are established by founding treaties, a close legal relationship between decisions of IOs and their founding treaties exists. This relationship justifies the presumption that the domestic legal status of decisions of IOs is to a large extent comparable to the domestic status of international treaties. In this chapter, the legal status of international treaties within the domestic legal orders of the selected EU Member States and the European legal order will be examined.

1 International treaties within domestic law

In this section the legal status of international treaties is examined in the domestic legal orders of Germany, the Netherlands and France. The focus will be on three issues, namely: the legal rank of international treaties in the domestic legal order, their possible supremacy and their possible direct effect.

1.1 Germany

Article 59 (2) GG provides that:

> 'Treaties which regulate the political relations of the Federation or relate to matters of federal legislation require the consent or participation, in the form of a federal statute, of the bodies competent in any specific case for such federal legislation. As regards administrative agreements, the provisions concerning the federal administration apply mutatis mutandis.'[1]

---

1 Original German text:
Art. 59
(2) Verträge, welche die politischen Beziehungen des Bundes regeln oder sich auf Gegenstände der Bundesgesetzgebung beziehen, bedürfen der Zustimmung oder der Mitwirkung der jeweils für die Bundesgesetzgebung zuständigen Körperschaften in der Form eines Bundesgesetzes.
Für Verwaltungsabkommen gelten die Vorschriften über die Bundesverwaltung entsprechend.

This provision simply states that (most) international agreements must first be transposed into the domestic legal order through a federal statute before they become applicable in Germany.[2] Since the international treaty is directly linked with the transformation act, the legal status of the treaty is equalized with the legal status of the transformation act, which means that international treaties have the same legal status as federal laws, i.e. below the *Grundgesetz* but equal to other federal statutes (*Doppelfunktion des Vertragsgesetzes*).[3] International treaties can be superseded by a subsequent federal law on the basis of the *lex posterior* rule or by provisions of the *Grundgesetz*. Hence, international treaties neither enjoy supremacy over the German constitution nor over other federal statutes. Moreover, since only the transformation statute and not the international treaty itself is applied in Germany, the issue of direct effect of international treaties does not arise.

This situation must be seen in the light of the general jurisprudence of the *Bundesverfassungsgericht* (BVerfG) concerning the legal status of international treaties within the *Grundgesetz*. The *BVerfG* concluded on the basis of the preamble of the *Grundgesetz* and Article 24 GG which allows for the transfer of powers to IOs, that the *Grundgesetz* anticipates the active participation of Germany in IOs (principle of *'Völkerrechtsfreundlichkeit'*).[4] It considers the principle of *'Völkerrechtsfreundlichkeit'* to be a central approach of the *Grundgesetz*,[5] which forms a guideline for the interpretation of the provisions of the *Grundgesetz*.[6]

More specifically, the *BVerfG* derived from that principle the concept of *'völkerrechtsfreundliche Auslegung'*, which means that conflicts between international law and domestic law must be avoided – as far as possible – by interpreting domestic law in the light of international law in order to prevent a violation of German international obligations.[7] This method of interpretation applies to general principles of public international law[8] as well as to provisions of international treaties.[9]

2 See for details: BVerfGE 77, 170 (210); Von Münch/Kunig (2000) Art. 59, no. 34.

3 Geiger (2002) at 170-177; Frowein (1987) at 67.

4 BVerfGE 58, 1 (41).

5 BVerfGE 73, 339 (386); Mosler (1992) at 603 ff.

6 See: Geiger (2002) at 190.

7 BVerfGE 58, 1 (34): 'Im Rahmen seiner Gerichtsbarkeit hat das BVerfG dabei allerdings in besonderem Maße darauf zu achten, daß Verletzungen des Völkerrechts, die in der fehlerhaften Anwendung oder Nichtbeachtung völkerrechtlicher Normen durch deutsche Gerichte liegen und eine völkerrechtliche Verantwortlichkeit der BRD begründen könnten, *nach Möglichkeit* verhindert oder beseitigt werden.' (emphasis added); reaffirmed in BVerfGE 59, 63 (89); see also: Steinberger (1988); Frowein/Oellers-Frahm (1996) at 85.

8 See regarding general principles of public international law: BVerfGE 75, 1 (18 f.).

9 See regarding provisions of international treaties: BVerfG 74, 358 (370).

Despite this conflict-avoiding approach, international treaties could still be superseded by a subsequent federal statute according to the principle of *lex posterior*. But the *BVerfG* has limited the application of the *lex posterior* rule by arguing that it must be assumed that the German legislature does not intend to violate international norms by issuing a subsequent conflicting law – except if the legislature explicitly stated that it indeed intends to do so.[10] Therefore, one can characterize the general approach of the *BVerfG* in the sense that German courts are under an obligation to interpret German domestic laws as far as possible in a way that avoids legal conflicts with international norms.[11]

Finally, in the context of the legal status of international law within the German legal order, it should also be noted that, during the ratification process of the Treaty of Maastricht, the *Grundgesetz* was amended by the addition of a completely new provision (Article 23 GG) dealing specifically with the domestic legal status of the EC/EU Treaties.[12] Hence, the *Grundgesetz* contains an explicit distinction between international law and European law and also applies different rules to them, thereby accepting the special characteristics of European law.

1.2 The Netherlands

It is generally assumed that since the revision of the *Grondwet* in 1953, international treaties are internally applicable.[13] Articles 93, 94 Gw. of the Dutch *Grondwet* state that international treaties and decisions of IOs which are binding on anyone enjoy primacy over conflicting national laws – including constitutional law – and can have direct effect if certain conditions are fulfilled.[14]

Article 93

'Provisions of treaties and of resolutions by international institutions which may be binding on all persons by virtue of their contents shall become binding after they have been published.'[15]

---

10 BVerfGE 74, 358 (370): 'Auch Gesetze - hier die Strafprozeßordnung - sind im Einklang mit den völkerrechtlichen Verpflichtungen der BRD auszulegen und anzuwenden, selbst wenn sie zeitlich später erlassen worden sind als ein geltender völkerrechtlicher Vertrag; denn es ist nicht anzunehmen, daß der Gesetzgeber, sofern er dies nicht klar bekundet hat, von völkerrechtlichen Verpflichtungen der BRD abweichen oder die Verletzung solcher Verpflichtungen ermöglichen will.'

11 See for an overview of the case-law of the Federal Admininistrative Court on international agreements: Rojahn, (2000).

12 See: Scholz (1996) Art. 23, no. 3; Everling (1993); Classen (1993).

13 See for details: Brouwer (1992) at 145-149, 158, 268.

14 Brölmann/Vierdag (1996) at 448; Vlemminx/Boekhorst (2000) at 465. See for an extensive analysis of the development of the Dutch constitution regarding international treaties: Brouwer (1992); Schermers (1987).

Article 93 Gw. explicitly states that provisions of international treaties are legally binding on individuals if their content is suitable for it.[16] The *Hoge Raad* considers a provision of an international treaty as 'binding on anyone' if it is unconditional, precise and needs no further implementing acts.[17] In practice, 'binding on anyone' is understood as meaning direct applicability.[18]

Article 94

'Statutory regulations in force within the Kingdom shall not be applicable if such application is in conflict with provisions of treaties that are binding on all persons or of decisions of international organizations.'[19]

Article 94 Gw. governs the legal rank of international treaties and decisions of international organizations within the Dutch legal order. This provision pronounces the primacy of international treaties and decisions of international organizations over statutes in case of conflict between the two.[20] This primacy applies to all levels of domestic law – including the *Grondwet*.[21]

While Articles 93, 94 Gw. contain the conditions for the supremacy and direct effect of international treaties and decisions of IOs, it is the domestic courts which determine whether a provision of an international treaty or decision of an IO fulfils the required conditions, i.e. whether the provision is clear, sufficiently precise and intended to give rights to individuals, in order to be directly applicable.[22] Yet, even though Article 94 Gw. seems to predetermine the legal consequences of a directly applicable provision of international treaties/decisions of international organizations, i.e. that in case of conflicts with national law the international treaty or decision of an IO prevails, the courts do not always set aside the national legislation in question.[23] Before the courts

---

[15] Original Dutch text:

Art. 93

Bepalingen van verdragen en van besluiten van volkenrechtlijke organisaties, die naar haar inhoud een ieder verbinden, hebben verbindende kracht nadat zij zijn bekendgemaakt.

[16] Brölmann/Vierdag (1996) at 444.

[17] See e.g.: Hoge Raad (Harmonisatiewet), judgment of 14.4.1989, AB 1989, 207; Vierdag (1995) at 118-123.

[18] Van Bijsterveld (1992) at 866-872.

[19] Original Dutch text:

Art. 94

Binnen het Koninkrijk geldende wettelijke voorschriften vinden geen toepassing, indien deze toepassing niet verenigbaar is met een ieder verbindende bepalingen van verdragen en van besluiten van volkenrechtelijke organisaties.

[20] Vierdag (1995) at 124.

[21] Kortmann (1997) at 168; Brölmann/Vierdag (1996) at 448; Schermers (1987) at 112-114.

[22] See for some examples: Besselink (1995) at 44-46; Vierdag (1995) at 97; Kortmann (1997) at 166.

[23] See: Besselink (1995) at 46-47; Brouwer (1992) at 275-278.

take this 'serious' step to disregard national laws and thus side step a decision of the legislature, they will try to interpret the national law as far as possible in conformity with the international treaty/decision of an IO.[24] However, if the conflict between national law and the provision of an international treaty/ decision of an IO is so serious that it cannot be resolved by way of interpretation, Dutch courts will have to set aside the conflicting national law.[25] However, Dutch courts are cautious of doing so if that leads to a gap in the legal order. In such a situation, courts prefer not to take up the role of the legislature but rather recommend to the legislature that it take the necessary legal measures in order to solve the legal conflict.[26]

1.3 France

In the French legal order, Article 55 of the *Constitution Française* (CF) of 1958 is the central provision concerning international treaties.[27]

Article 55

'Treaties or agreements duly ratified or approved shall, upon publication, prevail over Acts of Parliament, subject, in regard to each agreement or treaty, to its application by the other party.'[28]

Article 55 CF explicitly determines the legal rank of treaties within the French legal order, i.e. international treaties prevail over acts of Parliament. Nevertheless, the discussion on the legal status of international treaties within the French legal order has been long and intense, marked in particular by a divergent case-law between the *Conseil d'Etat* and the *Cour de Cassation*.[29] In a number of recent decisions of principle adopted by both courts in full plenary sessions, a process

---

[24] The Hoge Raad stated in the judgment of 16.11.1990, NJ 1991, 475, that Dutch judges are obliged if possible to interpret Dutch law in such a way as to ensure that the Netherlands fulfils its international obligations; see also: Heringa (1993) at 172-176.

[25] Kortmann (1997) at 168.

[26] Heringa (1994) at 860-861.

[27] See generally: Kronenberger (2000); Gundel (1999); Richards (2000); Bell/Boyron/Whittaker (1998); Decaux/Eisemann/Goesel-Le Bihan/Stern (1996); Dutheil de la Rochère (1987).

[28] Original French text:
Art. 55
Les traités ou accords régulièrement ratifiés ou approuvés ont, dès leur publication, une priorité supérieure à celle des lois, sous réserve, pour chaque accord ou traité, de son application par l'autre partie.

[29] See: Alland (1998).

of convergence of the case-law has been set in motion. The current situation can be summarized as follows.[30]

The first issue concerns the question of whether treaties enjoy primacy over subsequently adopted laws. While the *Cour de Cassation* decided in 1975 in its *Vabre*[31] judgment that this is indeed the case, the *Conseil d'Etat* followed this line only in 1989 in its *Nicolo*[32] ruling. The second issue relates to the question whether treaties enjoy primacy over the French constitution. In its *Sarran*[33] judgment, the *Conseil d'Etat* established that the supremacy conferred by Article 55 CF upon treaties over domestic laws is not applicable to provisions of constitutional order. Treaties enjoy supremacy over laws but not over the French constitution or other norms of constitutional value (*dispositions de valeur constitutionnelle*).[34] The *Cour de Cassation* followed this line in its *Fraisse*[35] judgment adopted shortly after the *Sarran* decision by the *Conseil d'Etat*. Thus, there is now a convergence between the two supreme courts as regards the hierarchy of norms in the French legal order.[36] As to the direct effect of international treaties in the French legal order, the provision of the treaty must be sufficiently precise and confer rights to individuals, which is determined by the French courts on a case-by-case basis.[37]

1.4 Summary

From the foregoing sections it has become clear that the rank of international treaties differs in the constitutional systems of Germany, the Netherlands and France. International treaties enjoy the highest rank in the Netherlands (higher than the constitution), followed by France (below the constitution but primacy over statutes) and Germany (below constitution and equal to federal statutes). The approach of the domestic courts is generally friendly towards international treaties, based on the principle of interpreting national provisions as much as possible in the light of international agreements.[38] In France and the Netherlands, the issue of direct effect of provisions of international treaties is dealt with by using the criteria of clear, precise and uncondi-

---

30 See: Remy-Granger (2001); Prétot (2000a).

31 Cour de Cassation, 24.5.1975, RGDIP 1976 at 960.

32 Conseil d'Etat, 20.10.1989, Rec. CE, 190.

33 Conseil d'Etat, 30.10.1998, RFDA 1998, 1081-1090.

34 See: Prétot (2000a) at 1044-1045.

35 Cour de Cassation, 2.6.2000, RGDIP 2000, 1067-1094.

36 See for a detailed analysis: Ondoua (2000).

37 See e.g.: Conseil d'Etat, 21.6.2002, no. 240239; Cour de Cassation, 10.3.1993, no. 91-11310; Decaux/Eisemann/Goesel-Le Bihan/Stern (1996) at 258-259.

38 See also: Frowein/Oellers-Kahn (1996).

tional, while in Germany this issue does not arise because, rather than applying the treaty, the federal implementing statute is applied.

2 International treaties within the European legal order

In this section, the legal status of international treaties within the European legal order is analysed by focusing on the same three issues as in the previous section, namely, the legal status of international treaties, their supremacy and their possible direct effect. Moreover, due to the fact that the ECJ plays a central role in determining in particular the criteria for direct effect of international treaties, it is necessary to discuss the extent of the jurisdiction of the ECJ regarding the various types of international treaties. Accordingly, in a first step an inventory of the various types of international treaties that can be found in the European legal order is made. In a second step, the extent of the jurisdiction of the ECJ regarding the various types of international treaties is defined. Based on that, the jurisprudence of the ECJ and CFI on the direct effect of the various types of international agreements will be analyzed.

2.1 Various types of international treaties

For the purpose of this analysis the various types of international treaties are subdivided into five groups.[39] The first group deals with international treaties concluded by the EC alone. The second group concerns treaties concluded by the EU. The third group comprises international treaties concluded by the EC together with some or all Member States (mixed agreements). The fourth group refers to treaties concluded by the EU and its Member States covering matters of the II. and III. pillars (mixed EU agreements). Finally, the fifth group deals with treaties concluded by the Member States alone.

2.1.1 Treaties concluded by the EC alone

The starting point for answering the question of the legal status of international treaties concluded by the EC alone in the Community legal order is Article 300 EC Treaty. According to Article 300 (7) EC Treaty, agreements concluded by the EC alone are binding on the EC institutions and the Member States. However, this provision does not provide a clear answer regarding the legal status of those treaties in the Community legal order. Consequently, one must turn to the case-law of the ECJ. The ECJ has held that international agreements concluded according to the procedure of Article 300

39 See for details: Eeckhout (2004); Ott (2001); De Witte (2001).

EC Treaty are an integral part of EC law.[40] More specifically, in the *International Dairy* case, the ECJ stated that international treaties concluded by the EC alone enjoy primacy over secondary Community legislation.[41] Although the ECJ did not deal with the question of which legal rank international agreements have in relation to primary EC law, the general opinion in the legal literature assumes that international treaties are placed between primary and secondary EC law, with the result that they prevail over conflicting secondary EC law but not over primary EC law (the EC Treaty).[42] The ECJ explicitly stated in the same ruling that Community law must be interpreted as far as possible in the light of international treaties.[43] As a result of the fact that international treaties are an integral part of the Community legal order, they also enjoy primacy over all national law, including constitutional law, of the EU Member States.

In sum, it can be ascertained that international treaties concluded by the EC alone are integral part of EC law and enjoy supremacy over conflicting secondary Community law and all national law, including constitutional law, of the EU Member States.

2.1.2 Treaties concluded by the EU alone

Articles 24, 38 (Article 38 refers back to Article 24) TEU provide for the possibility of concluding agreements between the EU and other states and IOs covering issues of the II. and III. pillars. Article 24 TEU as amended by the Nice Treaty reads as follows:

> '1. When it is necessary to conclude an agreement with one or more States or international organisations in implementation of this Title, the Council may authorise the Presidency, assisted by the Commission as appropriate, to open negotiations to that effect. Such agreements shall be concluded by the Council on a recommendation from the Presidency.
>
> 2. The Council shall act unanimously when the agreement covers an issue for which unanimity is required for the adoption of internal decisions.
>
> 3. When the agreement is envisaged in order to implement a joint action or common position, the Council shall act by a qualified majority voting in accordance with Article 23 (3).

[40] Case 181/73 *Haegeman* v. *Belgium* [1974] ECR 449; Case 12/86 *Demirel* v. *Stadt Schwäbisch Gmünd* [1987] ECR 3719; Case C-192/89 *Sevince* [1990] ECR I-3461; see also: Pescatore (1987) at 179-180.

[41] See: Case C-61/94 *Commission* v. *Germany* [1996] ECR I-3989, para. 52; Manin (1997) at 403; Peters (1998).

[42] Martenczuk (2001) at 155; Streinz (2001) at no. 605; Oppermann (1999) at no. 1673; Geiger (1995) Art. 228, no. 23.

[43] Case C-61/94 *Commission* v. *Germany* [1996] ECR I-3989; Opinion of AG Alber in Case C-93/02 P *Biret* of 15.5.2003, para. 42.

4. The provisions of this Article shall also apply to matters falling under Title VI [Provisions on Police and Judicial Cooperation in criminal matters, III. pillar]. When the agreement covers an issue for which a qualified majority voting is required for the adoption of internal decisions or measures, the Council shall act by qualified majority in accordance with Article 34 (3).

5. No agreement shall be binding on a Member State whose representative in the Council states that it has to comply with the requirements of its own constitutional procedure; the other members of the Council may agree that the agreement shall nevertheless apply provisionally.

6. Agreements concluded under the conditions set out by this article shall be binding on the institutions of the Union.'

Despite the existence of this provision, a lot of legal uncertainty exists as to the legal status and effect of such agreements in the European legal order. Some legal scholars even reject the idea that such agreements are concluded on behalf of the EU, but rather claim that they are concluded by the Council on behalf of the EU Member States.[44]

But the wording of Article 24 TEU does not contain any indication that would support such a position. Article 24 TEU expressly empowers the Council to authorize the Presidency to negotiate such an international agreement and provides for the Council to conclude the agreement on behalf of the EU and not on behalf of the Member States.[45] If the EU Member States had the intention to let the Council negotiate on their behalf, they certainly would have made this clear in Article 24 TEU by inserting a phrase to that effect – for instance at the last treaty revision conference in Nice. The recent practice of the EU, which has concluded several international agreements on its behalf, confirms the finding that such treaties are concluded on behalf of the EU.[46]

---

44 See for the various views: Neuwahl (1998); Cremona (1999); Koenig/Pechstein (1998) at 169; Streinz (2001) at 173; Marquardt (2001).

45 This view is supported by the Legal Advisor of the Conference of the Representatives of the Governments of the Member States, SN 5332/1/00, Brussels, 24.11.2000, Comments on the draft to Article 24 TEU; and Mr Piris, Legal Advisor of the Council, Speaking note, SN 1620/00, Brussels, 16.2.2000; see also: Craig/De Búrca (2003) at 37; Wouters (2002) at 67; Marquardt (2001) at 340-344; V. Bogdandy (1999) at 894.

46 Agreement on extradition between the European Union and the USA, OJ 2003 L 181/27-33; Agreement on mutual legal assistance between the European Union and the USA, OJ 2003 L 181/34-42; Agreement between the European Union and the Republic of Albania on the activities of the European Union Monitoring Mission (EUMM) in the Republic of Albania, OJ 2003 L 093/50-52; Agreement between the European Union and Bosnia Herzegovina (BiH) on the activities of the European Union Police Mission (EUPM) in BiH, OJ 2002 L 293/2; Agreement between the European Union and the Federal Republic of Yugoslavia on the activities of the European Union Monitoring Mission (EUMM) in the Federal Repub-

While the Treaty of Nice added paragraph 6 to Article 24 TEU, thereby explicitly stating that the agreements concluded on the basis of Article 24 (and Article 38) TEU are binding on the institutions of the EU, this still does not resolve much of the legal uncertainty regarding the issue on whose behalf those agreements are concluded.

This situation will be clarified by the new provisions contained in the draft text of a new European Constitution.[47] Article III-204 provides as regards the Common Foreign and Security Policy that:

> 'The Union may conclude agreements with one or more States or international organisations pursuant to this Chapter, in accordance with the procedure described in Article III-227.'

Moreover, Article III-225 states generally that:

> '1. The Union may conclude agreements with one or more third countries and international organisations where the Constitution so provides or where the conclusion of an agreement is necessary in order to achieve, within the framework of the Union's policies, one of the objectives fixed by the Constitution, where there is a provision for it in a binding Union legislative act or where it affects one of the Union's internal acts.
>
> 2. Agreements concluded by the Union are binding upon the institutions of the Union and on its Member States.'

The procedure described in Article III-227 indicates that the agreements are negotiated and concluded solely by the various organs of the Union without any involvement of the Member States. Thus, the argument that agreements concluded within the CFSP and JHA are concluded on behalf of the Member States will lose any possible basis.

As regards the existing differences concerning treaties concluded according to the procedure of Article 300 EC Treaty and Articles 24, 38 TEU, the creation of a single legal personality of the EU – as is now provided for in Article 6 of the draft European Constitution – logically requires the application of one legal regime for all agreements concluded by the EU. Consequently, the regime of Article 300 EC Treaty and the case-law of the ECJ should be extended to agreements concluded on the basis of Articles 24, 38 TEU. Accordingly, in line with Article 300 EC Treaty, treaties concluded on the basis of Articles 24, 38 TEU that cover matters falling within the exclusive competence of the EU, would have

---

lic of Yugoslavia, OJ 2001 L 125/2-4; Agreement between the European Union and the Former Yugoslav Republic of Macedonia on the activities of the European Union Monitoring Mission (EUMM) in the Former Yugoslav Republic of Macedonia, OJ 2001 L 241/2-4.

47 Draft Treaty establishing a Constitution for Europe, CONV 850/03, 18.7.2003.

a legal rank between primary EU law (TEU) and secondary EU law. Hence, they would enjoy supremacy over conflicting secondary EU law and all national law, including constitutional law, of the EU Member States and could have direct effect if they fulfil the criteria developed by the ECJ regarding treaties concluded by the EC.

2.1.3 Treaties concluded by the EC together with its Member States (mixed agreements)

The EC has concluded many so called 'mixed agreements', that is, treaties concluded by the EC together with its Member States.[48] Mixed agreements are a special type of international treaties because they simultaneously encompass the EC and its Member States competences. They are a means to overcome difficulties in the delineation between the competences of both the EC and the Member States.[49] Often it is not possible to make a clear-cut distinction between the two.[50] The conclusion of the WTO Agreement is a case in point. In this case, the EC Commission was of the opinion that it had the exclusive competence to ratify all three main treaties annexed to the WTO Agreement, i.e. the GATT 1994, GATS and TRIPS Agreement. The Member States strongly disputed the existence of a an exclusive Community competence for the GATS and TRIPS Agreement. The dispute was resolved by requesting an opinion of the ECJ.[51] The ECJ decided that the EC has only exclusive competence over the GATT 1994, while for the GATS and TRIPS Agreement, the competence is shared between the EC and the Member States.[52] Consequently, the WTO Agreement was signed as a mixed agreement.

As to the legal status of mixed agreements within the European legal order, the case-law of the ECJ indicates that they are treated similar to treaties concluded by the EC alone.[53] Accordingly, mixed agreements that have been

---

48 See for a detailed analysis: Rosas (1998); *ibid.* (2000a); Heliskoski (2001).

49 Bleckmann (1983); Neuwahl (1991); *ibid.* (1996).

50 Macleod/Hendry/Hyett (1996) at 145.

51 ECJ Opinion 1/94 *WTO* [1994] ECR I-5267; see also the critical discussion of that opinion by: Bourgeois (1995); Pescatore (1999).

52 ECJ Opinion 1/94 *WTO* [1994] ECR I-5267.

53 Regarding mixed agreements see: Case 12/86 *Demirel* v. *Stadt Schwäbisch Gmünd* [1987] ECR 3719 and Case C-192/89 *Sevince* v. *Staatssecretaris van Justitie* [1990] ECR I-3461; for a treaty concluded by the EC alone see: Case C-432/92 *Anastasiou* [1994] ECR I-3087; Pescatore (1983) at 665; Peters (1998) at 21; Macleod/Hendry/Hyett (1996) at 156. The ECJ recently explicitly stated in case C-13/00 *Commission* v. *Ireland* [2002] ECR I-2943: '14. The Court has ruled that mixed agreements concluded by the Community, its Member States and non-member countries have the *same status* in the Community legal order as purely Community agreements, as these are provisions coming within the scope of Community competence (see, to that effect, Case 12/86 *Demirel* [1987] ECR 3719, para. 9)', emphasis added.

concluded on the basis of Articles 133 or 310 EC Treaty are an integral part of the Community legal order. They enjoy supremacy over all conflicting national law of the EU Member States and secondary Community law. However, due to the special nature of mixed agreements, namely that they touch upon the competence of the EU and its Member States, the supremacy of mixed agreements does not apply to matters that belong to the exclusive competence of the EU Member States. Those matters are governed by the respective constitutional rules of the EU Member States as if they belong to an international treaty concluded by the EU Member States alone.

2.1.4 Treaties concluded by the EU together with its Member States (mixed EU agreements)

It is conceivable that the EU concludes mixed EU agreements that touch on issues falling within the competence of the EU in the fields of CFSP and JHA and the competence of the Member States. Such agreements would have to be concluded as mixed EU agreements by the EU and its Member States. As has been stated above, the Community law rules applicable on treaties concluded by the EC should also be applied to treaties concluded by the EU. Consequently, mixed EU agreements would be concluded and ratified by both the EU (with regard to the matters falling within its competence) and the EU Member States (with regard to the matters falling in their competence). Moreover, mixed EU agreements – excluding the matters falling within the scope of exclusive competence of the EU Member States – would enjoy primacy over conflicting secondary EU law and all national law, including constitutional law, of the EU Member States and could have direct effect according to the criteria developed by the ECJ.

The same principles would be applicable to so-called 'cross-pillar' EU agreements, i.e. treaties that touch on issues of the I., II. and/or III. pillars and 'cross-pillar' mixed EU agreements, which in addition touch on Member States competence. Accordingly, all issues that do not fall within the exclusive competence of the Member States would be governed by Community law principles such as supremacy and possible direct effect, while those issues that remain with the EU Member States' competence would be treated as being part of 'normal' treaties of public international law governed by their respective constitutional provisions.

2.1.5 Treaties concluded by the Member States alone

In principle, international treaties concluded by the Member States without EC involvement are not part of the body of EC law. They are governed by the rules of public international law and the constitutional laws of each

Member State. However, there are international treaties that – even though the EC is not a party to them – come into the 'orbit'[54] of EC law.[55]

The first example is the GATT 1947. Even though the GATT 1947 was concluded before the establishment of the EC and, despite the fact that the EC never was a contracting party to it, its provisions nevertheless became an integral part of EC law. This happened due to the fact that the EC obtained exclusive competence over trade issues and thus *de facto* replaced the Member States in the GATT 1947.[56] As a result of this replacement, the GATT 1947 has been treated as being part of Community law from the moment the EC gained exclusive competence with respect to trade related matters within the scope of Article 133 EC Treaty.[57] Consequently, the GATT 1947 obtained supremacy over all national law of the EU Member States by virtue of the fact that the GATT became part of the exclusive competence of the EC.

The second example is the European Convention on Human Rights (ECHR) that was also concluded before the EC existed and to which all Member States are party, except the EC.[58] The ECJ established that fundamental rights form an integral part of the general principles of Community law that are protected by the ECJ.[59] As a source for these general principles, the ECJ draws 'inspiration from the constitutional traditions common to the Member States'.[60] The ECJ further explained 'similarly, international treaties for the protection of human rights, on which the Member States have collaborated or of which they are signatories, can supply guidelines which should be followed within the framework of community law'.[61] Thus, not only the ECHR but also other international treaties protecting fundamental rights to which the Member States are parties, such as the International Covenant on Civil and Political Rights or the International Covenant on Economic, Social and Cultural Rights, can be used as tools for the interpretation and application of Community law. Moreover, in the last years the ECJ not only indirectly draws on the ECHR but also explicitly applies the provisions of the ECHR in its judgments.[62] In this way, the ECJ treats the ECHR as

---

54 I borrowed the expression 'within the 'orbit' of Community law' from De Witte.

55 See: Uerpmann (2003).

56 Case 21-24/72 *International Fruit Company* v. *Produktschap voor Groenten en Fruit* [1972] ECR 1219; Joint cases 267-269/81 *Amministrazione delle finanze dello Stato* v. *SPI and SAMI* [1983] ECR 801; Schmid (1998) at 192.

57 *Ibid.*

58 For detailed analysis see: Alston (1999); Weiler (1996); Binder (1995); Oliver (2000).

59 See for a general discussion: Craig/De Búrca (2003) at 317-370; Jacobs (1994); Lawson (1994).

60 Case 4/73 *Nold* v. *Commission* [1974] ECR 491.

61 *Ibid.*

62 See for example: Case C-260/89 *ERT* [1991] ECR I-2925; Case C-404/92 *X* v. *Commission* [1994] ECR I-4737; Case C-368/95 *Familiapress* [1997] ECR I-3689; Case C-7/98 *Krombach* [2000] ECR I-1935; Case C-274/99 P *Connolly* v. *Commission* [2001] ECR I-1611; Case C-60/00 *Carpenter* [2002] ECR I-6279.

being linked to a certain extent with Community law.[63] The EU Member States have further 'integrated' the ECHR into the 'orbit' of Community law by the Maastricht Treaty which explicitly allows the ECJ to use the ECHR when reviewing all acts of the institutions (Article 6 (2) TEU in conjunction with Article 46 (d) TEU).[64] Indeed, in the *Schmidberger*[65] case, the ECJ emphasized the special position of the ECHR within the Community legal order as follows:

> '73. It follows that measures which are incompatible with observance of the human rights thus recognised are not acceptable in the Community (see, *inter alia*, *ERT*, cited above, paragraph 41, and Case C-299/95 *Kremzow* [1997] ECR I-2629, paragraph 14).
>
> 74. Thus, since both the Community and its Member States are required to respect fundamental rights, the protection of those rights is a legitimate interest which, in principle, justifies a restriction of the obligations imposed by Community law, even under a fundamental freedom guaranteed by the Treaty such as the free movement of goods.'[66]

As a consequence thereof, the ECHR – as far as it is applied by the ECJ – obtains supremacy over conflicting Community law – even over the fundamental freedoms guaranteed by the EC Treaty – and all national law of the EU Member States and can have direct effect if the criteria of the ECJ are met.

As a third example, reference can be made to the CITES which has been ratified by all EU Member States but not by the EC because it is only open to states. However, the EC copied the CITES into Regulation 3626/82,[67] thereby transforming it from a treaty based on public international law into a Community law measure. In this way a treaty to which the EC is not a contracting party, and therefore would fall outside EC law, suddenly is brought into the Community legal order.

These examples illustrate that the legal status of international treaties is not static for all times but rather can evolve over time. The legal status of international treaties can be modified by Community law even when the EC is not a party to them. This is especially the case when the EC assumes exclusive external competence over a certain policy area, when the EC incorporates a treaty through Community legislation or when the ECJ applies it in its case-law. In these cases, the international agreements are modified by virtue of Community law and obtain supremacy over all national law of the EU Member States that, prior to the modification, was not necessarily the case.

---

63 Callewaert (2001); Jacobs (1994) at 563; Lawson (1994).

64 See: Duvigneau (1998); Alston/Weiler (1999).

65 Case C-112/00 *Schmidberger* [2003] ECR I-5659.

66 *Ibid.*

67 OJ 1982 L 384/1-61; replaced by Regulation 338/97, OJ 1997 L 61/1-69.

In summary, it can be stated that the legal status of the various international treaties depends on the extent of the involvement of the EC. Accordingly, all international treaties that have been concluded by the EC alone or together with the Member States are an integral part of the Community legal order. Thus, they enjoy supremacy over secondary EC law and all national law of the Member States. Similarly, also international treaties that fall within the exclusive competence of the EC – even if the EC has not signed and ratified the treaty – also are integral part of the Community order. The legal status of treaties concluded within the framework of the II. and III. pillar is less clear but it is argued that they should be treated similar to treaties concluded within the I. pillar. All other treaties concluded by the Member States and which do not fall within the exclusive competence of the EC are not integral part of the Community legal order. Their legal status is determined by the respective constitutional law of each Member State.

2.2 The jurisdiction of the ECJ over international treaties

According to Article 220 EC Treaty, the task of the ECJ is to ensure that the law is observed in the interpretation and application of the EC Treaty. In addition, Article 234 EC Treaty provides that the ECJ has jurisdiction to interpret the EC Treaty and secondary Community law acts (Article 234 (a) EC Treaty) and to rule on the validity of acts of the Community institutions (Article 234 (b) EC Treaty). But these provisions say nothing with regard to the jurisdiction of the ECJ over international treaties.[68] The ECJ has seized jurisdiction over international treaties by interpreting the term 'acts of the Community institutions' broadly when it argued with respect to the Association Agreement EEC-Greece and EEC-Turkey that the:

> '[...] agreement was concluded by the Council under Articles 228 and 238 of the Treaty as appears from the terms of the [Council] Decision [...] therefore, in so far as concerns the Community, [it is] an act of one of the institutions of the Community within the meaning of subparagraph (b) of the first paragraph of Article 177 [now 234]'.[69]

The ECJ's main argument justifying its jurisdiction over international treaties is that only when it has broad jurisdiction can the provisions of international treaties be applied uniformly and effectively in all Member States.[70]

68 See generally: Hancher (1994).

69 Case 181/73 *Haegeman* [1974] ECR 449, para. 3, 4; Case 12/86 *Demirel* v. *Stadt Schwäbisch Gmünd* [1987] ECR 3719, para. 7.

70 Case 104/81 *Hauptzollamt Mainz* v. *Kupferberg* [1982] ECR 3641; Case C-61/94 *Commission* v. *Germany* [1996] ECR I-3989.

Accordingly, the ECJ has jurisdiction in the following cases:[71]

2.2.1 Treaties concluded by the EC alone

It is obvious that the jurisdiction of the ECJ extends to all international agreements that have been concluded by the EC alone on the basis of Articles 133, 310 EC Treaty.[72]

2.2.2 Treaties concluded by the EU alone and mixed EU agreements

Currently, Article 46 TEU states that the jurisdiction of the ECJ is excluded regarding treaties concluded by the EU on the basis of Articles 24, 38 TEU. Consequently, the ECJ is prohibited from reviewing those agreements. However, the 'Working Group on Legal Personality' recommended to the European Convention to extend the jurisdiction of the ECJ so that also agreements concluded on the basis of Articles 24, 38 TEU by the EU alone or together with the EU Member States, could be reviewed by the ECJ.[73] But such a far-reaching extension of the jurisdiction of the ECJ has not been included in the draft text of the European Constitution.[74] Article III-282 explicitly excludes the provisions on CFSP, so that agreements also covering CFSP issues must be considered to be excluded from the scope of the jurisdiction of the ECJ. In contrast, Article III-283 only excludes the jurisdiction of the ECJ regarding the validity or proportionality of operations carried out by police or other law enforcement services. Accordingly, it can be assumed that mixed EU agreements covering III. pillar issues but excluding police or law enforcement service would fall within the jurisdiction of the ECJ.

2.2.3 Treaties concluded by the EC together with its Member States (mixed agreements)

The twofold character of mixed agreements also comes into play with respect to the jurisdiction of the ECJ.[75] The main question is whether the jurisdiction of the ECJ extends also to areas of shared competence, i.e. areas that have not yet become the exclusive competence of the EC.

Before the *Demirel*[76] judgment, many authors doubted that the jurisdiction of the ECJ would extend to areas that – although shared with the EC – still

[71] See: Pescatore (1983) at 664-669; Peters (1998).

[72] Case 104/81 *Hauptzollamt Mainz* v. *Kupferberg* [1982] ECR 3641.

[73] Final Report of Working Group III on Legal Personality, 1.10.2002, CONV 305/02.

[74] CONV 850/03, 18.7.2003.

[75] See fore a recent extensive analysis: Koutrakos (2002); Heliskoski (2000).

[76] Case 12/86 *Demirel* v. *Stadt Schwäbisch Gmünd* [1987] ECR 3719.

remained within the competence of the Member States.[77] In the *Demirel*[78] case, the ECJ was explicitly requested to deal with the issue of whether its jurisdiction extends also to the provisions that – according to some Member States – belong to their competence. However, the ECJ found a way to interpret the provision of the Association Agreement with Turkey without determining how far its jurisdiction reaches.[79] After the *Demirel* ruling and up until now, the ECJ has not yet explicitly decided this issue. The practice of the ECJ concerning for example Article 50 (6) TRIPS[80] agreement illustrates that the ECJ interprets provisions of a mixed agreement without delineating the exact distribution of competences between the EC and its Member States. Thus, the ECJ interprets Article 50 (6) TRIPS Agreement despite the fact that, in its *Opinion 1/94*, it declared that the TRIPS Agreement belongs for the most part to the competence of the Member States.[81] One of the arguments used by the ECJ to justify its broad jurisdiction is the concept of ensuring the uniform application of international treaties within the Community legal order.[82] According to this concept, the function of Article 234 EC Treaty is 'to ensure the uniform application throughout the Community of all provisions forming part of the Community legal system and to ensure that the interpretation thereof does not vary according to the interpretation accorded to them by the various Member States'.[83] Thus, in light of the above, it can be concluded that the jurisdiction of the ECJ extends to all provisions of a mixed agreement which fall within areas of shared competence.[84] In other words, the jurisdiction of the ECJ encompasses all provisions except those that fall within the exclusive competence of the Member States.[85]

2.2.4 Treaties concluded by the EU Member States alone

In principle, international treaties concluded by the EU Member States alone and which do not fall within the exclusive competence of the EC are outside the scope of Community law and thus outside the jurisdiction of the ECJ.[86] However, the Member States are free to extend the jurisdiction of the ECJ to such treaties. This can be done, for example, through an additional

---

77 See: Nolte (1988) at 407, footnote 10.

78 Case 12/86 *Demirel* v. *Stadt Schwäbisch Gmünd* [1987] ECR 1987 3719.

79 See for a discussion of the Demirel case: Vedder (1988).

80 Case C-53/96 *Hermès* [1998] ECR I-3603; Joined Cases C-300/98 *Dior* and C-392/98 *Assco* [2000] ECR I-11307; Case C-89/99 *Schieving-Nijstad* [2001] ECR I-5851; see also: Lavranos (2002c).

81 ECJ Opinion 1/94 *WTO* [1994] ECR I-5267; see also: Ott (2001) at 107-109; Lavranos (2002b).

82 See: Case 104/81 *Kupferberg* [1982] ECR 3641; Case C-61/94 *Commission* v. *Germany* [1996] ECR I-3989.

83 Case C-192/89 *Sevince* v. *Staatssecretaris van Justitie* [1990] ECR I-3461, para. 11.

84 Koutrakos (2002) at 34.

85 De Witte (2001) at 128; Dashwood (2000).

86 Case C-379/92 *Peralta* [1994] ECR I-3453.

protocol to the international treaty as has been the case with the Brussels Convention 1968.

But there are two cases in which the ECJ exerts a sort of 'implied jurisdiction' to international treaties concluded by the EU Member States alone. The first case concerned the GATT 1947 that fell within the exclusive competence of the EC (Article 133 EC Treaty). In this case the ECJ was able to extend its jurisdiction due to the fact that the EC *de facto* replaced the Member States as regards the GATT 1947. The second case in which the jurisdiction of the ECJ comes into play is the ECHR concerning fundamental rights. Regarding the extent of its jurisdiction in utilising the ECHR, the ECJ not only considers itself competent to review Community measures in light of the general principles, but under certain conditions even Member States' measures.[87] In the *ERT*[88] case, the ECJ stated that:

> 'it has no power to examine the compatibility with ECHR if national rules do not fall within the scope of EC law. On the other hand, where such rules fall within the scope of Community law, it must provide all the criteria of interpretation needed to determine whether those rules are compatible with fundamental rights the observance of which the court ensures and which derives in particular from the ECHR.'[89]

Thus, the ECJ uses the 'general principles' as a means to expand its jurisdiction to interpret also the ECHR that primarily is the task of the Strasbourg Court. Moreover, the Maastricht Treaty has further reinforced the legal links between Community law and ECHR law by giving the ECJ the explicit possibility to review – within its jurisdiction – acts of the EC and EU as to their compatibility with the ECHR.[90] Indeed, in its more recent case-law, the ECJ applies the ECHR even directly without using the 'general principles' detour.[91] In fact, in the *Schmidberger* judgment, the ECJ accepted that the ECHR can even restrict the fundamental freedoms (free movement of goods, workers, services and capital) guaranteed by the EC Treaty.[92] Nonetheless, it must be pointed out that the application of the ECHR by the ECJ is not without problems and can lead to divergent interpretations of the ECHR between the ECJ and the European Court of Human Rights.[93]

---

87 Jacobs (1994) at 563-564.

88 Case C-260/89 *ERT* [1991] ECR I-2925.

89 *Ibid.*, para. 42.

90 See for details: Duvigneau (1998).

91 Case C-60/00 *Carpenter* [2002] ECR I-6279; Case C-413/99 *Baumbast* [2002] ECR I-7091.

92 Case C-112/00 *Schmidberger* [2003] ECR I-5659; see also above.

93 See for a detailed discussion of this point: Chapter 4; see also: Spielmann (1999); Lawson (1994).

2.3 The case-law of the ECJ on the direct effect of international treaties

One of the main issues of the interaction between international law, Community law and national law is the question of direct effect.[94] In the following sections, the conditions of direct effect of treaties in the European legal order will be analysed by discussing two elements. First, the criteria of clear, precise and unconditional and second, the 'additional' criteria.

2.3.1 Clear, precise and unconditional

In order to determine whether a provision of a treaty enjoys direct effect, the ECJ uses the same criteria as for determining whether a provision of Community law has direct effect.[95] The ECJ analyses whether a provision is clear, precise and unconditional.[96] This is the case when the 'provision contains a clear and precise obligation which is not subject, in its implementation or effects, to the adoption of any subsequent measure'.[97]

2.3.2 'Supplemental' criteria

In addition to the textual based criteria (clear, precise and unconditional), the ECJ also takes into account supplemental criteria such as the economic and political implications of the various international agreements, i.e. whether and to what extent the treaties establish an 'asymmetry of obligations', 'special relations of integration with the Community' or are 'reciprocal and mutually advantageous'. Accordingly, in the *Portugal* v. *Council*[98] case, the ECJ emphasized this point when it argued:

> 'As regards, more particularly, the application of the WTO agreements in the Community legal order, it must be noted that, according to its preamble, the agreement establishing the WTO, including the annexes, is still founded, like GATT 1947, on the principle of negotiations with a view to 'entering into reciprocal and mutually advantageous arrangements' and is thus *distinguished, from the viewpoint of the Community, from the agreements concluded between the Community and non-member countries which introduce a certain asymmetry of obligations,*

---

94 See extensively: Eeckhout (2004).

95 Manin (1997) at 422.

96 See e.g.: Case T-115/94 *Opel Austria* [1997] ECR II-39.

97 Case C-162/00 *Pokrzeptowicz-Meyer* [2002] ECR I-1049, para. 19.

98 C-149/96 *Portugal* v. *Council* [1999] ECR I-8395; see for details: Desmedt (2000); Zonnekeyn (2000b); Rosas (2000b).

> *or create special relations of integration with the Community*, such as the agreement which the Court was required to interpret in *Kupferberg* (para. 42).'[99]

Moreover, despite the fact that the ECJ uses the same criteria in order to examine whether a provision of Community law is directly applicable, the ECJ has repeatedly emphasized that it does not necessarily follow that a similar provision of an international treaty must be interpreted in the same way as a Community law provision, but rather takes the specific characteristics of each treaty into account.[100] Thus, when the ECJ has to determine whether a provision of an international agreement can have direct effect, it analyzes the wording of the provision as well as the specific characteristics of the treaty. In this way the application of these supplemental criteria creates some flexibility for the ECJ to determine on a case-by-case basis whether provisions of an international agreement concluded by the EC can be relied upon before a national court.[101]

With regard to the direct effect of the various types of international agreements, the case-law of the ECJ can be summarized as follows.

2.3.3 Direct effect of GATT/WTO law

The ECJ has always rejected any direct effect of GATT provisions both under the GATT 1947 as well as under the WTO regime.[102] Concerning the question of whether GATT 1947 provisions could have direct effect, the ECJ held in the *International Fruit Company*[103] case that:

> '20 For this purpose, the spirit, the general scheme and the terms of the general agreement must be considered.
>
> 21 This agreement which, according to its preamble, is based on the principle of negotiations undertaken on the basis of "reciprocal and mutually advantageous arrangements" is characterized by the great flexibility of its provisions, in particular those conferring the possibility of derogation, the measures to be taken when confronted with exceptional difficulties and the settlement of conflicts between the contracting parties.'

In contrast, the Italian Constitutional Court, before it had to follow the ECJ case-law, was of the opinion that certain GATT 1947 provisions could be directly applicable.[104] Nonetheless, from 1972 up until the entering into force of the

---

99 Case C-149/96 *Portugal* v. *Council* [1999] ECR I-8395, emphasis added.

100 Case 104/81 *Hauptzollamt Mainz* v. *Kupferberg* [1982] ECR 3461.

101 See: Van den Broek (2001); Ott (2001) at 95-140.

102 See for a detailed study: Eeckhout (2004); Snyder (2003); Van den Broek (2001); Kuilwijk (1996).

103 Case 21-24/72 *International Fruit Company* v. *Produktschap voor Groenten en Fruit* [1972] ECR 1219.

104 See: Stoll (1997) at 128; Giardina (1987) at 266; Pescatore (1983) at 673.

WTO Agreement,[105] the ECJ has repeated its position that the provisions of the GATT 1947 are not directly applicable. With regard to the agreements annexed to the WTO Agreement, in particular GATT 1994, GATS and TRIPS, the ECJ observed in the *Portugal* v. *Council* case:

> '36 While it is true that the WTO agreements, as the Portuguese Government observes, differ significantly from the provisions of GATT 1947, in particular by reason of the strengthening of the system of safeguards and the mechanism for resolving disputes, the system resulting from those agreements nevertheless accords considerable importance to negotiation between the parties.
>
> 37 Although the main purpose of the mechanism for resolving disputes is in principle, according to Article 3(7) of the Understanding on Rules and Procedures Governing the Settlement of Disputes (Annex 2 to the WTO), to secure the withdrawal of the measures in question if they are found to be inconsistent with the WTO rules, that understanding provides that where the immediate withdrawal of the measures is impracticable compensation may be granted on an interim basis pending the withdrawal of the inconsistent measure.
>
> 38 According to Article 22(1) of that Understanding, compensation is a temporary measure available in the event that the recommendations and rulings of the dispute settlement body provided for in Article 2(1) of that Understanding are not implemented within a reasonable period of time, and Article 22(1) shows a preference for full implementation of a recommendation to bring a measure into conformity with the WTO agreements in question.
>
> 39 However, Article 22(2) provides that if the member concerned fails to fulfil its obligation to implement the said recommendations and rulings within a reasonable period of time, it is, if so requested, and on the expiry of a reasonable period at the latest, to enter into negotiations with any party having invoked the dispute settlement procedures, with a view to finding mutually acceptable compensation.
>
> 40 Consequently, to require the judicial organs to refrain from applying the rules of domestic law which are inconsistent with the WTO agreements would have the consequence of depriving the legislative or executive organs of the contracting parties of the possibility afforded by Article 22 of that memorandum of entering into negotiated arrangements even on a temporary basis.
>
> 41 It follows that the WTO agreements, interpreted in the light of their subject-matter and purpose, do not determine the appropriate legal means of ensuring that they are applied in good faith in the legal order of the contracting parties.
>
> 42 As regards, more particularly, the application of the WTO agreements in the Community legal order, it must be noted that, according to its preamble, the agreement establishing the WTO, including the annexes, is still founded, like GATT 1947, on the principle of negotiations with a view to "entering into recipro-

[105] See e.g.: Case C-280/93 *Germany* v. *Council* [1994] ECR I-4973; Case C-469/93 *Amministrazione delle finanze dello Stato* v. *Chiquita Italia* [1995] ECR I-4533.

cal and mutually advantageous arrangements" and is thus distinguished, from the viewpoint of the Community, from the agreements concluded between the Community and non-member countries which introduce a certain asymmetry of obligations, or create special relations of integration with the Community, such as the agreement which the Court was required to interpret in *Kupferberg*.

43 It is common ground, moreover, that some of the contracting parties, which are among the most important commercial partners of the Community, have concluded from the subject-matter and purpose of the WTO agreements that they are not among the rules applicable by their judicial organs when reviewing the legality of their rules of domestic law.

44 Admittedly, the fact that the courts of one of the parties consider that some of the provisions of the agreement concluded by the Community are of direct application whereas the courts of the other party do not recognise such direct application is not in itself such as to constitute a lack of reciprocity in the implementation of the agreement (*Kupferberg*, paragraph 18).

45 However, the lack of reciprocity in that regard on the part of the Community's trading partners, in relation to the WTO agreements which are based on "reciprocal and mutually advantageous arrangements" and which must *ipso facto* be distinguished from agreements concluded by the Community, referred to in paragraph 42 of the present judgment, may lead to disuniform application of the WTO rules.'[106]

Thus, while the ECJ acknowledged that the WTO Agreement strengthened the system of safeguards and the dispute settlement mechanism, it still rejects any direct effect.[107] The only exception to that is the so-called *Nakajima/Fediol* rule. This rule allows for the possibility of direct effect of WTO law if a Community law act explicitly refers to the agreements annexed to the WTO Agreement or is intended to implement obligations arising out of these agreements.[108]

The ECJ uses two different arguments for rejecting a direct effect of WTO law. First, the ECJ argues that accepting direct effect would limit the ability of the EC legislature to use the – albeit temporary – alternative possibility of negotiating an agreement for compensation with the other party of the dispute as provided for by Article 22 (2) DSU. Second, the ECJ refers to the argument of reciprocity in the sense that other important trade partners of the EC, i.e. the US and Japan, also do not accord any direct effect to the agreements annexed to the WTO Agreement.

[106] Case C-149/96 *Portugal* v. *Council* [1999] ECR I-8395.

[107] *Ibid.*, para. 36; see also more recently: Case T-174/00 *Biret* [2002] ECR II-17, paras. 60-68. See also Rosas (2001) who supports the line of argument of the ECJ.

[108] Case C-69/89 *Nakajima* [1991] ECR I-2069; Case 70/87 *Fediol* [1989] ECR 1781; see also: Zonnekeyn (2001); Louis (2000). Recently confirmed in the judgment in Case C-76/00 P *Petrotub* [2003] ECR I-79, see case-note by: Zonnekeyn (2003).

However, a closer look at Article 22 DSU illustrates that the argument of the ECJ concerning the temporary alternative for the implementation of a dispute settlement report provided by Article 22 DSU is not very convincing. Article 22 (1) DSU provides for two temporary alternative measures, (i) compensation and (ii) suspension of concessions, in the event that the dispute settlement report is not implemented within a reasonable period of time.[109]

As regards compensation, it should be first noted that Article 22 (1) last sentence DSU states that compensation is voluntary. Second, the parties to the dispute must come to an agreement concerning the level of compensation (Article 22 (2) first sentence DSU). That means if the EC decides to offer temporarily compensation until it implements the dispute settlement report it has to negotiate an agreement with the other party to the dispute. In other words, the EC depends on the willingness of the other party to accept compensation. It is thus not an option the EC can unilaterally adopt but rather depends on the agreement of the other party.

As regards the temporary alternative of suspension of concessions, the decision to opt for this measure is completely out of the hands of the EC in case the EC fails to implement a dispute settlement report within the prescribed deadline and no agreement on compensation was reached. In this case, it is the other party that can request an authorization from the DSB to suspend concessions (Article 22 (2) second sentence DSU). As this decision is adopted unless all Members of the DSB decide not to authorize the suspension of concessions, the EC could not block such a decision.

Hence, it can be concluded that the use of the alternative temporary possibilities provided for by Article 22 DSU essentially depends on the attitude and actions of the other party to the dispute. Consequently, there is not much room for manoeuvre available for the EC executive and legislature that could be limited by granting direct effect to WTO law or more generally by judicial interference or judicial activism of the ECJ.[110] This is even more so since, as AG Alber correctly pointed out in the *Biret*[111] case, at the end of the day there is no alternative than implementing the dispute settlement report.

Moreover, also the argument of reciprocity is open to criticism.[112] In particular the concern of the ECJ that granting direct effect to WTO law would lead to disuniform application of WTO rules is not very convincing. In fact, it can equally be argued that granting direct effect would help to ensure the proper and thus uniform application of WTO law. Moreover, as the ECJ itself stated in the *Kupferberg* case, reciprocity is not a bar for direct effect.[113] Indeed, as AG

---

[109] See for details: Van den Bossche (2004) at 327.

[110] Opinion of AG Alber in the Case C-93/02 P *Biret* of 15.5.2003, para. 96.

[111] *Ibid.*, para. 81.

[112] See for details: Van den Broek (2001).

[113] Opinion AG Alber in Case C-93/02 P *Biret* of 15.5.2003, para. 101.

Alber argued, it is difficult to conceive how the negotiation position of the EC vis-à-vis the other WTO Members could be affected by granting direct effect to WTO law in the Community legal order.[114] If for instance the US violates WTO law but excludes any direct effect of WTO law in US law, the EC (acting also in the name of affected European companies) would still be able to start a dispute settlement procedure against the US in order to challenge that situation. Conversely, if the EC violates WTO law and direct effect would be possible within EC law, then all affected companies – whether non-EC or EC companies – could challenge that situation before the European Courts. This would not affect the right of other WTO Members to start a WTO dispute settlement procedure against the EC. Accordingly, the reciprocity argument is more a trade than a legal argument.[115] In fact, granting direct effect to WTO law would enhance the rule of law within the Community legal order which strengthens the authority of WTO law and even serves as an example that could be copied by other WTO Members.[116] It is for these reasons that AG Alber pleaded for accepting direct effect of WTO law for the purpose of being able to start a procedure against the EC if the EC has failed to implement a WTO dispute settlement report after the deadline has passed.[117] In this context, it should be noted that while the ECJ agreed with the outcome of the judgment of the CFI in the *Biret* case, in its appeal judgment in the *Biret*[118] case, the ECJ criticized the CFI for failing to properly examine whether in this case direct effect of a dispute settlement report for the purpose of obtaining damages from the EC for failing to implement a dispute settlement report is possible. More interestingly, the ECJ explicitly left the question open whether in a case in which the factual circumstances were different direct effect of a WTO dispute settlement report could be possible.[119] Thus, it can be seriously questioned whether the case-law regarding the GATT 1947 should be equally applied to the agreements annexed to the WTO Agreement.[120] More generally, it can be concluded that there are no convincing reasons for the European Courts not to accept a direct effect of WTO law.

---

114 *Ibid.*, para. 102.

115 *Ibid.*

116 *Ibid.*, para. 109.

117 See for details Chapter 4.

118 Case C-93/02 P *Biret*, judgment of 30.9.2003, para. 57.

119 *Ibid.*, para. 64; see for a detailed discussion on this point Chapter 4.

120 Van den Bossche (1996); Lavranos (1999).

2.3.4 Direct effect of FTAs, Co-operation and Association Agreements

As regards provisions of Free-Trade Agreements (FTAs), the ECJ accepted a direct effect if the context of the agreement supports such an outcome. In the *Metalsa* case the ECJ summed up its case-law as follows:

> '10 In certain cases the Court has considered it appropriate to extend the interpretation of a provision of the EEC Treaty to an identical or similar provision of an agreement concluded with a non Member State (see Case 17/81 *Pabst & Richarz v Hauptzollamt Oldenburg* [1982] ECR 1331 and Case 163/90 *Administration des Douanes* v *Legros and Others* [1992] ECR 4625), while in other cases the Court has considered such an extension neither possible nor appropriate (see Case 270/80 *Polydor* v *Harlequin Record Shops* [1982] ECR 329 and Case 104/81 *Hauptzollamt Mainz* v *Kupferberg* [1982] ECR 3641).
>
> 11 It is clear from that case-law that the extension of the interpretation of a provision in the Treaty to a comparably, similarly or even identically worded provision of an agreement concluded by the Community with a non-member country depends, inter alia, on the aim pursued by each provision in its particular context and that a comparison between the objectives and context of the agreement and those of the Treaty is of considerable importance in that regard.
>
> 12 An international treaty must not be interpreted solely by reference to the terms in which it is worded but also in the light of its objectives. Article 31 of the Vienna Convention of 23 May 1969 on the law of treaties stipulates in that respect that a treaty is to be interpreted in good faith in accordance with the ordinary meaning to be given to its terms in their context and in the light of its object and purpose (*Opinion 1/91* [1991] ECR I-6079, paragraph 14).'[121]

The ECJ has also accepted the direct effect of provisions of Co-operation Agreements, for instance, with Morocco[122] and Algeria.[123] The ECJ summarized the case-law in the *Krid*[124] case as follows:

> '21 [...] the Court added that the object of the Cooperation Agreement [is] to promote overall cooperation between the contracting parties, in particular in the field of labour, [which] confirms that the principle of non-discrimination enshrined in Article 41(1) is capable of governing the legal situation of individuals.

---

121 Case C-312/91 *Metalsa* [1993] ECR I-3751.

122 Case C-18/90 *Kziber* [1991] ECR I-199; Case C-58/93 *Yousfi* [1994] ECR I-1353; Case C-416/96 *El Yassini* [1999] ECR I-1209.

123 Case C-103/94 *Krid* [1995] ECR I-719.

124 *Ibid.*

22 The Court concluded (see the judgments in *Kziber*, cited above, paragraph 23 and *Yousfi*, cited above, paragraph 17) that that provision was capable of being applied directly.

23 Article 39(1) of the Cooperation Agreement between the EEC and Algeria is drafted in the same terms as Article 41(1) of the Cooperation Agreement between the EEC and Morocco, and the two agreements pursue the same object.

24 Accordingly, the direct effect which Article 39(1) of the Agreement must be recognized as entailing that persons to whom that provision applies are entitled to rely on it in proceedings before national courts.'[125]

This applies also to a multilateral Cooperation Agreement such as the Cotonou Agreement between the EC, its Member States and the ACP countries.[126] In the *Bresciani*[127] case, the ECJ simply argued that:

'25 By expressly referring, in Article 2 (1) of the Convention, to Article 13 of the Treaty, the Community undertook precisely the same obligation towards the associated states to abolish charges having equivalent effect as, in the Treaty, the Member States assumed towards each other.

Since this obligation is specific and not subject to any implied or express reservation on the part of the Community, it is capable of conferring on those subject to Community law the right to rely on it before the courts and to do so with effect from 1 January 1970.'

Moreover, the ECJ has accepted the direct effect of provisions of the Association Agreements with Turkey[128] (in particular provisions of Decisions 1/80 and 3/80 of the EC-Turkey Association Council) and of the Association Agreement with Cyprus.[129] For instance, in the *Sürül* case, the ECJ observed that:

'60 It is settled case-law that a provision in an agreement concluded by the Community with non-member countries must be regarded as being directly applicable when, regard being had to its wording and to the purpose and nature of the agreement itself, the provision contains a clear and precise obligation which is not subject, in its implementation or effects, to the adoption of any subsequent measure (see, in particular, Case 12/86 *Demirel* [1987] ECR 3719, paragraph 14 Case C-18/90 *Kziber* [1991] ECR I-199, paragraph 15, and Case C-162/96 *Racke*

[125] *Ibid.*, emphasis added.

[126] See for an overview on the Cotonou Agreement: Arts (2003).

[127] Case 87/75 *Bresciani* [1976] ECR 129.

[128] See e.g.: Case 12/86 *Demirel* v. *Stadt Schwäbisch Gmünd* [1987] ECR 3719; Case C-192/89 *Sevince* [1990] ECR I-3461; Case C-65/98 *Eyüp* [2000] ECR I-4747; Case C-37/98 *Savas* [2000] ECR I-2927; Case C-329/97 *Ergat* [2000] ECR I-1487; Case C-340/97 *Nazli* [2000] ECR I-957.

[129] Case C-312/91 *Metalsa* [1993] ECR I-3751.

> [1998] ECR I-3655, paragraph 31). In Case C-192/89 *Sevince* v *Staatssecretaris van Justitie* [1990] ECR I-3461, paragraphs 14 and 15, the Court made it clear that the same conditions apply in determining whether the provisions of a decision of the EEC-Turkey Association Council may have direct effect.
>
> 61 In deciding whether Article 3(1) of Decision No 3/80 meets those criteria, it is necessary first to examine its terms.
>
> 62 That provision lays down in clear, precise and unconditional terms a prohibition of discrimination, based on nationality, against persons residing in the territory of any Member State to whom the provisions of Decision No 3/80 are applicable.
>
> 65 That interpretation is also confirmed by settled case-law of the Court (see *Kziber*, cited above, paragraphs 15 to 23, confirmed by Case C-58/93 *Yousfi* [1994] ECR I-1353, paragraphs 16 to 19 Case C-103/94 *Krid* [1995] ECR I-719, paragraphs 21 to 24 Case C-126/95 *Hallouzi-Choho* v *Bestuur van de Sociale Verzekeringsbank* [1996] ECR I-4807, paragraphs 19 and 20 and Case C-113/97 *Babahenini* [1998] ECR I-183, paragraphs 17 and 18) relating to the principle of equal treatment contained in Article 39(1) of the Cooperation Agreement between the European Economic Community and the People's Democratic Republic of Algeria, signed in Algiers on 26 April 1976 and concluded on behalf of the Community by Council Regulation (EEC) No 2210/78 of 26 September 1978 (OJ 1978 L 263, p. 1) and to Article 41(1) of the Cooperation Agreement between the European Economic Community and the Kingdom of Morocco, signed in Rabat on 26 April 1976 and concluded on behalf of the Community by Council Regulation (EEC) No 2211/78 (OJ 1978 L 264, p. 1).'[130]

Finally, the ECJ has also accepted the direct effect of provisions of the Association Agreements between EC and Poland, Czech Republic and Bulgaria on the basis of the same criteria as applied for the Association Agreement with Turkey.[131]

In sum, it can be concluded that the ECJ applies the textual criteria (clear, precise and unconditional) as well as the 'supplemental' ones in the sense that it examines whether the object, purpose and nature of the agreement supports the acceptance of direct effect. More specifically, with regard to the agreements annexed to the WTO Agreement, the ECJ also applies the reciprocity argument and the argument of judicial restraint vis-à-vis the negotiation position of the EC. In this way the ECJ is able to decide on a case-by-case basis whether direct effect of a provision of an international agreement should be accorded or not.

---

130 Case C-262/96 *Sürül* [1999] ECR I-2685.

131 Case C-268/99 *Jany* [2001] ECR I-8615; Case C-235/99 *Kondova* [2001] ECR I-6427; Case C-257/99 *Barkoci and Malik* [2001] ECR I-6557; Case C-63/99 *Gloszczuk* [2001] ECR I-6369; Case C-162/00 *Pokrzeptowicz-Meyer* [2002] ECR I-1049; see for details: Staples (2002); Van Ooik (2002); Van Ooik/ Staples (2001); Govaere (1997); Van Ooik (1997); see also in general: Maresceau (1997).

Accordingly, the fact that a provision of an international treaty is clear, precise and unconditional does not automatically lead to the acceptance of direct effect within the Community legal order.

3 Summary

The previous sections illustrated that the legal status and effect of international treaties is substantially affected by the influence of Community law, in particular by the case-law of the ECJ regarding treaties concluded by the EC alone, mixed agreements and certain agreements to which the EC is not even party but which belong to the 'orbit' of the EC legal order. As a consequence thereof, these treaties become 'integral' parts of the Community legal order, ranked between primary and secondary Community law. Hence, international treaties that are integral part of the Community legal order enjoy supremacy over all conflicting national law – including constitutional law – of the Member States and conflicting secondary EC law. Moreover, as regards their possible direct effect, it appears from the case-law of the ECJ that two interrelated elements are taken into account when determining the direct effect of provisions of international treaties.[132] Besides, considering the specific characteristics of the agreement, the ECJ also examines the wording of the provision of the agreement,[133] which must be clear, precise and unconditional, i.e. no subsequent implementation measures are required.[134] Only when the ECJ is satisfied that both sets of conditions are met is it willing to grant direct effect to international agreements. Consequently, the ECJ determines the legal status of those international treaties and the conditions for their direct effect in the legal order of the EC as well as of the Member States. Moreover, these conclusions are in principle also applicable to treaties concluded by the EU either alone or as mixed EU agreements.

In this way, the ECJ is able to circumvent the existing constitutional differences regarding the legal status of treaties in the EU Member States, thereby ensuring a uniform and effective application of them within all the EU Member States. Similarly, the criteria used by the ECJ to decide whether provisions of international agreements can have direct effect are now uniformly determined by the ECJ. While the textual criteria used by the ECJ to establish whether a

---

[132] See for a detailed analysis: Bebr (1983); Bourgeois (1984); Peters (1998).

[133] Case 21-24/72 *International Fruit Company* v. *Produktschap voor Groenten en Fruit*) [1972] ECR 1219; Case 9/73 *Schlüter* v. *Hauptzollamt Lörrach* [1973] ECR 1135; Case 87/75 *Bresciani* [1976] ECR 129; Case C-163/90 *Legros* [1992] ECR I-4625; Case C-312/91 *Metalsa* [1993] ECR I-3751; Case C-432/92 *Anastasiou* [1994] ECR I-3087; Case C-18/90 *Kziber* [1991] ECR I-199; Case C-126/95 *Hallouzi-Choho* v. *Bestuur van de Sociale Verzekeringsbank* [1996] ECR I-4807.

[134] Case C-192/89 *Sevince* v. *Staatssecretaris van Justitie* [1990] ECR I-3461; Case C-58/93 *Yousfi* [1994] ECR I-1353; Case C-432/92 *Anastasiou* [1994] ECR I-3087; Case C-103/94 *Krid* [1995] ECR I-719.

provision of an international treaty can have direct effect are comparable to the ones applied by Dutch and French courts, the additional criteria are not. One exception is the reciprocity element that is also applied by the French courts since it is mentioned in Article 55 CF. For the German courts the impact is again particularly great since the issue of direct effect of international law does not arise in the German constitutional system. So, German courts are confronted by the case-law of the ECJ with specific criteria concerning the supremacy and direct effect of treaties in their legal order which are not foreseen in the *Grundgesetz* and thus would otherwise not arise.

Finally, the involvement of the ECJ also affects the jurisdiction of the national courts of the EU Member States to review international agreements. Due to the extensive jurisdiction of the ECJ regarding the review of international agreements, the national courts have lost their jurisdiction to review those treaties or the provisions thereof that fall within the scope of competence of the EC.

In summary, this means that the constitutional provisions of the EU Member States regarding the legal status and effect of international treaties in their domestic legal order are – by virtue of the influence of EC law – superimposed by Community law rules and the case-law of the ECJ – except for matters that fall within the exclusive competence of the EU Member States.

CHAPTER 3

The Domestic Legal Status of Decisions of International Organizations

In this chapter the influence of Community law on the legal status and effect of binding decisions of regional fisheries organizations, the EC-Turkey Association Council, Multilateral Environmental Agreements, UN Security Council and the ICAO Council will be analysed. The sections of the various IOs examine the decisions as applied on the international, European and national law level covering the three selected EU Member States (Germany, the Netherlands and France).

Before starting with the analysis, the general position of decisions of IOs within the domestic legal orders of the three selected EU Member States is outlined below. This will illustrate the classic legal situation 'law of IOs-national law' that exists in the selected EU Member States if the influence of EC law is left out. In addition, also the general position of decisions of IOs in the European legal order will be determined.

1 The general position of decisions of IOs within domestic law

1.1 Germany

Article 24 GG provides for the participation of Germany in international organizations and the possibility of transferring sovereign rights to IOs. The scope of Article 24 GG is broadly interpreted, thus covering all sorts of IOs in all three main legal branches.[1] However, neither Article 24 GG nor any other provision of the *Grundgesetz* deals with decisions of IOs or their legal status and effect in the German legal order. Perhaps three aspects can explain this situation. First, at the time the *Grundgesetz* was drawn up, only very few IOs existed that could adopt binding decisions, thus there was no apparent need to regulate that issue.[2] Second, since the generally accepted interpretation of Articles 24 and 59 (2) GG is that a transformation act is required before becoming applicable in the domestic legal order – be it for international treaties or binding decisions of IOs – no specific provision seemed necessary.[3] Third, since Germany gained full sovereignty only in 1955, membership in IOs was probably not an important issue when the *Grundgesetz* was drawn up in the late 1940s. However, as will be discussed in the following sections, due to the close legal

1 See: Randelzhofer (1992); Bleckmann (1975) at 229.

2 Bleckmann (1975) at 155 writes in this context: 'Die Rechtssetzungsbefugnis einer Organisation gegenüber ihren Mitgliedstaaten kann von einer unverbindlichen Empfehlung über die Mitwirkung beim Abschluß völkerrechtlicher Verträge bis zum Erlaß von Vorschriften gehen, welche für die einzelnen Mitgliedstaaten unmittelbar verbindlich sind. Solche Entscheidungsbefugnisse sind allerdings selten.'

3 See: Frowein/Oellers-Frahm (1996) at 90-92; Schreuer (1977) at 188; Geiger (2002) at 179.

relationship between decisions of IOs and international agreements, decisions of IOs are treated to a large extent in a similar manner to international treaties. Thus, Article 59 (2) GG is also applied to decisions of IOs, i.e. they must be incorporated by a domestic legal act before being internally applicable.[4] Consequently, the decisions enjoy the same legal status within the German legal order as the transformation act itself, which can be a federal statute but can also be a *Rechtsverordnung* (executive order), which is below the rank of a federal statute.

1.2 The Netherlands

The Dutch constitution is one of the very few which explicitly deals with the legal effect of decisions of IOs.[5] Before 1953, the Dutch constitution did not contain any reference to the legal effect of decisions of IOs. However, in 1953 the Dutch constitution was substantially revised and for the first time the term 'decisions by organizations based on international law' was introduced.[6] Since Articles 93, 94 Gw. are very similar to the Articles 65-67 of the 1953 Dutch constitution[7], reference is made to the discussion in section 1.2 of Chapter 2. Accordingly, decisions of IOs that are 'binding on anyone' (*ieder verbindend*) can be invoked by natural or legal persons before a Dutch court and enjoy primacy over conflicting national law. Whether a provision is binding on anyone depends on whether it is sufficiently clear and precise and does not require a further implementation act. This is determined by the national judge on a case-by-case basis.[8]

The sweeping legal effects granted to decisions of IOs must be seen in the light of the developments right after WW II. At that time, several IOs were set up with the competence to adopt binding decisions. Reference can be made to the UN Security Council, NATO, Council of Europe, OEEC (later renamed OECD), the IMF and World Bank as well as the ECSC. In addition, even before the creation of these IOs, for the Netherlands a relevant example existed, namely, the International Rhine Commission that could also adopt binding decisions.[9] The Commission for the revision of the Dutch constitution Eysinga explicitly referred to the development of the increasing establishment of IOs having the competence of adopting binding decisions and, therefore, emphasized that it was important that the Dutch constitution dealt with this phenomenon appropriately.[10] He argued that the Dutch constitution should contain explicit provi-

---

4 Geiger (2002) at 178-179.

5 See for details: Kuijper (1979).

6 See for an overview: Brouwer (1992).

7 See for an English text of the provisions of the 1953 constitution: Van Panhuys (1953) at 540.

8 See for a detailed discussion: Tammes (1962).

9 See generally: Haak (1988).

10 See: Eindrapport van de Commissie nopens de samenwerking tussen regering en Staten-Generaal inzake het buitenlands beleid, 9.7.1951; see critically: Duynstee (1954).

sions determining the legal status and effect of international treaties as well as decisions of IOs within the Dutch legal order. More specifically, by 1953, Eysinga distinguished between decisions of intergovernmental and supranational organizations, i.e. a decision of the International Rhine Commission (as an example of a classic intergovernmental organization) as opposed to a decision of the High Authority of the ECSC (as an example of a supranational organization). In this context, he emphasized the difference in the legal effect of these decisions. While decisions of the International Rhine Commission belong to a classical intergovernmental organization that can be controlled by the member states, the High Authority of the ECSC constituted an organ with supranational features to which the member states irreversibly had transferred sovereign rights. Because it was apparent that decisions of the High Authority of the ECSC would enjoy (automatically) primacy over all Dutch law, Eysinga called for explicit provisions in the *Grondwet* in order to address this development. Nonetheless, although the supranational character of the EEC (the preparations for negotiating the EEC Treaty were started at around the same time) became evident, no differentiation between decisions of intergovernmental and supranational organizations was introduced into the *Grondwet*.

In summary, since 1953 – that is before the establishment of the EEC but after the creation of the ECSC – the Dutch constitution has explicitly recognized the existence of decisions of IOs and determined their legal status within the Dutch legal order. Moreover, the Dutch constitution has accepted right from the beginning – without the influence of EC law – the primacy of decisions of IOs (in case they are binding on anyone) over conflicting national law if they fulfil the required criteria.

1.3 France

The French constitution of 1958 does not contain any explicit provisions regarding the legal status of decisions of IOs. This was also the case with the previous French constitutions.[11] However, decisions of IOs could fall within the scope of Article 55 CF that provides that treaties properly ratified and published enjoy primacy over conflicting laws.[12] In this context, two interpretations are possible. A restrictive textual interpretation would argue that because only international treaties are mentioned in Article 55 CF and not decisions of IOs, they do not fall within the scope of Article 55 CF. An extensive interpretation would argue that decisions of IOs are derived acts from international treaties, and are so closely connected with them that they should be treated similar to treaties and thus should fall within the scope of Article 55 CF.[13] In fact,

[11] Lanfranchi (1997) at 38.

[12] Decaux/Eisemann/Goesel-Le Bihan/Stern (1996) at 270-273.

[13] Poirat (2000) at 548.

a study concluded by the *Conseil d'Etat* indicates that decisions of IOs adopted for the purpose of implementing international treaties could fall within the scope of Article 55 CF.[14] Similarly, the *Conseil Constitutionnel* stated in a decision of 1986 that the scope of Article 55 CF includes *'les obligations internationales de France'* without any distinction or limitation attached to that general statement.[15] Further evidence for the equal treatment of treaties and decisions of IOs can be found in a decree from 1953 regarding the ratification and publication of engagements in international affairs by France, which mentions treaties as well as *'les règlement internationaux par lesquels la France se trouve engagée'*.[16] Similar as regards treaties, the decree prescribes that *'ces règlements doivent être publiés au Journal officiel de la Republique française (Lois et décrets) s'ils sont de nature à affecter par leur application les droits et obligations des particuliers'*. Accordingly, there is sufficient evidence to conclude that binding decisions of IOs could fall within the scope of Article 55 CF and thus enjoy primacy over conflicting French statutes.

1.4 Summary

From the discussion above, it can be concluded that the legal status of decisions of IOs is explicitly regulated only in the Netherlands where they enjoy supremacy over all national and direct effect if they fulfil the conditions of Articles 93, 94 Gw. In Germany and France, the provisions that are used to determine the legal status and effect of international treaties are also applicable to binding decisions of IOs. Accordingly, decisions of IOs enjoy primacy over conflicting national law – excluding constitutional provisions – in France, while in Germany they are implemented by a transformation act before becoming part of the domestic legal order, enjoying the same legal status as the transformation act, i.e. similar to a federal statute or an executive regulation. Hence, the legal status and effect of decisions of IOs is treated differently in the three selected EU Member States. This conclusion should be kept in mind in the course of the analysis of the following examples.

---

[14] Lanfranchi (1997) at 42 refers to a study concluded by the Conseil d'Etat in 1985.

[15] Conseil Constitutionnel, judgment no. 86-207, 25.6.1986; see also: Lanfranchi (1997) 42.

[16] Décret no. 53-192, 14.3.1953, revised by Décret 86-707, 11.4.1996, summarized by Circulaire du Premier Ministre, 30.5.1997, RGDIP 1997, 591-608.

2 The general position of decisions of IOs within the European legal order

The EC Treaty does not specify the legal status of decisions of IOs within the Community legal order. Accordingly, one must examine the case-law of the European courts. Whilst the jurisprudence of the European courts so far has not determined generally the legal status and effect of decisions of IOs, there is case-law concerning some decisions of IOs. For instance, the ECJ determined in the *Sevince* case that, due to the close relationship between the Decisions of the Association Council and the Association Agreement itself, the Decisions must be treated in the same way as the Association Agreement.[17] Similarly, the CFI stated in its *Biret* judgment that there is 'an inescapable and direct link between the [AB] decision and the plea alleging infringement of the SPS Agreement [as part of the WTO Agreement], and the decision could therefore only be taken into consideration if the Court had found that Agreement to have direct effect [...]'.[18] Also, Advocate General Alber opined in its Opinion in the appeals case of *Biret* that the WTO dispute settlement reports are a concretization of the WTO Agreement and therefore should be treated in the same way.[19] Indeed, the following case-studies illustrate that generally binding decisions of IOs are treated in the Community legal order in the same way as agreements concluded by the EC. Accordingly, they are an integral part of the Community legal order and thus enjoy primacy over conflicting secondary Community law and all domestic law of the EU Member States and may have direct effect.[20]

3 Decisions of Regional Fisheries Organizations

As will be explained below, the EC has exclusive competence in the field of fisheries and has also replaced the EC Member States in the various fisheries organizations, which results in a legal relationship 'decisions of regional fisheries organizations–EC law'.[21] Consequently, at first sight, there appears to be not much of a transformation that would lead to an 'EC law transformed' legal relationship 'decisions of fisheries organization–European

[17] The ECJ stated in case C-192/89 *Sevince* [1990] ECR I-3461: '9 The Court has also held that, since they are directly connected with the Agreement to which they give effect, the decisions of the Council of Association, *in the same way* as the Agreement itself, form an integral part, as from their entry into force, of the Community legal system (see judgment in Case 30/88 *Greece* v. *Commission*, supra, paragraph 13).' Empahsis added.

[18] Case T-174/00 *Biret* [2002] ECR II-17, para. 67.

[19] Opinion AG Alber in case C-93/02 P *Biret*, para. 120.

[20] See for details: Chapter 2.

[21] See section 3.2.

law–national law'. Nevertheless, the inclusion of this case-study is justified for two reasons. First, fisheries policy is in the daily practice of the EC an important issue. Second, for the sake of completeness, it is included in the research in order to examine also the impact of the exclusive competence of the EC and sole membership of the EC in the regional fisheries organizations and thus the complete transformation of these decisions by Community law before they enter the domestic legal orders of the selected EC Member States.

3.1 International law level

There are numerous regional fisheries organizations such as the North-East Atlantic Fisheries Commission (NEAFC), North Atlantic Salmon Conservation Organization (NASCO), Indian Ocean Tuna Commission (IOTC), International Baltic Sea Fishery Commission (IBSFC), Northwest Atlantic Fisheries Organization (NAFO), International Commission for the Conservation of Atlantic Tunas (ICCAT) and the Commission for the Conservation of Antarctic Marine Living Resources (CCAMLR).

Generally speaking, most regional fisheries organizations have a comparable institutional structure consisting of a Council, a (Fisheries) Commission, sometimes a Secretariat and one or more scientific advisory bodies.[22] In the case of the NASCO, three regional Commissions exist. The main task of the Fisheries Commissions is to adopt recommendations determining the total allowable catches (TACs) for the various fish stocks. In most cases the recommendations are adopted by majority voting (NAFO, ICCAT), qualified majority voting (IOTC) or by a 2/3 majority (IBSFC). Only in the case of the NASCO is unanimity required, while in the case of the CCAMLR decisions on matters of 'substance shall be taken by consensus' and all other decisions by simple majority. The problem whether an issue is a matter of substance shall be treated as a matter of substance, i.e. is decided by consensus. It is assumed that fixing TACs is a matter of substance. In all regional fisheries organizations each contracting party has one vote. Thus, in most cases the Fisheries Commissions can adopt with some sort of majority voting binding quotas for the catching of the respective fish stocks. However, the entering into force of adopted recommendations is subject to complicated, slightly differing opting-out procedures.[23]

Essentially, the contracting parties of the various regional fisheries organizations can raise an objection against the adopted TAC within a certain period of time, ranging from 50 days up to 6 months. Thus, any contracting party can

---

[22] See for details: Koers (1984); Churchill (1987) at 184-191.

[23] An exception in this regard is the Convention for the Conservation of the Southern Bluefin Tuna (CCSBT) which does not contain an opt-out procedure, but simply states that the decisions of the Commission reached by unanimity (Article 7) are binding on the parties (Australia, New Zealand, Japan are the only parties, Article 8 (7)).

avoid being bound by recommendations through using the opting-out procedure.[24] This simple way of avoiding the binding effect of recommendations is the main cause why the Fisheries Commissions have not been very successful in preventing over-fishing and the reduction of the fish stocks.[25] Another factor for the limited success of the Fisheries Commissions is the introduction of the Exclusive Economic Zone (EEZ) by most coastal states, thereby extending their sovereignty to fish from the prior 12 to 200 miles.[26] This in turn reduced the competence of the regional fisheries organizations since they are only allowed to fix TAC quotas beyond the 200 miles EEZ zone.[27]

3.2 European law level

Since the *Kramer*[28] judgment of the ECJ, it is generally accepted that the EC has exclusive external competence in the field of fisheries.[29] The exclusive competence of the EC regarding fisheries resulted in 1983 in the establishment of a Common Fisheries Policy (CFP)[30], which was revised in 1992 by EC Regulation 3760/92.[31] More recently, Regulation 3760/92 has been replaced by EC Regulation 2371/2002 establishing a new Common Fisheries Policy of the EC.[32] Due to its exclusive competence in the field of fisheries, the EC is alone a member of the regional fisheries organizations, either as a founding member or as a substitute for the EU Member States that were originally members. An exception is the Commission for the Conservation of Antarctic Marine Living Resources (CCAMLR) that covers policy areas falling outside the exclusive fisheries competence of the EC. Also in certain cases, Denmark remains alongside

---

24 See for details: Churchill (1999a).

25 *Ibid.*, at 465.

26 *Ibid.*, at 465-467.

27 For instance, Article I (2) NAFO Convention states:
'[...] "the Regulatory Area" is that part of the Convention Area which lies beyond the areas in which Coastal States exercise fisheries jurisdiction'. The only exception is the Baltic Sea Convention which defines in Article II the 'Convention area' as 'all waters of the Baltic Sea and the Belts, excluding internal waters'.

28 See: Joined cases 3 ,4, and 6/76 *Officier van Justitie* v. *Kramer* [1976] ECR 1279; subsequently confirmed in Case C-258/89 *Commission* v. *Spain* [1991] ECR I-3977; Case C-25/94 *Commission* v. *Council* [1996] ECR I-1469. See for extensive analysis: Koers (1977); *ibid.*, (1984); Churchill (1980); *ibid.*, (1987), Chapter 5, at 167-202; *ibid.*, (1999a); *ibid.*, (1999b).

29 Churchill (1999a) at 468-469.

30 Council Regulation 170/83, OJ 1983 L 24/1.

31 OJ 1992 L 389/1-14.

32 Council Regulation, No. 2371/2002 on the conservation and sustainable exploitation of fisheries resources under the Common Fisheries Policy, OJ 2002 L 358/59-80; see also: Le Bihan (2003).

the EC as a member of some fisheries organizations because of Denmark's responsibility for the Faeroe Islands and Greenland. Similarly, France is also a member in some regional fisheries organizations alongside the EC because of its responsibility for some overseas territories and because, in accordance with Article 299 EC Treaty, many relevant provisions of the EC Treaty (including fisheries) are not or are only partly applicable in those territories.[33]

Since the EC is member of most regional fisheries organizations, the treaties establishing them have become an integral part of the Community legal order, thereby obtaining Community law characteristics. Likewise, from the moment the TACs adopted by the various Fisheries Commissions enter into force, they also become integral part of the Community legal order. As a result, they are modified from decisions adopted under public international law into Community law measures, enjoying primacy over all national law and having direct effect if they meet the criteria established by the ECJ.

As to the implementation of binding TACs, the overall majority of them are implemented by EC Council Regulations based on Article 8 (4) of Regulation 3760/92.[34]

An example is Council Regulation 49/1999[35] fixing the TACs for certain highly migratory fish stocks. As the preamble of the Regulation states, the ICCAT adopted recommendations on catch limitations that have become binding for all contracting parties, including the EC. Accordingly, the TACs as determined by the ICCAT are simply copied into the EC Regulation, thereby transforming them into EC law measures, so they also become binding by virtue of Community law. Moreover, the European Commission is also involved in the implementation of the fisheries policy. It issues Commission Regulations that forbid the fishers of the Member States from continuing to fish if they have reached the limits of their fishing quotas and thus they are no longer allowed to fish for that particular sort of fish.[36]

Over the years the ECJ has dealt several times with cases in which Member States challenged the validity of the fixing of TACs.[37] However, in all these cases only 'communitarized' TACs transposed by Community law measures were

---

33 See: Chuchill (1987) at 55-67; Schröder (1997).

34 Van Rijn (1997) at 1041.

35 OJ 1999 L 13/54-58.

36 See e.g.: Commission Regulation (EC) No. 2050/2001 of 19.10.2001 prohibiting fishing for haddock by vessels flying the flag of Sweden, OJ 2001 L 277/4; Commission Regulation (EC) No. 1826/2001 of 17.9.2001 prohibiting fishing for monkfish by vessels flying the flag of the Netherlands, OJ 2001 L 248/16; Commission Regulation (EC) No. 1970/2001 of 9.10.2001 prohibiting fishing for common sole by vessels flying the flag of Belgium, OJ 2001 L 269/4.

37 See e.g.: Case C-120/99 *Italy* v. *Council* [2001] ECR I-7997; Case C-206/97 *Sweden* v. *Council* [1999] ECR I-3885; Case C-179/95 *Spain* v. *Council* [1999] ECR I-6475; Case C-4/96 *NIFPO* [1998] ECR I-681; Joined cases C-63/90 and 67/90 *Portugal and Spain* v. *Council* [1992] ECR I-5073.

at issue. Generally, the ECJ has rejected the complaints by the Member States. There has been one recent case in which a French fishing company challenged before the Court of First Instance (CFI) an EC fishery Regulation directly on the basis of Article 230 (4) EC Treaty.[38] The interesting aspect of this judgment is that the CFI adopted a broader concept of the *locus standi* before European courts than the ECJ, which would give individuals much easier access to the CFI and ECJ, in order to challenge directly the validity of Regulations before the European courts.[39] However, the ECJ rejected the expansive approach of the CFI in a subsequent ruling.[40] This view has also been adopted in the Opinion of the Advocate General in the appeals procedure of the *Jégo-Quéré* case before the ECJ.[41] Consequently, the possibility of individuals to challenge the validity of Regulations fixing TACs remains very limited.[42] Although, the formulation of Article III-270 (4) of the draft European Constitution would extend the possibilities of individuals to challenge acts of the Union before the European courts.[43]

In summary, it can be concluded that due to the exclusive competence of the EC in the area of fisheries, all binding decisions of the regional fisheries organizations are implemented by secondary Community legislation, thus are an integral part of EC law.

3.3 National law level

Since all binding TACs decisions of the Regional Fisheries Organizations are implemented by EC Regulations and thus are generally applicable in all EU Member States, national implementation measures are not required in order to give effect to EC Regulations. The ECJ accepts national implementation measures for EC Regulations only if they do not alter, obstruct or obscure the nature of the Community Regulations.[44]

3.3.1 Germany

The German authorities apply the EC Regulations determining the TACs directly and not on the basis of a separate domestic act. However, paragraph 2 of the *Seefischereigesetz*[45] (SeefFischG) provides for the possibility to

---

38 Case T-177/01 *Jégo-Quéré* [2002] ECR II-2365.

39 See: Barents (2003).

40 Case C-50/00 P *UPA* [2002] ECR I-6677; see also case-note by: Prechal/Parret (2003).

41 Opinion of Advocate General Jacobs in case C-263/02 P *Jégo-Quéré* of 10.7.2003.

42 See for a detailed study: Biernat (2003).

43 *Ibid.*

44 Case 50/76 *Amsterdam Bulb* [1977] ECR 137; Craig/De Búrca (2003) at 191-192.

45 BGBl. I, 1984, 876, republished in: BGBl. I, 1998, 1791.

issue – with the consent of the *Bundesrat – Rechtsverordnungen* for the purpose of implementing the Common Fishery Policy of the EC as well as obligations arising out of international fisheries agreements.[46] An example for this is the *Verordnung zur Durchsetzung des gemeinschaftlichen Fischereirechts*[47] that was issued for the purpose of implementing EC Regulations concerning technical fishery aspects.

According to an enquiry by the author at the *Bundesanstalt für Landwirtschaft und Ernährung*, which supervises the implementation of the German TACs, no German case-law exists challenging EC Regulations imposing the TACs. The reason is that it has been very difficult to challenge EC Regulations[48] and there is an absence of German implementation measures against which German fishers could start judicial procedures. Thus, the exclusive competence of the EC in the fisheries policy results in the absence of both German implementation measures and German case-law.

3.3.2 The Netherlands

In the Netherlands, fishery policy is regulated in the *Visserijwet 1963*[49] (Fisheries Act). Article 3a provides for the implementation of international fisheries obligations arising out of international treaties or decisions of IOs by adopting *algemene maatregel van bestuur*. However, TACs imposed by EC Regulations – whether or not adopted within regional fisheries organizations – are implemented by *ministeriële regeling* modifying the *Regeling Vangstbeper-*

---

46 Paragraph 2 SeeFischG Das Bundesministerium für Verbraucherschutz, Ernährung und Landwirtschaft wird ermächtigt, durch Rechtsverordnung mit Zustimmung des Bundesrates zur Erhaltung und wirtschaftlichen Nutzung von Fischbeständen, zur Durchführung des gemeinschaftlichen Fischereirechts oder zur Erfüllung von Verpflichtungen aus internationalen Seefischerei-Übereinkommen
1. zu verbieten, Fische bestimmter Arten zu fangen, an Bord zu behalten, anzulanden oder zu verkaufen,
2. die Ausübung der Seefischerei mengenmäßig, zeitlich, räumlich oder in anderer Weise zu beschränken,
3. die Benutzung von Fanggeräten, Fang- und Verarbeitungsvorrichtungen sowie die Anwendung von Fangmethoden vorzuschreiben, zu verbieten oder zu beschränken,
4. die Pflicht zu Aufzeichnungen, Auskünften oder sonstigen Meldungen aufzuerlegen, soweit es erforderlich ist, um die Einhaltung der Beschränkungen überwachen, den Fischereiaufwand feststellen oder die Entwicklung der Fischbestände verfolgen zu können.

47 BGBl. I, 1996, 736.

48 Despite the hopes raised by the judgment of the CFI in the case T-177/01 *Jégo-Quéré* [2002] ECR II-2365, which were eliminated by the ECJ in its judgment in case C-50/00 P *UPA* [2002] ECR I-6677; see also: Opinion of AG Jacobs in the appeals procedure in case C-263/02 P *Jégo-Quéré* of 10.7.2003.

49 Staatsblad 2002, 4, version of 12.7.2002.

kingen.[50] While an *algemene maatregel van bestuur* must be adopted by the whole government, a *ministeriële regeling* can be issued by the responsible Minister. Consequently, a much easier procedure is provided for the implementation of 'communitarized' TACs.

In a few cases,[51] Dutch courts dealt with issues involving the conformity of domestic acts with EC Regulations imposing TACs. However, in all those cases the courts rejected any challenge against the EC Regulations. Thus, it can be concluded that executive regulations are used to implement the EC Regulations, while Dutch courts are rarely confronted with cases concerning the conformity of domestic legislation with the EC Regulations determining the TACs.

3.3.3 France

The *Loi d'orientation sur la pêche maritime et les cultures marines*[52] which was adopted in 1997 reorganized the French fishery policy.[53] Article 4 of the *Loi* modifies Article 3 of the *Décret* of 9.1.1852 by inserting a new paragraph authorizing the Council of State to issue *Décrets* for implementing the TACs as determined by Community legislation. In practice, the Minster of Agriculture issues *Arrêtés* implementing the TACs as contained in the relevant EC Regulations.[54] Similarly, *Arrêtés* are issued to impose TACs for fish stocks which are within the French jurisdiction but not covered by Community legislation[55] as well as implementing TACs issued by the NAFAO to which France is member along with the EC because of the special position of Saint-Pierre-et-Miquelon.[56]

---

50 See for instance: Wijziging Regeling Vangstbeperkingen, 14.11.2001, Staatscourant, 16.11.2001, nr. 223, 12.

51 See e.g.: Hoge Raad, judgment of 23.5.1989, NJ 1989, 759; Hoge Raad, judgment of 1.10.1991, NJ 1992, 266; Raad van State, Afdeling Rechtspraak, judgment 4.12.1990, AB 1991, 687; Case 46/86 *Romkes* [1987] ECR 2671.

52 J.O., No. 268, 19.11.1997, 16723.

53 See for details: Proutière-Maulin (1998a); *ibid.*, (1998b).

54 See e.g.: Arrêté du 28.3.2002 portant répartition de certains quotas de pêche accordés à la France pour 2002, J.O., No. 88, 14.4.2002, 6630; Arrêté du 20.3.2001 portant répartition de certains quotas de pêche accordés à la France pour 2001, J.O., No. 78, 1.4.2001, 5149.

55 Arrêté du 25.10.1994 modifiant l'arrêté du 7.6.1994 fixant le poids ou la taille minimale de capture de certains poissons et autres animaux marins dans les eaux maritimes qui relèvent de la souveraineté ou de la juridiction française mais qui ne sont pas couvertes par la réglementation communautaire de conservation et de gestion, J.O., No. 254, 1.11.1994, 15570.

56 Arrêté du 25.3.2002 fixant pour l'année 2002 certains prélèvements totaux autorisés de captures dans la sous-division 3Ps de l'Organisation des pêches de l'Atlantique du Nord-Ouest, J.O., No. 75, 29.3.2002, 5570; Arrêté du 5.4.2001 fixant pour l'année 2001 certains prélèvements totaux autorisés de captures dans la sous-division 3 PS de l'Organisation des pêches de l'Atlantique du Nord-Ouest, J.O., No. 87, 12.4.2001, 5648.

As regards France, no relevant case-law regarding the TACs could be found. In sum, in France executive regulations are also adopted in order to implement the TACs as imposed by EC Regulations.

3.4 Summary

In conclusion, it can be stated that all regional fisheries organizations can adopt binding decisions. All treaties – with one exception – provide for an opt-out procedure enabling contracting parties to avoid being legally bound by the recommendations.

Since the EC has obtained exclusive competence with regard to fisheries, the treaties establishing the regional fisheries organizations and the binding decisions adopted by the Fisheries Commissions are an integral part of the Community legal order. Consequently, they obtain Community law characteristics such as supremacy and possible direct effect. The EC implements the TACs adopted by the regional fisheries organizations by using Council Regulations, which usually simply copy the contents of the decisions. In this way, the TACs that used to be decisions adopted under public international law are modified (communitarized) into Community law measures. For the EU Member States, the 'communitarization' of the fisheries recommendations results in a modification of their legal nature and effect in the sense that they are transformed into binding EC law legislation with the result that they enjoy supremacy over all domestic law. In addition, the EU Member States are no longer able to avoid being bound by the recommendations by using the opting-out procedures.

On the national law level, the exclusive competence of the EC results in a very limited role for the national administrations and courts. In principle, EC Regulations do not have to be implemented or republished by domestic acts of the Member States. Nonetheless, the Netherlands and France issue executive regulations containing the contents of the EC Regulations and publish them in their official gazettes, while Germany does not issue any additional acts. It appears that the domestic courts of the selected Member States are practically never faced with cases involving TACs.

In summary, it can be concluded that the exclusive competence of the EC does not create an 'EC law transformed' legal relationship 'Decisions of regional fisheries organizations–European law–national law' but rather replaces the previous classic legal situation 'Decisions of regional fisheries organizations–national law' by a new legal situation 'Decisions of regional fisheries organizations–EC law'. As a consequence, the domestic law of the EU Member States does not play a great role in the implementation of TACs.

4 EC-Turkey Association Council Decisions

4.1 International law level

The Association Agreement concluded between the E(E)C, its Member States and Turkey dates back to 1964.[57] The main object of the treaty is to forge closer economic relations between the contracting parties and improve the living standards in Turkey which would subsequently facilitate the accession of Turkey to the E(E)C. Article 22 of the Association Agreement provides that:

> 'in order to attain the objectives of this Agreement the Council of Association shall have the power to takes decisions in the cases provided therein...'
> In addition, it gives the Association Council the power to:
> 'adopt appropriate decisions where, in the course of implementation of the Association arrangements, attainment of an objective of this Agreement calls for joint action by the Contracting Parties but the requisite powers are not granted in this agreement.'

According to Article 23 of the Association Agreement, the Association Council consists of members of the governments of the EC Member States, members of the Council and the Commission as well as members of the Turkish government. The Association Council Decisions are adopted with unanimity (Article 23).

The Association Council can thus be qualified as an organ established by the Association Agreement endowed with the competence to adopt binding decisions independently from the contracting parties. The question still arises whether the Association Council is an organ of an IO. If so, of which IO? Some legal authors doubt whether the Association Council can be qualified as an organ of an IO because – it is argued – they cannot act independently from the contracting parties, in particular since the decisions of the Association Council are adopted unanimously.[58] However, the fact that decisions are adopted unanimously is not a convincing argument because in many IOs, decisions are adopted with unanimity without putting their qualification as an IO into doubt. Rather, the decisive factor is whether the contracting parties intended to establish an organ that can adopt binding decisions independently from them. Considering the broad competences granted to the Association Council by Article 22 of the Association Agreement, it is clear that the contracting parties intended to establish an organ that can adopt binding decisions.[59] Indeed, the

---

57 OJ 1964 217/3687 (Dutch version).

58 See: Weber (1997b); Vedder (1994) at 209-210; Rohde/Kaltenborn (1993).

59 See: Von Bogdandy/Bast/Arndt (2002) at 147; Martenczuk (2001).

ECJ came to the same conclusion with regard to the legal effect of Association Council Decision 1/80 when it stated:

> '18 In so far as they implement the objectives set by the Agreement, such decisions are directly connected with the Agreement and, as a result of the second sentence of Article 22(1) thereof, have the effect of binding the Contracting Parties.
>
> 19 By virtue of the Agreement, the Contracting Parties agreed to be bound by such decisions and if those parties were to withdraw from that commitment, that would constitute a breach of the Agreement itself.
>
> 20 Consequently, contrary to the contention of the defendants in the main proceedings and the Governments of the Member States which have submitted observations to the Court, the binding effect of decisions of the Association Council cannot depend on whether implementing measures have in fact been adopted by the Contracting Parties.'[60]

So, the only issue that remains to be addressed is the question of which IO is the Association Council an organ? One possible answer is to consider the Association Council itself as the IO, being at the same time its only organ. However, that seems difficult to sustain as an IO requires some infrastructure as, for instance, a Secretariat, a seat of a headquarter etc. A less formal and more functional approach could lead to a more appropriate answer, namely, that the Association Agreement must be considered an institutionalized arrangement.[61] In other words, while the Association Agreement does not establish an IO in the formal sense, it does create an institution or organ endowed with powers that are comparable to an organ of an IO. Accordingly, the Association Council is considered to be an organ that can adopt binding decisions that can *de facto* be compared with an organ of IO.

The Association Council has adopted three important decisions. Decision 1/80 implements measures for the progressive free movement of Turkish workers, while Decision 2/80 determines the conditions for implementing the special aid to Turkey. Finally, Decision 3/80 concerns the application of the social security schemes of the Member States to Turkish workers and their family members.

4.2 European law level

The case-law of the ECJ regarding Association Council Decisions can be characterised as very *effet utile*-orientated. The following three

---

[60] Case C-277/94 *Taflan-Met* [1996] ECR I-4085.

[61] See on the institutionalized arrangements within the context of MEAs: Churchill/Ulfstein (2000); Röben (2000).

[62] Case 12/86 *Demirel* [1987] ECR 3719.

points can be highlighted. First, the ECJ – starting with the *Demirel* case[62] – asserted its jurisdiction to interpret Association Council Decisions even if certain provisions of them potentially fall within the competence of the Member States.[63] Second, the ECJ explicitly stated in the *Sevince* case that due to the close relationship between the Decisions of the Association Council and the Association Agreement itself, the Decisions must be treated in the same way as the Association Agreement.[64] Accordingly, Association Council Decisions are an integral part of the Community legal order and thus enjoy primacy over all domestic law of the EU Member States as well as over conflicting secondary Community law. Third, in a number of cases the ECJ ruled that certain provisions of Association Council Decisions can have direct effect, i.e. Turkish workers and their family members can rely on them in order to challenge national laws that restrict their rights granted under the Association Council Decisions. In the *Eroglu* case the ECJ summed up its case-law on the interpretation of Articles 6 and 7 of Association Council Decision 1/80 as follows:

> '17 Like Article 6(1) of Decision No 1/80, Article 7 clearly, precisely and unconditionally embodies the rights of those children of Turkish workers who have completed a course of vocational training in the host country to respond to any offer of employment there, irrespective of the length of time they have been resident in that Member State, provided one of their parents has been legally employed in the Member State concerned for at least three years. Like Article 6(1), the second paragraph of Article 7 has direct effect in the Member States of the European Community.
>
> 18 It is noteworthy that in *Sevince*, in the context of the third indent of Article 6(1) of Decision No 1/80, the Court held that even if that provision merely governs the circumstances of the Turkish worker as regards employment and makes no reference to the right of residence, those two aspects of the personal situation of a Turkish worker are closely linked and that by granting to such a worker, after a specified period of legal employment in the Member State, access to any paid employment of his choice, the provision in question necessarily implies - since otherwise the right granted by it to the Turkish worker would be deprived of any effect - the existence, at least at that time, of a right of residence for the person concerned (paragraph 29).
>
> 19 In *Kus*, the Court applied the same reasoning to the first indent of Article 6(1) of Decision No 1/80, since, without a right of residence the grant to a Turkish worker of the right to renewal of his permit to work for the same employer after

[63] Koutrakos (2002) at 30-34.

[64] The ECJ stated in case C-192/89 *Sevince* [1990] ECR I-3461: '9 The Court has also held that, since they are directly connected with the Agreement to which they give effect, the decisions of the Council of Association, *in the same way* as the Agreement itself, form an integral part, as from their entry into force, of the Community legal system (see judgment in Case 30/88 *Greece* v. *Commission*, supra, paragraph 13).' Empahsis added.

> one year' s legal employment would likewise be deprived of any effect (paragraph 30).
>
> 20 Since the right of residence is essential to access to and the pursuit of any paid employment, whether for the same employer in connection with renewal of a work permit or for another employer, chosen freely or subject to the priority given to workers of the Member States of the Community, it must also be accepted that the right conferred on a person by the second paragraph of Article 7 of Decision No 1/80 to respond to any offer of employment necessarily implies the recognition of a right of residence for that person.'[65]

This case-law has been confirmed and extended by the ECJ in its more recent case-law.[66]

While the ECJ ruled since the beginning of the 1990s that Articles 6 and 7 of Association Council Decision 1/80 have direct effect, the case-law of the ECJ regarding the provisions of Association Council Decision 3/80 has been much more cautious.[67] In the *Taflan-Met* case, the ECJ ruled for the first time on provisions of Association Council Decision 3/80. The ECJ stated that:

> '37 It follows from all the foregoing considerations that, even though some of its provisions are clear and precise, Decision No 3/80 cannot be applied so long as supplementary implementing measures have not been adopted by the Council.
>
> 38 The reply to be given to the national court' s second question must therefore be that, so long as the supplementary measures essential for implementing Decision No 3/80 have not been adopted by the Council, Articles 12 and 13 of that decision do not have direct effect in the territory of the Member States and are therefore not such as to entitle individuals to rely on them before the national courts.'[68]

A few years later, in the *Sürül* case the ECJ adopted a more dynamic approach when it ruled:

> '97 In that connection, it is important to emphasise first that the principle laid down in Article 3(1) of Decision No 3/80, prohibiting all discrimination based on nationality in the field covered by that decision, means that a Turkish national to whom that decision applies must be treated in the same way as nationals of the

---

65 Case C-355/93 *Eroglu* v. *Baden-Würtemberg* [1994] ECR I-5113 (emphasis added).

66 See e.g.: Joined cases C-317/01 *Abatay et. al.* and C-369/01 *Sahin*, judgment of 21.10.2003; Case C-171/01 *Wählergruppe Gemeinsam Zajedno/Birlikte Alternative und Grüne GewerkschafterInnen/UG*) [2003] ECR I-4301; Case C-188/00 *Kurz* [2002] ECR I-10691; Case C-65/98 *Eyüp* [2000] ECR I-4747; Case C-329/97 *Ergat* [2000] ECR I-1487; Case C-340/97 *Nazli* [2000] ECR I-957.

67 See: Keunen (2001) at 295-301.

68 Case C-277/94 *Taflan-Met* [1996] ECR I-4085.

> host Member State, so that the legislation of that Member State cannot impose upon such a Turkish national more or stricter conditions than those applicable to its own nationals (see, by analogy, Case 186/87 *Cowan* v *Trésor Public* [1989] ECR 195, paragraph 10, *Kziber*, paragraph 28, and *Hallouzi-Choho*, paragraphs 35 and 36, both cited above).
>
> 98 It follows that a Turkish national who has been authorised to enter the territory of a Member State in order to reunite the family of a Turkish migrant worker and who lawfully resides there with that worker must be able to obtain in the host Member State a social security benefit provided for by the legislation of that State under the same conditions as the nationals of the Member State concerned.'[69]

Thus, while not all provisions of Association Council Decision 3/80 are directly applicable, the non-discrimination clause contained in Article 3 of Association Council Decision 3/80 is directly applicable.[70] Hence, Turkish nationals can rely upon Article 3 of Association Council Decision 3/80 before the domestic courts of the EU Member States. However, in view of the potentially high financial repercussions for the budgets of the Member States, the ECJ limited the legal effect of its ruling by restricting its application to future cases and proceedings that were already started before the delivery of the judgment.

In summary, it can be concluded that the ECJ accepted that certain provisions of Association Council Decisions 1/80 and 3/80 can have direct effect and thus can be invoked by individuals to challenge conflicting national laws of the Member States.[71] In this way, these provisions of those Association Council Decisions have been transformed by the jurisprudence of the ECJ into Community law measures. Thus, the classic legal situation 'Association Council Decision–national law' is modified into an 'EC law transformed' legal situation 'Association Council Decision–European law–national law'. This in turn substantially affects the legal situation in the Member States as the following sections illustrate.

4.3 National law level

4.3.1 Germany

In Germany, the legal status of foreigners is regulated by the *Ausländergesetz* (Aliens act).[72] Since the Association Council Decisions were not implemented in Germany by specific legislation, the *Ausländergesetz* (AuslG)

69 Case C-262/96 *Sürül* [1999] ECR I-2685.

70 See also: Case C-171/01 *Wählergruppe Gemeinsam Zajedno/Birlikte Alternative und Grüne GewerkschafterInnen/UG* [2003] ECR I-4301.

71 Staples (1997); *ibid.*, (1999a); *ibid.*, (1999c).

72 BGBl. I, 1990, 1354. 9.7.1990.

also applies to Turkish nationals. Since the year 2000, the application of the *Ausländergesetz* is guided by general administrative rules (*Allgemeine Verwaltungsvorschrift zum Ausländergesetz, AuslG-VwV*), which are internal guidelines for the administration explaining in detail how the provisions of the AuslG should be applied.[73] Those guidelines refer where appropriate to the provisions of Association Council Decision 1/80.

A huge number of cases involving Association Council Decisions have come before German administrative courts. That can be explained by the fact that from the late 1960s on, Germany 'invited' Turkish workers to come to Germany and fill up mostly low-paid jobs. Over time several million Turkish workers and their family members established themselves in Germany. Naturally, Turkish workers were eager to enjoy the rights granted to them in the Association Agreement and the subsequently adopted Association Council Decisions. Accordingly, the Association Agreement and the Association Council Decisions have played a prominent role in many German (administrative law) cases involving working permits, resident permits, social benefits etc.[74] In addition, the high number of cases is also caused by the diverging approaches of the German authorities and the ECJ as regards the extent of the rights granted to Turkish workers and their family members.[75] While the German authorities pursue a restrictive policy by encouraging the return of Turkish workers and discouraging new immigration from Turkey, the ECJ has over time extended the rights of Turkish workers, especially by holding that certain provisions of the Decisions of the Association Council are directly applicable.[76] The consequence of this contrasting tendency becomes most visible before the German administrative courts since they are faced with, on the one hand, the restrictive German Alien laws and, on the other hand, are bound by Association Council Decisions as interpreted by the ECJ.

The following case is an illustration of the impact of the Association Council Decision as interpreted by the ECJ on the German AuslG. The case concerns the right of residence of a child of a Turkish worker.[77] The applicant is a Turkish national who lived from 1973 until 1976 with his parents in Germany. He then returned to Turkey and completed his school education there. In July 1979, the applicant entered Germany again and in 1981 began to study engineering at a German university. He completed the studies in March 1990. In August 1979, the applicant obtained his first limited residence permit (*Aufenthaltserlaubnis*), which was subsequently renewed several times until April 1991. Since July 1987 the residence permit included the explicit restriction 'for study purposes only'. Whether the residence permits issued before also contained this restriction is disputed between the parties. The father of the applicant was legally employed

---

73 Allgemeine Verwaltungsvorschrift zum Ausländergesetz of 28.6.2000, BAnz. Nr. 188a, of 6.10.2000.

74 See the overview of: Kemper (1995); see also the cases published in: NVwZ 1995, 1110-1125.

75 See: Gutmann (1996).

76 Nachbaur (1995) at 344-345.

77 BVerwG, judgment of 12.12.1995, NVwZ 1996, 1116-1117.

as a worker at a company in Germany from 1971 until 1996. In June 1990, the applicant married a Turkish national. Due to this marriage, his restricted residence permit (*Aufenthaltserlaubnis*) was replaced by an unrestricted residence permit (*Aufenthaltsberechtigung*), valid until April 1993. In the meantime, the applicant worked since January 1991 as an engineer. In May 1991, the wife of the applicant informed the authorities that the marriage was dissolved. Due to this new situation, the German authorities revoked – on the basis of the applicable provisions of the AuslG – with retrospective effect his residence permit and requested him to leave Germany within two months or otherwise be expelled. The applicant appealed against this order but was rejected. In turn, he successfully challenged this decision at the *Verwaltungsgericht* (administrative court of first instance). The authorities appealed against that ruling but were rejected. A final appeal of the authorities at the *Bundesverwaltungsgericht* (Federal Administrative Court) remained also unsuccessful.

The *Bundesverwaltungsgericht* (BVerwG) examined the case in a two-step procedure.

In a first step, it analysed the relevant provisions of the *Ausländergesetz* (AuslG)[78] (Aliens act). According to paragraph 12 (2) AuslG,[79] a residence permit can be retroactively restricted if a significant condition for issuing the permit does not exist anymore. As the marriage was the crucial condition for granting an unrestricted residence permit, and since it lasted less than a year and therefore less than the minimum period for a marriage of 4 years (or exceptionally 3 years), the dissolution of the marriage eliminated the significant condition for granting the unrestricted permit. Consequently, the applicant could not derive his own right of residence on the basis of the marriage (19 AuslG).[80] In addition, the applicant could not derive his own right of residence independently from his

---

78 BGBl. I, 1990, 1354. 9.7.1990.

79 § 12 AuslG

(2) Die Aufenthaltsgenehmigung wird befristed oder, wenn es gesetzlich bestimmt ist, unbefristed erteilt. Ist eine für die Erteilung, die Verlängerung oder Bestimmung der Geltungsdauer wesentliche Voraussetzung entfallen, kann die befristete Aufenthaltsgenehmigung nachträglich zeitlich begrenzt werden.

80 § 19 AuslG

(1) Die Aufenthalserlaubnis des Ehegatten wird im Falle der Aufhebung der ehelichen Lebensgemeinschaft als eigenständiges, von dem in § 17 Abs. 1 bezeichneten Aufenthalszweck unabhängiges Aufenthalsrecht verlängert, wenn

1. die eheliche Lebensgemeinschaft seit mindestens 4 Jahren rechtmäßig im Bundesgebiet bestanden hat,

2. sie seit mindestens 3 Jahren rechtmäßig im Bundesgebiet bestanden hat und es zur Vermeidung einer besonderen Härte erforderlich ist, dem Ehegatten den weiteren Aufenthalt zu ermöglichen, oder

[....].

It should be noted that paragraph 19 was modified in 2000. The required number of years in no. 1 has been reduced from 4 to 2 years and the 3 years in no. 2 have been deleted.

marital status, as he did not possess an unrestricted residence permit for more than 5 years, as in the time between 1987 and 1990 the permits granted were all restricted (24 (1) AuslG).[81] Thus, the applicant did not have a right to obtain another residence permit on the basis of the German *Ausländergesetz*.

In a second step, the *BVerwG* turned its attention towards the Association Agreement, in particular, Article 7 (2) of Association Council Decision 1/80.[82] According to Article 7 (2), the children of Turkish workers who have completed a vocational training can apply to any job in that Member State, irrespective of how long the child has been resident in that Member State. But the wording of this provision does not mention anything regarding the right of residence; it merely grants a right to apply to any employment offers. However, the *BVerwG* had to take into account the case-law of the ECJ concerning Articles 6, 7 of Association Council Decision 1/80.[83] The ECJ decided in the *Eroglu* case that 'to respond to any offer of employment *necessarily* implies the recognition of a right of residence for that person.'[84] Furthermore, the ECJ held in this case that Article 7 (2) like Article 6 (1) of Association Council Decision 1/80 has direct effect.[85] Thus, the *BVerwG* had to conclude that the legal status obtained by a Turkish worker on the basis of Article 7 of Association Council Decision 1/80 was capable of preventing the withdrawal – with retrospective effect – of an already granted residence permit.[86]

The following observations can be made on the basis of this case. Without hesitation, the *BVerwG* reaffirmed the findings of the lower courts that the applicant did not have any right under the German Aliens law to keep his unrestricted residence permit. Consequently, if the Association Council Decision had been adopted within the classic legal situation, the legal analysis of the

---

81 § 24 AulG
(1) Die Aufenthalserlaubnis ist unbefristet zu verlängern, wenn der Ausländer
1. die Aufenthalserlaubnis seit 5 Jahren besitzt [...].

82 Article 7 (2):
Children of Turkish workers who have completed a course of vocational training in the host country may respond to any offer of employment there, irrespective of the length of time they have been resident in that Member State, provided one of their parents has been legally employed in the Member State concerned for at least three years.

83 'Wie der Senat *im Anschluß an die Rechtsprechung des EuGH* näher dargelegt hat, läßt sich aus den zunächst rein beschäftigungsrechtlich konzipierten Vorschriften der Art. 6 und 7 ARB 1/80 ein ausländerrechtliches Aufenthalsrecht ableiten (BVerwGE 97, 301; BVerwGE 98, 31, BVerwG, NVwZ 1995, 1119 und 1123)', emphasis added, NVwZ 1996, 1116-1117.

84 Case C-355/93 *Eroglu* v. *Baden-Würtemberg* [1994] ECR I-5113, para. 20, emphasis added.

85 *Ibid.*, para. 17.

86 'Deswegen sind Rechtspositionen, die türkische Staatsangehörige in Anwendung dieser Vorschrift erworben haben, grundsätzlich geeignet, der Entziehung einer bereits erteilten Aufenthaltserlaubnis entgegenzuwirken'. NVwZ 1996, 1117.

BVerwG would have stopped here because the AuslG would overrule the internal guidelines for the administration. However, due to the case-law of the ECJ and thus the creation of the 'EC law transformed' legal situation 'Association Council Decision–European law–national law', the *BVerwG* was forced to take a second step in its analysis, namely, to turn to the Association Council Decision 1/80 and the interpretation of the ECJ given to it in the *Eroglu* case.[87] Due to this judgment, the *BVerwG* and subsequently all other administrative courts had to give up their resistance and accept the concept of a direct link between employment and residence rights, which until the *Eroglu* ruling, was clearly rejected.[88] In fact, it was only after the *Eroglu*[89] ruling of the ECJ that several higher administrative courts[90] explicitly changed their interpretation of Article 7 (1) of Association Council Decision 1/80. Nonetheless, the continuous resistance of German courts[91] against establishing a link between employment and residence rights was also apparent by the fact that the ECJ – in unusually strong and explicit terms – reprimanded Germany and advised it to stop interpreting and applying the provisions of Association Council Decision 1/80 in such way as to render them useless.[92] Finally, the ECJ specifically stated in the *Eyüp* case that

---

87 See annotation of the Eroglu case by: Zuleeg (1996).

88 See for a general discussion: Mallmann (1995); Rumpf (1995).

89 Case C-355/93 *Eroglu* v. *Land Baden-Würtemberg* [1994] ECR I-5113; see also: Weber (1995); Nachbaur (1995) at 344-345.

90 Oberverwaltungsgericht Münster (OVG), judgment of 21.12.1994, NVwZ 1995, 820-821; Verwaltungsgerichtshof Mannheim (VGH), judgment of 7.11.1994, NVwZ 1995, 821-822; VGH Baden-Würtemberg, judgment of 14.9.1994, InfoAuslR 1995, 51-53.

91 See for details the examples mentioned by: Gutmann (1996).

92 See: Case C-98/96 *Ertarnir* v. *Land Hessen* [1997] ECR I-5179: 'Moreover, the wording of Article 6 (1) is general and unconditional: it does not permit the Member State to deprive certain categories of Turkish workers of the rights which that provision confers directly on them or to restrict or attach conditions to such rights. (para. 33). It follows that the answer to the first of those questions, as rephrased, must be that Article 6 (3) of Decision No. 1/80 is to be interpreted as meaning that it does not permit Member States to adopt national legislation which excludes at the outset whole categories of Turkish migrant workers, such as specialist chefs, from the rights conferred by the three indents of Article 6 (1), (para. 37). It follows from paras. 31-35 of this judgment that such restrictions on the rights deriving from Decision No. 1/80 must be considered to be incompatible therewith and are therefore not relevant for the purposes of interpretation.' (para. 46); Case C-36/96 *Günaydin* v. *Freistaat Bayern* [1997] ECR I-5143: 'None the less, Article 6 (1) cannot be construed as permitting a Member State to modify unilaterally the scope of the system of gradual integration of Turkish workers in the host State's labour force, by denying a worker who has been permitted to enter its territory and who has lawfully pursued a genuine and effective economic activity for more than three-and-a-half years the rights which the three indents of that provision confer on him progressively according to the duration of his employment. (para. 37). The effect of such an interpretation would be to render Decision No. 1/80 meaningless and deprive it of any practical effect.' (para. 38); restated in Case C-329/97 *Ergat* [2000] ECR I-1487, para. 41.

Member States no longer have any right to change their legislation in such a way that it would restrict the rights explicitly granted to them by Association Council Decision 1/80.[93] The ECJ found a similar 'standstill' provision in Article 41 (1) of the Additional Protocol to the Association Agreement.[94]

In summary, this case clearly illustrates the impact of European law on the Association Council Decisions and the effect it has on the application of the German *Ausländergesetz*. Due to the communitarization of Association Decisions they obtain the highest legal status in the German legal order. As a consequence thereof, German courts had to apply the German *Ausländergesetz* in a way which they otherwise would not have done. Hence, the 'EC transformer' amplified the 12 Volt of the Association Council Decisions into a 220 Volt current before they enter the domestic electric circuit. As a result, German courts were forced to interpret German law in accordance with the jurisprudence of the ECJ.

4.3.2 The Netherlands

In the Netherlands, the legal status of foreigners is laid down in the *Vreemdelingenwet* (Aliens Act),[95] supplemented by *Vreemdelingencirculaire* containing further details.

Although a much smaller number of Turkish 'guest workers' and their family members settled in the Netherlands than in Germany, the general question of their rights granted under the Association Agreement has also been a critical issue in the Netherlands.[96] Until 1993, the general approach of the Dutch administrative authorities and courts, regarding the right of Turkish workers and their family members to obtain residence and working permits, was restrictive.[97] Until 1984, the *Raad van State* was of the opinion that the Association

---

93 Case C-65/98 *Eyüp* ECR 2000 I-4747, para. 41: 'In that respect, it is settled case-law that a Member State cannot unilaterally modify the scope of the system of gradually integrating Turkish workers into the host Member State's labour force, so that that State no longer has the power to adopt measures such as to impede the exercise of the rights expressly granted by Decision No 1/80.'; see also: Case C-340/97 *Nazli* v. *Stadt Nürnberg* [2000] ECR I-957, para. 30; see also: Staples (2000a).

94 Case C-37/98 *Savas* [2000] ECR I-2927, para. 69: 'It should also be noted that the standstill clause in Article 41(1) of the Additional Protocol precludes a Member State from adopting any new measure having the object or effect of making the establishment, and, as a corollary, the residence of a Turkish national in its territory subject to stricter conditions than those which applied at the time when the Additional Protocol entered into force with regard to the Member State concerned.' See also: Staples (2000b).

95 Vreemdelingenwet 2000, Staatsblad 2000, 495, 1.

96 See for detailed overviews: Groenendijk (1992); *ibid.*, (1994); Staples (1999b).

97 According to Groenendijk (1994) at 206, up until 1993 practically all cases relying on Association Agreement rules were rejected, either because the rules were not applicable in the specific case, or the

Agreement was – due to its structure – not capable of being directly applicable.[98] Only after the ECJ decided in 1987 in the *Demirel*[99] case that the Association Agreement was capable of being directly applicable, did the Dutch courts start to change their case-law. However, it still took a couple of other far-reaching rulings of the ECJ, notably *Sevince*[100] and *Kus*[101], to finally convince the Dutch courts that, indeed, Turkish nationals could rely on Articles 6, 7 of Association Council Decision 1/80.[102]

The following example illustrates the influence of Association Council Decision 1/80 as interpreted by the ECJ on the Dutch courts and their application of Dutch laws.

The applicant, a Turkish national born in 1972, has been living since August 1992 as an illegal in the Netherlands.[103] In January 1993, he requested a residence permit in order to live with his wife. In March 1993, the residence permit was granted. However, in October 1995, the marriage was dissolved. In February 1997, the applicant requested a residence permit in order to work as an employed person. In March 1997, that request was rejected and the objection raised by the applicant was declared as unfounded by the State Secretary of Justice. In November 1997, the applicant appealed against that decision at the *Rechtbank 's-Gravenhage.*

The applicant claims to have a right to obtain a residence permit, based *inter alia* on provisions of the Association Agreement EC-Turkey, in particular, since he was legally employed for one year before his marriage was dissolved. The respondent State Secretary of Justice denied that the applicant fulfilled the necessary condition of having sufficient means laid down in the *'hoofdstuk B1/4.5.2. van de Vreemdelingencirculaire 1994* (VC)'. According to Article 11 (5) *Vreemdelingenwet* (Aliens Act) – applicable at that time[104] – granting a residence permit can be denied based on the general interest of the Netherlands.[105]

---

rules were too vague or because they were considered not to be directly applicable. However, Groenendijk does not substantiate this statement with any references.

98 'Naar het oordeel van de Afd. rechtspraak zijn de door appellant aangehaalde artikelen niet rechtstreeks toepasselijk.', 9.8.1984, AB 1985, 159.

99 Case 12/86 *Demirel* [1987] ECR 3719.

100 Case C-192/89 *Sevince* [1990] ECR I-3461.

101 Case C-237/91 *Kus* [1992] ECR I-6781.

102 See: Groenendijk (1993); Verschueren (1997); Sewandono (1998a); *ibid.* (1998b); Verboom (1998).

103 Rechtbank 's-Gravenhage, judgment 10.6.1999, AWB 97/13082.

104 The Vreemdelingenwet has been revised completely in 2000, Vreemdelingenwet 2000, Staatsblad 2000, 495, 1.

105 '4. Ingevolge artikel 11, vijfde lid, Vw kan het verlenen van een vergunning tot verblijf aan een vreemdeling worden geweigerd op gronden aan het algemeen belang ontleend.'

The court determined that the marriage lasted less then 3 years and that the applicant worked prior to 2 October 1995 part time, earning a certain amount of income. In these circumstances, chapter *B1/4.5.2. of the Vreemdelingencirculair* enumerates a number of conditions for obtaining a residence permit.[106] The court concluded that the applicant did not have sufficient means in the relevant period and thus could not obtain a residence permit on the basis of the Dutch Alien rules.[107]

In a second step, the court turned to Article 6 Association Council Decision 1/80.[108]

The court noted that the respondent State Secretary did not examine (either in the first decision or in the reviewed decision) whether the applicant qualified for a residence permit on the basis of the 1st indent of Article 6 (1) Association Council Decision 1/80. Article 6 (1), 1st indent, grants the right to extend the residence permit after having been legally employed for a year by the same employer. Since the applicant worked for one year for the same employer, he fulfilled the conditions of the 1st indent of Article 6 (1) Association Council Decision 1/80. Consequently, the applicant could successfully rely on Article 6 Association Council Decision 1/80, so the court found that the decision was not in conformity with Article 7:12 Awb (General act on administrative law), which requires that a decision be properly motivated. Thus, the State Secretary had to adopt a new decision.

---

[106] '7. Het beleid met betrekking tot voorgezet verblijf na verbreking relatie korter dan drie jaar is neergelegd in hoofdstuk B1/4 Vc en in het bijzonder, gelet op de nationaliteit van eiser in hoofdstuk B1/4.5.2. Ingevolge dit beleid komt een Turkse onderdaan die is toegelaten in het kader van een relatie, na de verbreking van deze relatie voor voortgezet verblijf in aanmerking indien aan de volgende vereisten is voldaan:

- de vreemdeling moet reeds gedurende één jaar onafgebroken arbeid in loondienst hebben verricht op basis van een vergunning tot verblijf en een tewerkstellingsvergunning, dan wel zonder dat een tewerkstellingsvergunning ex artikel 4 Wet arbeid vreemdelingen (Wav) vereist was;
- en de werkgever heeft nog voortgezette werkgelegenheid;
- en de vreemdeling beschikt over voldoende middelen van bestaan; (norm Algemene bijstandswet voor de desbetreffende categorie)
-en er mag geen sprake zijn van gevaar voor of inbreuk op de openbare rust, de openbare orde of nationale veiligheid.'

[107] '8. De peilperiode als bedoeld in het eerste gedachtestreepje van genoemd beleid loopt van 2 oktober 1994 tot 2 oktober 1995. Met verweerder is de rechtbank van oordeel dat eiser niet heeft aangetoond dat hij gedurende deze periode over voldoende middelen van bestaan heeft beschikt in de zin van genoemd beleid. Eiser heeft dit ook niet betwist. Aldus heeft verweerder terecht vastgesteld dat eiser ingevolge genoemd beleid niet in aanmerking komt voor de gevraagde vergunning.'

[108] '9. Eiser heeft zich voorts beroepen op artikel 6 van Besluit 1/80 van de Associatieovereenkomst.'

After having determined that the decision should be revised, the court considered it necessary to emphasize the following points.[109] The *Rechtbank* recalls that according to the case-law of the ECJ (*Sevince* and *Kus*), Article 6 of Association Council Decision 1/80 is directly applicable.[110] According to that case-law the term 'legal employment' requires that the employment situation of the Turkish worker must be stable and based on a valid permit. It is apparent that the applicant worked since 1993 as well as after 1995 for the same employer. Consequently, on the basis of these facts, the reasoning of the respondent concerning the lack of stability could not be accepted.[111] Finally, the court noted that Member States are prohibited from restricting the precise and unconditional rights granted to Turkish workers.

This case is an illuminating example of how the Association Council Decision 1/80 overruled the national provisions. While the applicant did not fulfil the Dutch rules for obtaining a renewed residence permit, he could successfully obtain a permit on the basis of the Association Council Decision. More generally, it is interesting to note the explicit criticism of the court regarding the failure of the Dutch authorities to take into account the rules of the Association Agreement and Association Decision. Thus, similar to the German case discussed above, the involvement of European law amplified the legal status of the Association Council Decision which in turn directly influenced the application of the domestic aliens laws in respect to Turkish migrant workers.

4.3.3 France

In contrast to the situation in Germany and the Netherlands, the number of cases involving EC-Turkey Association Council Decisions before French courts has been very limited and of recent date.

Moreover, in contrast to Germany and the Netherlands, the focus of the cases concerns Association Council Decision 3/80 and not Association Council Decision 1/80. Indeed, only one recent case was found concerning the application of Association Council Decision 1/80.[112] In that case a Turkish national tried to enter France but was rejected and ordered to go back to Turkey where he came from. In his appeal against that decision he relied on Article 6 of Association Council Decision 1/80. However, the *Conseil d'Etat* rejected his plea by concluding that he did not fulfil any of the conditions of Article 6 of Association Council Decision 1/80.

---

[109] 'De rechtbank hecht er aan daaromtrent het volgende op te merken.'

[110] 'Blijkens arresten van het Hof van justitie (Sevince en Kus) komt aan voornoemd besluit rechtstreekse werking toe.'

[111] 'Reeds hierom kan naar het oordeel van de rechtbank het gestelde in het verweerschrift met betrekking tot de stabiliteit van de door eiser verrichtte werkzaamheden de toets der kritiek niet doorstaan.'

[112] Conseil d'Etat, 10.10.2003, no. 245342.

Instead, the *Cour de Cassation* has been recently confronted with several cases involving Association Council Decision 3/80 concerning social security rights. As mentioned above, the case-law of the ECJ on Association Council Decision 3/80 has been much more cautious than on Association Council Decision 1/80. So far, the ECJ has only accepted a direct effect of the non-discrimination clause contained in Article 3 of Association Council Decision 3/80.[113] This probably explains why the series of nearly identical cases in which Article 3 of Association Council Decision 3/80 was invoked started only after the delivery of the Opinion of the Advocate General, who came to the same conclusion, and the ruling of the judgment in the *Sürül* case.

Accordingly, between 1999 and 2001, the *Cour de Cassation* rendered several nearly identical rulings on similar cases in which Turkish workers or their family members were denied supplementary payments from the national social solidarity fund (*allocation supplémentaire du Fonds national de solidarité*), the special fund for invalidity (*Fonds spécial d'invalidité*) and the fund for handicapped adults (*allocation aux adultes handicapés*) solely on the basis of their nationality, i.e. not having French nationality, whereas it is not disputed that they otherwise fulfilled all the conditions for receiving the supplement.[114]

The lower courts argued in line with the *Taflan-Met* decision of the ECJ that since the grant of the benefits are expressly excluded from the scope of application of Association Council Decision 3/80, they could not be invoked by Turkish nationals.[115] Thus, while the rulings of the lower courts were all delivered before the *Sürül* judgment and thus were in accordance with the law as it stood at that time,[116] it should be noted that three rulings were delivered after the Opinion

---

113 Case C-262/96 *Sürül* [1999] ECR I-2685.

114 Cour de Cassation, chambre civile, 4.10.2001, no. 00-11755; 25.1.2001, no. 99-16462; 31.10.2000, no. 99-11878; 13.7.2000, no. 99-11358; 21.10.1999, no. 97-22040; 21.10.1999, no. 97-22039; 14.1.1999, no. 97-12487.

115 See e.g.: Cour de Cassation, 4.10.2001, no. 00-11755: 'Que, pour rejeter le recours de l'intéressé contre la décision de la Caisse primaire d'assurance maladie qui lui a refusé le bénéfice de cette prestation en raison de sa nationalité étrangère, la cour d'appel, par motifs adoptés, énonce essentiellement que l'allocation litigieuse est expressément exclue du champ d'application matériel de la décision 3/80 du Conseil d'association du 19 septembre 1980, prise en application de l'accord d'association entre la Communauté économique européenne et la Turquie, et qu'elle ne répond pas non plus aux exigences de la Convention internationale du travail n° 118 de l'Organisation internationale du travail du 28 juin 1962, de sorte qu'en l'absence de convention de réciprocité entre la France et la Turquie portant sur cette prestation, l'article L. 815-5 du Code de la sécurité sociale exclut qu'elle puisse être accordée; [...].'

116 Cour de Cassation, 13.7.2000, no. 99-11358: '[...] la cour d'appel retient que les dispositions de la décision n° 3/80 du Conseil d'association du 19 septembre 1980, prise en application de l'accord d'association entre la Communauté économique européenne et la Turquie du 23 décembre 1963, relatives à la vieillesse et à l'invalidité, *telles qu'interprétées par la Cour de justice des communautés européennes, n'ont pas d'effet direct sur le territoire des Etats membres,* [...].' (emphasis added).

of the Advocate General in the *Sürül* case was rendered. Hence, those courts already had an indication that Article 3 of Association Council Decision 3/80 could possibly be directly applicable.

In contrast, the *Cour de Cassation* took note of the outcome of the *Sürül* judgment and applied it instantly to those cases. Consequently, it simply stated that since the applicants fulfilled the conditions for obtaining the benefits, the refusal on the sole basis of their nationality violated the non-discrimination clause of Article 3 of Association Council Decision 3/80.[117] Accordingly, all the rulings of the lower courts were overturned. However, it should also be noted that in three cases the *Cour de Cassation* overturned the ruling of the lower courts that had accepted a direct effect of Association Council Decision 3/80. In one case, the *Cour de Cassation* came to the conclusion that the Community had not yet adopted necessary implementing measures;[118] in the other case, it concluded that the payment in question was considered to be outside the scope of Association Council Decision 3/80;[119] while in the third case, the *Cour de Cassation* considered that Association Council Decision 3/80 did not apply to non-contributory payments[120].

Nonetheless, similar to the situation in Germany and the Netherlands, the involvement of Community law, in particular the case-law of the ECJ, transformed the Association Council Decisions into EC law acts that forced the French courts to accept their supremacy and direct effect. In other words, only due to the transformation of Association Council Decision 3/80 by the 'EC law transformer' were Turkish nationals able to enforce their rights before French courts that otherwise were not prepared to grant those rights.

4.4 Summary

It summary, it can be concluded that the example of Association Council Decisions illustrates the modification of the classic legal situa-

[117] Cour de Cassation, 4.10.2001, no. 00-11755: 'Attendu qu'en statuant ainsi, alors qu'il n'était pas contesté que M. Aydin remplissait toutes les conditions exigées pour l'attribution de cette prestation, en sorte que la décision de refus, uniquement fondée sur sa nationalité étrangère, n'était pas justifiée, la cour d'appel a violé les textes susvisés; [...].'

[118] Cour de Cassation, 21.10.1999, no. 98-10030, '[...] qu'en l'absence de l'adoption par le Conseil des Communautés des mesures mise en oeuvre de la décision 3/80 du Counseil d'association [...] ses dispositions ne sont pas directement applicables dans les Etats membres et ne son pas de nature à engendrer pour les particuliers le droit de s'en prévaloir devant les juridictions nationales [...]'.

[119] Cour de Cassation, 14.1.1999, no. 97-14757, '[...] que la décision 3/80 du Conseil d'association qui en avait fixé les dispositions excluit expréssement cette prestation du champ d'application de l'accord [...]'.

[120] Cour de Cassation, 21.10.1999, no. 97-22039, '[...] que l'allocation aux adultes handicapés, prestation non-contributive, ne peut être assimilée à une prestation d'invalidité, au sens de l'article 12 de la décision 3/80 [...]'.

tion into an 'EC law transformed' legal situation, which results in a number of important consequences. First, Association Council Decisions obtain supremacy over all national law and some provisions enjoy direct effect. Second, as a consequence thereof, Turkish nationals and their family members could rely on those provisions of Association Council Decision 1/80 and 3/80 and thereby have been able to successfully challenge conflicting national laws, administrative measures and court decisions that were adopted on the basis of the conflicting national laws. Third, the transformation of Association Council Decisions into Community law resulted in a high degree of uniform legal status and effect in all EU Member States since Association Council Decisions enjoy the same highest legal status in all EU Member States and since all courts and administrations of the Member States are bound by the jurisprudence of the ECJ, the provisions of Association Council Decisions that enjoy direct effect in the view of the ECJ enjoy that effect also in all Member States regardless of the existing constitutional differences. In this way, Turkish workers are able to effectively enforce their rights that have been granted by the Association Council Decisions in all Member States. Thus, the modification of the current of the Association Council Decisions from 12 Volt into a 220 Volt by the European law transformer has had a strong impact on the application of Association Council Decisions in the EU Member States.

5 Decisions adopted by COPs/MOPs

Over the past decades a large number of international agreements covering practically all aspects of environmental law have been concluded on the global as well as on the regional level.[121] Most of those multilateral environmental agreements (MEAs) establish organs that are able to adopt binding decisions. Moreover, the EC has adopted extensive legislation in the field of environmental law and is also – often besides the EC Member States – party to many MEAs and thus involved in the implementation of the decisions adopted within MEAs.[122]

This section will first shortly describe the legal structure that is common to most MEAs[123] before discussing the question of whether the Conference of Parties (COPs) and Meeting of Parties (MOPs) which adopt the decisions within MEAs can be qualified as organs of IOs.[124] Based on that, the implementation of those decisions on the European level and in the selected EU Member States is examined.

---

121 See: Morrison/Wolfrum (2000); Weiss (1992); Gehring/Oberthür (1997).

122 See: Nollkaemper (1987); Leefmans (1998); Jans (2000); Lavranos (2002a).

123 See for description of several MEAs: Ott (1998).

124 See two recent excellent studies: Churchill/Ulfstein (2000); Röben (2000).

5.1 International law level

5.1.1 General legal structure of most MEAs

International environmental law may be seen as a continuing dynamic process of the collective solving of common environmental problems.[125] Indeed, as Handl states:

> 'International legislation under this guise is no longer a single well-defined product carried by expectations of stability for a foreseeable future. It is rather a fragile, temporary sign-post in an institutionalized process in which legal positions are subject to constant review and susceptible to frequent and speedy alteration.'[126]

Accordingly, flexible amendment procedures have been developed to accommodate this process.[127] As a consequence thereof, the autonomous legal structure of MEAs has developed.[128] These MEAs provide for the possibility of adopting binding decisions according to distinctive procedures that are usually not found in most traditional IOs.[129] In order to overcome the cumbersome treaty-adoption and -amendment procedures normally applicable to international instruments, most MEAs are based on a three-tiered approach.[130]

First, states conclude a so-called framework agreement that sets out the general obligations. Second, states agree upon a separate protocol that implements the framework agreement by containing more detailed obligations. Third, these protocols are in turn implemented through annexes or appendices containing the technical details, for instance, a list of substances or species that are controlled by the protocol and the framework agreement.

All MEAs or protocols thereto provide for the establishment of a plenary organ usually denominated as Conference of Parties (COP) or Meeting of Parties (MOP) as the plenary body in which all contracting states are represented.[131] The COPs/MOPs of the MEAs do not have a permanent seat but meet regularly once a year. The COP/MOP is the supreme body of the framework agreement, having the power to adopt all necessary internal and external deci-

---

125 See: Ott (1998) at 91.

126 Handl (1990) at 6-7.

127 Handl (1990) at 4-5; Gehring, (1990) at 37.

128 See for details: Churchill/Ulfstein (2000); Röben (2000).

129 It is for this reason that Churchill/Ulfstein prefer to use the term 'autonomous institutional arrangements'. See for an analysis of various decisions of IOs: Schermers/Blokker (2004), Chapter 8, at 765-832. See for a critical analysis: Bodansky (1999).

130 Gehring (1990) at 47-50.

131 Churchill/Ulfstein (2000) at 626.

sions, including, in particular, adjusting the annexes/appendices of the treaties/protocols.[132]

The decision-making process within MEAs can be differentiated into two aspects.[133] One aspect concerns the process of treaty-making, treaty-adoption and treaty-amendment, while the second aspect refers to the adoption of binding COP/MOP decisions which adjust the annexes/appendices attached to the treaties or protocols.

In the law-making phase, many MEAs[134] provide the possibility for the COPs/MOPs to amend or adjust the annexes/appendices attached to the framework agreement or protocol.[135] These annexes usually contain the technical details, which can be updated as a result of changing circumstances and/or new scientific evidence.

In this context, three points are of particular importance. First, in contrast to primary treaty law, most amendments or adjustments to the annexes/appendices do not need to be ratified by the states.[136] Second, with regard to many MEAs, such amendments or adjustments are binding on all states unless objected to within a certain period of time. In the case of the Montreal Protocol, contracting parties do not even have that option; the only option they have is to denounce the protocol if they do not wish to accept the amendments.[137] Thus, a majority of contracting parties can adopt amendments or adjustments that can bind the other contracting parties even against their will. However, in practice this does not happen because in most MEAs the search for consensus exists either as a non-written tradition or is explicitly required in the rules of procedure before one moves on to majority voting.[138] Third, amendments or adjustments of annexes/appendices can have far reaching effects even to the extent that substantive obligations of the contracting parties are changed.[139] In sum, COPs/MOPs have genuine law-making powers when adopting binding COP/MOP decisions.

---

[132] See in general: Werksman (1996).

[133] See for details: Werksman (1996) at 56-57; Széll (1996) at 210-214; Ott (1998) at 148-200.

[134] Such as the Convention on International Trade in Endangered Species of Wild Fauna and Flora (CITES), the Vienna Convention for the Protection of the Ozone Layer, the Montreal Protocol on Substances that deplete the Ozone Layer and the Basle Convention on the control of transboundary movements of hazardous wastes and their disposal.

[135] See e.g.: CITES (Art. XV); Vienna Convention (Art. 10); Montreal Protocol (Art. 11); Basle Convention (Art. 15).

[136] See e.g.: CITES (Art. XV (1)); Climate Change Convention (Art. 16); Churchill/Ulfstein (2000) at 638.

[137] Art. 2 (9) (d) Montreal Protocol; see also: Ott (1998) at 155-156.

[138] Széll (1996) at 212.

[139] See for some examples: Churchill/Ulfstein (2000) at 638-639; Ott (1998) at 193-200; Gehring (1990) at 48-49.

5.1.2 COPs/MOPs: organs of IOs?

On the basis of the above, it appears that COPs/MOPs could be qualified as (organs of) IOs created by the framework agreements or the protocols thereto. Indeed, Sands simply states, in passing, that:

> 'These institutional arrangements [MEAs] are, in effect, international organisations. They have international legal status, rules of procedure and membership, and enumerated powers relating to decision-making and dispute settlement and, occasionally, enforcement powers.'[140]

However, that this conclusion might be too simple is indicated by the differentiated conclusion of Churchill and Ulfstein when they state:

> 'In spite of their formal denomination, we nevertheless conclude that these self-governing, treaty-based AIAs [Autonomous Institutional Arrangements] of MEAs may be considered to be IGOs, albeit of a less formal, more ad hoc nature than traditional IGOs. This conclusion is based on Schermers and Blokker's definition of an international organization as a form of cooperation founded on an international agreement (the MEA), creating at least one organ with a will of its own (the COP) established under international law. This conclusion is further supported by the character, functions, and practice of these AIAs. Thus, while due account should be taken of the special characteristics of these arrangements, international institutional law should apply to them and supplement the law of the treaties when it comes to assessing their powers. ... We must emphasize however, that one should not lose sight of the special characteristics of these arrangements and that, accordingly, the powers of AIAs are not necessarily identical to those of formal IGOs in all respects.'

Doubts, however, seem justified as the view of Röben indicates:

> 'The international community's ability to form a will of its own through the Meetings of Parties makes it necessary to rethink the traditional definition of an international organisation. Meetings of Parties can, as well as the organs of international organisations, occasionally take majority decisions. The main difference appears to be the degree to which the institution is rendered independent in its operational mode. The international environmental agreements considered here are different from the treaties constituting traditional international organisations in that they do not bring about a separate entity with defined objectives and approaches, finite instruments and a premium on stability. [...] Yet, they perform functions that few, if any, international organisations can match. [...] In addition to

[140] Sands (1995) at 92.

> international organisations, international administrative unions and international negotiating conferences, there are now institutionalised international agreements.'[141]

And Gehring and Oberthür are even more outspoken on this point when they conclude:

> 'Internationale Umweltregime können also als Institutionen betrachtet werden, mit deren Hilfe eine Gruppe von Staaten ein gemeinsames Umweltproblem zu bearbeiten sucht, indem sie gemeinsamen Interessen durch eine geeignete Organisation des kollektiven Entscheidungsprozesses gezielt fördert. Obwohl sie in der Regel über kleine Sekretariate verfügen, sind Umweltregime deshalb – im Gegensatz zu klassischen internationalen Organisationen – keine selbständig handelnden Akteure. Sie erlauben keinen gegen die Einzelinteressen der Mitgliedstaaten gerichtete internationale Umweltpolitik, sonder stellen zur Förderung der gemeinsamen Interessen der beteiligten Akteure einen regimespezifischen Entscheidungsapparat zur Verfügung, der zum Kern einer problemfeldspezifischen 'Regelungsmaschinerie' wird.'[142]

Hence, it appears that the main difference between these statements lies in the evaluation of the element 'organ with a will of its own' as a condition for qualifying COPs/MOPs as IOs.

Whereas Churchil/Ulfstein qualify COPs/MOPs as organs with a will of their own, Röben and Gehring/Oberthür stress the point that the main difference between traditional international agreements and MEAs is the fact that they do not establish a separate organ with a will of its own. Indeed, international organizations – as defined by Schermers and Blokker[143] – have at least one organ that can be clearly distinguished in terms of its composition, tasks and powers from the contracting parties of an international agreement. Schermers and Blokker emphasize this point when they state:

---

[141] Röben (2000) at 439.

[142] Gehring/Oberthür (1997) at 17: 'International environmental regimes can be considered as institutions within which groups of states attempt to solve a common environmental problem by promoting the common interests through the useful organisation of the decision-making process. Although environmental regimes generally have a small Secretariat, they are – in contrast to classic international organizations – not independent actors. They do not permit an international environmental policy to be taken against the individual interests of member states, but rather provide a regime specific decision-making apparatus, which develops into a core of a problem specific "regulatory machine" for the promotion of the common interests of the participating actors.' (own translation).

[143] Schermers/Blokker (2004) at 26-37.

> 'The requirement that the organ in question has a will of its own (*volenté distincte*) distinguishes organizations from bilateral or multilateral treaties, whereby parties lay down a common will, which remains their own, however, and is not entrusted to a newly created body.'[144]

In my view, a functional approach to this issue offers the best answer to the question whether COPs/MOPs can be considered to be organs established by international treaties. While it is true that states have purposely developed less complex, 'light'-versions of traditional IOs, because it was felt that constantly establishing new IOs with huge overhead costs and overlapping tasks would prevent quick action and increase costs[145], the fact remains that at the same time COPs/MOPs have been endowed with the competence to adopt binding decisions. Thus, although formally COPs/MOPs do not fulfil the criteria of IOs, in practice the binding decisions of COPs/MOPs are comparable to the binding decisions of organs of traditional IOs. Or as put by Gehring:

> 'International environmental regimes constitute a particular type of institution, distinct from both multilateral treaties and international organizations. Like treaties, they compromise a specific normative framework of prescriptions that are particularly suitable to organizing internationally coordinated behavior within a limited issue-area. Like international organizations, they provide a permanent mechanism for changing these normative prescriptions.'[146]

Therefore, COPs/MOPs must be qualified as organs established by international treaties endowed with the competence to adopt binding decisions, while at the same time no formal IOs are established. This conclusion also fits the broad definition of IOs proposed by Gaja which considers the ability to exercize governmental functions as the main element for qualifying a structure as an IO.[147]

5.2 European law level

The EC has become party – together with some or all of the EC Member States – to many important MEAs[148], for instance, the Vienna Convention for the Protection of the Ozone Layer[149] and the Montreal Protocol on

---

[144] Schermers/Blokker (2004) at 35.

[145] Churchill/Ulfstein (2000) at 629; Ott (1998) at 131-133.

[146] Gehring (1990) at 54-55.

[147] See discussion in Chapter 1.

[148] See: Nollkaemper (1987); Leefmans (1998); Jans (2000), Chapter II, at 69-98; Eberle (2001).

[149] OJ 1988 L 297/8-10.

Substances that Deplete the Ozone Layer[150], the Basle Convention on the Control of Transboundary Movements of Hazardous Wastes and their Disposal[151] and the United Nations Framework Convention on Climate Change[152]. Since most MEAs are concluded by the EC together with its Member States as mixed agreements, the legal implications of mixed agreements must be kept in mind.[153] In accordance with the principles applicable to mixed agreements, all parts of the MEAs that do not fall within the exclusive competence of the Member States become an integral part of the Community legal order. As a result, they obtain the Community law characteristics of supremacy over conflicting secondary Community law and all national law of the EU Member States as well as possible direct effect if they fulfil the criteria established by the ECJ.[154] The ECJ appears to treat international environmental agreements different than, for instance, the WTO agreements regarding their suitability to be used as a basis to review the conformity of Community law with them. In the *Biotechnology Directive* case, the ECJ emphasized the differences between the WTO agreements on the one hand and the MEAs on the other hand, when it argued:

> '52. It is common ground that, as a rule, the lawfulness of a Community instrument does not depend on its conformity with an international agreement to which the Community is not a party, such as the EPC. Nor can its lawfulness be assessed in the light of instruments of international law which, like the WTO agreement and the TRIPS and TBT agreements which are part of it, *are not in principle, having regard to their nature and structure, among the rules in the light of which the Court is to review the lawfulness of measures adopted by the Community institutions* (Case C-149/96 *Portugal* v *Council* [1999] ECR I-8395, paragraph 47).
>
> 53. However, such *an exclusion cannot be applied to the CBD* [Convention on Biodiversity], which, unlike the WTO agreement, is not strictly based on reciprocal and mutually advantageous arrangements (see *Portugal* v *Council*, cited above, paragraphs 42 to 46).
>
> 54. Even if, as the Council maintains, the CBD contains *provisions which do not have direct effect*, in the sense that they do not create rights which individuals can rely on directly before the courts, *that fact does not preclude review by the courts*

---

150 OJ 1988 L 297/8 and 21, as amended by OJ 1991 L 377/30; amended by OJ 1994 L 033/3 and as amended by OJ 2000 L 272/27.

151 OJ 1993 L 039/1-3, as mended by OJ 1997 L 272/46.

152 OJ 1994 L 033/11-13.

153 See for detailed discussions: Neuwahl (1991); *ibid.*, (1996); Okowa (1997); Rosas (1998); O'Keeffe, (1999); Thieme (2001); Leefmans (1998), Chapter 5, at 245-277; Temple Lang (1986); see also: Opinion 2/00 [2001] ECR I-9713 concerning the Cartagena Protocol to the Biodiversity Convention.

154 See e.g. Raad van State, Afdeling bestuursrechtspraak, judgment of 11.6.2003, JM 2003/95.

> *of compliance with the obligations incumbent on the Community as a party to that agreement* (Case C-162/96 *Racke* [1998] ECR I-3655, paragraphs 45, 47 and 51)."[155]

Thus, provisions of MEAs, including – in my view – binding COPs/MOPs decisions – can be used by the ECJ to review Community law irrespective of whether they have direct effect or not. This is in clear contrast to the WTO agreements that are *per se* excluded as a basis for review because they are considered by the ECJ not to have any direct effect. In other words, even if a provision of an MEA or a COP/MOP decision does not have direct effect, this would not exclude the possibility that the ECJ might use that provision to review the compatibility of Community law acts with them.

In any case, the EC is required – within the limits of its competence – to fulfil the obligations arising out of those agreements by implementing the respective binding decisions of the COPs/MOPs. The instruments used by the EC for implementing COP/MOP decisions vary depending on the specific requirements of the respective MEA.[156] For instance, Regulation 2037/2000[157] implements the latest amendments and adjustments to the Montreal Protocol made at the seventh and ninth MOP. The Regulation further delegates powers to the European Commission to decide on specific details, such as the allocation of quantities of controlled substances.[158] Further, the EC also uses Council Decisions in order to implement COP decisions. For instance, adjustments to the appendices of the Bonn Convention on the conservation of migratory species of wild animals decided by COP-5 were implemented by Council Decision 98/145.[159]

In certain cases, the power to implement COP decisions has been delegated by an EC Regulation to the European Commission. For example, the adjustments to the appendixes of the CITES adopted by COP-11 were implemented by Commission Regulation 2724/2000.[160] In this context, it should be remembered that, although the EC is not a contracting party to the CITES, it copied the

---

155 Case C-377/98 *Netherlands* v. *EP/Council* [2001] ECR I-7079.

156 See for numerous examples: Eberle at 230-274.

157 OJ 2000 L 244/1-23.

158 Commission Decision 2001/333/EC of 13.2.2001 on the allocation of quantities of controlled substances allowed for essential uses in the Community in 2001 under Regulation (EC) No 2037/2000 of the European Parliament and of the Council on substances that deplete the ozone layer, OJ 2001 L 118/57-60.

159 Council Decision 98/145/EC of 12.2.1998 on the approval, on behalf of the EC, of the amendments to Appendices I and II to the Bonn Convention on the conservation of migratory species of wild animals as decided by the fifth meeting of the COP to the Convention, OJ 1998 L 46/6-7.

160 Commission Regulation (EC) No 2724/2000 of 30.11.2000 amending Council Regulation (EC) No 338/97 on the protection of species of wild fauna and flora by regulating trade therein, OJ 2000 L 320/1.

CITES into Regulation 3626/82,[161] thereby implementing the decisions of the COP of the CITES by Community legislation.

5.3 National law level

In this section, the implementation of COP/MOP decisions in the selected three EU Member States will be examined. Of particular interest is the issue of how COP/MOP decisions are implemented in the EU Member States and whether the involvement of the EU affects the way in which they are implemented in the domestic legal orders of those EU Member States.

5.3.1 Germany

In principle, according to Articles 74, 75 GG, environmental policy broadly defined falls either within the concurrent competence or within the *'Rahmenkompetenz'* (framework competence) of the Federal State. Thus, the Federal State does not have a comprehensive competence to legislate in the environmental area but rather shares it with the *Länder.* As a result, the protection of the environment is regulated in numerous sector specific laws and regulations, which depending on the competence, can be federal, regional or sometimes local.[162]

An example of a federal environmental statute that refers to the implementation of the obligations arising out of bilateral, multilateral or regional agreements is paragraph 11 of the *Gesetz über die Überwachung und Kontrolle der grenzüberschreitenden Verbringung von Abfällen* (AbfVerbrG)[163] (Act on controlling cross-border waste transport), which provides for exceptions on the prohibition of waste transports. Paragraph 11 of the AbfVerbrG authorizes the Federal Government to adopt executive regulations (*Rechtsverordnungen*) – with the consent of the *Bundesrat* – for the purpose of implementing COP/MOP decisions adopted for instance within the framework of the Basle Convention on the control of transboundary movements of hazardous wastes.[164]

---

[161] OJ 1982 L 384/1-61; replaced by Regulation 338/97, OJ 1997 L 61/1-69.

[162] It should be noted that a comprehensive environmental law act (Umweltgesetzbuch) is currently discussed within the German government on the basis of a draft text, see: http://www.bmu.de/fset800.php.

[163] BGBl I, 1994, 2771.

[164] Paragraph 11 AbfVerbrG
Die Bundesregierung wird ermächtigt, durch Rechtsverordnung mit Zustimmung des Bundesrates
1. Ausnahmen hinsichtlich der Verbringungsverbote und der Verbringungsverfahren festzulegen, um in Umsetzung von zweiseitigen, mehrseitigen oder regionalen Übereinkünften oder anderen Vereinbarungen, die nach Artikel 11 des Basler Übereinkommens und der EG-Abfallverbringungsverordnung

Similarly, paragraph 37 *Bundesimmissionsschutzgesetz* (BImSchG)[165] (Federal Emissions Act) authorizes the Federal Government to adopt – with the consent of the *Bundesrat* – *Rechtsverordnungen* for the purpose of implementing obligations arising out of international agreements or Community law determining the specific conditions for the operation of installations, products etc.[166]

Finally, also paragraph 6a of the *Wasserhaushaltsgesetz* (WSH)[167] (Water Resources Act) authorizes the Federal Government to adopt – with the consent of the *Bundesrat* – *Rechtsverordnungen* for the purpose of implementing obligations arising out of international agreements or Community law concerning the conditions and use of water as well as of water installations.[168] Thus, in all these cases, the Federal Government can adopt executive regulations in order to implement obligations arising out of international agreements and/or Community law. Hence, the same provision can be used for the implementation of international obligations and EC law obligations. In other words, whether or not the EC first implements a COP/MOP decision before it enters the German domestic legal order does not make a difference regarding the legal basis for the adoption of the implementing *Rechtsverordnungen*.

---

zulässig sind, die schadlose Verwertung oder gemeinwohlverträgliche Beseitigung von Abfällen zu fördern,

2. weitere Verbote der Verbringung bestimmter Abfälle in den, aus dem oder durch den Geltungsbereich dieses Gesetzes zu erlassen, soweit dies erforderlich ist, um eine schadlose Verwertung oder gemeinwohlverträgliche Beseitigung sicherzustellen, insbesondere auch um Verbringungsverbote anderer Staaten durchzusetzen. Diese Rechtsverordnungen können auch zur Durchführung oder Umsetzung von entsprechenden zweiseitigen, mehrseitigen oder regionalen Übereinkünften oder anderer Vereinbarungen, die nach Artikel 11 des Basler Übereinkommens und der EG-Abfallverbringungsverordnung zulässig sind, erlassen werden.

165 BGBl. I, 1990, 880.

166 Paragraph 37 Erfüllung von zwischenstaatlichen Vereinbarungen und Beschlüssen der EG Zur Erfüllung von Verpflichtungen aus zwischenstaatlichen Vereinbarungen oder von bindenden Beschlüssen der Europäischen Gemeinschaften kann die Bundesregierung zu dem in § 1 genannten Zweck durch Rechtsverordnung mit Zustimmung des Bundesrates bestimmen, daß Anlagen, Stoffe, Erzeugnisse, Brennstoffe oder Treibstoffe gewerbsmäßig oder im Rahmen wirtschaftlicher Unternehmungen nur in den Verkehr gebracht werden dürfen, wenn sie nach Maßgabe der §§ 32 bis 35 bestimmte Anforderungen erfüllen. [...]

167 BGBl. I, 1996, 1695.

168 Paragraph 6a WSH Supra- und Internationale Anforderungen

Soweit es zur Erfüllung bindender Beschlüsse der Europäischen Gemeinschaft oder zwischenstaatlicher Vereinbarungen notwendig ist, kann die Bundesregierung durch Rechtsverordnung mit Zustimmung des Bundesrates Vorschriften über die Bewirtschaftung der Gewässer nach den Grundsätzen des § 1a Abs. 1 erlassen, insbesondere Anforderungen an die Beschaffenheit und die Benutzung von Gewässern sowie den Bau und Betrieb von Anlagen im Sinne des § 18b Abs. 1, des § 19a Abs. 1 und des § 19g Abs. 1 und 2 festlegen.

As examples for the implementation of international obligations through *Rechtsverordnungen*, reference can be made to the *Bundesartenschutzverordnung*[169] implementing the modifications of the CITES, while the prohibition of certain CFC substances imposed by modifications of the Montreal protocol was implemented by a specific CFC regulation.[170]

Decisions of COPs/MOPs do not arise *directly* before German courts since they first need to be implemented by a domestic incorporation act (Article 59 (2) GG), so that only the domestic incorporation act is applied by the German courts. Accordingly, it is not surprising that Rest comes to the conclusion that 'aspects of international environmental law remained outside of the consideration or played only a marginal role when an international convention directly was concerned'.[171] This conclusion is also confirmed by a review of the German environmental case-law covering the last years which does not mention a single case directly involving international environmental agreements or COP/MOP decisions of IOs.[172] However, German courts interpret domestic law in the light of international obligations as the decision of the *Bundesverwaltungsgericht* (BVerwG) in the *Lingen*[173] case illustrates.

In this case, a Dutch national living in the Netherlands challenged the construction of a nuclear power plant in Germany close to the Dutch border. The administrative court of first instance rejected the claim by arguing that the public international law principle of territoriality limits German acts to German territory, thereby excluding a right of foreigners to appeal against the construction of the nuclear power plant if they are not residing or owning land in Germany. The *BVerwG* took a different approach by focusing in particular on paragraph 1 Nr. 4 *Atomgesetz* (AtomG, Nuclear power Act) that states that one of the purposes of the act is to implement the international obligations of Germany related to nuclear energy. Without mentioning any specific international agreement or decision of an IO, the *BVerwG* concluded that an interpretation compatible with public international law of the AtomG is indispensable, thus accepting the appeal of the Dutch national.

In summary, it can be concluded that the same legal basis can be used for the implementation of COP/MOP decisions coming directly from MEAs and for COP/MOP decisions that have been 'communitarized' by secondary EC legislation. Hence, those provisions make no distinction between international obligations and Community law obligations. However, the difference between COP/MOP decisions that are not communitarized and those that are communi-

---

169 BGBl. I, 1999, Nr. 47, 21.10.1999, 1955.

170 Verordnung zum Verbot von bestimmten die Ozonschicht abbauenden Halogenkohlenwasserstoffen (FCKWHalonVerbV), BGBl. I, 1991, 1090, 6.5.1991.

171 Rest (1997) at 420.

172 Schmidt (2001); *ibid.*, (1999); *ibid.*, (1997).

173 BVerwGE 75, 285. See for details: Jans (1987).

tarized lies in the fact that communitarized COP/MOP decisions enjoy primacy over all German law and can be directly applied if they fulfil the criteria developed by the ECJ. So, the involvement of Community law upgrades the legal rank of communitarized COP/MOP decisions within the German legal order.

5.3.2 The Netherlands

Also in the Netherlands, environmental legislation is spread over numerous sectoral legislative acts. Some of these acts contain explicit provisions enabling the responsible Minister to adopt executive regulations (*ministeriële regelingen*) for the purpose of implementing international obligations. For example, Article 1a *Wet houdende regelen omtrent de verontreiniging van oppervlaktewateren*[174] (Act on pollution of surface waters) authorizes the responsible Minister to adopt executive regulations concerning the levels of substances and their measurement for the purpose of fuflilling obligations arising out of international agreements and binding rules of international organizations.[175] In this context, it should be noted that the procedure for adopting the executive regulations for the purpose of implementing international obligations deviates from the procedure for adopting domestic regulations which are not required by international or European law. For domestic regulations, an *algemene maatregel van bestuur* that must be adopted by the whole government is required, whereas a *ministeriële regeling* can be adopted by the responsible Minister alone.

Another example is Article 10.34 *Wet milieubeheer*[176] (Act on environmental management) which authorizes the responsible Minister to adopt rules concerning the collection and transport of waste water for the purpose of implementing obligations arising out of decisions of IO and international agreements. Finally, Article 3 *Flora- en faunawet*[177] (Act on Flora and Fauna) provides that the desig-

---

[174] Staatsblad, 13.11.1969, 536.

[175] Artikel 1a Wet houdende regelen omtrent de verontreiniging van oppervlaktewateren

[...]

3. In afwijking van het eerste en het tweede lid geschiedt de vaststelling van grenswaarden, regels inzake metingen van stoffen en termijnen ter uitvoering van een voor Nederland verbindend verdrag of een voor Nederland verbindend regeling van een volkenrechtelijke organisatie door Onze Minister van Volkshuisvesting, Ruimtelijke Ordening en Milieubeheer bij in het *Staatsblad* bekend te maken regeling.

[176] Staatsblad, 13.6.1979, 442,

Art. 10.34

Onze Minister stelt regels over het ontwerpen, bouwen, aanpassen en onderhouden van de voorzieningen voor de inzameling en het transport van afvalwater ter uitvoering van een voor Nederland verbindend verdrag of een voor Nederland verbindend besluit van een volkenrechtelijke organisatie.

[177] Staatsblad, 25.05.1998, 402,

Art. 3

[...]

nation of plant species as protected domestic plant species required by binding decisions of IOs or the EC must be implemented by *ministeriële regeling*. For instance, a *ministeriële regeling* on the basis of Article 3 (2) *Flora- and Faunawet* was used for implementing modifications of the list of endangered species of the Berne Convention 1979.[178] Similarly, a *ministeriële regeling* was adopted for implementing modifications of the Montreal protocol.[179]

Since most obligations arising out of MEAs and COP/MOP decisions are first implemented by domestic executive regulations, Dutch courts rarely apply them directly.[180] In most cases, international environmental agreements are applied indirectly by interpreting national laws in the light of international obligations.[181]

An example of a direct application of an international agreement is the following case concerning the permission for a building project that endangered hamsters.[182] The hamster is listed as an endangered species by EC Directive 92/43 as well as the Convention on the Conservation of European Wildlife and Natural Habitats (Berne Convention 1979). Several environmental NGOs challenged the validity of the building permission claiming *inter alia* that obligations arising out of the Berne Convention 1979 would conflict with the permission. The *Raad van State* quashed the decision of the regional authority granting the permission because it did not sufficiently take into account the obligations arising out of the Berne Convention (and EC Directive 92/43).

In summary, in the Netherlands binding COP/MOP decisions – whether communitarized or not – are also implemented through *ministeriële regelingen*, and thus are treated in the same way. Moreover, since Articles 93, 94 Gw. accept the primacy of international agreements and decisions of IOs over conflicting Dutch law, including constitutional law, if certain conditions are fulfilled, there is no difference in the legal status between communitarized and non-communitarized COP/MOP decisions. However, the involvement of EC law potentially has an impact with regard to the criteria to be applied by Dutch courts when determining whether a provision of an international treaty or binding decision of an IO has direct effect or not. While the criteria developed by the ECJ for determining whether a provision of an international agreement has direct effect or not are to a large extent comparable with the ones applied by Dutch courts,

---

2. De aanwijzing van een plantensoort als beschermde inheemse plantensoort geschiedt in afwijking van het bepaalde in het eerste lid bij ministeriële regeling indien die aanwijzing noodzakelijk is ter uitvoering van internationale verplichtingen of bindende besluiten van organen van de Europese Unie of andere volkenrechtelijke organisaties.

[178] Regeling aanwijzing dier- en plantensoorten, Staatscourant 13.3.2002, nr. 51, 30.

[179] Regeling ozonlaagafbrekende stoffen Wms 2001, Staatscourant, 9.11.2001, nr. 218, 13.

[180] See generally: Nollkaemper (1998).

[181] See: Nollkaemper (2002).

[182] Afdeling bestuursrechtspraak van de Raad van State, judgment of 26.10.1999, JM 1999, 165.

this is not the case for decisions of IOs. Whereas the ECJ ruled that the decisions of organs established by international agreements must be treated in the same way as the agreement, Dutch constitutional law requires that extra conditions must be fulfilled before a decision of an IO is considered to have direct effect, for instance, that the decision is published in the Dutch official gazette and that it is binding on everyone (*ieder verbindend*). Hence, communitarized COP/MOP decisions could be applied by Dutch courts more readily than non-communitarized COP/MOP decisions. Nonetheless, due to the fact that most COP/MOP decisions need to be implemented by domestic measures, Dutch courts apply the domestic implementing measures rather than the COP/MOP decisions.

5.3.3 France

Until recently, environmental issues in France were also regulated in numerous sectoral legislative acts.[183] However, this situation substantially changed with the adoption of a comprehensive *Code de l'environnement*[184] which merges numerous legislative acts covering, for instance, the atmosphere, air, water, fauna and flora, etc.[185] The implementation of international obligations is not specifically mentioned in the *Code de l'environnement*.[186] It merely contains generally formulated provisions delegating to the Council of Ministers the competence to determine the details by issuing *décrets* (executive decrees).[187]

However, the *décrets* used for implementing COP/MOP decisions are not specifically based on a law but, in their preamble, simply refer to Articles 52-55 CF and the law relating to the publication of international agreements of 1953. That is, for example, the case for the amendments of the Annex of the Marpol

---

[183] See generally: Dutheil de la Rochère (1999).

[184] J.O., 21.9.2000.

[185] See generally: Prieur (2001).

[186] See for details: Prieur (2000).

[187] See e.g.:

Article L. 211-2

I - Les règles générales de préservation de la qualité et de répartition des eaux superficielles, souterraines et des eaux de la mer dans la limite des eaux territoriales sont déterminées par décret en Conseil d'Etat.

[...]

Article L. 211-3

I - En complément des règles générales mentionnées à l'article L. 211-2, des prescriptions nationales ou particulières à certaines parties du territoire sont fixées par décret en Conseil d'Etat afin d'assurer la protection des principes mentionnés à l'article L. 211-1.

Convention adopted in 1997,[188] the amendments of the Montreal protocol[189] or the modifications of the Annexes of the CITES.[190] In contrast to that, *décrets* implementing EU decisions concerning the environment refer to the relevant secondary Community law decisions and the specific domestic laws[191] or more recently to the *Code de l'environnement.*[192] Accordingly, the implementation of COP/MOP decisions is directly based on the provisions concerning the ratification and publication of international treaties, thereby indicating the close legal relationship between the COP/MOP decisions and their founding treaties.

The general application of international environmental treaties by French courts started in the 1990s and concentrates mainly on cases concerning the hunting of various species that are protected by the CITES,[193] Berne Convention 1979,[194] and Ramsar Convention.[195] It can be concluded from the cases found that the *Conseil d'Etat* consistently denies any direct effect of provisions of the CITES or the Berne Convention.[196] However, in a recent case the *Conseil d'Etat* ruled that French regional authorities who were intending to extend an existing motorway in a area protected by the Ramsar Convention and EC law *'commis une erreur manifeste d'appréciation en inscrivant dans le schéma ce projet d'infrastructure*

[188] Décret no. 2001-186, 20.2.2001 portant publication des amendements à l'annexe du protocole de 1978 relatif à la Convention internationale de 1973 pour la prévention de la pollution par les navires (résolution MEPC.7540), J.O., No. 49, 27.2.2001, 3118.

[189] Décret no. 96-905, 9.10.1996 portant publication des ajustements au protocole de Montréal du 16 septembre 1987 relatif à des substances qui appauvrissent la couche d'ozone, J.O., No. 243, 17.10.1996, 15188; Décret no 96-824, 16.9.1996 portant publication des ajustements au protocole de Montréal du 16 septembre 1987 relatif à des substances qui appauvrissent la couche d'ozone, J.O., No. 221, 21.9.1996, 14032.

[190] Décret no. 93-251, 23.2.1993 portant publication des amendements aux annexes I, II, III à la convention de Washington du 3 mars 1973 sur le commerce international des espèces de faune et de flore sauvages menacées d'extinction, J.O. No. 49, 27.2.1993.

[191] Décret no. 99-55, 26.1.1999 relatif à l'application du règlement (CEE) no. 793/93 du 23.3.1993 concernant l'évaluation et le contrôle des risques présentés par les substances existantes et du règlement (CE) no. 3093/94 du 15.12.1994 relatif à des substances qui appauvrissent la couche d'ozone, J.O. No. 23, 28.1.1999, 1447.

[192] Décret no. 2002-213, 15.2.2002 portant transposition des directives 1999/30/CE du Conseil du 22.4.1999 et 2000/69/CE du Parlement européen et du Conseil du 16.11.2000 et modifiant le décret no 98-360 du 6.5.1998, J.O., No. 42, 19.2.2002, 3198.

[193] Conseil d'Etat, 8.6.1990 (no. 82146, 82147, 82154); Conseil d'Etat, 30.1.1995 (no. 130238); Conseil d'Etat, 6.11.1998 (no. 172563).

[194] Conseil d'Etat, 12.2.1993 (no. 115468); Conseil d'Etat, 19.6.1998 (no. 137404); Conseil d'Etat 14.4.1999 (no. 185954, 197159-197162).

[195] Conseil d'Etat, 6.1.1999 (no. 161403); Conseil d'Etat, 30.6.2000 (no. 98NT01333).

[196] See for an exception: Tribunal administratif de Saint-Denis-de-la Réunion, 19.2.1997 (SOPTOM-Réunion); see case note by: Le Cornec (1999).

routière', because they failed to take the relevant Ramsar Convention and Community law provisions appropriately into account.[197]

An example of how French courts apply an international environmental agreement in relation to domestic legislation is the following case concerning the hunting of wolves.[198] A number of French communities decided to allow the hunting of wolves whose population has been increasing in their area. The regional *préfet* started a procedure at the administrative court in Nice requesting the annulment of a decision that held that wolves are protected by the Berne Convention 1979. The *Tribunal administratif de Nice* ruled that the decision was indeed contrary to the Berne Convention and therefore annulled the decision. On appeal, the *Cour administratif d'appel de Marseille* upheld the ruling of the court of first instance for the same reason.[199] The decisions of the lower courts were in contrast to the long-standing case-law of the *Conseil d'Etat* which had repeatedly rejected any direct effect of the Berne Convention as it addressed only the contracting parties.[200] Accordingly and in line with its case-law, the *Conseil d'Etat* on final appeal annulled the rulings of the lower courts.[201] It argued that the provisions of the Berne Convention do not produce any direct effect within the domestic order and thus cannot be invoked, hence the lower courts erred in law.[202] Thus, the *Conseil d'Etat* did not consider the Berne Convention to be applicable in the present case. However, it then turned to EC Directive 92/43[203] on the conservation of natural habitats and of wild fauna and flora (habitat directive) that also listed the wolf as protected species. The *Conseil d'Etat* concluded that the hunting of the wolf was covered by the exception contained in Article 16 of the Directive, which provided an exception in order:

> '(b) to prevent serious damage, in particular to crops, livestock, forests, fisheries and water and other types of property or (c) in the interests of public health and public safety, or for other imperative reasons of overriding public interest, includ-

---

[197] Conseil d'Etat, 30.6.2000 (no. 98NT01333).

[198] See for the details of the case: Bohbot (1999).

[199] Cour administrative d'appel de Marseille statuant au contentieux, 28.12.1998 (N° 97MA00640), '[...] que de telles dispositions, qui autorisent la destruction systématique des loups sur le territoire national, excédent, par leur généralité, les possibilités de dérogation prévues par l'article 6 de la convention de Berne; qu'elles sont par conséquent incompatibles avec ladite convention [...]'.

[200] Conseil d'Etat, 23.10.1995 (Association Artus et autres); Conseil d'Etat, 17.11.1995 (Union juridique Rhône-Méditerranée); Conseil d'Etat, 6.2.1998 (Ministre de l'Environnement c/ ASPAS); Conseil d'Etat, 30.12.1998 (Association Artus).

[201] Conseil d'Etat, 8.12.2000 (no. 204756), see case-note by: Férvrier (2001).

[202] *Ibid.*, 'Considérant toutefois que ces stipulations ne créent d'obligations qu'entre les Etats parties à la convention et ne produisent pas d'effet direct dans l'ordre juridique interne;[...] la cour a entaché son arrêt d'une erreur de droit [...]'.

[203] OJ 1992 L 206/7.

ing those of a social or economic nature and beneficial consequences of primary importance for the environment'.

This case is also an example of the different treatment of international agreements and secondary Community law. While the *Conseil d'Etat* could avoid the application of the Berne Convention by arguing that it cannot be invoked before the national court because it lacks direct effect, it was forced by virtue of Community law to determine whether the national measures were compatible with the EC Directive.[204]

In sum, France uses *décrets* for 'communitarized' as well as non-communitarized COP/MOP decisions, thus treating both types of decisions equally. As to the French case-law, it appears that in most cases international environmental agreements are considered to be addressed only to the contracting parties, and thus do not contain rights that can be invoked before national courts. However, the involvement of EC law does upgrade the legal status of communitarized COP/MOP decisions since they enjoy primacy over all French law, including constitutional law, which is not the case with non-communitarized COP/MOP decisions. Moreover, as regards communitarized COP/MOP decisions, French courts have to apply the criteria of direct effect developed by the ECJ, which are different than the French criteria. For instance, Article 55 CF requires reciprocity and publication of the international agreement in the French official gazette, whereas this is obviously not required by the ECJ. Hence, Community law and, in particular, the ECJ make a difference regarding the legal status and effect of communitarized COP/MOP decisions.

5.4 Summary

The institutional architecture of many MEAs prevents one from fitting them into the traditional categories of public international law. They are 'more' than traditional international agreements, but at the same time they create institutional arrangements that are 'less' than classic international organizations. As COPs/MOPs decisions can *de facto* result in substantive changes to the legal obligations of the contracting parties – often even against the will of a minority of parties – they must be considered to perform essentially the same functions as organs of IOs.

On the European law level, it appears that many MEAs are concluded as mixed agreements by both the EC and its Member States. As a consequence, the obligation to implement COP/MOP decisions is shared between the EC and its Member States depending on whether an issue falls within the Community's or Member States' competence. However, since the EC has legislated in many areas of environmental law, it is competent to implement most COP/MOP decisions.

[204] Férvrier (2001) at 778-779.

As a result, those COP/MOP decisions become an integral part of the Community legal order, thereby acquiring supremacy over all national law of the EU Member States as well as having the possibility of direct effect.[205] Consequently, from the point of view of the EU Member States, there is no difference any longer in terms of the legal status between 'communitarized' COP/MOP decisions and original secondary Community legislation.

As regards the national level, the unclear qualification of COPs/MOPs as *de facto* organs of IOs or as international treaties is important in order to determine their legal status in the domestic legal order. For Germany, the distinction could be important because COPs/MOPs could fall either within Article 24 GG or Article 59 (2) GG. In the former case, Germany would transfer powers to the COPs/MOPs, while in the latter case, Germany first needs to transpose COPs/MOPs decisions by formal act. For France, the qualification of COPs/MOPs as international agreements is easier to accommodate with Article 55 CF, since Article 55 CF does not explicitly mention decisions of IOs, thereby casting doubt whether they could fall within the scope of Article 55 CF. While for the Netherlands, the issue is less relevant since Articles 93, 94 Gw. apply equally to both decisions of IOs and international agreements.

Moreover, it is interesting to note that the same national law provision is used for the implementation of obligations arising out of international agreements and EC law. Thus, no distinction is made as to whether a COP/MOP decision is implemented directly by the EU Member State or whether it first is communitarized by being implemented by the EC first before it enters the domestic legal level. In all three EU Member States, environmental obligations arising out of international agreements or from the EC are implemented by the issuance of executive orders by the responsible Minister. Finally, since in most cases COP/MOP decisions are implemented by domestic executive regulations, national courts rarely apply MEAs or COP/MOP decisions directly, but rather interpret the domestic legislation in the light of the international obligations.

In summary, it can be concluded that the modification of the classic legal situation 'COP/MOP decisions–national law' into an 'EC law transformed' legal situation 'COP/MOP decisions– European law–national law' is in practice not very visible with regard to the implementation of international environmental obligations in the selected EU Member States. Nonetheless, the 'EC law transformer' transforms all those COP/MOP decisions that fall within the competence of the EC from 12 Volt to 220 Volt before they enter the domestic circuit of the Member States.

---

[205] See generally: Sands (1991).

6 Security Council Resolutions

6.1 International law level

Since the end of the Cold War, the Security Council has been – at last – able to fulfil its assigned tasks effectively. According to Article 24 UN Charter, the Security Council is responsible for the maintenance of international peace and security, while Chapters VI and VII of the UN Charter indicate the various possible measures the Security Council can take if the international peace is threatened (Article 39 UN Charter). One of these measures entails the imposition of economic sanctions (Article 41 UN Charter) against a state.[206] Since 1990, the Security Council has increasingly used sanctions to respond to serious political crises such as in the Gulf War against Iraq and in the Balkan wars against the former Yugoslavia (FRY).[207]

Although the Security Council adopts the sanction measures, it is on the national level where the implementation measures must be taken. The Security Council has to rely on the UN member states for their actual implementation according to Article 25 UN Charter. Consequently, the effectiveness of Security Council Resolutions depends largely on the degree of implementation by the UN member states.[208] This situation can thus be described as a classic legal interaction 'Security Council Resolutions–national law'.

6.2 European law level

This classic legal interaction does not apply to the EU and its Member States. In their case, a third legal layer (EU law) is inserted between the international and national law level, thereby modifying it into an 'EC law transformed' legal situation 'Security Council Resolutions–European law–national law'.[209]

The EU is not a member of the UN and it cannot currently become a member because the UN is only open to nation-states (Article 4 UN Charter). Thus, from a formal legal point of view, the EU is not obliged to implement Security Council obligations.[210] However, in several cases Security Council Resolutions have also called upon non-member states and international organizations to implement Security Council Resolutions.[211] Accordingly, not being a

---

206 See in general the contributions in: Gowlland-Debbas (2001); Uerpmann (1995).

207 Rydelski (1995).

208 Brandl (1999) at 167; Uerpmann (1995) at 111.

209 See for a detailed analysis: Kuijper (2003); Bethlehem (2001).

210 Bethlehem (2001) at 295; Puissochet (1997) at 1568-1569.

211 See for example: UN Security Council Resolution 687 (1991) on Iraq which states: '27. Calls upon all States to maintain such national controls [...], and calls upon international organizations to take all

member of the UN is apparently not considered to be an obstacle to creating an obligation to implement Security Council Resolutions. Indeed, despite the fact that the UN Charter and Security Council Resolutions are not an integral part of the Community legal order, the EC/EU has, since the beginning of the 1990's, implemented most Security Council Resolutions, thereby indicating that it is ready to implement them even without being a member of the UN.[212] The basis for the implementation of Security Council Resolutions imposing economic and financial sanctions by the EC can be found in the exclusive competence of the EC in external trade matters. Since the entry into force of the Maastricht Treaty in 1993, the implementation of Security Council Resolutions imposing economic sanctions has been formalized in the EU and EC Treaty in a two-step procedure.[213]

In a first step within the CFSP decision-making process, the EU Member States reach a common position (Article 15 TEU) or agree on a joint action (Article 14 TEU).[214] In a second step, the Council of the EC adopts the appropriate legal measures (mostly a Regulation) on the basis of Article 301 EC Treaty and, if the sanctions touch on the movement of capital and payments, on the basis of Article 60 EC Treaty.[215] The EC Regulation is then published in the *Official Journal of the EU* and it is from that moment on directly applicable in all EU Member States. Accordingly, the classic legal situation is modified because Security Council Resolutions are first implemented by European legislation before they enter the domestic legal order of the EU Member States.

There is some ECJ case-law on the implementation of Security Council Resolutions within the EU and its Member States.[216] Two groups of cases can be distinguished. The first group concerns cases involving the implementation of UN Security Council Resolutions by the EU and its Member States. The second group of more recent cases involves the question of non-contractual liability for unlawful acts adopted by the EU organs. These cases will not be discussed in this study.[217]

---

appropriate steps to assist in ensuring such full compliance.' See also: Security Council Resolutions 1199 (Kosovo), 1244 (Kosovo), all available at the UN server at: http://www.un.org/Docs/sc.htm.

212 See for the pre-Maastricht situation: Bohr (1993).

213 See: Auvert-Finck (2003); Pavoni (1999); Canor, (1998); Naud (1997).

214 See for details: Wessel (1999) at 154-182.

215 See e.g.: Council Regulation (EC) No 2580/2001 of 27.12.2001 on specific restrictive measures directed against certain persons and entities with a view to combating terrorism, OJ 2001 L 344/70-75; Council Regulation (EC) No 1146/2001 of 11.6.2001 concerning certain restrictive measures in respect of Liberia, OJ 2001 L 156/1-6.

216 See: Kapteyn (2003); Puissochet (1997).

217 See e.g.: Case T-220/96 *EVO* [2002] ECR II-2265; Case C-237/98 P *Dorsch Consult* [2000] ECR I-4549; Case T-184/95 *Dorsch Consult* [1998] ECR II- 667.

In the following cases, two issues are of central importance. First, the question is whether and, if so, to what extent the EU Member States still have some residual competence concerning the implementation of Security Council Resolutions. Second, the question is what is the extent of the jurisdiction of the ECJ to interpret Security Council Resolutions.

One of the first cases involving the interpretation of EU acts implementing a UN Security Council Chapter VII Resolution was the *Bosphorus*[218] case. Bosphorus Airways is a Turkish charter company which leased – before sanctions were imposed against the Federal Republic of Yugoslavia (FRY) – for a period of 4 years two aircrafts owned by the national Yugoslav airline JAT. EC Regulation No. 990/93[219] based on Article 133 EC Treaty (as a pre-Maastricht Treaty measure) intended to implement certain aspects of sanctions imposed against the FRY by Security Council Resolution 820 (1993)[220] that provides in paragraph 24:

> 'that all States shall impound all vessels, freight vehicles, rolling stock and aircraft in their territories in which a majority or controlling interest is held by a person or undertaking in or operating from the FRY [...]'.

Article 8 of Regulation 990/93 contains the same wording:

> 'All vessels, freight vehicles, rolling stock and aircraft in which a majority or controlling interest is held by a person or undertaking in or operating from the Federal Republic of Yugoslavia (Serbia and Montenegro) shall be impounded by the competent authorities of the Member States.'

The main issue was whether the term 'majority or controlling interest' was applicable in the present case where Bosphorus was solely responsible for the day-to-day operations of the leased aircrafts, while JAT remained owner of the planes without being involved in the operation of them. The ECJ – emphasizing the importance of the aims pursued by the UN Sanctions and the Regulation – applied a broad interpretation of the term 'majority or controlling interest' and concluded that Article 8 of Regulation 990/93 is applicable also in the present circumstances.[221]

Soon afterwards, the *Centro-Com* case came before the ECJ.[222] This case involved the implementation of UN Security Council Resolution 757 (1992)

[218] Case C-84/95 *Bosphorus* [1996] ECR I-3953.

[219] Council Regulation (EEC) No 990/93 of 26.4.1993 concerning trade between the EEC and the Federal Republic of Yugoslavia (Serbia and Montenegro) OJ 1993 L 102/14.

[220] UN Security Council Resolution, 17.4.1993, available at: http://www.un.org/Docs/scres/1993/820e.pdf.

[221] Case C-84/95 *Bosphorus* [1996] ECR I-3953, para. 23 ff.

[222] Case C-124/95 *Centro-Com* [1997] ECR I-81.

by EC Regulation No. 1432/92[223] prohibiting Serbian or Montenegrian funds deposited in its territory from being released in order to pay for goods exported to those areas.

Article 4 (c) of Resolution 757 provides that all states shall prevent:

> 'The sale or supply by their nationals or from their territories or using their flag vessels or aircraft of any commodities or products, whether or not originating within their territories – but not including supplies intended strictly for medical purposes and foodstuffs notified to the Security Council Committee established pursuant to Resolution 724 (1991) – to any person or body in the FRY (Serbia and Montenegro) [...]'.

Article 5 of Resolution 757 states that:

> 'no state shall make available to the authorities of FRY (Serbia and Montenegro) or to any commercial, industrial or public utility undertaking in the FRY, any funds or any other financial or economic resources and shall prevent their nationals and any persons within their territories from removing from their territories or otherwise making available to those authorities or to any such undertaking any such funds or resources and from remitting any other funds to persons or bodies within the FRY (Serbia and Montenegro), except payments exclusively for strictly medical or humanitarian purposes and foodstuffs'.

EC Regulation 1432/92 implemented those measures in the following way:

> **'Article 1**
> As from 31 May 1992, the following shall be prohibited:
> [...]
> b) the export to the Republics of Serbia and Montenegro of all commodities and products originating in or coming from the Community [...]
> **Article 2**
> The prohibitions of Article 1 shall not apply to:
> a) the export to the Republics of Serbia and Montenegro of commodities and products intended for strictly medical purposes and foodstuffs notified to the Committee established pursuant to Resolution 724 (1991) of the United Nations Security Council [...]'.

Centro-Com is an Italian company that exported pharmaceutical goods and blood-testing equipment to Montenegro. The bills were to be paid from funds deposited with Barclays bank in the UK. The UK implemented Security Coun-

---

[223] Council Regulation (EEC) No 1432/92 of 1.6.1992 prohibiting trade between the EEC and the Republics of Serbia and Montenegro, OJ 1992 L 151/4.

cil Resolution 757 (based on the UN Act 1946) by 'Order 1992' which prohibits any person from supplying or delivering any goods to a person connected with Serbia and Montenegro – with the exception of medical supplies. Following reports of abuse of the authorization procedure established by the Sanctions Committee for the export of goods to Serbia and Montenegro, the UK Treasury decided to change its policy. Henceforth, payments from Serbian and Montenegrian funds held in the UK for exports of goods exempted from the sanctions, such as medical products, were to be permitted only where those exports were made from the UK. Since Centro-Com operated from Italy, Barclays bank was no longer allowed to transfer the requested funds to Centro-Com. The central issue in this case was whether the UK still retained some residual competence to adopt such measures after the EC had adopted Community law measures implementing Security Council Resolution 757. The ECJ accepts that:

> '24 The Member States have indeed retained their competence in the field of foreign and security policy. At the material time, their cooperation in this field was governed by inter alia Title III of the Single European Act.'[224]

But then concludes that:

> '27 Consequently, while it is for Member States to adopt measures of foreign and security policy in the exercise of their national competence, those measures must nevertheless respect the provisions adopted by the Community in the field of the common commercial policy provided for by Article 113 of the Treaty.'[225]

Thus, the remaining competence of the Member States to adopt measures in this policy area is severely limited in the sense that they must be in accordance with the relevant Community law measures.

A few weeks later the ECJ handed down its judgment in the *Ebony*[226] case concerning – like the *Bosphorus* case – the implementation of Security Council Resolution 820 (1993) by Regulation 990/93. The Resolution and Regulation require all states to detain all vessels within their territory that might violate the embargo. A vessel flying the Maltese flag that was on its way to the FRY was detained by Italian authorities in international waters. The main issue in this case was whether the action on international waters was covered by the sanctions laid down in the Resolution and the Regulation. The ECJ concluded that for an effective implementation of the sanctions all traffic in Yugoslavian waters

---

[224] Case C-124/95 *Centro-Com* [1997] ECR I-81.

[225] *Ibid.*

[226] Case C-177/95 *Ebony Maritime* [1997] ECR I-1111.

must be prevented, which includes also attempted entries into those waters by vessels that are still in international waters.[227]

More recently, an action against the Council and the Commission has been brought before the Court of First Instance (CFI) by a number of Swedish nationals of Somali origin.[228] On 15 October 1999, the UN Security Council adopted Resolution 1267 (1999), calling for *inter alia* sanctions against the Taliban, which were extended by Resolution 1333 (2000) to cover Osama Bin Laden and persons and bodies associated with him. On 6 March 2001, the Council adopted Regulation (EC) No 467/2001.[229] Under Article 2 of that Regulation all funds and other financial resources belonging to any natural or legal person, entity or body listed in Annex I are to be frozen. The Taliban Sanctions Committee of the Security Council decided to amend the list by adding several individuals and bodies, including the applicants. On the basis of Article 10 of the Regulation, the Commission adopted Regulation (EC) No 2199/2001[230] giving effect to that decision.

The applicants submitted that the Council Regulation, which required that the applicants' funds were to be frozen and that resources were not to be made available to them, exceeds the powers of the Council under Articles 60 and 301 EC Treaty and is in breach of Article 249 EC Treaty. They argued that, by automatically copying the decision of the Sanctions Committee, the Council and the Commission have *de facto* delegated the power to the Taliban Sanctions Committee to determine which persons or organisations are included in Annex I. They further claimed that the Council and Commission had not examined the reasons why the Taliban Sanctions Committee included the applicants in its list nor were the applicants given any opportunity to apprise themselves of and refute the allegations on which the decision to include them in Annex I was based. The applicants had onerous sanctions imposed on them without any opportunity to defend themselves. The fundamental legal principle of the right to a fair and equitable hearing had been disregarded. Accordingly, the applicants asked the CFI in an interim procedure to annul the measures adopted by the Council and the Commission. However, the President of the CFI refused in the *Aden* as well as the *Sison* case to do so in the interim procedure because it did not considered it necessary to provide for interim measures in order to protect the rights of the applicants. Thus, it remains to be seen what the outcome will be in the main procedure and perhaps in a subsequent appeal procedure before the ECJ.[231]

---

[227] *Ibid.*, paras. 25 ff.

[228] Case T-306/01 R *Aden a.o.* [2002] ECR II-2387; see also a similar more recent case: T-47/03 R *Sison*, Order of the President of the CFI of 15.5.2003.

[229] Council Regulation, 467/2001 of 6.3.2001, OJ 2001 L 67/1.

[230] Commission Regulation No. 2199/2001, OJ 2001 L 295/16.

[231] See generally: Bartelt/Zeitler (2003).

In summary, it can be concluded that despite the fact the EU is not member of the UN, most Security Council Resolutions imposing sanctions are implemented by first adopting a Common Position and then a Regulation. In this way, Security Council Resolutions are incorporated in the Community legal order. Moreover, the ECJ interprets the EC Regulations implementing Security Council Resolutions very broadly with a view to ensuring the full effectiveness of them. Finally, by emphasizing the exclusive competence of the EC for external trade, the ECJ reduces to a minimum the residual competence of the EU Member States to adopt their own measures.

6.3 National law level

In this section the implementation and application of Security Council Resolutions in the selected EU Member States is examined.[232] The focus will be on the issues of legal rank and direct effect of Security Council Resolutions as well as the effect of EU involvement in the domestic legal orders.

6.3.1 Germany

The central law regulating the export from Germany and import into Germany of goods and services is the *Außenwirtschaftsgesetz* (AWG) (foreign trade act) dating from 1961.[233] Paragraph 1 (1) AWG states that trade in goods, services, capital, etc. with foreign countries is free. However, for the purpose of implementing obligations arising out of international agreements to which the competence to restrict trade has been transferred by a federal statute, the external trade can be restricted (paragraph 5 AWG).[234] Since Germany became a member of the UN by adopting the UN Charter through a federal statute, Germany also accepted the competence of the Security Council to impose trade restrictions. More specifically, paragraph 27 AWG determines that, for the purpose of implementing international obligations within the meaning of paragraph 5 AWG, the Minister of Economics can adopt *Rechtsverordnungen* (executive regulations) without the consent of the *Bundesrat*. Those *Rechtsverordnungen* are incorporated into the *Verordnung zur Durchfühung des Außenwirtschaftsgesetzes* (AWV) of 1986 that works out the details of the AWG.[235] For

[232] See also: generally: De Wet/Nollkaemper (2002).

[233] BGBl. I, 1961, 481. See for a detailed analysis: Schneider (1999).

[234] Paragraph 5 AWG

Zur Erfüllung zwischenstaatlicher Vereinbarungen, denen die gesetzgebenden Körperschaften in der Form eines Bundesgesetzes zugestimmt haben, können Rechtsgeschäfte und Handlungen im Außenwirtschaftsverkehr beschränkt und bestehende Beschränkungen aufgehoben werden.

[235] In the version of 2.7.2001, BAnz. Nr. 130, 17.7.2001, 14621.

example, paragraph 69e AWV prohibits capital movements between the EC and Iraq on the basis of Security Council Resolution 661, while paragraph 69g AWV deals with restrictions concerning air traffic and trade in weapons against Sierra Leone on the basis of Security Council Resolutions 1132 (1997) and 1171 (1998). These provisions do not distinguish between Security Council Resolutions implemented directly or via Community legislation.

Finally, the AWG also contains various penalties if the AWG is infringed. The penalties vary from administrative offences (*Ordnungswidrigkeiten*) with fines of up to 500.000 euros to prison sentences of up to 5 years (paragraphs 33, 34 AWG). However, paragraph 34 (4) AWG contains a higher prison sentence (not less than 2 years) for the infringement of laws or regulations that implement economic sanctions imposed by Security Council Resolutions based on Chapter VII UN Charter.[236] Hence, there is a direct reference to Security Council Resolutions in the AWG and the higher prison sentence indicates that infringements of Security Council sanctions are considered to be particularly serious.

The following two cases illustrate the practice of German courts dealing with Security Council sanctions. The cases indicate that under German law, Security Council Resolutions have no direct effect and require a national implementation act before being able to affect individuals.

In the first case,[237] the two accused organized bus trips transporting mostly guest workers and their family members from Germany into Serbia and back. After the imposition of sanctions by the UN Security Council and the EC against Serbia, they organized the bus trips with an interruption at the Hungarian-Serbian border, i.e. they provided the bus service from Germany to the Hungarian-Serbian border while Serbian bus companies organized the rest of the trip. In a first instance ruling, the accused were sentenced for violating paragraph 34 (4) AWG in conjunction with paragraphs 69h, 69k AWV of 1992, which implemented UN Resolution 757 (1992) and EC Regulation 1432/92. However, in an appeal before the *Bundesgerichtshof* (BGH), they successfully challenged the judgment of the lower court.

The *BGH* began its analysis by stating that sanctions adopted by the Security Council within the scope of Chapter VII UN Charter were only binding on

---

[236] Paragraph 34 (4) AWG states:

Mit Freiheitsstrafe nicht unter zwei Jahren wird bestraft, wer einer Vorschrift dieses Gesetzes oder einer auf Grund dieses Gesetzes erlassenen Rechtsverordnung oder einem im Bundegsesetzblatt oder im Bundesanzeiger veröffentlichten Rechtsakt der EG zur Beschräkung des Außenwirtschaftsverkehrs, *die der Durchführung einer vom Sicherheitsrat der Vereinten Nationen nach Kapitel VII der Charta der Vereinten Nation beschlossenen wirtschaftlichen Sanktionsmaßnahmen dienen*, zuwiderhandelt. In minder schweren Fällen ist die Strafe Freiheitsstrafe von drei Monaten bis zu fünf Jahren. (emphasis added).

[237] BGH, judgment of 21.4.1995, NJW 1995, 2174-2176.

the member states and not on their citizens.[238] The *BGH* continued by stating that paragraph 34 (4) AWG is a *'Blankettstrafvorschrift'* (carte blanche provision) enabling Germany to penalize violations of UN sanctions.[239] This provision assumed that it is only the Security Council that is competent to determine the type and extent of the sanctions,[240] which are constitutive and strictly binding on the UN member states.[241] Furthermore, the imposition of a prohibition by a *Rechtsverordnung* must be strictly related to the sanction measure and not go beyond it.[242] Turning to Resolution 757 (1992) the *BGH* concluded that the transport of persons within the territory of Serbia and Montenegro was not covered by it.[243] The Resolution merely prohibited in paragraph 5 'to make available any commercial, industrial or public utility undertaking on the FRY, any funds or any other financial economic resources'. According to the interpretation of the *BGH*, FRY nationals are merely prevented from receiving any funds,[244] but not from receiving (paid) services.[245] Finally, the *BGH* also turned to EC Regulation 1432/92 that was adopted for the purpose of implementing Security Council Resolution 757 and contained similar provisions. Accordingly, the Regulation could have been used as a basis for charging the accused. However, paragraph 34 (4) AWG prescribes that the minimum penalty of two years in prison can only be imposed for violations of EC acts adopted for the purpose of implementing Security Council Resolutions if they have been published in the official German gazettes.[246] Since Regulation 1432/92 was not published in the

[238] 'Im Hinblick darauf, dass eine nach Kapitel VII der UN-Charta vom Sicherheitsrat der Vereinten Nationen beschlossene wirtschaftliche Sanktionsmassnahme für die Bürger der Mitgliedstaaten keine unmittelbaren Rechtswirkungen entfaltet, sondern nur die Mitgliedstaaten bindet [...]', NJW 1995, 2175.

[239] '[...] eröffnet [...] paragraph 34 IV AWG als Blankettstrafvorschrift der BRD eine rechtliche Handhabe, vom Sicherheitsrat der Vereinten Nationen beschlossene, für sie als Mitgliedstaat der Vereinten Nationen verbindliche wirtschaftliche Sanktionsmassnahme innerstaatlich mit Strafbewehrung umzusetzen', NJW 1995, 2175.

[240] 'Die Vorschrift geht davon aus, dass nur der Sicherheitsrat der Vereinten Nationen die Kompetenz besitzt, Art und Umfang der zukünftigen und gebotenen Embargo-Massnahmen zu bestimmen, [...]', NJW 1995, 2175.

[241] '[...] dass derartige Beschlüsse des Sicherheitsrats gem. Art. 41 UN-Charta konstitutiv sind und strikte Bindungswirkung gegenüber die Mitgliedstaaten entfalten.'

[242] 'Ein durch die Rechtsverordnung statuiertes Verbot muss im strikten Regelungsbezug zu den vom Sicherheitsrat beschlossenen Sanktionsmassnahmen stehen; insbesondere darf es in seinem Regelungsgehalt nicht über die in dem Beschluss des Sicherheitsrats verhängten Massnahmen hinausgehen.'

[243] 'Die Beförderung von Privatpersonen auf dem Gebiet der Republiken Serbien und Montenegro ist von der UN-Resolution Nr. 757 (1992) nicht erfasst.'

[244] 'Privatpersonen sind lediglich vom Empfang 'sonstiger Gelder' auszuschliessen.'

[245] 'Die Zuwendung von – auch entgeldlichen – Dienstleistungen an Privatpersonen fällt hierunter nicht.'

[246] 'In diesem Sinne hätte auch die Verordnung (EWG) Nr. 1432/92 v. 1.6.1992 verwendet werden können, soweit und sofern sie als Durchführungsvorschrift zu den vom UN-Sicherheitsrat beschlossenen wirt-

German gazettes, the EC Regulation could not be used as a basis. In sum, the *BGH* concluded that the accused could not be punished either on the basis of paragraph 34 (4) AWG or on the basis of Regulation 1432/92.

In the second case,[247] the accused organized a number of transports of goods from and into Serbia after the imposition of the UN embargo against the FRY. The court of first instance based its sentence on the basis of paragraph 34 (4) AWG in conjunction with paragraphs 69h (1) and 69i AWV. The accused appealed by arguing that sentencing on the basis of paragraph 69h (1) AWV required that the products had to be produced in the FRY in order to be applicable, whereas according to him, the products were not produced in Serbia but were only en route from Serbia.

Similar to the first case, the *BGH* repeated that UN sanctions are only binding on the UN member states and not on individuals. Germany implemented the sanctions by issuing a *Rechtsverordnung* that was incorporated into the AWV. Paragraph 69h (1) AWV uses the term *'aus oder mit Ursprung'* FRY, i.e., 'from or originating from' the FRY. The court of first instance concluded that it did not matter where the products were produced but only that they were imported from Serbia. The *BGH* agreed with that conclusion but noted that the lower court could not base that conclusion only on the text of paragraph 69h (1) AWV.[248] Since the German legislature was limited in implementing the UN sanctions, the national measure could not go beyond the UN measure.[249] Thus, it was necessary to determine the scope of the UN sanction. Resolution 757 used the term 'originating in' which according to the *BGH* means both produced in as well as coming from a certain place.[250] The *BGH* based its final conclusion on the interpretation of that provision given by the Security Council itself in Resolution 838 (1993) in which the term 'originating in or exporting from FRY' is used. According to the *BGH* this is the only authentic interpretation of the provi-

---

schaftlichen Sanktionsmassnahmen erlassen worden ist und sich in diesem Rahmen hält. Hierzu hätte sie jedoch nach der von den EG-Organen veranlaßten Veröffentlichung im Amtsblatt der EG – zusätzlich – aufgrund einer autonomen, gerade im Hinblick auf § 34 IV AWG getroffenen Entscheidung des zuständigen deutschen Organs auch im Bundesgetzblatt oder im Bundesanzeiger veröffentlicht werden müssen.', NJW 1995, 2175.

[247] BGH judgment of 28.9.1995, NJW 1996, 602-605.

[248] 'Auf den Text des § 69 H I Nr. 1 AWV allein durfte die Strafkammer allerdings nicht abstellen.'

[249] 'Der deutsche Verordnungsgeber hatte sich nämlich auf die Durchfürhung der vom Sicherheitsrat der VN in der Resolution 757 (1992) beschlossenen wirtschaftlichen Sanktionsmassnahmen zu beschränken. Die Verbote der Verordnung durften somit nicht über die wirtschaftliche Sanktionen der VN hinausgehen.', NJW 1996, 602.

[250] '"Originating in" bedeutet nämlich auch "herstammen aus"; der Begriff erfasst somit nach seinem Sinngehalt auch die Bedeutung, dass auf das Gebiet verwiesen wird, aus dem die Ware herkommt.', NJW 1996, 603.

sion that is in conformity with the aim and purpose of the sanctions.[251] While the *BGH* did not turn to Regulation 1432/92 in its judgment, the *BGH* could have found support for its reasoning in the text of the Regulation which uses the terms 'originating in or coming from'. Hence, the *BGH* rejected the claim of the accused and applied a broad interpretation that covered both products that had been produced in the Republics of Serbia and Montenegro as well as products that were merely en route through those republics.

In summary, it can be concluded that Security Council Resolutions have no direct effect in Germany as they are first implemented by executive regulations. The implementation of Security Council Resolutions – whether communitarized or not – takes place on the same legal basis, so no distinction is made between them. The only difference is the heavier penalty for the violation of Security Council Resolutions. Also, as regards the cases discussed in this section, it appears that they were dealt with on the basis of the classic legal relationship 'Security Council Resolutions–national law'. The reason for that can be found in the fact that the EU is not member of the UN, while all EU Member States are and thus are also legally obliged to implement binding Security Council Resolutions. The involvement of the EU is solely based on the fact that the EC has obtained exclusive competence in external trade matters without being legally bound to implement Security Council Resolutions. Thus, from the point of view of the EU Member States, the implementation of Security Council Resolutions imposes a dual legal obligation: one vis-à-vis the UN and the other one vis-à-vis the EU. So, in this case, Community law leaves the classic legal relationship 'Security Council Resolutions–national law' intact and creates an additional one 'EC law–national law'. Thus, Germany is obliged to implement Security Council Resolutions by virtue of UN law and EC law.

6.3.2 The Netherlands

In 2000, the *Sanctiewet* of 1977[252] was substantially revised.[253] Under the revised *Sanctiewet*, Security Council Resolutions are implemented by *ministeriële regeling* adopted by the Foreign Minister (Article 2 section 2 *Sanctiewet*).[254] Thus, sanctions can be implemented by using one single instrument

[251] 'Nur diese vom Sicherheitsrat vorgenommene Auslegung entspricht dem Sinn und Zweck der Sanktionen.', NJW 1996, 603.

[252] Staatsblad of 15.2.1980, 93; see for details: Kuijper (1980); Coomans/Grünfeld/Hartogh/Jansen (1995) and more recently: Bulterman (1999).

[253] Wet van 13 april 2000 tot wijziging van de Sanctiewet 1977 en van de In- en uitvoerwet tot vereenvoudiging van de implementatie van internationale verplichtingen, Staatsblad of 13.4.2000, 196; see for a detaild analysis: Wijmenga (2002).

[254] Under the old Sanctiewet a three-step system in which three different instruments had to be used, i.e. (i) sanctieregeling (Article 7) with a maximum time limit of 10 months, (ii) sanctiebesluit (Article 8 (2))

that can also be used for the implementation of EC Regulations implementing Security Council Resolutions.[255] The applicable penalties are regulated by the *Wet op economische delicten* (Act concerning economic delicts) of 1950.[256] This Act distinguishes between crimes and offences (*misdrijven* and *overtredingen*). According to Article 2 (1) in conjunction with Article 1 (no.1), crimes are penalised with a maximum sentence of 6 years (Article 6 (1) no.1) or fines of the 5th category, while offences are penalised by a maximum of 2 years (Article (1) no.2) in prison or fines of the 4th category.

The Dutch case-law regarding Security Council sanctions mainly concerned the residual competence of the Member State regarding national implementation measures and the direct effect of Security Council Resolutions.

The first case concerned the prohibition of the Dutch port authorities to unload a Yugoslav-owned ship carrying a cargo of Colombian coal arriving in the port of Rotterdam.[257] The prohibition was based on Dutch measures implementing the embargo imposed by Security Council Resolutions against FRY, which were also implemented by EC Regulation 1432/92. In an interim injunction procedure, the owner of the ship appealed against the Dutch measure. The main argument of the owner was that Article 9 (1) of the *Sanctiewet* contained a relevant exception that should be applied in the present case. The court began its analysis by examining EC Regulation 1432/92, which does not contain a relevant exception. While the court accepted that Article 9 (1) of the *Sanctiewet* gave the Minister of Economics the possibility to grant exceptions, it concluded that the EC Regulation prevented Dutch authorities from using this possibility.[258] The owner of the ship challenged that decision before the President of the Rotterdam court.[259] The President began his analysis by emphasizing that the Netherlands is obliged to give full effect to Security Council Resolutions, in particular those based on Chapter VII.[260] The Security Council is competent to determine which

---

if the sanction is intended to have effect after 10 months with a maximum time limit of 3 years, (iii) a formal Act for a duration beyond 3 years, was applicable.

[255] See e.g.: Sanctieregeling terrorisme 2003, Staatscourant, 7.4.2003, nr. 68, 11; Sanctieregeling Irak 2003 II, Staatscourant, 21.7.2003, nr. 137, 10; see also: Bulterman (2002); Wijmenga (2002) at 49. It should be noted that the Raad van State criticized this new system in its advisory opinion. See: Advies Raad van State en Nader Rapport, TK, vergaderjaar 1998-1999, 26 2000 VI, B.

[256] Staatsblad of 22.6.1950, 258.

[257] Voorzitter College van Beroep voor het Bedrijfsleven, 11.9.1992, AB 1993, 317.

[258] 'Naar voorlopig oordeel stelt verweerder zich terecht op het standpunt dat de Vo. hem geen mogelijkheid biedt tot het verlenen van ontheffing, als door verzoekster gevraagd en dus evenmin voor een belangenafweging, als door verzoekster voorgestaan. Daaraan doet niet af dat de Sanctiewet de mogelijkheid tot verlenen van ontheffing wel kent.'

[259] President Rechtbank Rotterdam, 10.2.1993, AB 1993, 318.

[260] 'Wij stellen voorop, dat Nederland tot uitvoering van mandatoire resoluties van de Veiligheidsraad verplicht is op grond van het Handvest der Verenigde Naties, waarin - en in het bijzonder in hoofdstuk

measures should be taken for restoring peace.[261] Having said that, the President noted that the cargo was 'neutral' when it came from Colombia on the way to Rotterdam. The violation of the embargo lies simply in the fact that a Yugoslavian ship was chartered.[262] Accordingly, the President of the court concluded that the cargo of the ship is allowed to be unloaded. In other words, this case did not constitute a violation of the imposed sanctions. The President of court considered the case to fall outside the scope of the EC Regulation and thus was able to apply the exception.

The second case concerned the release of assets within a liquidation procedure of a company in the Netherlands established by an Iraqi national.[263] Security Council Resolution 778 imposed sanctions against Iraq and stated *inter alia* that 'no assets shall be released except to an escrow account' (an escrow account is a blocked account controlled by the UN). This Resolution was implemented by the adoption of a *sanctiebesluit* on the basis of the *Sanctiewet*. In contrast to the absolute wording of the Resolution, Article 1 of the *sanctiebesluit* as well as Article 9 of the *Sanctiewet* gave the responsible Minister the possibility to grant exceptions.

Nevertheless, in accordance with the Security Council Resolution, the assets of an Iraqi company in the Netherlands were frozen. The trustee in bankruptcy who was in charge of liquidating the company requested the release of the funds in order to pay open bills. The Ministers of Finance and Foreign Affairs rejected that request. The trustee in bankruptcy argued that he is unable to fulfil his task – imposed by Dutch law – without the release of the assets. The Dutch Ministers claimed that the relevant provision of Security Council Resolution 778 was absolute without allowing for any room for exceptions. The *College van Beroep voor het Bedrijfsleven* began its analysis by remarking that the relevant Security Council Resolution did not contain any provisions that are 'binding on anyone' and thus fell outside the scope of Articles 93, 94 Gw. Consequently, the Security Council Resolution did not form an obstacle to the utilization of the exception contained in Article 1 of the *sanctiebesluit*.[264] As the Dutch authorities implemented the sanctions by adopting the *sanctiebesluit* in conjunction with Article 9 *Sanctiewet*,

---

VII - bepalingen zijn opgenomen die een optreden van de organen van de Verenigde Naties mogelijk moeten maken ingeval van bedreiging van de vrede en daden van agressie.'

[261] 'Aan de Veiligheidsraad is de bevoegdheid gegeven in voorkomend geval aanbevelingen te doen en te beslissen welke maatregelen moeten worden genomen om de internationale vrede en veiligheid te handhaven of te herstellen. De ten processe bedoelde resoluties vallen daaronder.'

[262] 'De overtreding van het embargo ligt dus alleen in het feit dat voor het vervoer van de kolen een Joegoslavisch schip is gecharterd.'

[263] College van Beroep voor het Bedrijfsleven, 19.8.1999, AB 1999, 472.

[264] 'Het college overweegt te dien aanzien in de eerste plaats dat de bedoelde resoluties van de Veiligheidsraad geen bepalingen bevatten die een ieder kunnen verbinden en als zodanig in de weg staan aan de toepasselijkheid van de bij art. 1 van het sanctiebesluit voorziene ontheffingsmogelijkheid.'

they also incorporated the possibility to grant an exception.[265] Consequently, if one requests an exception based on the Dutch implementation measure, every such request must be examined by balancing the various interests and giving reasons for the rejection of such a request.[266] The court considered that simply referring to the Resolutions was not sufficient.[267] This is even more so since, in this case, a special situation existed, namely, that the request came from a Dutch liquidation officer concerning the liquidation of a company registered in the Netherlands.[268] The Dutch Ministers did not give any reasons that would form an obstacle to granting an exception under the condition that no payments are made in the direction of Iraq. Consequently, the rejection was not properly motivated (violating Art. 7:12 (1) *Awb*) and thus had to be revised.

In summary, it can be concluded that also in the Netherlands, Security Council Resolutions fall outside the scope of Articles 93, 94 Gw., thus they neither have direct effect nor do they enjoy primacy over conflicting national law. As in Germany, Security Council Resolutions are implemented in the Netherlands by executive regulations. Thus, while the classic legal relationship 'Security Council Resolutions–national law' remains intact, a new relationship 'EC law-national law' is created when Security Regulations are implemented. Hence, the Netherlands must implement Security Council Resolutions due to its legal obligations arising out of UN law and EC law.

6.3.3 France

Sanctions are implemented in the French legal order on the basis of two legal instruments.[269] First, Article 21 of the *Code des Douanes* enables the Council of Ministers to adopt *décrets* in order to restrict the import and export of goods in case of external tensions. Second, a *Décret-loi* of 1939 determines that trade in military goods, arms and munitions is regulated on the basis of prior authorisation and control by the state authorities.[270] For example,

[265] 'De wetgever heeft de in de resoluties neergelegde afspraken geïmplementeerd in de Nederlandse wetgeving door deze op te nemen in het sanctiebesluit. De in het sanctiebesluit in samenhang met art. 9 Sanctiewet 1977 opgenomen ontheffingsmogelijkheid maakt van deze implementatie deel uit.'

[266] 'Wordt daarop een beroep gedaan dan zal ten aanzien van ieder verzoek moeten worden aangegeven welke bijzondere belangen bij afweging tegen de door de aanvrager gestelde belangen nopen tot afwijzing daarvan.'

[267] 'De enkele verwijzing naar de resoluties, waarvan de ontheffingsmogelijkheid - als gezegd - mede de implementatie is, volstaat daartoe niet.'

[268] 'Een en ander klemt te meer nu in dit geval sprake is van een bijzondere situatie in die zin dat het verzoek is ingediend door de Nederlandse vereffenaar van een rechtspersoon naar Nederlands recht in liquidatie.'

[269] See for an overview: Dutheil de la Rochère (1992).

[270] Décret-loi du 18.4.1939 fixant le régime des matériels de guerre, armes et munitions, J.O., 13.6.1939.

Security Council Resolution 757 imposing sanctions against the FRY was implemented by *Décret* no 92-489 referring to Article 21 *Code des Douanes* as well as Articles 11-13 of the *Décret-loi* 1939. Both the *Code des Douanes* as well as the *Décret-loi* contain a complex system of penalties ranging from fines to several years of imprisonment.[271] More recent *décrets* giving effect to EC Regulations which implement Security Council Resolutions only refer to the Common Position and EC Regulation,[272] but sometimes also to the *Decret-loi* of 1939.[273]

The French case-law on Security Council Resolutions revolves around the question of whether or not individuals can challenge them before French courts. The following two cases illustrate in particular the difference between the *Conseil d'Etat* and the *Cour de Cassation* concerning their competence to review Security Council Resolutions.[274]

In the first case, the *Counseil d'Etat* had to deal with a decision of the *Ministre du budget* refusing the renewal of a temporary authorization to allow the export of military materials for two helicopters, combined with the request to 're-import' from Libya those helicopters.[275] The measures were adopted in order to implement Security Council Resolution 748 (1992) prohibiting the supply to Libya of any aircraft or aircraft components as well as any arms and related materials of all types. Société Heli-Union appealed against the decision at the *Tribunal Administratif de Paris* that rejected the appeal. An appeal against that ruling at the *Conseil d'Etat* was also turned down. The *Conseil d'Etat* concluded that the decision of the Minister could not be detached from the conduct of the international relations of France and thus was outside the jurisdiction of the courts (*actes de gouvernement*).[276] Accordingly, administrative courts are not competent to annul the decision of the Minister as an *ultra vires* act.[277] This case is an illustration of the separation of powers doctrine as understood by the

---

[271] Articles 408 ff. Codes de Douanes and Articles 25 ff. Decret-loi.

[272] See e.g.: Décret n° 2002-1019 du 24 juillet 2002, Décret abrogeant le décret n° 92-489 du 5 juin 1992 relatif à l'application au régime des matériels de guerre, armes, munitions et matériels assimilés de la résolution 757 du Conseil de sécurité des Nations unies concernant la République fédérale de Yougoslavie, available at: www.legifrance.gouv.fr.

[273] Décret n° 2002-1018 du 24 juillet 2002, Décret modifiant le décret n° 92-387 du 14 avril 1992 relatif à l'application de la résolution 748 du Conseil de sécurité des Nations unies, available at: www.legifrance.gouv.fr.

[274] Guillaume (1998) at 541-549.

[275] Conseil d'Etat, 12.3.1999 (Société Heli-Union), RGDIP 2000, 541-542.

[276] '[...] que dans les circonstances où elle a été prise, cette décision du ministre du budget n'est pas détachable de la conduite des relations internationales de la France et échappe, pas suit, à tout contrôle jurisdictionnel [...]', RGDIP 2000, 542; see also: Dutheil de la Rochère (1992) at 82.

[277] '[...] que la juridiction administrative n'est dès lors pas compétente pour connaître de la requête par laquelle la Société Heli-Union demande l'annulation pour excès de pouvoir de cette décision.', RGDIP 2000, 542.

Conseil d'Etat with the result that it considers the implementation of Security Council Resolutions as an *'acte de gouvernement'*, which courts are not allowed to review and thus cannot be challenged by individuals, let alone have possible direct effect.

In the second case, the *Cour de Cassation* had to determine whether Iraq had to pay its debts arising from unpaid bills for work done by Dumez GTM for the Iraqi Ministry of Defence.[278] The *Tribunal de grande instance de Nanterre* ruled in a judgment – which could not be appealed ('devenu irrevocable') – that Iraq had to pay for the work done by Dumez GTM. However, during the procedure of executing this judgment, Iraq refused to pay by claiming immunity as the funds would have to be channelled through the Iraqi Embassy in France. Moreover, Iraq claimed that the execution of the judgment would touch on the sanctions imposed by the Security Council. The *Cour de Cassation* rejected that argument by referring to paragraph 17 of Resolution 687 (1991) that required Iraq to 'adhere scrupulously to all of its obligations concerning servicing and repayment of its foreign debt'. Consequently, the immunity argument could not be invoked by Iraq for refusing to pay its debts.[279] Thus, the *Cour de Cassation* annulled the ruling of the Paris court. The question of direct effect of Security Council Resolutions was not at issue in this case.

The two cases clearly illustrate the divergent approach of the *Conseil d'Etat* and the *Cour de Cassation* (and the *Cour d'Appel de Paris*). While the *Conseil d'Etat* qualified the implementation of the Security Council as an *'acte de gouvernement'* and thus did not consider itself competent to review that measure, the *Cour de Cassation* and the *Cour d'Appel de Paris* apparently had no difficulties in considering themselves competent to adjudicate this case involving the consequences of Security Resolution 687.[280] It is especially remarkable since Security Council Resolution 687 was not implemented by a specific national measure and not even published. Thus, Poirat rightly concludes that this ruling:

> 'marque sans doute à cet égard une étape décisive puisque la Cour de Cassation admet l'invocabilité d'une décision du Conseil de Sécurité'.[281]

[278] Cour de Cassation, 15.7.1999, J.D.I. 2000, 45-55, with case-note of Cosnard (2000).

[279] 'Attendu qu'en statuant ainsi, sans réprondre aux conclusions invoquant les limitations apportées à la souveraineté de l'Etat Iraquien découlant des sanctions internationales et, notament, de la résolution 687 imposant à l'Iraq d'honorer scrupuleusement toutes ses obligations au titre du service et du remboursement de sa dette extérieure, de sorte que cet Etat ne pourrait plus opposer son immunité d'exécution la cour d'appel a violé le texte susvisé [...]', J.D.I. 2000, 47.

[280] See also: Cour de Cassation, 9.2.2000, no. 99-88054.

[281] Poirat (2000) at 553.

However, it remains to be seen whether the *Conseil d'Etat* will soon follow the case-law of the *Cour de Cassation* and create a convergence similar to the one that has recently been established regarding the status of international treaties within the French constitutional order.

In summary, it can be concluded that the legal status of Security Council Resolutions in the French legal order remains unclear due to the divergent approach of the French courts. If one follows the *Conseil d'Etat*, Security Council Resolutions would fall outside the scope of Article 55 CF, thus neither would have supremacy over conflicting domestic laws nor possible direct effect. If one follows the approach of the *Cour de Cassation*, Security Council Resolutions could be considered to fall within the scope of Article 55 CF, thus could enjoy supremacy over conflicting domestic laws and have direct effect if they fulfil the conditions. In practice, Security Council Resolutions are implemented by executive regulations. Also, in France, the implementation and application of Security Resolutions is dealt with on the basis of the classic legal situation 'Security Council Resolutions–national law'. However, the involvement of Community law adds another legal relationship 'EC law–national law' to the existing one, which creates a double legal obligation for France vis-à-vis the UN and the EC.

6.4 Summary

In summary, it can be concluded that the involvement of European law in the implementation of Security Council Resolutions leaves the existing legal relationship 'Security Council Resolutions–national law' intact, while adding at the same time a new legal relationship 'EC law (transformed Security Council Resolutions)–national law'. Consequently, the EU Member States are thus obliged to implement Security Council Resolutions by virtue of UN law as well as European law. Accordingly, this example shows that in this case rather than creating one new legal relationship 'Security Council Resolution–EC law–national law', two parallel legal relationships are established. This can be explained by the fact that while the EU is not member of the UN, the EU implements most Security Council Resolutions imposing sanctions on the basis of Articles 14, 15 EU Treaty (Common Position) in conjunction with Articles 301, 60 EC Treaty (Regulation). As a consequence thereof a new legal relationship 'Security Council Resolutions–European law' is created which in turn establishes a new legal relationship 'EC law (transformed Security Council Resolutions)–national law'. This 'communitarization' of Security Council Resolutions means that they enjoy primacy over all domestic law of the EU Member States, regardless of which legal rank and effect the respective constitutions of the EU Member States grant to Security Council Resolutions. Moreover, the implementation of Security Council Resolutions through EC Regulations also creates a jurisdiction for the ECJ to interpret those acts.[282] The ECJ case-law covering

[282] The EU Treaty excludes the jurisdiction of the ECJ regarding acts adopted within the framework of the CFSP.

the pre-Maastricht Treaty situation (with the exception of the recent *Aden* and *Sison* cases which are still pending) highlights two important aspects. First, the exclusive competence of the EC regarding common commercial policy cannot be undermined by Member States' measures adopted under their foreign policy competence. Second, the ECJ places particular importance on the effective implementation of the UN sanctions. As the *Ebony* case illustrates, the ECJ is prepared to interpret the Community law acts implementing Security Council Resolutions in a dynamic and teleological way so as to ensure their maximum effectiveness.

As regards the national level, it must be emphasized that despite the transformation of Security Council Resolutions by Community law, the Member States are still obliged to fulfil their legal obligations created by UN law. Accordingly, the classic legal relationship 'Security Council Resolutions–national law' still remains intact. Moreover, the research indicates that in all three selected EU Member States, executive regulations are adopted for the purpose of enforcing Security Council Resolutions and EC Regulations implementing Security Council Resolutions. Besides, in all three selected EU Member States, no direct effect or supremacy over domestic law is accepted for Security Council Resolutions. The examined case-law indicates that the EU measures implementing the Security Council Resolutions did not play the important role as could be expected. The reason is that in those cases the EU measures implementing the Security Council Resolutions could – for various reasons – be left outside when deciding the cases. This however does not mean that the 'EC law transformed' legal interaction does not take place, rather that it did not show up in the few existing cases that were discussed.

7 Decisions of the ICAO Council

7.1 International law level

The central forum for organizing the international aviation law is the ICAO, which was established in December 1944 by the Chicago Convention.[283] At the moment, practically all states (187) are members of the ICAO, including all EU Member States. The EU itself is not member of the ICAO. According to the preamble of the Chicago Convention, the purpose of the ICAO is to facilitate the development of international civil aviation in a safe and orderly manner and to help the establishment of international air transport services on the basis of equal opportunity, operating on a sound economic basis.[284] The ICAO has been set up with a number of organs, in particular, the Assembly

[283] UN Treaty Series, No. 102, 1948, 296 ff.; see for an overview: Diedericks-Verschoor (1993).

[284] See for detailed overviews: Buergenthal (1969); Erler (1967); Weber (1981).

and the Council plus several sub-commissions.[285] The ICAO Council, currently composed of 33 states,[286] is the central decision-making body of the ICAO. It has three different functions of legislative, judicial and administrative nature. The legislative (law-making) function, which is relevant for our purposes, includes the power of the Council to adopt various types of rules.[287]

On the basis of Article 37 (2), the ICAO can adopt two main different types of decisions, namely, international standards and recommended practices (abbreviated as SARPS, Standards And Recommended PracticeS) in the areas enumerated in Article 37.[288] According to Article 54 (l) Chicago Convention, the Council shall adopt international standards and recommended practices that are designated as 'Annexes' to the Convention. The Chicago Convention does not define the terms 'international standards' and 'recommended practices'. The ICAO distinguishes them in the following way:[289]

> **International standard**: Any specification for physical characteristics, configuration, matériel, performance, personnel or procedure, the uniform application of which is recognized as *necessary* for the safety or regularity of international air navigation and to which Contracting States will conform in accordance with the Convention; in the event of impossibility of compliance, notification is compulsory under Article 38.
>
> **Recommended practice**: Any specification for physical characteristics, configuration, matériel, performance, personnel or procedure, the uniform application of which is recognized as *desirable* in the interest of safety, regularity or efficiency of international air navigation, and to which Contracting States will endeavour to conform in accordance with the Convention.

The two instruments differ as to the extent of the legal obligations they impose on the Contracting States.[290] International standards oblige the Contracting

---

[285] Erler (1967) at 17-32; Buergenthal (1969) at 3-12.

[286] Algeria, Argentina, Australia, Brazil, Cameron, Canada, Chile, China, Costa Rica, Cuba, Czech Republic, Egypt, Ethiopia, France, Germany, India, Ireland, Italy, Japan, Lebanon, Mauritius, Mexico, Nigeria, Pakistan, Paraguay, Korea, Russian Federation, Saudi Arabia, Senegal, Singapore, South Africa, Spain, Sweden, UK, US, Venezuela. It should be noted that on its 28th session the Assembly of the ICAO adopted a new Article 50a that has been inserted into the Chicago Convention which increased the number of members of the Council to 36, see: Memorandum on ICAO, 15th ed., published by the ICAO, Montreal 1994, 13.

[287] See for details: Erler (1967) at 107-154; Buergenthal (1969) at 57-62.

[288] See: Abeyratne (1992) at 387-394.

[289] See e.g.: the definitions in Annex 14 (Aerodromes), Vol. II (Heliports) 1st. ed., July 1990; see also the slightly different earlier definitions of Assembly Res. A 15-8, Appendix E, ICAO Doc. 8528 (A15-P/6) (1965), as quoted by Buergenthal (1969) at 61 and of Erler (1967) at 116-117, who refers to an even earlier definition adopted by the ICAO.

[290] Erler (1967) at 116-122.

States to implement them, while the implementation of recommended practices is only seen as desirable and, therefore, Contracting States are only required to endeavour to implement them.

The difference in the legal obligations attached to the instruments is evidenced by Article 38 Chicago Convention, which requires Contracting States to notify 'immediately' the Council if they find it 'impractical' to comply fully with adopted international standards or if they need to keep domestic regulations in force that differ from the international standards. This obligation to notify legal differences between national legislation and international standards does not apply to recommended practices.[291] Thus, Article 38 Chicago Convention gives the Contracting States a margin of appreciation for determining whether or not it is possible for them to implement international standards.[292] Since this decision is fully within the discretion of the Contracting States themselves, Buergenthal concluded that 'the Contracting States have no legal obligation to implement or to comply with provisions of a duly promulgated Annex or amendment thereto, unless they find it practicable to do so'.[293] Erler goes only as far as describing the obligation to implement international standards as a *'gelockerter Rechtspflicht'* for the Contracting States.[294] I agree with Erler since the fact that the Contracting States have an opt-out possibility does not affect the legal obligation created from the moment the Annex has been formally adopted. However, it is true that in practice the procedure for the opt-out possibility makes it easy for the Contracting States to use it.

The adoption of ICAO Annexes and amendments thereto is regulated by Article 90 (a) Chicago Convention.[295] According to Article 90 (a) Chicago Convention, two thirds of the votes of the Council are required for the adoption of an Annex.[296] The coming into force of adopted Annexes and amendments thereto, raised questions by some Contracting States that were clarified by the

---

291 *Ibid.*, at 117; Buergenthal (1969) at 78.

292 See: Buergenthal (1969) at 76-80.

293 *Ibid.*, at 76.

294 Erler (1967) at 135-136.

295 So far 18 Annexes have been adopted: Annex 1 (Personnel Licensing); Annex 2 (Rules of the Air); Annex 3 (Meteorological service for international air navigation); Annex 4 (Aeronautical charts); Annex 5 (Units of measurement to be used in air ground operations); Annex 6 (Operation of Aircraft); Annex 7 (Aircraft nationality and registration marks); Annex 8 (Airworthiness of aircraft); Annex 9 (Facilitation); Annex 10 (Aeronautical telecommunications); Annex 11 (Air Traffic services); Annex 12 (Search and Rescue); Annex 13 (Aircraft accident and incident investigation); Annex 14 (Aerodromes); Annex 15 (Aeronautical information services); Annex 16 (Environmental protection); Annex 17 (Security); Annex 18 (The safe transport of dangerous goods by air).

296 However, it should be noted that the ICAO Council determined that this provision must be understood as 2/3 of the total membership of the Council, thus not depending on the numbers of members participating in such a meeting; see: Erler (1967) at 124-125.

ICAO.[297] Whereas Article 90 (a) Chicago Convention states that an adopted Annex 'shall become effective within 3 months', unless a majority of Contracting States in the mean time register their disapproval of the Annex, Article 90 (b) provides that the Council shall immediately notify all Contracting States of the coming into force of the Annex or amendment thereto. The ICAO Council clarified the legal meaning of the terms 'shall become effective' and 'coming into force' by adopting the 'Revised form of resolution of adoption of an Annex' of 1953.[298] The ICAO Council concluded that, since the ICAO does not have the power to decide for the Contracting States how an adopted Annex should enter into force in their domestic legal systems, the terms could only apply for the coming into force of the Annexes on the international level. Consequently, the Annexes contain three different dates that must be distinguished: (i) date of adoption, (ii) date of effectiveness (coming into force) and (iii) date of applicability.[299] The date of adoption is the date when the Council adopted the decision with the required two-thirds majority. The date of effectiveness is of importance since it marks the date until which Contracting States are allowed to express their disapproval of the decision. If a majority of the Contracting States did not disapprove of the decision, the decision comes into force on the international level. The date of applicability is the recommended date when the Contracting States would make the ICAO decision applicable in their domestic legal order.

In summary, it can be concluded that the ICAO Council is able to take legally binding decisions by a two-thirds majority (two thirds of 33, which in fact represents a very small minority of the 189 Contracting States). However, a Contracting State that is unwilling or unable to accept an Annex can avoid its implementation by notifying of the lack of acceptance.

7.2 European law level

Despite the fact that the EU is not member of the ICAO, it is involved in the implementation of ICAO decisions.[300] Until the ECJ judgment in case 167/73,[301] the EC was not considered to be competent in the area of air transport. Although this judgment did not deal with air transport but rather with sea transport, the judgment has had equal effect on air transport.[302] The ECJ clarified in this case, and confirmed this view in later cases,[303] that:

---

297 See: Buergenthal (1969) at 69-76.

298 *Ibid.*, at 74.

299 See: Erler (1967) at 128.

300 See for a detailed analysis: Balfour (1998) at 172-176; *ibid.*, (1995); Van der Esch (1988); Weber (1981).

301 Case 167/73 *Commission* v. *France* [1974] ECR 359; see for an analysis, Weber (1981) at 97-105.

302 Weber (1981) at 3 and 128-143.

303 See: Joined cases 209-213/84 *Ministère Public* v. *Lucas Asjes* [1986] ECR 1425; Case C-389/96 *Aher-Waggon GmbH* v. *Germany* [1998] ECR I-4473.

> '31. Far from excluding the application of the Treaty to these matters, it provides only that the special provisions of the Title relating to transport shall not automatically apply to them.
>
> 32. Whilst under Article 84 (2) [now Article 80 (2)], therefore, sea and air transport, so long as the Council has not decided otherwise, is excluded from the rules of Title IV [now Title V] of part two of the Treaty relating to the common transport policy, it remains, on the same basis as the other modes of transport, subject to the general rules of the Treaty.'

From that moment on, the Commission started to table an increasing number of proposals for legislation in the field of air transport law, resulting in the nearly complete liberalization of the internal air transport market by 1993.[304] However, the exact extent of the internal as well as external competence of the EC in the field of air transport still remains disputed between the Commission and the Member States.[305] The Commission has always argued for a broad and exclusive internal as well as external competence, but has been facing strong opposition by the Member States.[306]

In its ruling on the open skies agreements concluded between most EU Member States and the USA, the ECJ rejected the argument of an overall exclusive competence of the EC.[307] According to the ECJ, the EC is only exclusively competent in the areas that have been completely harmonized by Community legislation and, therefore, would be affected by the individual conduct of the Member States.[308] All other issues of air transport law remain within the competence of the EU Member States.[309] This also means that the EC is competent and obliged to implement those ICAO Annexes (as of their date of effectiveness) that fall within its exclusive competence. If the EC implements ICAO Annexes, they become an integral part of the EC legal order, thereby obtaining Community law features such as supremacy over all national law and possible direct effect.

As the following examples illustrate, the EC implements ICAO Annexes by adopting secondary Community law acts, which essentially copy the contents of the ICAO Annex. As regards the method of implementation, a distinction can be made between 'indirect' implementation of an ICAO Annex by reference in the preamble and 'direct' implementation by referring explicitly to the ICAO Annex in the provisions of the EC Directive/Regulation.

---

[304] See for an overview: Balfour (1995) at 13-30; Erdmenger (1997).

[305] See: Wassenbergh (2000); Balfour (1997); Weber (1981) at 249-262.

[306] Van der Esch (1988) at 47-50.

[307] See: Cases C-466/98, C-467/98, C-468/98, C-469/98, C-471/98, C-472/98, C-475/95, C-476/98 [2002] ECR I-9427; see for details: Sevinga (2003); Lavranos (2003); Middeldorp/van Ooik (2003).

[308] *Ibid.*

[309] *Ibid.*; see also: Bentzien (1998).

An example of an 'indirect' implementation can be found in the preamble of Council Directive 94/56,[310] which refers to Annex 13 as one of the reasons for the adoption of this Directive:

> 'Whereas account should be taken of the Convention on International Civil Aviation, signed in Chicago on 7 December 1994, which provides for implementation of the measures necessary to ensure the safe operation of aircraft; whereas particular account should be taken of Annex 13 to this Convention which lays down recommended international standards and practices for aircraft accident investigation;
>
> Whereas, according to the international standards in Annex 13, the investigation of accidents is to be carried out under the responsibility of the State where the accident occurs;'

An example of a 'direct' implementation of an ICAO Annex can be found in Council Directive 80/51,[311] which expressly refers in its provisions to Annex 16 of the ICAO and thus makes compliance compulsory for the Member States as a matter of Community law.

> **'Article 1**
>
> Each Member State shall ensure that any civil aircraft falling within one of the categories set out in Annex 16 to the Convention on international civil aviation, third edition (July 1978) and registered in its territory may not be used therein unless it has granted noise certification on the basis of satisfactory evidence that the aircraft complies with requirements which are at least equal to the applicable standards specified in Part II, Chapters 2, 3, 5 or 6 of Volume I of Annex 16/5.'

EC Directive 83/206,[312] which amends the above-mentioned Directive 80/51, was specifically issued in order to implement new standards adopted by Annex 16/5 of the ICAO. The text of Directive 83/206 explicitly refers to the changes made by the ICAO to Annex 16:

> 'Whereas changes made by the International Civil Aviation Organization to Annex 16 of the Convention on international civil aviation, which specifies aircraft noise emission standards, and other action in the international area on aircraft noise

---

[310] Council Directive 94/56/EC of 21.11.1994 establishing the fundamental principles governing the investigation of civil aviation accidents and incidents, OJ 1994 L 319/14-19; Regulation of 16.12.1991 on the harmonization of technical requirements and administrative procedures in the field of civil aviation, OJ 1991 L 373/4-8.

[311] Council Directive of 20.12.1979 on the limitation of noise emissions from subsonic aircraft, OJ 1980 L 018/26-28.

[312] Council Directive 83/206, OJ 1983 L 117/15-17.

have made it necessary to make certain amendments to Council Directive 80/51/EEC of 20 December 1979 on the limitation of noise emissions from subsonic aircraft (3).

Whereas it is necessary to clarify the intention of Articles 1 and 5 of Council Directive 80/51/EEC;

[...]

Article 1

Directive 80/51/EEC shall be amended as follows:

1. Article 1 shall be replaced by the following:

Article 1

Each Member State shall ensure that any civil subsonic jet or propeller-driven aeroplane registered in its territory and falling within one of the categories set out in Volume I (Aircraft Noise) of Annex 16 to the Convention on international civil aviation, as applicable from 26 November 1981, in accordance with Amendment 5, (hereinafter referred to as Annex 16/5) may not be used in the territory of Member States unless it has granted noise certification on the basis of satisfactory evidence that the aeroplane complies with requirements which are at least equal to the applicable standards specified in Part II, Chapters 2, 3, 5 or 6 of Volume I of Annex 16/5.'

Similarly, EC Directive 98/20[313] was adopted for implementing more stringent noise standards as agreed upon within the framework of the ICAO. More recently, the EC implemented the newest noise standards (Chapter 4 standard of Annex 16) adopted by the ICAO by issuing EC Directive 2002/30.[314]

Since the EC implements the ICAO Annexes that fall within its competence, the ECJ also acquires jurisdiction to review these ICAO Annexes and the implementing Community law acts. So far, it appears that the ECJ has only rarely dealt with cases involving ICAO law.[315] Despite the fact that in the *Omega Air*[316] and *Aher Waggon*[317] cases, the noise standards as contained in ICAO Annex 16 were at issue, the ECJ only dealt with the EC Directives implementing the ICAO noise standards, thus deciding the cases purely on the basis of Community law.

7.3 National law level

As the Chicago Convention does not prescribe how its decisions have to be implemented by the Contracting States, every Contracting State

[313] OJ 1998 L 107/4.

[314] OJ 2002 L 85/40.

[315] See e.g.: Joined cases C-27/00 and C-122/00 *Omega Air* [2002] ECR I-2569; Case C-346/97 *Braathens Sverige* [1999] ECR I-3419; Case C-389/96 *Aher-Waggon* [1998] ECR I-4473.

[316] Joined cases C-27/00 and C-122/00 *Omega Air* [2002] ECR I-2569.

[317] Case C-389/96 *Aher-Waggon* [1998] ECR I-4473.

can freely chose how to implement the ICAO decisions in accordance with its domestic law. Due to the fact that the domestic legal situation differs in the various Contracting States, a range of different ways of implementing ICAO Annexes can be found.[318] Accordingly, the following section will examine how ICAO Annexes are implemented and applied in the selected EU Member States, focusing in particular on the issues of legal status, supremacy and direct effect of ICAO Annexes in the domestic legal order.

7.3.1 Germany

In Germany, aviation issues are regulated by the Aviation Law Act (*Luftverkehrsgesetz,* LuftVG).[319]

Paragraph 32 (1) LuftVG[320] enables the Federal Minister of Transport to issue – with the consent of the *Bundesrat* – executive regulations (*Rechtsverordnungen*) for the purpose of implementing the LuftVG and the relevant EC Regulations (but not EC Directives). However, § 32 (3) LuftVG allows the Minister to issue executive regulations (*Rechtsverordnungen*) without the consent of the *Bundesrat* if they are adopted for the purpose of implementing international standards and recommended practices (SARPS) of the ICAO:

> § 32 (3) first sentence
> Rechtsverordnungen bedürfen nicht der Zustimmung des Bundesrates, wenn sie der Durchführung von Richtlinien und Empfehlungen der ICAO dienen [...]'.

So, the same legal basis can be used for the implementation of international standards (*Richtlinien*) and recommended practices (*Empfehlungen*) without making a distinction as to their legal nature. The LuftVG does not contain an explicit provision for the implementation of EC Directives implementing ICAO Annexes. However, paragraph 32 (4) LuftVG allows the Minister of Transport to adopt executive regulations without the consent of the *Bundesrat* for the purpose of defining the technical specifications of airplanes. In practice, the *Luftverkehrs-Ordnung* (Luft-VO)[321] is an executive regulation that was amended for the purpose of implementing EC Directives that implement ICAO Annexes. For instance, paragraph 11c of the Luft-VO implements the amendments of

---

[318] See for a few examples: Buergenthal (1969) at 102-107; Erler (1967) at 150-152.

[319] BGBl. I, 266, 2001, in the version of 27.3.1999 as amended; see for details: Schwenk (1995); Giemulla/ Schmid (2000).

[320] German text of § 32 (1) LuftVG
Das Bundesministerium für Verkehr erlässt mit Zustimmung des Bundesrates die zur Durchführung dieses Gesetzes und von Verordnungen des Rates oder der Kommission der EG notwendigen Rechtsverordnungen [...].

[321] BGBl. I, 580, 27.3.1999.

Annex 16 as required by EC Directive 98/20. Another example is § 28a (4) of the *Luftverkehrs-Zulassungs-Ordnung* (LuftVZO)[322] concerning the recognition of licenses of other EU Member States that refers to ICAO Annex 1 (Personnel Licensing):

> '(4) Erlaubnisse für Luftfahrzeugführer, die von einem Mitgliedstaat der Europäischen Gemeinschaft gemäß den Anforderungen des Anhangs 1 zu dem Abkommen von Chicago über die internationale Zivillufftfahrt erteilt wurden, werden anerkannt, wenn der Inhaber den in der Anlage 4 zur Luftverkehrs-Zulassungs-Ordnung aufgeführten besonderen Anforderungen genügt.'

Similarly, § 42 of the same LuftVZO refers in (2) no. 4 to ICAO Annex 14 (Aerodromes):

> '(1) Die Genehmigung des Flughafens ist für seine Anlegung und seinen Betrieb zu erteilen; sie kann mit Auflagen, insbesondere zur Einschränkung von Lärmauswirkungen auf die Umgebung des Flughafens, verbunden und befristet werden.
> (2) Die Genehmigungsurkunde muß enthalten
> [...]
> 4. die Angabe, zu welcher Klasse des Anhangs 14 des Abkommens über die Internationale Zivilluftfahrt der Flughafen, gegebenenfalls entsprechend seiner ersten Ausbaustufe, gehört,'

Thus, in practice, the *Rechtsverordnungen* that implement ICAO SARPS simply refer to them in their provisions.[323] The Minister of Transport can implement ICAO Annexes through the adoption of *Rechtsverordnungen*, regardless of whether or not they have been previously implemented by the EC.[324] This in turn means that ICAO Annexes enjoy the same legal rank as the implementing measure, that is, either at the level of a federal law or at the level of an executive regulation.

German courts have dealt several times with cases involving ICAO Annexes, in particular, concerning the proper application of German and ICAO noise standards.[325] One case concerned the question of whether the mandatory retirement of pilots at the age of 60 was justified. The Federal Labour Court (*Bundesarbeitsgericht*) decided that this it was indeed justified and, moreover, also required by ICAO Annex 1.[326] However, none of the cases found involved

[322] BGBl. I, 610, in the version of 27. 3.1999.

[323] Giemulla (2000) at § 32, Rn. 9.

[324] *Ibid.*, § 32, Rn. 8 ff.

[325] BVerwG, judgment of 5.10.1990, NVwZ-RR 1991, 118-129; BVerwG, judgment of 29.1.1991, NWvZ-RR 1991, 601-623.

[326] BAG, judgment of 12.2.1992, ZLW 1993, 199-208.

communitarized ICAO Annexes. Nevertheless, the following case is interesting as it illustrates how German courts deal with an ICAO Annex.

This case[327] arose before the *BVerwG* in which a measure by the Government of Bavaria prohibiting on the Nuremberg Airport flights during the night hours for certain aircrafts was challenged on appeal.[328] The measure uses a so-called 'bonus-list' enumerating certain types of quiet aircrafts that were excluded from the prohibition. A number of airlines complained that their aircrafts were not included in the 'bonus-list' despite the fact that they fulfilled the criteria of Chapter 3 of ICAO Annex 16 (at the time the most stringent international noise standard). Thus a differentiation between 'bonus-aircrafts' and 'Chapter 3 aircrafts' was established. The airlines questioned whether it was allowed to exclude aircrafts that met the ICAO Annex 16 Chapter 3 standard that Germany had accepted. The *BVerwG* rejected the argument of the airlines by stating that the fact that the aircrafts met the Chapter 3 standard did not grant a right to land in the night at any German airport. In addition, the airlines claimed that their legitimate expectations were violated because they could expect – as was the case in the past – that any modifications of the rules would affect all planes of the same category – i.e. all Chapter 3 aircrafts. However, the *BVerwG* did not consider this a valid argument. It merely noted that there existed no legal provision that would prevent airlines using noisy Chapter 3 aircrafts from being able to land at night, while other less noisy airplanes of the same category are allowed to do so. Thus, the *BVerwG* considered the noise standards as determined by the ICAO as minimum standards only that do not prevent Contracting States from imposing more stringent standards.

In summary, it can be concluded that the legal relationship between ICAO Annexes, EC law and national law is not very visible in the German legislation or in the jurisprudence.

7.3.2 The Netherlands

The Netherlands' legal system regulates the aviation issues in two statutes.[329] The general legal basis is the *Luchtvaartwet* (Aviation Law), which regulates all issues of aviation law with the exception of air traffic control.[330] The *Luchtverkeerswet* (Aviation Traffic Law) regulates all air traffic control.[331] The Ministry of Transport is responsible for the implementation of the aviation rules. For that purpose, either *'algemene maatregel van bestuur'*

[327] BVerwG, judgment of 12.6.1998, DVBl. 1998, 1184-1188; judgment of the lower instance, VGH München, 25.2.1998, ZLW 1999, 260-271.

[328] See for the legal background: Geisler (1997); Pieroth/Görisch (2000); Giemulla (2000).

[329] See for details: Scholens (2001).

[330] Staatsblad, 1999, 235.

[331] Staatsblad, 1997, 256.

(AMvB) or *'ministeriële regeling'* can be issued. The difference between the two instruments is that AMvB must be adopted by the entire government, while a *ministeriële regeling* can be issued by the responsible Minister alone.

The *Luchtvaartwet* does not explicitly refer to the implementation of ICAO decisions. However, a few provisions (e.g. Articles 2.8, 3.28, 4.1) provide for the possibility that the Minister can issue *ministeriële regeling* on the basis of international treaties or decisions of international organizations. For instance Article 2.8 states:

> 'Onze Minister van Verkeer en Waterstaat kan op grond van internationale overeenkomsten of besluiten van volkenrechtelijke organisaties bewijzen van bevoegdheid of bewijzen van gelijkstelling [...], zijn afgegeven door a.) de bevoegde autoriteit van een door hem bij ministeriële regeling aangewezen staat [...]'.

Similarly, Article 3.28 provides:

> 'Onze Minister van Verkeer en Waterstaat kan op grond van een internationale overeenkomst of een besluit van een volkenrechtelijke organisatie natuurlijke of rechtspersonen, die bedrijven voeren, welke op grond van eisen, welke gelijkwaardig zijn aan de krachtens artikel 3.25 gestelde eisen, [...]'.

An important AMvB adopted on the basis of Articles 5.5, 5.11, 5.12 *Luchtvaartwet* is the *Luchtverkeersreglement*.[332] The *Luchtverkeersreglement* regulates in detail all major rules applicable to air traffic on the ground and in the air. It also delegates powers to the Minister of Transport to determine the details on certain issues through *ministeriële regeling*. Whereas the *Luchtverkeersreglement* does not explicitly mention the implementation of ICAO Annexes, the explanatory section of the *ministeriële regeling* on *burgerluchtvaartinlichtingen*[333] (aeronautical information) states that the reason for adopting the executive regulation was to implement the obligations arising out of ICAO Annexes.[334]

---

[332] Besluit van 18.12.1992, houdende regelen ter bevordering van de veiligheid en de regelmaat van het luchtverkeer (Luchtverkeersreglement), Staatsblad 2000, 501, in the version of 1.12.2000.

[333] Regeling burgerluchtvaartinlichtingen, Staatscourant 1998, nr. 246, 12.

[334] 'Artikel 61 LVR geeft de minister de mogelijkheid om internationaal gemaakte afspraken met betrekking tot de luchtvaartinlichtingen uit te voeren door middel van een ministeriële regeling. De verplichtingen voor de lidstaten van ICAO zoals die zijn opgenomen in bijlagen 4 en 15 worden in deze regeling uitgevoerd. Voor de interpretatie van de genoemde Annexen wordt gebruik gemaakt van de onderliggende ICAO documenten zoals [...]'. Artikel 61 Luchtvaartreglement in the version of 1.12.2000. Staatsblad 2000, 501 reads as follows:

'Met betrekking tot luchtvaartinlichtingen stelt Onze Minister van Verkeer en Waterstaat regels betreffende: a) de gegevens welke zij dienen te bevatten; b) de wijze van verstrekking; c) de plaatsen waar en de perioden gedurende welke zij dienen te worden verstrekt; d) de instanties en personen waaraan zij dienen te worden verstrekt.'

Accordingly, several provisions of the *ministeriële regeling* on *burgerluchtvaart-inlichtingen* simply refer to the ICAO Annexes 4 and 15. For instance:

> **'Artikel 4**
> 1. Luchtvaartinlichtingen van blijvende aard die essentieel zijn voor de vluchtu-itvoering binnen het vluchtinformatiegebied Amsterdam, worden door de LVB-organisatie verstrekt middels de luchtvaartgids, overeenkomstig bijlagen 4 en 15. [...]
>
> **Artikel 5**
> Permanente aanpassingen van de luchtvaartgids worden verstrekt middels een amendement, overeenkomstig bijlagen 4 en 15.'

In summary, the implementation of ICAO Annexes takes place in the Netherlands on the basis of executive regulations. There is no explicit provision regarding the implementation of ICAO Annexes that have been previously implemented by the EC. Accordingly, communitarized as well as non-communitarized ICAO Annexes are implemented in the same way.

As regards the Dutch jurisprudence involving ICAO law, the central issue is whether an ICAO Annex falls within the scope of Articles 93, 94 Gw. and thus can be qualified as a decision of an IO that is binding on anyone. If that would indeed be the case, than an ICAO Annex would enjoy primacy over conflicting Dutch law and could have direct effect. In the practice of the Dutch courts, ICAO law has only been a few times at issue. Similar as in Germany, in one case the mandatory retirement of pilots at the age of 60 was also challenged.[335] However, the *Raad van State* confirmed that the age limit is justified and also referred to the fact that while discussions within the ICAO are currently taking place to increase the age limit, so far no decision to that effect has been adopted by the ICAO. However, none of the cases found involved communitarized ICAO Annexes.

The case that will be discussed below is nevertheless interesting as it concerned the question of whether or not Dutch authorities properly took into account ICAO requirements.[336]

The case decided by the court of Rotterdam is an example of the application of a provision of an ICAO Annex in relation to domestic laws and decisions.[337] The main issue of the case concerned the question of whether the granting of permission to cut trees in the vicinity of the airport was valid or not. The permission to cut the trees was granted because the trees formed an obstacle for planes that take-off or land at the Rotterdam Airport. The permission was

---

335 Raad van State (Afdeling Rechtspraak), judgment of 21.8.1993, AB 1994/15.

336 Raad van State (Afdeling bestuursrechtspraak), judgment of 11.9.2002, JB 2002/306.

337 Rechtbank Rotterdam, 27.6.2000, JB 2000/240.

issued in order to fulfil Article 4.2.23 of ICAO Annex 14 that requires that a certain amount of area around the landing tracks must be free of obstacles. The court of Rotterdam started its analysis by qualifying Article 4.2.23 of Annex 14 as a provision of a decision of an international organization, i.e., a decision of the ICAO Council.[338] Since the Netherlands did not indicate to the ICAO that it would be unable to implement Annex 14, it became binding on the Netherlands.[339] However, the court did not determine whether the provision of the ICAO Annex could be considered a decision of an IO that is binding on everyone within the meaning of Articles 93, 94 Gw., since the text of Annex 14 was published according to the rules laid down in the Act concerning the ratification and publication of treaties (*Rijkswet goedkeuring en bekendmaking verdragen*) only in June 1999, that is, after the decision to grant the permission was adopted.[340] Consequently, whether the decision was binding on everyone is irrelevant as it could not have direct effect anyway.[341] Nonetheless, the absence of direct effect of Annex 14 does not affect the fact that the Netherlands was still bound by it by virtue of public international law.[342] Accordingly, the court concluded that since there are no conflicting national provisions, all organs of the state must – within their discretionary competence – act in conformity with Annex 14.[343] The important point of this ruling is the fact that the court considered that all state organs

---

338 'De rechtbank stelt vast dat de in artikel 4.2.23 van Bijlage 14 bij het Verdrag vastgestelde internationale norm als bedoeld in artikel 37, tweede volzin, van het Verdrag moet worden aangemerkt als een bepaling van een besluit van een volkenrechtelijke organisatie, te weten de Raad.'

339 'Dat besluit - en daarmee die bepaling – is, nu het Koninkrijk der Nederlanden terzake niet een kennisgeving als bedoeld in artikel 38 van het Verdrag aan de Internationale Burgerluchtvaartorganisatie heeft gedaan, voor het Koninkrijk der Nederlanden bindend geworden.'

340 'De rechtbank laat in het midden of artikel 4.2.23 van Bijlage 14 bij het Verdrag op zichzelf zou kunnen worden aangemerkt als een eenieder verbindende bepaling van een besluit van een volkenrechtelijke organisatie in de zin van artikel 93 van de Grondwet. Aangezien - de actuele tekst van - die bepaling eerst op 26 juni 1999 op de in de Rijkswet goedkeuring en bekendmaking verdragen voorgeschreven wijze is bekendgemaakt, kon gelet op artikel 93 van de Grondwet ten tijde van het nemen van het bestreden besluit immers hoe dan ook geen sprake zijn van zogeheten rechtstreekse werking van artikel 4.2.23 van Bijlage 14 bij het Verdrag.'

341 *Ibid.*

342 'Het feit dat geen sprake is van rechtstreekse werking van artikel 4.2.23 van Bijlage 14 bij het Verdrag laat vervolgens echter onverlet dat het Koninkrijk der Nederlanden daaraan volkenrechtelijk is gebonden.'

343 'Nu voorts geen sprake is van met die bepaling strijdige nationale bepalingen, kan die bepaling doorwerken in de rechtsorde van het Koninkrijk der Nederlanden. Dat betekent dat de Nederlandse wetgevende en bestuursorganen, ongeacht of het gaat om organen van de Staat dan wel van andere overheden, gehouden zijn om binnen de grenzen van hun bevoegdheid artikel 4.2.23 van Bijlage 14 bij het Verdrag in acht te nemen.'

must act in accordance with ICAO law even if it was not yet binding on the Netherlands at the time the decision was taken on the domestic level – irrespective of whether the provision had direct effect or not. In sum, it can be noted that also in the Netherlands the legal interplay regarding the implementation and application of ICAO law is not very visible in the cases that were discussed.

7.3.3 France

In France, aviation issues are regulated in the *Code de l'Aviation civile*.[344] The code does not contain one general provision regarding the implementation of ICAO decisions, but rather specific provisions referring to international norms. For instance, Article 133-1-3 provides:

> 'Les entreprises détenant un certificat d'agrément, ou sollicitant un tel certificat, en application de l'article R. 133-1-1, font l'objet d'un contrôle de l'Etat portant sur l'application des dispositions fixées par les conventions internationales, les lois et les règlements en vigueur dans les domaines prévus aux articles R. 133-1, R. 133-1-1 et R. 133-2.'

The Minister of Transport implements ICAO decisions by issuing executive regulations in the form of *Arrêtés*. Accordingly, for instance, the *Arrêté* of 26.11.1981[345] implements the noise standards of ICAO Annex 16:

> 'Le ministre d'Etat, ministre des Transports,
> Vu la convention [Chicago Convention] [...];
> Vu l'annexe XVI à ladite convention;
> Vu le code d l'Aviation civile, notamment ses articles R. 133-1 à R.133-10; [...]'

Similarly, the *Arrêté* of 14.12.1993[346] implements the more stringent noise standards imposed by Chapter 3 of ICAO Annex 16. Moreover, an *Arrêté* has been used to implement EC Directive 83/206 through which the EC implemented amendments made to ICAO Annex 16.[347] Accordingly, the same executive measures are adopted for the implementation of ICAO Annexes, whether or not previously implemented by the EC.

---

344 Available at: www.legifrance.gouv.fr.

345 Arrêté du 26.11.1981 concernant les certificats de limitation de nuisances destines aux avions à hélices de masse maximale au décollage supérieure à 5700 kg, Revue Française de droit aérien 1982, 79-81.

346 Arrêté, 14.12.1993, Arrêté du 14.12.1993 relatif au retrait progressif d'exploitation des avions à réaction subsoniques non conformes aux normes du chapitre 3 de l'annexe 16, volume 1, deuxième édition (1988), de l'Organisation de l'aviation civile internationale, J.O., No. 296, 22.12.1993, 17853.

347 Arrêté, 16.11.1990 relatif à l'exploitation des avions à réaction subsoniques en vue limiter leur émissions sonores, J.O., 28.11.1990, 14636.

The central issue of ICAO Annexes in the French jurisprudence is the question of whether ICAO Annexes can be considered as binding decisions and, if so, whether they can be directly applicable or not. The *Conseil d'Etat* always rejected the possibility of invoking ICAO Annexes because it did not consider them to be binding decisions due to the opting-out procedure contained in Article 38 Chicago Convention.[348] The *Conseil d'Etat* stated that:

> 'Considérant, en dernier lieu, qu'il ressort de la Convention de Chicago en date du 7 décembre 1944 relative à l'aviation civile internationale, et notamment de ses articles 37 et 38 relatifs aux 'normes et practiques recommendées internationales', que les normes adoptées par l'organisation de l'aviation civile internationale, compte tenu de leur nature et notamment des possibilités de dérogations qu'elles comportent, constituent des recommendations s'adressant aux États et ne preuvent être invoquées utilement à l'appui d'un recours pour excès de pouvoir; [...]'.'[349]

In 1992, the *Conseil d'Etat* repeated this position[350] that was confirmed by a ruling of the *Cour Administrative d'appel de Paris* (CAA Paris).[351] More recently, the *Conseil d'Etat* reconfirmed this position again.[352] The *Conseil d'Etat* decided two similar cases in which the recognition of aviation licences of pilots from other EU nationals was at issue. In these cases,[353] EC Directive 91/670[354] requires that the recognition of licences obtained in other EU Member States should take due account of all relevant facts. Article 4 (5) of the Directive states that:

> '5. Notwithstanding the above, with respect to pilot's licences and notwithstanding paragraphs 1 to 4, a Member State shall accept any licence issued in accordance with the requirements of Annex 1 to the Chicago Convention on International Civil Aviation if the bearer satisfies the special validation requirements laid down in the Annex to this Directive.'

---

348 Conseil d'Etat, 20.11.1981 (Syndicat national des officiers mécaniciens de l'aviation civile), Lebon 1981, 428-429, '[...] qu'il ne comporte aucun caractère normatif; qu'en outre la circonstance que les dérogations instituées par l'arrêté attaqué à certaines normes édictées par l'organisations de l'aviation civile internationale n'auraient pas été notifiées à cette organisation, en méconnaissance de l'article 38 de cette convention, est, en tout état de cause, sans influence sur la légalité de l'arrêté attaqué; [...]'.

349 Conseil d'Etat, 7.10.1998 (Larquetoux), RFDAS 1999, 363.

350 Conseil d'Etat, 13.4.1992, Lebon 1992, 547.

351 CAA Paris, 10.2.1998 (Compagnie nationale Air France), ADJA 1998, 227-228.

352 Conseil d'Etat, 23.11.2001 (no. 19550).

353 Conseil d'Etat, 28.7.1998 (no. 96PA02797) and (96PPA00484).

354 OJ 1991 L 373/21.

Referring to that provision, the *Conseil d'Etat* concluded that the authorities failed to take into account all relevant facts, and that the lower court violated Community law and thus indirectly also ICAO Annex 1, although the *Counseil d'Etat* did not deal explicitly with ICAO Annex 1.

In contrast, the situation with regard to ICAO Annexes before the *Cour de Cassation* developed differently. In 1963, the *Cour de Cassation* accepted the interpretation of the *Cour d'appel de Dakar* that considered that the inspection of the luggage of a traveller who is travelling as a transit passenger on an international flight was incompatible with chapter 5-3 of Annex 9.[355] In a judgment in 1972, the *Cour de Cassation* explicitly stated that:

> '1. Si, au regard notamment des articles 5, 16, 23, 24, 35, 37, 38, et 90 de la Convention de Chicago, les normes et pràctiques recommandées, définies dans l'Annexe 9 de la dite Convention par l'organisation de l'aviation civile internationale sont directement et immédiatement applicables sur le territoire français;
> 2. Si, dans l'affirmative, les conditions de réciprocité édictées par l'article 55 de la Constitution se trouvaient réunies, en l'espace, tant en ce qui concerne les dispositions de la Convention elle-même que celles de l'Annexe 9;
> Attendu qu'il appartenait aux juges d'interroger le Ministre des Affaires Étrangères sur ces points précis avant de se prononcer sur le bien-fonde de la poursuit; [...]'[356]

Accordingly, and in contrast to the *Conseil d'Etat*, the *Cour de Cassation* accepted that SARPS adopted on the basis of Annex 9 were directly and immediately applicable in France, and that Annex 9 fell within the scope of Article 55 CF, which means that they could have direct effect. However, in this case the lower court failed – although at that time all French courts were required to obtain such an opinion before handing down a judgment which involves the interpretation of international treaties – to ask the Minister of Foreign Affairs to determine whether the condition of reciprocity mentioned in Article 55 was fulfilled or not. The Minister stated in both cases that: *'l'Annexe 9 à la Convention de Chicago n'est pas immédiatement applicable sur le territoire national'*.[357] This position was also then adopted by the *Cour de Cassation* in a ruling of 1973.[358]

Consequently, ICAO Annexes cannot be invoked by natural or legal persons before French courts, either because they are considered as not legally binding or, if that is the case, because they are not directly applicable. Finally, also in the French jurisprudence the involvement of the EC in the implementation of

355 Cour de Cassation, ch. crim., 8.11.1963, Bulletin crim. 1963, no. 315.

356 Cour de Cassation, ch. crim., 29.6.1972 (no. 71-91581), confirmed in: Cour de Cassation, ch. crim., 29.6.1972 (no. 71-91821).

357 Quoted in: RFDAS 1999, 365.

358 Cour de Cassation, 27.6.1973 (no. 73-90057).

ICAO Annexes that fall within its competence does not play any role. So, also in France, the transformation of ICAO Annexes through EC law is hardly visible in the implementation and application of ICAO Annexes.

7.4 Summary

As regards the international level, it should be noted that while the ICAO Council can adopt binding decisions, their binding legal effect is mitigated by the possibility for states of avoiding their implementation by simply notifying the ICAO Council. This point plays a crucial role for the French courts in rejecting their direct applicability.

As regards the European level, it appears that the EC has exclusive competence for certain aviation matters and thus – without being member of the ICAO – is competent to implement ICAO Annexes. In fact, in a number of cases the EC implements ICAO Annexes by either referring to them or copying them into EC legislation. In this way, these ICAO Annexes are transformed by EC law into Community law acts, thus attaching supremacy and possible direct effect to them. Moreover, the ECJ obtains jurisdiction to interpret these 'communitarized' ICAO Annexes despite the fact that the EC is not even a member of the ICAO.

As regards the national level, the communitarization of ICAO Annexes could not be substantiated by jurisprudence or domestic legislation. Nonetheless, this does not mean that the legal interaction between 'ICAO Annexes–European law–national law' does not exist. Rather, the reason must be found in the fragmentary character of ICAO law and its implementation that touches on very different European and domestic norms. The important point to keep in mind is that when the EC implements an ICAO Annex through a Community law act, the ICAO Annex is transformed into a Community law measure attached with EC law characteristics that it previously did not have. Thus, even though the EC is not a member of the ICAO, a transformation of ICAO Council decisions can take place if they fall within the competence of the EC.

8 Concluding remarks

The various examples of decisions of IOs discussed in the preceding sections illustrate that a transformation of these decisions by Community law takes place. As consequence thereof, the legal status and effect of the 'communitarized' decisions of IOs is modified by attached supremacy over all national law and possible direct effect to them. This transformation in turn affects their legal status and effect on the national law level. Whereas previously the constitutional system of each individual state determined what the domestic legal status and effect of decisions of IOs is, this determination is now superimposed by Community law. In this way, the legal status of 'communitarized' decisions of IOs is equalized in all EC Member States, thereby overcoming the existing constitutional differences.

However, a nuance to this general conclusion needs to be made because the effect of the transformation of decisions of IOs is not equally visible in all cases. Indeed, the case-studies show that the extent of the transformation of decisions of IOs depends on the extent of the competence of the EC. For instance, in the case of complete exclusive competence of the EC (fisheries), the transformation of the decisions of the regional fisheries organizations by Community law is complete so that no involvement of the domestic law of the Member States is possible. That is also the case regarding the implementation of Security Council Resolutions even though the EU is not a member of the UN and thus formally not required to implement Security Council Resolutions. In contrast, in the case of concurrent competence between the EC and its Member States, the impact of the transformation of decisions of IOs is much more visible on the national law level. This is particularly the case of Association Council Decisions, whereas it appears less visible with regard to COP/MOP decisions and ICAO Annexes. This can be explained by the fact that there have been more legal conflicts regarding Association Council Decisions than COP/MOP decisions and ICAO Annexes. This in turn is due to the fact that the direct effect of several provisions of Association Council Decisions has been accepted whereas this is not the case for COP/MOP decisions and ICAO Annexes. Consequently, conflicts between the legal orders do not manifest themselves in the jurisprudence of the courts.

Moreover, it should be noted that the fact whether or not the EC is member of an IO is an important factor for the way in which decisions of those IOs are transformed by EC law. If the EC is not member of an IO, the involvement of EC law results in the creation of another legal relationship 'EC law (transformed decision of IO)–national law' next to the already existing relationship 'law of IOs–national law'. Hence, in these cases, the obligations of the Member States vis-à-vis the IO remain intact on the basis of the classic legal relationship, while the involvement of the EC creates a second legal relationship for the Member States towards the EC. If the EC is member of the IO, the transformation takes place through the European law level, i.e. 'law of IOs–European law–national law'. Thus, when the impact of the transformation of decisions of IOs in the national legal order of the Member States is examined, it is necessary to take into account the fact whether or not the EC is member of an IO and what the extend of the competence of the EC in a given policy area is.

CHAPTER 4

Judicial and Quasi-judicial Binding Decisions

In this Chapter two cases in which the decisions are adopted by independent judicial and quasi-judicial organs will be assessed. The decisions discussed in this Chapter differ in terms of their nature and function compared with the previous Chapter. While the decisions discussed in Chapter 3 are more of an administrative, executive or legislative nature with a general scope of application, the WTO dispute settlement reports and the judgments of the European Court of Human Rights (ECrtHR) discussed below, are of a dispute settling nature resolving specific disputes between WTO Members and individuals against ECHR Members on a case-by-case basis. Moreover, the (quasi)judicial decisions are of an interpretative nature of existing obligations whereas the examples in Chapter 3 are more of a decision-making nature by creating new legal obligations for the members of the IOs. In addition, the WTO dispute settlement reports and the judgments of the ECrtHR are formally only binding on the parties involved in the specific dispute,[1] whereas the decisions discussed in the previous Chapter are binding on all members of the IO, except if opted out.

As regards WTO dispute settlement reports, reference must first be made to Article 3 (2) DSU which states inter alia that the dispute settlement system

> '[...] serves to preserve the rights and obligations of Members under the covered agreements, and to clarify the existing provisions of those agreements in accordance with customary rules of interpretation of public international law. Recommendations and rulings of the DSB cannot add to or diminish the rights and obligations provided in the covered agreements.'

Similarly, Article 19 (2) DSU states

> 'In accordance with paragraph 2 of Article 3, in their findings and recommendations, the panel and Appellate Body cannot add or diminish the rights and obligations provided in the covered agreements.'

Second, the Appellate Body (AB) noted in the *Japan – Taxes on Alcoholic Beverages*[2] case that

> '[...] Adopted panel reports are an important part of the GATT *aquis*. They are often considered by subsequent panels. They create legitimate expectations among WTO Members, and, therefore should be taken into account where they

[1] See: AB report *Japan – Taxes on Alcoholic Beverages* (WT/DS8/AB/R, WT/DS10/AB/R, WT/DS11/AB/R) of 8.11.1996; Art. 44 ECHR.

[2] See: AB report *Japan – Taxes on Alcoholic Beverages* (WT/DS8/AB/R, WT/DS10/AB/R, WT/DS11/AB/R) of 8.11.1996.

> are relevant to a dispute. However, they are not binding except with respect to resolving the particular dispute between the parties to the dispute.'[3]

Accordingly, two aspects should be noted in this context. First, WTO dispute settlement reports only clarify the existing provisions without creating new legal obligations for the WTO Members. Second, WTO dispute settlement reports are only binding on the parties involved in the dispute.[4] Thus, if the EC is involved as an applicant or respondent party in a dispute that falls within its exclusive competence for external trade matters (Art. 133 EC Treaty), the dispute settlement report is addressed to the EC only but is binding on the EC as well as on its Member States. Accordingly, an 'EC law transformed' legal situation 'WTO dispute settlement report–European law–national law' is created in which problems between the European and national level can arise when it comes to the implementation of WTO dispute settlement reports.

Regarding the judgments of the ECrtHR, it must be noted that Article 46 (1) ECHR states that:

> 'The High Contracting Parties undertake to abide by the final judgment of the Court in any case to which they are parties.'

This suggests that the judgments of the ECrtHR are only binding on the contracting parties involved in a certain case.[5] In other words, a judgment that finds Germany to have violated the ECHR in a specific case is formally not binding on the Netherlands or France or any other contracting party of the ECHR. This was also the generally accepted opinion in the legal literature as is reflected by Ress when he wrote in 1981:

> 'Die Entscheidungen des EGMR haben – grundsätzlich nicht anders als die Entscheidungen eines obersten nationalen Gerichts – über den Einzelfall hinausgehend bezüglich der gegebenen Auslegung nur Überzeugs- bzw. Orientierungswirkung. Die Rechtskraft im eigentlichen Sinne bleibt auf den entschiedenen Fall *inter partes* bschränkt.'[6]

More recently, however, Ress has adopted a more dynamic approach when he writes that:

---

3 *Ibid.*, at 9.

4 Van den Bossche (2004) at 66; McNelis (2003).

5 See: Ress (1983) in particular at 726 ff.

6 Ress (1983) at 731.

> 'Für Staaten, die nicht an dem Fall beteiligt sind (also für die dem Wortlaut nach die Rechtsfolge aus Art. 46 [ex 53] EMRK nicht einschlägig ist), haben die Urteile des Gerichtshofs Orientierungswirkung, da die darin vertretene Auslegung, auch wenn sie keine objektive oder erga ommnes-Wirkung hat, *dennoch Autorität bei der Auslegung der Konvention i.S. von Art, 1 EMRK entfaltet.*'[7]

Thus, Ress now accepts that ECrtHR judgments carry some authority by providing an orientation as to the interpretation of the ECHR provisions. Indeed, in order to ensure that the ECHR is properly applied in all contracting parties it is submitted that the relevant observations of the ECrtHR regarding a specific ECHR provision made in a judgment, i.e. the operative parts, are generally applicable to similar situations in all other contracting parties.[8] In fact, in many cases, contracting parties, who were not involved in a case, have modified their domestic legislation after the ECrtHR found that a certain measure is inconsistent with the ECHR.[9] Nevertheless, it must be accepted that formally speaking ECHR judgments are binding only *inter partes.*

Second it must be noted that the EC is not party to the European Convention of Human Rights (ECHR). Consequently, it is formally not bound by the judgments of the ECrtHR. Nevertheless, as has been discussed above, the ECJ and CFI regularly apply the ECHR and the case-law of the ECrtHR.[10] However, the European courts are free to decide whether or not they apply the ECHR and the case-law of the ECrtHR in a concrete case. If they do so, an 'EC law transformed' legal situation 'ECHR–European law–national law' is created, which might affect the existing classic legal situation between the ECHR and the EU Member States that are all parties to the ECHR.

Thus, despite the differences between the decisions discussed in the previous Chapter and those discussed below, their inclusion in this analysis is justified because an 'EC law transformed' legal situation, that is, the interaction between decisions adopted on the international law level, European law and national law, is created in certain cases. The main focus in this Chapter will be to examine whether and, if so, to what extent the involvement of European law creates an 'EC law transformed' legal situation, which can be detected in particular concerning the legal rank, supremacy and possible direct effect of WTO dispute settlement reports and judgments of the ECrtHR.

---

7 Ress (1996) at 350, emphasis added.

8 See: Bernhardt (2000) at 153-154; Lawson (1999a) at 92-93; *ibid.* (1999b) at 106-111.

9 See: Barkhuysen/Emmerik (1999) at 9.

10 See Chapter 2.

1 WTO dispute settlement reports

1.1 International law level

The WTO Agreement establishing the WTO encompasses several agreements, in particular, the GATT (for goods), the GATS (for services), the TRIPS (for intellectual property rights) and the SPS (for sanitary/phytosanitary matters).[11] Moreover, the WTO Agreement created a unique quasi-judicial dispute settlement system compared to other international organizations.[12] The dispute settlement system of the WTO is regulated in the Dispute Settlement Understanding (DSU), which essentially provides for a two-tier system of review allowing the Members of the WTO to bring their complaints against another Member of the WTO before a Panel of three experts, whose decisions can then be appealed at the Appellate Body.[13] The Appellate Body (AB) is a standing independent quasi-judicial organ that resolves a specific dispute by issuing a final report on the interpretation and application of the various treaties falling under the WTO Agreement.[14] However, it should be noted that the reports of the Appellate Body and Panels become binding only after they have been adopted by the Dispute Settlement Body (DSB) in which all WTO Members are represented. The unique feature of the WTO dispute settlement procedure as compared to the way in which other binding decisions within the WTO and within most other IOs are adopted is the special mode of adoption of Panel and AB reports in the DSB. A Panel or AB report becomes binding unless the DSB decides by consensus not to adopt the report (reversed consensus, Art. 16 (4) DSU for Panel reports, Art. 17 (14) DSU for Appellate Body reports). In other words, only if all Members, including the one who 'won' the case, would object to the adoption of the Panel/AB report would it not become binding. Since this is highly unlikely, Panel/AB reports can *de facto* be considered to be binding from the moment they are circulated to the members of the DSB, despite the fact that formally speaking they first have to be adopted by the DSB.[15] Moreover, since the AB has been established by the WTO Agreement as an independent organ endowed with the task of rendering quasi-judicial decisions, the AB fulfils the conditions of an organ of an IO as defined in the introduction of this research.[16]

---

[11] See for details: Van den Bosshe (2004).

[12] See: Van den Bossche (2004); Petersmann (1997b); Lavranos (2002d).

[13] See: Van den Bossche/Marceau (1998).

[14] See for a detailed analysis: Vermulst/Mavroidis/Waer (1999).

[15] The term 'WTO dispute settlement reports' is used to denominate Panel and AB reports that have been adopted by the DSB and thus have become formally binding on the WTO members involved in the dispute.

[16] See Chapter 1.

1.2 European law level

As the ECJ determined in its Opinion concerning the ratification of the WTO Agreement, the EC has only exclusive competence on the basis of Article 133 EC Treaty for trade in goods under GATT 1994 and trade in services when supplied cross-border (i.e. when neither the service provider nor the service receiver, but only the service itself, moves across the border) and also the provisions of the TRIPS Agreement concerning measures against counterfeit trade, while the Member States retain their competence for most of the parts of the GATS and TRIPS.[17]

However, in the meantime the Amsterdam and Nice Treaty revisions have modified the situation as follows.[18] The Amsterdam Treaty included a new paragraph 5 into Article 133 EC Treaty which allowed the use of the procedure of Article 133 EC Treaty for treaties covering intellectual property rights and services. Since the decision to that effect requires a unanimous vote by the Council and since the Member States did not consider such a move necessary, this possibility has not been used.[19] The Nice Treaty again modified Article 133 EC Treaty in a very complex manner. In short, the following points can be mentioned.[20] First, it should be noted that paragraph 5 first sentence of Article 133 EC Treaty now explicitly states that paragraph 1–4 of Article 133 EC Treaty also apply to the negotiation and conclusion of agreements in the fields of trade in services and the commercial aspects of intellectual property rights in so far as they are not covered by paragraph 6 of Article 133 EC Treaty. This means that regarding those agreements the Council acts with qualified majority voting (Article 133 (4) EC Treaty) instead of with unanimity. However, paragraph 6 of Article 133 EC Treaty takes agreements that cover trade in cultural, audiovisual, educational, social and human health services out of the exclusive competence of the EC by providing that they fall within the shared competence of the EC and its Member States. Consequently, those agreements must be concluded and ratified by both the EC and its Member States. Second, paragraph 5 second sentence of Article 133 EC Treaty modifies the requirement of qualified majority voting into a requirement of unanimity if an agreement covers an area for which unanimity is required for internal EC legislation or if areas are covered for which the EC has not yet adopted legislation. Moreover, paragraph 5 third sentence provides that the Council shall act unanimously in case of horizontal agreements, i.e. covering trade in goods and services, and also in case treaties touch on areas mentioned in paragraph 6 of Article 133 EC Treaty.

---

17 See: Opinion 1/94 *WTO* [1994] ECR I-5267.

18 Leal-Arcas (2003); Herrmann (2002).

19 *Ibid.*, at 6-8.

20 See for details: Herrmann (2002).

Thus, whereas the modification of Article 133 EC Treaty introduced by the Amsterdam Treaty seemed to start a process of making it easier to extend the scope of Article 133 EC Treaty in order to cover more subject-matters and thus extend the exclusive competence of the EC, the Nice Treaty in fact resulted in making it even more difficult than it was to apply Article 133 EC Treaty.[21]

The draft text on the European Constitution has slightly reduced the complexity of the provisions governing common commercial policy.[22] Whereas Article I-12 states that the Union shall have exclusive competence for common commercial policy, Article III-217 is the provision that substitutes Article 133 EC Treaty. It reads as follows:

Article III-217

1. The common commercial policy shall be based on uniform principles, particularly with regard to changes in tariff rates, the conclusion of tariff and trade agreements relating to trade in goods and services and the commercial aspects of intellectual property, foreign direct investment, the

achievement of uniformity in measures of liberalisation, export policy and measures to protect trade such as those to be taken in the event of dumping or subsidies. The common commercial policy shall be conducted in the context of the principles and objectives of the Union's external action.

[...]

4. For the negotiation and conclusion of agreements in the fields of trade in services involving the movement of persons and the commercial aspects of intellectual property, the Council of Ministers shall act unanimously where such agreements include provisions for which unanimity is required for the adoption of internal rules.

The Council shall also act unanimously for the negotiation and conclusion of agreements in the field of trade in cultural and audiovisual services, where these risk prejudicing the Union's cultural and linguistic diversity.

The negotiation and conclusion of international agreements in the field of transport shall be subject to the provisions of Section 7 of Chapter III of Title III and Article III-227.

5. The exercise of the competences conferred by this Article in the field of commercial policy shall not affect the delimitation of internal competences between the Union and the Member States, and shall not lead to harmonisation of legislative or regulatory provisions of Member States insofar as the Constitution excludes such harmonisation.

---

21 Leal-Arcas (2003) at 12-13.

22 CONV 850/03 of 18.7.2003.

The text of Article III-217 clarifies a number of issues. First, the exclusive competence of the EC will encompass treaties covering trade in services, the commercial aspects of intellectual property rights and foreign direct investment. Second, the requirement of unanimity will be prescribed only for cultural and audiovisual treaties as well as those that cover services and intellectual property rights for which unanimity is required for the adoption of internal Community legislation. Hence, treaties covering education, social and human health will not require unanimity anymore but can be concluded by qualified majority voting. Third, the use of the external competence by the Union may not lead to an extension of its internal competence as prescribed by the Constitution. Finally, Article III-227 specifies that qualified majority voting is the standard voting procedure unless unanimity is explicitly required. Thus, Article III-217 of the draft text of a European Constitution will extend the exclusive competence of the EC by explicitly including a broad range of subject-matters in the scope of the common commercial policy and will simplify the conclusion of such agreements by the Council by prescribing qualified majority voting as the standard voting procedure.

In any case, the WTO Agreement was ratified as a mixed agreement by the EC and its Member States, which means that within their respective competence, both the EC and its Member States are responsible for the proper implementation of all obligations arising out of the agreements annexed to the WTO Agreement. Moreover, as has been discussed above, the agreements annexed to the WTO Agreement are an integral part of the Community legal order, which means that they enjoy supremacy over conflicting secondary EC law as well as all national law of the Member States.[23]

The EC, being one of the biggest economies of the world, has been actively involved in the WTO dispute settlement system, both as a complaining and as a respondent party as well as an interested third party. So far, more than 20 WTO dispute settlement reports involving the EC have been circulated and adopted by the DSB, including the well-known disputes on bananas, hormones, steel, asbestos and sardines.[24] One of the notorious cases of the WTO dispute settlement system has been the case on bananas that was brought before the WTO by the US and a number of Latin-American states against the EC.[25] The banana dispute was sparked by the adoption of Regulation 404/93 by the EC.[26] Before the adoption of that Regulation, the banana market within the EC was fragmented. Every Member State applied its own banana regime with different tariffs, quotas and import licences. Regulation 404/93 aimed at creating a single

---

[23] See: Chapter 2; Opinion AG Alber in Case C-93/02 P *Biret* of 15.5.2003.

[24] All panel and AB reports are available at: http://www.wto.org/english/tratop_e/dispu_e/distab_e.htm.

[25] In fact the case was already instigated under the old GATT 1947 dispute settlement system, but the EC blocked the adoption of the panel report. See for an extensive analysis: Komuro (2000).

[26] OJ 1993 L 47/1.

European banana market. However, the Regulation distinguished between so-called dollar-bananas from Latin America and ACP-bananas from the ACP countries by introducing tariff quotas and a system of import licences. The result was that ACP-bananas became much more competitive while at the same time the traditionally very competitive dollar-bananas lost much of their competitive advantage. Another effect of the banana Regulation was that German banana importers who traditionally imported large amounts of dollar-bananas practically lost all of their business, while importers of ACP bananas profited from the new banana regime. This is the reason why the banana Regulation was fiercely opposed by Germany and German banana importers.[27]

The US and several Latin American states considered this banana regime to be incompatible with WTO law and thus started a WTO dispute settlement case against the EC. Indeed, several WTO dispute settlement reports have ruled that the banana regime and its revised version are incompatible with WTO law.[28] On the European level, the ECJ and CFI ruled in a series of cases that an individual as well as a Member State cannot invoke GATT/WTO law in order to challenge the lawfulness of a Community act.[29] Subsequently, the ECJ even stated that 'the WTO agreements are not in principle among the rules in the light of which the Court is to review the legality of measures adopted by the Community institutions.'[30] The only exception to that is the *Nakajima/Fediol* rule, i.e. if Community legislation explicitly refers to the agreements annexed to the WTO Agreement or if Community legislation intends to implement WTO law obligations. Accordingly, the European Courts have so far not ruled on the substance of whether the banana regime is compatible with GATT/WTO law. However, on the national level, several German courts expressed serious doubts about the consistency of the banana regime with GATT/WTO law as well as fundamental rights.[31]

Besides the banana dispute, the hormones dispute is another more recent example which involves similar issues. In this dispute the EC adopted legislation which prohibits the importation of hormone-treated meat.[32] The US challenged these measures by starting a WTO dispute settlement procedure against the EC. The Appellate Body ruled that the measures of the EC were inconsistent with the SPS agreement.[33] The report was adopted by the DSB and thus became bind-

---

27 See for details: Lavranos (1999); Everling (1996); Weber (1997a); Petersmann (1997a); Kuschel (1996).

28 See: WT/DS27/R; WT/DS27/AB/R; WT/DS27/ARB, all available at: http://www.wto.org/english/tratop_e/dispu_e/distab_e.htm.

29 See e.g.: Case C-280/93 *Germany* v. *Council* [1994] ECR I-4973; Case C-465/93 *Atlanta* [1995] ECR I-3761; Joined cases C-364/95 and 365/95 *T.Port* [1998] ECR I-1023; Case C-104/97 P *Atlanta* [1999] ECR I-6983. See also: Everling (1996); Cassia/Saulnier (1997b); Lavranos (1999); Mengozzi (2000).

30 Case C-149/96 *Portugal* v. *Council* [1999] ECR I-8395.

31 FG Hamburg, EuZW 1995, at 413-416; BFH, EuZW 1996, at 126-128.

32 OJ 1996 L125/3.

33 AB report *EC – Measures concerning meat and meat products (Hormones)* (WT/DS26/AB/R) of 16.1.1998.

ing on the EC.[34] Although, the implementation deadline has passed, the EC has so far not implemented the WTO dispute settlement report. Biret International which imported hormone-treated meat started a procedure before the Court of First Instance to obtain damages from the EC for failure to implement the WTO dispute settlement report.[35] However, both the CFI and in appeal also the ECJ[36] rejected the claim of Biret.[37]

In the light of these developments, the following three issues will be discussed. First, what is the legal status of WTO dispute settlement reports in the EC legal order? Second, are the European courts bound by WTO dispute settlement reports? Third, do WTO dispute settlement reports have direct effect, i.e. can they be invoked by individuals before a court?

1.2.1 The legal status of WTO dispute settlement reports in the EC legal order

As mentioned before, according to the case-law of the ECJ international treaties that have been concluded by the EC are integral part of the Community legal order and enjoy supremacy over conflicting secondary EC legislation and all national law of the Member States.[38] Moreover, as regards decisions of organs established by an international agreement, for instance Association Council Decisions, the ECJ stated:

> '[...] that, since they [Association Council Decisions] are *directly connected with the Agreement to which they give effect*, the decisions of the Council of Association, in the *same way as the Agreement itself*, form an integral part, as from their entry into force, of the Community legal system'.[39]

In the *Biret* case the CFI argued that:

> '67. There is an inescapable and direct link between the decision [AB report] and the plea alleging infringement of the SPS Agreement, and the decision could therefore only be taken into consideration if the Court had found that Agreement to have direct effect in the context of a plea alleging the invalidity of the directives in question (see, with regard to a decision of the DSB finding that certain provi-

---

[34] WT/DS26/13 of 19.2.1998.

[35] Case T-174/00 *Biret* [2002] ECR II-17.

[36] Case C-93/02 P *Biret*, judgment of 30.9.2003; see also case-note by: Pitschas (2003); Lavranos (2004).

[37] See below.

[38] See Chapter 2.

[39] Case C-192/89 *Sevince* v. *Staatssecretaris van Justitie* [1990] ECR I-3461, para. 9, emphasis added.

> sions of Community law were incompatible with GATT 1994, Case C-104/97 P *Atlanta* v *European Community* [1999] ECR I-6983, paragraphs 19 and 20).'[40]

While, in contrast, in the appeals case AG Alber argued that:

> '120. Aufgrund der vorstehenden Erwägungen ist davon auszugehen, dass die Artikel 3 und 5 des SPS-Übereinkommens, konkretisiert durch die DSB-Empfehlungen vom 13. Februar 1998, mangels Umsetzung dieser Empfehlungen innerhalb des bis 13. Mai 1999 reichenden angemessenen Zeitraums unmittelbar anwendbar sind. Dies hat zur Folge, dass sich Biret auf eine Regelung berufen kann, die ihrem Schutz dient. Somit besteht im Gegensatz zu den Ausführungen im angefochtenen Urteil eine qualifizierte Rechtsverletzung.'[41]

It should be noted that when the ECJ rendered its judgment in this case, it could avoid discussing this issue because of the factual circumstances of the case.[42] In any case, the CFI indicated that the WTO dispute settlement reports are inescapably and directly linked with the SPS agreement, while the Advocate General referred to the WTO dispute settlement report as a concretization of the SPS agreement. So, both the CFI and the Advocate General consider the WTO dispute settlement reports to be part of the agreements annexed to the WTO Agreement rather than separate decisions of an independent (quasi)judicial body of the WTO. This position is also reflected in Articles 3 (2) last sentence and 19 (2) DSU as well as in the *Japan – Taxes on Alcohol Beverages* ruling of the AB as discussed above.[43]

Nonetheless, it is also possible to qualify WTO dispute settlement reports as decisions of an organ established by a treaty.[44] As mentioned above, the Appellate Body has been established by the WTO Agreement as an independent quasi-judicial organ to resolve disputes concerning the proper application of WTO law. The reports of the AB and the Panels when adopted by the DSB become binding for the parties involved in the disputes. Accordingly, WTO dispute settlement reports are directly connected with the agreements to which they give effect. Thus, WTO dispute settlement reports fit into the definition quoted above of the ECJ concerning the legal status of Association Council Decisions in the Community legal order. However, Zonnekeyn[45] rejects this by arguing that:

---

40 Case T-174/00 *Biret* [2002] ECR II-17.

41 Opinion AG in C-93/02 P *Biret* of 15.5.2003, not yet available in English.

42 Case C-93/02 P *Biret*, judgment of 30.9.2003.

43 See at 131-132.

44 Lavranos (1999).

45 Zonnekeyn (2000a).

> 'It is questionable, however, whether panel or Appellate Body reports can be assimilated with decisions taken by the Association Council. Certainly, there are formal similarities but they do not have or intend to have identical legal effects. The panels and the Appellate Body are judicial entities, whereas the Association Council rather acts as a kind of executive, administrative body. Even the decisions taken by the Association Council as a "dispute settlement body" under the Association Agreement would, in my view, not have the same status and/or effect as panel or Appellate Body reports since the dispute settlement system established in the framework of the Association Agreement with (for example) Turkey, does not have the same judicial characteristics as the WTO dispute settlement mechanism. For example, the jurisdiction of the Association Council is not compulsory and there is no possibility for appeal.'[46]

Indeed, it must be admitted that there are differences between Association Council Decisions and WTO dispute settlement reports. First, it is true that the nature of the two organs is different, while the Association Council is more of a legislative and executive nature, the Appellate Body and the Panels are of quasi-judicial nature. Second, it is also true that Association Council Decisions create new legal obligations for the contracting parties, while WTO dispute settlement reports do not but merely interpret and clarify the already existing legal obligations of the WTO Agreement and its annexed agreements.[47] Third, one must also point out – which Zonnekeyn does not mention – to the difference concerning their binding nature. Whereas Association Council Decisions bind all parties, WTO dispute settlement reports are binding only to the parties involved in the dispute.[48]

All these objections are certainly true, but they do not affect the conclusion that WTO dispute settlement reports which are addressed to the EC are integral part of the Community legal order and enjoy supremacy over conflicting secondary EC law. More importantly, the case-law of the ECJ on the legal status of international agreements and decisions of organs of IOs in the Community legal order does not distinguish them because of their executive, legislative or (quasi)judicial nature. Neither does the ECJ make a distinction as to whether decisions of IOs can be appealed or whether they are binding only *inter partes* or *erga omnes*. In fact, the ECJ has explicitly accepted that it considers itself bound by decisions of a court established by an international agreement by the EC Member States.[49] Consequently, all international agreements and decisions of

---

46 *Ibid.*, at 98.

47 See above at 131-132.

48 *Ibid.*

49 Opinion 1/91 [1991] ECR I-6079: '39 Where, however, an international agreement provides for its own system of courts, including a court with jurisdiction to settle disputes between the Contracting Parties to the agreement, and, as a result, to interpret its provisions, *the decisions of that court will be binding on*

IOs which are integral part of the Community legal order enjoy the same legal status in the EC legal order. Accordingly, in my opinion, WTO dispute settlement reports can be qualified as decisions of an independent quasi-judicial organ established by the WTO Agreement rather than being an incorporated part of the WTO Agreement and its annexed agreement.

Either way, it must be concluded that WTO dispute settlement reports enjoy the same legal status in the Community legal order as the WTO Agreement and the agreements annexed to it. Thus, they enjoy supremacy over conflicting secondary Community law and all national law of the Member States.

1.2.2 The bindingness of WTO dispute settlement reports on European Courts

As discussed above, WTO dispute settlement reports become legally binding to the parties of the dispute when they are adopted by the DSB. Moreover, WTO Members are legally required to implement the WTO dispute settlement reports and cannot escape their implementation by using the temporary alternative measures provided for in Article 22 DSU.[50]

As regards the bindingness of international law on the EC, the ECJ has explicitly affirmed that Community law must – as far as possible – be interpreted in the light of an international agreement.[51] More importantly, the ECJ has clearly stated that it considers itself bound by decisions of judicial bodies established by international agreements, which are integral part of the Community legal order.[52] Consequently, since the WTO Agreement and the agreements annexed to it as well as the WTO dispute settlement reports are integral part of the Community legal order, the EC and thus the European Courts are bound by those WTO dispute settlement reports which have become binding on the EC. Accordingly, the ECJ and CFI were required to interpret the banana and hormones legislation of the EC in the light of the relevant WTO dispute settle-

---

the Community institutions, including the Court of Justice, inter alia where the Court of Justice is called upon to rule on the interpretation of the international agreement, in so far as that agreement is an integral part of the Community legal order.

40 An international agreement providing for such a system of courts is in principle compatible with Community law. The Community's competence in the field of international relations and its capacity to conclude international agreements necessarily entails the power to submit to the decisions of a court which is created by such an agreement as regards the interpretation and application of its provisions.' (emphasis added). See more recently: Opinion 1/00 [2002] ECR I-3493 and case-note by Castillo de la Torre (2002). See also: Cottier (1998) at 371.

50 See discussion above. See also: Opinion of AG in Case C-93/02 P *Biret* of 15.5.2003; Kearns/Charnovitz (2002); Rosas (2001); Mengozzi (1999).

51 Case C-61/94 *Commission* v. *Germany* [1996] ECR I-3989.

52 See: Opinion 1/91 [1991] ECR I-6079; Opinion 1/00 [2002] ECR I-3493.

ment reports, which essentially means that they were required to invalidate them as far they are inconsistent with WTO law.[53]

1.2.3 Direct effect of WTO dispute settlement reports

After having established the legal status of WTO dispute settlement reports within the Community legal order and their binding effect on the European courts, it is now necessary to examine their possible direct effect.

The issue was first raised in the *Atlanta*[54] case, however the ECJ avoided dealing with it by arguing that this point should have been raised in an earlier stage in the proceedings before the Court of First Instance (CFI).[55]

Soon afterwards, the CFI was faced with this issue in three identical cases concerning the grant of import quotas for bananas.[56] The CFI started its analyses by repeating again the consistent case-law of the ECJ and its own that the 'WTO Agreement and its annexes are not intended to confer rights on individuals which they could rely on in court'.[57] The CFI then turned to the argument of the appellant who claimed that the adoption of another banana Regulation administering the basic banana Regulation which was judged in the WTO dispute settlement report as being inconsistent with WTO law, results into a continuing infringement of WTO law, in particular, the obligation to rectify such infringements. Thus, the appellant claimed that the adoption of such a Regulation constitutes a misuse of powers. The CFI rejected this argument by stating that:

> '58 In that regard, it is only where the Community *intends to implement* a particular obligation assumed in the context of the WTO, *or* where the Community measure *refers expressly to the precise provisions* of the agreements contained in the annexes to the WTO Agreement, that it is for the Court of Justice and the Court of First Instance to review the legality of the Community measure in question in the light of the WTO rules (see *Portugal* v *Council*, paragraph 49).
>
> 59 Neither the reports of the WTO Panel of 22 May 1997 nor the report of the WTO Standing Appellate Body of 9 September 1997 which was adopted by the Dispute Settlement Body on 25 September 1997 included any special obligations which the Commission 'intended to implement', within the meaning of the case-law, in Regulation No 2362/98 (see with regard to the 1947 GATT, Case C-69/89 *Nakajima* v *Council* [1991] ECR I-2069, paragraph 31). The regulation does not

---

53 See: Royla (2001) at 511; Berrod (2000); Weber/Moos (1999); Lavranos (1999); Cottier (1998) at 369.

54 Case C-104/97 P *Atlanta* [1999] ECR I-6983.

55 *Ibid.*, para. 22; see also: Zonnekeyn (1999).

56 Case T-18/99 *Cordis* [2001] ECR II-913; Case T-30/99 *Bocchi Food Trade* [2001] ECR II-943; Case T-52/99 *T.Port* [2001] ECR II-981; see also case-note by: Zonnekeyn (2002b); Peers (2001).

57 See above at 35-40; Case T-18/99 *Cordis* [2001] ECR II-913, para. 46.

> make express reference either to any specific obligations arising out of the reports of WTO Bodies, or to specific provisions of the agreements contained in the annexes to the WTO Agreement.'[58]

Two conclusions can be drawn from these remarks. First, only when a Community act intends to implement WTO obligations or refers explicitly to a specific WTO provision are the CFI and ECJ willing to review the legality of such a Community act with WTO law. Second and more specifically regarding WTO dispute settlement reports, the CFI seems not to exclude the possibility of reviewing Community legislation that intends to implement or refers explicitly to any specific obligations arising out of WTO dispute settlement reports. Accordingly, the CFI applies the *Nakajima/Fediol*-conditions also to WTO dispute settlement reports and thus treats them in the same way as the WTO agreements.

As to the reasoning of the CFI, it is submitted that it is not convincing for at least two reasons. First, this reasoning of the CFI would enable the EC organs to prevent any review of legality of their acts that are somehow connected with the WTO agreements and/or WTO dispute settlement reports by simply avoiding any explicit reference to them or concealing the fact that they are intended to implement WTO obligations. This purely formalistic approach can hardly be considered to be in line with the Community law principle that ensures full review of Community law acts by granting a right to an effective remedy as one of the fundamental rights protected by the ECJ and CFI. In a recent case the CFI itself emphasized the importance of this right by stating:

> '121. In this connection, the Court of Justice has stated that *access to justice is one of the constitutive elements of a Community based on the rule of law* and is guaranteed in the legal order based on the EC Treaty in that the Treaty has established a *complete system of legal remedies and procedures* designed to permit the Court of Justice to *review the legality of measures adopted by the institutions* (Case 294/83 *Les Verts* v *Parliament* [1986] ECR 1339, paragraph 23). The Court of Justice uses the constitutional traditions common to the Member States and Articles 6 and 13 of the European Convention for the Protection of Human Rights and Fundamental Freedoms as a basis for the right to obtain an effective remedy before a competent court (Case 222/84 *Johnston* [1986] ECR 1651, paragraph 18).'[59]

It is obvious that the formalistic approach of the CFI makes the actual exercise of the right of an effective remedy against Community law measures, which are somehow connected with WTO obligations but which do not explicitly state that, dependent on the preferences of the legislative and executive organs of

---

[58] *Ibid.*, emphasis added.

[59] Case T-377/00 *Philip Morris International* v. *Commission* [2003] ECR II-1, emphasis added.

the EC. This can hardly be reconciled with the basic task of the ECJ and CFI as enshrined in Article 220 EC Treaty, namely, to ensure that the law is observed.[60]

Second, while it may formally be true that Regulation 2362/98, which was at issue in the three cases before the CFI, neither explicitly refers to WTO agreements nor intends to implement obligations arising out of the WTO dispute settlement reports, it is perfectly clear from the context in which Regulation 2362/98 was adopted that it continues to administer the – WTO law inconsistent – banana regime.[61] Thus, a more contextual and teleological approach must come to the conclusion that Regulation 2362/98 *de facto* continued the violations of WTO law caused by Regulation 404/93.[62] Therefore, while the formalistic approach of the CFI and ECJ prevents – currently – individuals from invoking WTO dispute settlement reports, the important point to remember is that the CFI apparently accepts WTO dispute settlement reports against the EC as decisions which are legally binding on the EC and thus can be used to review Community law legislation – albeit only if the *Nakajima/Fediol*-conditions are met.

In the *Biret*[63] case the CFI was again requested to deal with the issue of direct effect of WTO dispute settlement reports. The CFI repeated the long-standing case-law of the ECJ and its own, that WTO law does not form part of the rules by which the European Courts review the legality of Community legislation and that individuals cannot rely on them.[64] More specifically, regarding the invocability of WTO dispute settlement reports, the CFI argued – by referring to the *Atlanta* case – that this point could only be taken into account if the SPS agreement would have direct effect. As this is not the case, Biret could not invoke the WTO dispute settlement report.[65] Accordingly, also in the *Biret* case the CFI stuck to the case-law that WTO dispute settlement reports cannot be invoked by legal or natural persons and thus cannot be used to rely on them before a court. As a consequence thereof they also do not have direct effect.

However, in his opinion in the appeals case of *Biret*, AG Alber deviated from this general exclusion of invocability and direct effect of WTO dispute settlement reports.[66] He concluded that in a case in which the EC is legally required by a WTO dispute settlement report to change its legislation in order to bring it in line with WTO law, while the EC fails to do so after the implementation period has passed, WTO dispute settlement reports can be invoked by natural or legal persons and thus have direct effect for the purpose of starting a

---

60 Krück (1997).

61 See for details: Zonnekeyn (2002b) at 151.

62 Peers (2001) at 615.

63 Case T-174/00 *Biret* [2002] ECR II-17.

64 *Ibid.*, para. 61.

65 *Ibid.*, para. 67.

66 Opinion of AG in Case C-93/02 P *Biret* of 15.5.2003.

case against the EC for obtaining compensation for failure of the EC to act.[67] Whether this new approach of the AG is followed by the ECJ is not yet decided since the ECJ could avoid dealing with this issue in that case because of the factual circumstances.[68]

Nonetheless, it should be emphasized that the ECJ criticized the CFI for failing to address the issue of the legal status and effect of WTO dispute settlement reports by simply referring to the judgment in the *Atlanta*[69] case. In that case, the applicant Atlanta submitted before the ECJ that the WTO dispute settlement report in the banana dispute clearly established that the banana regulation is incompatible with WTO law and therefore the ECJ should squash the ruling of the CFI which dismissed Atlanta's action as inadmissible in so far as it sought the annulment of provisions of the banana regulation. In other words, Atlanta tried to directly invoke the WTO dispute settlement report in order to request the annulment of the banana regulation. In this context, it should be noted that the WTO dispute settlement report in the banana dispute was adopted some months after Atlanta had lodged its appeal at the ECJ. Nevertheless, the ECJ rejected the submission of Atlanta by arguing that Atlanta could have claimed already in the proceedings before the CFI the direct effect of WTO dispute settlement reports.[70] Hence, the ECJ did not determine in the *Atlanta* judgment the legal status and effect of WTO dispute settlement reports in the Community legal order. Consequently, rather than referring to the *Atlanta* judgment of the ECJ, the CFI should have examined this aspect properly in its *Biret* judgment.[71] Moreover, the ECJ explicitly left it open whether WTO dispute settlement reports could have direct effect for the purpose of starting a procedure to obtain damages from the EC, if the factual circumstance were different than in the *Biret* case.[72] Consequently, as the case-law currently stands, WTO dispute settlement reports cannot be invoked before a court and do not have direct effect.

Nonetheless, another argument for direct effect of WTO dispute settlement reports can be found if one compares the legal nature of Association Council Decisions and WTO dispute settlement reports. Whereas Association Council Decisions create new legal obligations for the contracting parties, WTO dispute settlement reports merely interpret and clarify the existing obligations arising out of the WTO Agreements and the agreements annexed to it. Thus, even though the legal impact of Association Council Decisions on the obligations

---

67 *Ibid.* Already a few years ago, Eeckhout (1997) at 54, argued in this context: 'In other words, direct effect should be given to WTO dispute settlement decisions establishing a breach by the Community of its commitments.'

68 Case C-93/02 P *Biret*, judgment of 30.9.2003.

69 Case C-104/97 P *Atlanta* [1999] ECR I-6983.

70 *Ibid.*, paras. 21-22.

71 Case C-93/02 P *Biret*, judgment of 30.9.2003, para. 59.

72 *Ibid.*, para. 64.

of contracting parties is much greater than in the case of WTO dispute settlement reports, the ECJ has had very little difficulties in accepting direct effect and invocability of several provisions of Association Council Decision 1/80 and 3/80.[73] So from that point of view, a direct effect of WTO dispute settlement reports should be easy to accept for the ECJ and CFI.

Indeed, in spite of the longstanding restrictive approach of the European Courts towards WTO dispute settlement reports, the EC legislature has in the meantime taken a more open stance by adopting Regulation 1515/2001.[74] This Regulation concerns the measures that may be taken by the EC following a WTO dispute settlement report that has been adopted by the DSB concerning anti-dumping and anti-subsidy matters. The instrument provides for the Council and the Commission to easily repeal or amend Community anti-dumping and anti-subsidy legislation that have been found to be inconsistent with WTO law. The importance of this instrument lies in the fact that for the first time the EC formally recognizes WTO dispute settlement reports as binding decisions of an organ established by the WTO Agreement – albeit only with regard to anti-dumping and anti-subsidy measures.[75] As a consequence thereof, the EC accepts that it has to bring its legislation in line with WTO dispute settlement reports which find EC law to be inconsistent with WTO law.[76]

In summary, it can be concluded that WTO dispute settlement reports that cover issues which fall within the competence of the EC become an integral part of the Community legal order. Thus, due to the 'EC law transformer' WTO dispute settlement reports enjoy supremacy over conflicting secondary Community law and national law of the EU Member States and have direct effect if they fulfil the conditions. However, in view of the present case-law of the ECJ and CFI, any invocability and direct effect of WTO dispute settlement reports is strictly limited to the cases in which a secondary Community law act intends to implement obligations arising out of WTO dispute settlement reports or explicitly refers to them (*Nakajima/Fediol*-conditions).

73 See for details Chapter 3 on Association Council Decisions.

74 OJ 2001 L 201/10.

75 See: Zonnekeyn (2002a).

76 See: Blanchard (2003).

1.3 National law level

1.3.1 Germany

1.3.1.1 The legal status and effect of WTO dispute settlement reports in the German legal order

The GATT 1947 as well as the WTO Agreement and its annexed agreements were transposed into the German legal order by a federal statute (*Zustimmungsgesetz*).[77] Consequently, the WTO Agreement enjoys the same legal rank as a federal statute and thus below the *Grundgesetz*. While the *Grundgesetz* does not mention decisions of IOs, it has been argued in Chapter 3 that the same principle applies to decisions of IOs, namely, that they enjoy the same legal status as the domestic implementing act, i.e. in any case below the *Grundgesetz*.[78] Accordingly, WTO dispute settlement reports enjoy the same legal rank in the German legal order as the implementing act, which can be a federal statute but also an executive regulations (*Rechtsverordnung*).

This classic legal situation is modified by the involvement of EC law and in particular the case-law of the ECJ and CFI. As mentioned above, the WTO Agreement and its agreements annexed to it are an integral part of the Community legal order and enjoy supremacy over conflicting secondary EC law as well as all domestic law of the EC Member States. The same applies to WTO dispute settlement reports. As a result of their communitarization, they enjoy the highest legal rank within the German legal order. At the same time, German courts are bound by the case-law of the European Courts concerning the lack of direct effect and impossibility of invoking WTO dispute settlement reports before a court.

1.3.1.2 The effects of the ECJ case-law on the legal status and effect of WTO dispute settlement reports in the German legal order

Nonetheless, German banana importers tried to challenge the validity of the Community legislation which introduced the banana regime. The following case illustrates that German finance courts had strong doubts about the validity of the banana Regulation. Since the case arose before the WTO Agreement entered into force, the German courts could only take into account the Panel report on the consistency of the EC banana regime issued within the framework of the GATT 1947, which however was not adopted and therefore

[77] Zustimmungsgesetz for the GATT 1947, BGBl. II, 1951, at 173; Zustimmungsgesetz for the WTO Agreement, BGBl. II, 1994, at 1438.

[78] See above Chapter 2 on Germany; see also: Geiger (2002) at 178-179.

not binding on the EC. Nevertheless, the arguments of the German courts are illuminating and equally applicable to WTO dispute settlement reports adopted under WTO rules.

The applicant was a German banana importing company that intended to import dollar-bananas from Ecuador without having an import license as was required by the banana Regulation. The applicant requested from the German customs' authorities that the cargo be imported without imposing the higher tariff introduced by the banana Regulation. The request was rejected by the customs authorities. In turn, the applicant instituted a *Verfassungsbeschwerde* (constitutional complaint) before the *BVerfG* claiming that the banana Regulation was inapplicable in Germany and that it violated fundamental rights. The *BVerfG* declared the application inadmissible because the applicant failed to exhaust all available remedies, namely, to start proceedings before the competent ordinary courts.[79] However, the *BVerfG* remarked that proceedings before the competent ordinary courts cannot be considered to be entirely without any chance, since the banana Regulation could indeed be considered to be inconsistent with GATT rules. Accordingly, the applicant started an interim procedure at the *Finanzgericht Hamburg* (Court of Finance), requesting that the bananas be imported without the licence. Furthermore, the applicant claimed again that the banana Regulation was inconsistent with GATT law and thus should be declared inapplicable.[80] The *Finanzgericht Hamburg* accepted the claim of the applicant. At the same time, the *Finanzgericht Hamburg* requested a preliminary ruling from the ECJ on the legality of the banana Regulation.[81]

The customs authorities appealed at the *Bundesfinanzhof* (BFH, Federal Court of Finance) against the decision of the *Finanzgericht Hamburg*. The *Bundesfinanzhof* confirmed the ruling of the *Finanzgericht* and was equally doubtful with regard to the GATT 1947 conformity of the banana regime.[82] In this context, it should be noted that the *BFH* issued its ruling before the ECJ answered the preliminary questions of the *Finanzgericht*. Therefore, the *BFH* could not take into account the opinion of the ECJ, but included some hypothetical reasoning in its ruling concerning the possible consequences of the answer of the ECJ.

The *BFH* started its analysis by stating that it had serious doubts as to the validity of the decision not to grant extra licences. The doubts were based on the consideration that the banana Regulation could violate international law with the result that the Regulation could be – temporarily – inapplicable.[83] More

79 BVerfG, Beschluss, 26.4.1995, EuZW 1995 at 412-413.

80 FG Hamburg, Beschluss, 19.5.1995, EuZW 1995 at 413-416.

81 *Ibid.*

82 BFH, Beschluss, 9.1.1996, EuZW 1996 at 126-128.

83 'Der Senat hält begründete Zweifel an der Rechtmäßig des angefochtenen Bescheides für gegeben. Diese bestehen in Hinblick auf die Frage, ob die der Abgabenregelung zugrundeliegende Zollrege-

specifically, the *BFH* wondered whether the banana regime was in conformity with the GATT rules.[84] First, the *BFH* referred to the Panel report of 18.1.1994 that was conducted under the GATT 1947.[85] Despite the fact that the Panel report was not legally binding,[86] at the very least, the Panel report seemed to imply that the EC banana regime could be inconsistent with the GATT 1947.[87] Based on this assumption, the court argued that since the GATT 1947 is – according to the consistent case-law of the ECJ – an integral part of EC law, the fact that the banana Regulation apparently violated GATT rules, raised the question of whether the banana Regulation was still applicable.[88] Second, if the ECJ were to conclude in its answer to the preliminary questions of the *Finanzgericht Hamburg* that the banana regulation was consistent with the GATT, the *BFH* was faced with the question of whether the banana Regulation would then constitute an *'ausbrechender Gemeinschaftsakt'* as developed by the *BVerfG* in its *Maastricht*-judgment.[89] The *BFH* concluded that if the ECJ indeed considered the banana Regulation in conformity with the GATT, then the banana Regulation would not be covered by the federal statute under which Germany consented to join the EC, and therefore would constitute an *'ausbrechender Gemeinschaftsakt'*.[90] Consequently, the banana Regulation would no longer be

lung der Bananenmarktordnung gegen etwa vorrangig zu beachtendes Völkerrecht verstößt, und die Folgerung, die sich aus einem derartigen – vorläufigen – Befund für die Anwendbarkeit der Gemeinschaftsregelung ergibt.' EuZW 1996 at 127.

84 'Hinreichende Zweifel bestehen zunächst wegen der Frage, ob die Bananenmarktordnung GATT-konform ist.' *Ibid.*

85 'Die Zweifel des Senats gründen sich auf den im Rahmen des Streitschlichtungsverfahrens nach Art. XXIII Abs. 2 GATT am 18.1.1994 vorgelegten Panel-Bericht, nach dem die folgende Regelungen GATT-widrig sind [...]'. *Ibid.*

86 'Dieser Bericht ist, weil die Gemeinschaft als de-facto GATT-Mitglied die Zustimmung verweigerte, nicht einstimmig angenommen worden und dadurch nicht formell Bestandteil des GATT-Rechts geworden.' *Ibid.*

87 'Gleichwohl behalten die im [panel] Bericht getroffenen Feststellungen für die rechtliche Bewertung ihre Bedeutung. Sie lassen die Annahme, daß die Bananenmarktordnung in den entsprechenden Teilen GATT-widrig ist, zumindest als nicht fernliegend erscheinen.' *Ibid.*

88 'Ein Verstoß der Bananenmarktordnung gegen Verpflichtungen aus dem GATT, das nach der Rechtsprechung des EuGH integrierender Teil der Gemeinschaftsrechtsordnung ist, könnte nach Auffassung des Senats die Anwendbarkeit der maßgebenden Vorschriften des Gemeinschaftsrechts unbeschadet ihrer vom EuGH festgestellten gemeinschafts- rechtlichen Gültigkeit in Frage stellen.' *Ibid.*

89 BVerfGE 89, 155.

90 'Wäre davon auszugehen, daß eine durch den Anwendungsvorrang des Völkerrechts – hier des GATT – bestimmte und durch ihn begrenzte Gemeinschaftsgesetzgebung im Vertrag umschrieben und sie nur in diesem Umfang durch das nationale Zustimmungsgesetz gedeckt ist, so könnte – in letzter Linie – unter Berücksichtigung der bereits angesprochenen Bedenken in der Bananenmarktordnung ein sog.

applicable in Germany. Accordingly, in view of these serious doubts, the *BFH* confirmed the ruling of the *Finanzgericht Hamburg*.

However, in its answer to the request for a preliminary ruling of the *Finanzgericht Hamburg*, the ECJ stated that:

> '63 Furthermore, Ecuador was not a contracting party to GATT 1947 and did not become a member of the WTO, and therefore a party to GATT 1994, until 1996.
>
> 64 It follows that neither GATT 1947, concluded before the entry into force of the Treaty, nor GATT 1994 can be effectively relied on, in circumstances such as those of the present cases, to preclude the application, under the first paragraph of Article 307 [ex 234] of the Treaty, of provisions of Regulations Nos 404/93 and 478/95.
>
> 65 The answer to the first question and the second part of the second question must therefore be that the first paragraph of Article 307 [ex 234] of the Treaty must be interpreted as not applying to cases involving imports of bananas from a third country which is not a party to an international agreement concluded by Member States before the entry into force of the Treaty.'[91]

This answer did not end the discussion in Germany regarding whether or not the banana Regulation could be considered an *'ausbrechender Gemeinschaftsakt'* and thus be inapplicable in Germany.[92] Consequently, within the framework of yet another proceeding, the *Verwaltungsgericht Frankfurt* (Administrative court) considered the EC banana Regulation to be an *'ausbrechender Germeinschaftsakt'* and referred this question to the *BVerfG* for a final decision.[93] After 4 years (!) the *BVerfG* decided on the request of the Frankfurt Administrative court by declaring it inadmissible.[94] Consequently, the *BVerfG* did not deal with the issue raised by the Frankfurt court, but rather specified for the first time the conditions for requests of German courts which consider a Community act or an ECJ judgment to be an *'ausbrechender Gemeinschaftsakt'*. According to the *BVerfG*, the lower court must substantiate in detail in its request that the absolute minimum level of protection of fundamental rights is generally not guaranteed anymore by the Community law measure.[95] Since the request was declared

---

ausbrechender Rechtsakt gesehen werden, an dessen Anwendung in der BRD die deutschen Staatsorgane, auch die Gerichte, aus verfassungsrechtlichen Gründen gehindert wären (vgl. insb. BVerfGE 89, 155 (188).' (emphasis added), EuZW 1996 at 128.

91 Joined cases C-364/95 and C-365/95 *T.Port* [1998] ECR I-1023.

92 See: Kuschel (1996).

93 VG Frankfurt, EuZW 1997 at 182-192.

94 BVerfGE 102, 147; see: Limbach (2000); Mayer (2000).

95 The BVerfG sums up the requirements as follows: 'Sonach sind auch nach der Entscheidung des Senats in BVerfGE 89, 155 [Maastricht-Entscheidung] Verfassungsbeschwerden und Vorlagen von Gerichten von vornherein unzulässig, wenn ihre Begründung nicht darlegt, dass die europäische

inadmissible, the *BVerfG* did not determine whether this was the case with the banana Regulation. Therefore, the banana Regulation remained in the opinion of the *BVerfG* also fully applicable in Germany.

Thus, it can be concluded that at the end of the day, the *BVerfG* accepted the exclusive and supreme jurisdiction of the ECJ regarding the authoritative interpretation and application of WTO law vis-à-vis Community law and the domestic law of the EC Member States. In other words, due to the creation of the 'EC law transformed' legal situation, the German courts were unable to give full effect to the binding WTO dispute settlement report by setting aside the banana Regulation. Furthermore, as the ECJ remarked in its preliminary ruling for the *Finanzgericht Hamburg*, Ecuador was not a contracting party to the GATT 1947 prior to the date when the dispute arose, so that Article 307 EC Treaty, which enables EC Member States to set aside EC law in order to fulfil their obligations arising out of treaties ratified prior to the EC Treaty, was not applicable in this case. This, of course, does not exclude the possibility that Article 307 EC Treaty would be applicable in a case involving a contracting party that was party to the GATT 1947 before a dispute arose. However, as Article II:2 of the WTO Agreement states, the agreements annexed to it (GATT 1994, GATS, TRIPS, SPS, DSU etc.) are an integral part of it.[96] Moreover, while the introductory text of the GATT 1994 stipulates that it consists of the GATT 1947 and other instruments, Article II:4 of the WTO Agreement explicitly states that the GATT 1994 is legally distinct from the GATT 1947.[97] Besides, it should be noted that the GATT 1947 was terminated in 1996.[98] Consequently, Article 307 EC Treaty is not applicable to the agreements annexed to the WTO Agreement.[99] Thus, the German courts had no possibility to deviate from the case-law of the ECJ concerning the banana Regulation.

The question, however, arises whether this result would have been different without the case-law of the ECJ. Since the banana Regulation enjoys supremacy over all national law, including constitutional law, the German courts would have been required by virtue of the supremacy of Community law to apply the

---

Rechtsentwicklung einschließlich der Rechtsprechung des Europäischen Gerichtshofs nach Ergehen der Solange II-Entscheidung (BVerfGE 73, 339 (378 bis 381)) unter den erforderlichen Grundrechtsstandard abgesunken sei. Deshalb muss die Begründung der Vorlage eines nationalen Gerichts oder einer Verfassungsbeschwerde, die eine Verletzung in Grundrechten des Grundgesetzes durch sekundäres Gemeinschaftsrecht geltend macht, im Einzelnen darlegen, dass der jeweils als unabdingbar gebotene Grundrechtsschutz generell nicht gewährleistet ist. Dies erfordert eine Gegenüberstellung des Grundrechtsschutzes auf nationaler und auf Gemeinschaftsebene in der Art und Weise, wie das Bundesverfassungsgericht sie in BVerfGE 73, 339 (378 bis 381) geleistet hat.' (emphasis added).

96 See further: Van den Bossche (2004) at 54.

97 *Ibid.*, at 55-56.

98 *Ibid.*

99 See: Peers (2001) at 609-610.

banana Regulation. The only possible exception to this under German law would have been the application of the *'ausbrechender Gemeinschaftsakt'*-concept of the *BVerfG*. However, the conditions that need to be fulfilled in order to consider a Community law measure to be an *'ausbrechender Gemeinschaftsakt'* are so high, that they are presumably not met by the banana Regulation. Thus, even without the 'GATT-obstructive' jurisprudence of the ECJ, German courts would only be able to disregard the banana Regulation and thus give effect to the WTO dispute settlement report if the ECJ would declare the banana Regulation to be invalid. That result is also in line with the case-law of the ECJ which allows only for the ECJ to declare a Community law act invalid.[100]

Finally, the question could also be raised whether German courts would be bound by the ECJ and CFI jurisprudence in a case a WTO dispute settlement report addressed only to Germany concerning an issue that falls exclusively within the competence of Germany. Some guidance to answer this question can be found in the *Dior/Assco*-judgment of the ECJ.[101] In the *Dior/Assco* case, which involved the interpretation of Article 50 (6) TRIPS, the ECJ stated *inter alia* that:

> '48 [...] in a field in respect of which the Community has not yet legislated and which consequently falls within the competence of the Member States, the protection of intellectual property rights, and measures adopted for that purpose by the judicial authorities, do not fall within the scope of Community law. Accordingly, Community law neither requires nor forbids that the legal order of a Member State should accord to individuals the right to rely directly on the rule laid down by Article 50(6) of TRIPS or that it should oblige the courts to apply that rule of their own motion.'

In other words, in a case of a mixed agreement or binding decision of IOs, the domestic courts of the Member States are able to determine in accordance with their respective national laws whether or not to grant direct effect to them when they concern an aspect falling exclusively within the competence of the Member States. Accordingly, in such a case, the domestic courts would not be bound by the consistent case-law of the ECJ that rejects any direct effect of WTO law unless the *Nakajima/Fediol*-conditions are met. Hence, if a binding WTO dispute settlement report would be addressed only to Germany covering an issue that falls within the exclusive competence of Germany, for instance the TRIPS, than German courts would be able to give effect to it without being bound by the case-law of the ECJ. In view of the principle of *'völkerrechtsfreundliche Auslegung'* as established by the *BVerfG*,[102] German courts would be

[100] Case 314/85 *Foto-Frost* [1987] ECR 4199; Case C-465/93 *Atlanta* [1995] ECR I-3761.

[101] Joined cases C-300/98 and C-392/98 *Dior/Assco* [2000] ECR I-11307.

[102] See Chapter 2 on Germany.

required to interpret and apply German statutes as much as possible in light of a WTO dispute settlement report addressed to Germany.

Moreover, in light of the principle of *'völkerrechtsfreundliche Auslegung'*[103], German courts could declare WTO dispute settlement reports directly applicable in Germany. In practice, though, that would not happen since the WTO dispute settlement reports would first – in accordance with German constitutional law – have to be transposed by domestic legal acts before they could exert any legal effect within the German legal order.[104] Consequently, German courts would apply the domestic implementation act rather than the WTO dispute settlement report itself.

In any case, after years of proceedings, a convergence of opinion has been reached by both the highest European and German court despite the fact that, on the international level, the AB unequivocally concluded that the banana Regulation and even its revised version are inconsistent with WTO law. However, one must not fail to see the real issue underlying the final ruling of the *BVerfG* in the banana saga, which essentially amounts to the acceptance of the exclusive and supreme competence of the ECJ to invalidate Community law acts. This ruling must be seen as a conciliatory move of the *BVerfG* towards the ECJ, which reduces the application of the *'ausbrechender Gemeinschaftsakt'*-concept developed in the *Maastricht*-judgment to a theoretical possibility.[105] Or as Grewe put it, the ruling of *BVerfG* must be even seen as a 'peace treaty' offered to the ECJ.[106]

Thus, it must be concluded that German courts – including the *BVerfG* – have accepted the ECJ jurisprudence on GATT/WTO law and WTO dispute settlement reports vis-à-vis the banana Regulation. Consequently, in the cases before them, the German courts could not deviate from the case-law of the ECJ, so that the EC legislation which has been judged to be inconsistent with WTO law had to be applied in Germany. In other words, the 'EC law transformed' legal situation created by the involvement of the EC, which in turn established a jurisdiction of the ECJ to interpret WTO law, prevented German courts from giving effect to a binding WTO dispute settlement report and thus making them unable to ensure that Germany fulfils its legal obligations under WTO law.[107] Hence, the ECJ was able, by virtue of the supremacy of Community law, to determine *in fine* for the EC and its Member States the outcome of the legal interaction between 'WTO law–EC law–German (constitutional) law'.

---

[103] *Ibid.*

[104] *Ibid.*

[105] Pernice (2001); Mayer (2000).

[106] Grewe (2001).

[107] See: Bronckers (2001).

1.3.2 The Netherlands

Although, there are no cases in the Netherlands similar to those in Germany in which a conflict between the three legal orders 'WTO law–EC law–national law' arose, it appears from three cases that were raised by Dutch courts before the ECJ,[108] that they also had some difficulties with the ECJ's case-law rejecting a direct effect of any provision of WTO law. More specifically, the following three questions will be examined. First, what is the legal status and effect of WTO dispute settlement reports within the Dutch legal order? Second, does the 'EC law transformed' legal situation created by the involvement of the ECJ affect the legal status and effect of WTO dispute settlement reports in the Dutch legal order? Third, since the WTO Agreement has been ratified as a mixed agreement, the question arises: would the situation differ if a WTO dispute settlement report would be addressed only to the Netherlands concerning an issue which falls exclusively within the competence of the Netherlands?

1.3.2.1 The legal status of WTO dispute settlement reports in the Dutch legal order

According to Articles 93, 94 Gw. binding decisions of IOs enjoy primacy over conflicting Dutch law – including constitutional law – if they are binding on anyone (*'ieder verbindend'*).[109]

In the first place, it must be examined as to whether or not adopted WTO dispute settlement reports can be qualified as binding decisions of an organ of an IO within the scope of Articles 93, 94 Gw. As discussed above, two views on this point are possible. Either WTO dispute settlement reports are considered to be incorporated into the WTO Agreement and its annexes and thus should be treated as a treaty or they are qualified as decisions of a quasi-judicial organ of an IO. The provisions of the DSU, the ruling in the *Japan – Taxes on Alcohol Beverages* as well as the opinion of the CFI and AG Alber[110] seem to follow the former view, whereas the present author considers the latter view also possible.

From the point of view of Dutch law, the *Hoge Raad* accepted – as regards human rights treaties – the existence of a binding decision of an IO within the meaning of Articles 93, 94 Gw. when the Netherlands has transferred a competence by an international agreement to an organ established for the purpose of adopting decisions that are binding on the Netherlands.[111] In analogy to that,

---

[108] Case C-53/96 *Hermès* v. *FHT* [1998] ECR I-3603; Joined cases C-300/98 and C-392/98 *Dior/Assco* [2000] ECR I-11307; Case C-89/99 *Schieving-Nijstad* [2001] ECR I-5851.

[109] See Chapter 2 on the Netherlands.

[110] See above.

[111] Hoge Raad, judgment of 23.11.1984, NJ 1985/604.

it could be argued that by ratifying the WTO Agreement, including the DSU, the Netherlands transferred the competence to the Panels/Appellate Body and the DSB to render binding decisions on the interpretation of the agreements annexed to the WTO Agreement. As a result, WTO dispute settlement reports can be qualified as binding decisions of an organ of an IO from the point of view of Articles 93, 94 Gw.

However, alternatively, WTO dispute settlement reports could also be considered to be part of the WTO Agreement and its annexed agreements. The advantage of this incorporation theory is that the requirement for publication in the official Dutch gazette could be overcome since the WTO Agreement[112] had been published while WTO dispute settlement reports are not published. Consequently, if one adopts this view, WTO dispute settlement reports would enjoy the same legal status as the WTO Agreement enjoys within the Dutch legal order.

Nonetheless, it is submitted that WTO dispute settlement reports must be distinguished from the WTO Agreement or the agreements annexed to it, because the Appellate Body is a distinct and independent organ that determines its findings independently from the WTO Members. Although, it is admitted that the reports of the Panels and AB need to be adopted by the DSB, which includes all WTO Members, before they become binding, they are *de facto* already binding from the moment they are issued since their adoption is practically automatic. In other words, while it is obvious that the Appellate Body interprets and clarifies the agreements annexed to the WTO Agreement and thus there is a link between them, it is equally clear that they are two different sources that must be distinguished. This conclusion is moreover amplified by the fact that both WTO Agreement and WTO dispute settlement reports are different also in terms of their legal nature. While the WTO Agreement and the agreements annexed to it are primary law instruments that need to be ratified by all WTO Members and are binding on all WTO Members, WTO dispute settlement reports are secondary law instruments issued by the Panel/AB and adopted by the DSB but become binding only on the parties to a dispute. Thus, in my view, the incorporation theory is difficult to apply to WTO dispute settlement reports. Consequently, in the view of the present author, WTO dispute settlement reports should rather be qualified as binding decisions of an organ of an IO within the meaning of Articles 93, 94 Gw.

Moreover, it must be determined whether or not WTO dispute settlement reports are 'binding on anyone', so that a natural or legal person can rely on them before a Dutch court.[113] This would be the case if the main conclusions of a WTO dispute settlement report are clear, precise and unconditional and thus do not require any further implementation by the Netherlands. In general, if a WTO dispute settlement report concludes in a case that a measure of a WTO

---

[112] Tractatenblad 1995, 130.

[113] See above Chapter 2 on the Netherlands.

Member is inconsistent with WTO law, it requires that Member to do everything that is necessary in order to bring its domestic law in line with the findings of the WTO dispute settlement report.[114] Consequently, by its very nature, a WTO dispute settlement report always requires some sort of implementing measure from the WTO Member who is found to have violated WTO law, while at the same time leaving it up to the WTO Member to determine which measures must be taken in order to fulfil the obligations of the WTO dispute settlement report. Hence, WTO dispute settlement reports are not sufficiently clear, precise and unconditional and, therefore, cannot be considered to be 'binding on anyone' within the scope of Articles 93, 94 Gw. Accordingly, they cannot be invoked by individuals before Dutch courts and as a consequence thereof do not enjoy supremacy over conflicting Dutch laws.

1.3.2.2 The effects of the ECJ case-law on the legal status and effect of WTO dispute settlement reports in the Dutch legal order

As discussed above, WTO dispute settlement reports are integral part of the Community legal order and enjoy the same legal status as the WTO agreements.[115] Accordingly, WTO dispute settlement reports enjoy supremacy over all national law of the EC Member States. Consequently, the integration of WTO law, including WTO dispute settlement reports, into the Community legal order upgrades the legal status of WTO dispute settlement reports within the Dutch legal order to the highest norm – irrespective of the fact whether they are qualified to be 'binding on anyone' or not. However, it should be noted that the ECJ applies more stringent criteria than the Dutch courts as regards the issue of direct effect. While both the ECJ and Dutch courts essentially use the same criteria of clear, precise and unconditional in order to determine whether or not a provision of an international agreement or decision of an IO can have direct effect, the ECJ requires – additionally – that the *Nakijima/Fediol*-conditions are fulfilled.[116] So, the involvement of the ECJ makes

---

[114] The standard phrase used in the conclusion of AB reports is as follows:
'257. The Appellate Body recommends that the Dispute Settlement Body request the European Communities to bring the measures found in this Report and in the Panel Reports, as modified by this Report, to be inconsistent with the GATT 1994 and the GATS into conformity with the obligations of the European Communities under those agreements.' AB report on bananas, 9.9.1997. Similarly, in the AB report on Sardines, 26.9.2002, the report concludes: '316. The Appellate Body recommends that the DSB request the European Communities to bring the EC Regulation, as found in this Report and in the Panel Report, as modified by this Report, to be inconsistent with Article 2.4 of the TBT Agreement, into conformity with its obligations under that Agreement.'

[115] See above at 53.

[116] See above at 35-40.

it more difficult to invoke WTO dispute settlement reports before a Dutch court than would be the case under Dutch constitutional law. Thus, the case-law of the ECJ affects the legal status and effect of WTO dispute settlement reports within the Dutch legal order in two ways. On the one hand, WTO dispute settlement reports are upgraded to the highest norm, despite the fact that they are not 'binding on anyone'. On the other hand, the ECJ case-law adds the *Nakijima/ Fediol*-conditions to the criteria that are otherwise used by Dutch courts to determine whether or not decisions of IOs can have direct effect.

1.3.2.3 Mixed agreement situation

Finally, it remains to be examined whether the legal situation differs if a WTO dispute settlement report relates to an issue that falls exclusively within the competence of the Netherlands. This issue has been raised by Dutch courts in three separate cases before the ECJ. Apparently the Dutch courts disagreed with the ECJ's and CFI's case-law, which rejects any direct effect of WTO law, and wanted to see whether they could grant direct effect to WTO law provisions on the basis of Articles 93, 94 Gw.

Since the ECJ stated in its *Opinion 1/94* that '[...] the harmonization achieved within the Community in certain areas covered by TRIPS is only partial and that in other areas, no harmonization has been envisaged'[117] and that 'the Community institutions have not hitherto exercised their powers in the field of "enforcement of intellectual property rights", except in Regulation No. 3842/86 [...]',[118] the Dutch courts wondered whether they could deviate from the case-law of the European Courts. The underlying argument of the Dutch courts was: if the TRIPS Agreement, more in particular Article 50 (6) TRIPS, did indeed (also) fall within the competence of the Member States, should not the national courts be free to decide whether or not that provision has direct effect – irrespective of the case-law of the ECJ and CFI? This issue was raised before the ECJ in the course of three different cases all originating from Dutch courts within the preliminary ruling procedure of Article 234 EC Treaty.

In the first case, the *Hermès*[119] case, it is interesting to note how the ECJ prepared the ground to justify its jurisdiction to a provision that falls also within the competence of the Member States. The ECJ claimed jurisdiction on the basis of the following considerations:

> '24 It should be pointed out, however, that the WTO Agreement was concluded by the Community and ratified by its Member States *without any allocation between them of their respective obligations* towards the other contracting parties.

[117] Opinion 1/94 *WTO* [1994] ECR I-5267, para. 103.

[118] *Ibid.*, para. 104.

[119] Case C-53/96 *Hermès v. FHT* [1998] ECR I-3603; see also case-note by: Jans (1999).

25 *Equally, without there being any need to determine the extent of the obligations assumed by the Community* in concluding the agreement, it should be noted that when the Final Act and the WTO Agreement were signed by the Community and its Member States on 15 April 1994, Regulation No 40/94 had been in force for one month.

[...]

28 It is true that the measures envisaged by Article 99 and the relevant procedural rules are those provided for by the domestic law of the Member State concerned for the purposes of the national trade mark. However, since the Community is a party to the TRIPS Agreement and since that agreement applies to the Community trade mark, the courts referred to in Article 99 of Regulation No 40/94, when called upon to apply national rules with a view to ordering provisional measures for the protection of rights arising under a Community trade mark, are required to do so, as far as possible, in the light of the wording and purpose of Article 50 of the TRIPS Agreement (see, by analogy, Case C-286/90 *Poulsen and Diva Navigation* [1992] ECR I-6019, paragraph 9, and Case C-61/94 *Commission* v *Germany* [1996] ECR I-3989, paragraph 52).

29 It follows that the Court has, in any event, jurisdiction to interpret Article 50 of the TRIPS Agreement.

[...]

32 Second, where *a provision can apply both to situations falling within the scope of national law and to situations falling within the scope of Community law*, it is clearly in the *Community interest* that, in order to forestall future differences of interpretation, *that provision should be interpreted uniformly*, whatever the circumstances in which it is to apply (see, to that effect, Case C-130/95 *Giloy* v *Hauptzollamt Frankfurt am Main-Ost* [1997] ECR I-4291, paragraph 28, and Case C-28/95 *Leur-Bloem* v *Inspecteur der Belastingdienst/Ondernemingen* [1997] ECR I-4161, paragraph 34). In the present case, as has been pointed out in paragraph 28 above, Article 50 of the TRIPS Agreement applies to Community trade marks as well as to national trade marks.

33 The Court therefore has jurisdiction to rule on the question submitted by the national court.'[120]

The most important point to note for our purposes is the argument of the ECJ that, since no explicit distribution of powers between the EC and its Member States appears to have been made when the WTO Agreement was ratified, there is accordingly no need for the ECJ to embark on a clear distinction of the competences with regard to Article 50 TRIPS. That is insofar interesting since, in its *Opinion 1/94*, the ECJ explicitly indicated that there is barely any Community legislation in this area, so that most parts of the TRIPS fall within the competence of the Member States. Nonetheless, the ECJ argues, since Article 50 TRIPS

[120] *Ibid.*, emphasis added.

applies both to the EC and its Member States, both the ECJ and the national courts have jurisdiction to apply the provision. However, the ECJ goes on to claim that, since only the ECJ can ensure that Article 50 TRIPS is uniformly interpreted and applied in all Member States, it must exercise its jurisdiction in the present case. Thus, without deciding the main issue of whether or not Article 50 TRIPS falls within the competence of the EC or its Member States, the ECJ seized jurisdiction to interpret that provision anyway for the sake of ensuring uniformity of interpretation in all Member States.

In the second case, the *Dior/Assco*[121] case, the ECJ was faced with the question of whether or not Article 50 (6) TRIPS had direct effect as the Dutch courts apparently believed. Before dealing with this question, the ECJ – by referring to the *Hermès*-judgment – repeated that it has jurisdiction to interpret Article 50 (6) TRIPS. In particular, the ECJ emphasized again that:

> '38 Only the Court of Justice acting in cooperation with the courts and tribunals of the Member States pursuant to Article 234 [ex 177] of the Treaty is in a position to ensure such uniform interpretation.
>
> 39 The jurisdiction of the Court of Justice to interpret Article 50 of TRIPS is thus not restricted solely to situations covered by trade-mark law.'

As to the issue of direct effect, the ECJ argued as follows:

> '42 It is settled case-law that a provision of an agreement entered into by the Community with non-member countries must be regarded as being directly applicable when, regard being had to the wording, purpose and nature of the agreement, it may be concluded that the provision contains a clear, precise and unconditional obligation which is not subject, in its implementation or effects, to the adoption of any subsequent measure (see, in that regard, Case 12/86 *Demirel* v *Stadt Schwäbisch Gmünd* [1987] ECR 3719, paragraph 14, and Case C-162/96 *Racke* v *Hauptzollamt Mainz* [1998] ECR I-3655, paragraph 31).
>
> 43 The Court has already held that, having regard to their nature and structure, the WTO Agreement and the annexes thereto are not in principle among the rules in the light of which the Court is to review measures of the Community institutions pursuant to the first paragraph of Article 173 of the EC Treaty (now, after amendment, the first paragraph of Article 230 EC) (see Case C-149/96 *Portugal* v *Council* [1999] ECR I-8395, paragraph 47).
>
> 44 For the *same reasons* as those set out by the Court in paragraphs 42 to 46 of the judgment in *Portugal* v *Council*, the provisions of TRIPS, an annex to the WTO Agreement, are not such as to create rights upon which individuals may rely directly before the courts by virtue of Community law.'

---

[121] C-300/98 and C-392/98 *Dior/Assco* [2000] ECR I-11307; see also case-note by: Vanhamme (2001).

However, the ECJ then added the crucial point that:

> '48 [...] in a field in respect of which the Community has not yet legislated and which consequently falls within the competence of the Member States, the protection of intellectual property rights, and measures adopted for that purpose by the judicial authorities, do not fall within the scope of Community law. Accordingly, Community law neither requires nor forbids that the legal order of a Member State should accord to individuals the right to rely directly on the rule laid down by Article 50(6) of TRIPS or that it should oblige the courts to apply that rule of their own motion'.[122]

Thus, in the absence of Community legislation, the courts of the Member States are not prevented by Community law from according direct effect to a provision of an international agreement or binding decision of an IO that falls within their competence – regardless of the existence of a deviating case-law of the ECJ or CFI.[123]

Finally, in the third case, the *Schieving-Nijstad*[124] case, the ECJ confirmed the main points of its *Dior/Assco*-judgment. Accordingly, the ECJ still rejected any direct effect of Article 50 (6) TRIPS, but at the same time acknowledged that Community law cannot prevent Member States' courts from granting direct effect to such a provision in the absence of Community legislation on that point.[125]

In summary, it can be concluded that the preliminary questions posed by the Dutch courts resulted in an important clarification of the extent of the jurisdiction of the ECJ and thus on the extent of the effect of Community law on WTO dispute settlement reports within the Dutch legal order. On the one hand, Community law imposes on Dutch courts the conditions of the case-law of the ECJ as far as a provision of the WTO agreements or WTO dispute settlement reports covers areas that fall within the competence of the EC. On the other hand, in case a WTO dispute settlement reports concerns an issue that falls within the exclusive competence of the Netherlands, Dutch courts are free to give direct effect to them if the respective conditions of Articles 93, 94 Gw. are met. However, as has been discussed above, this is presumably not the case with regard to WTO dispute settlement reports since they are not 'binding on anyone'.

---

[122] *Ibid.*

[123] See for details: Neframi (2001).

[124] Case C-89/99 *Schieving-Nijstad* [2001] ECR I-5851; see case-note by: Lavranos (2002c).

[125] See: Desmedt (2001).

1.3.3 France

As regards France, only one relevant case involving WTO law in the French legal order was found.[126] Accordingly, the following sections will examine in an abstract manner the same three central issues as discussed in the case of the Netherlands.

First, what is the legal status and effect of WTO dispute settlement reports within the French legal order? Second, does the 'EC law transformed' legal situation created by the involvement of the ECJ affect the legal status and effect of WTO dispute settlement reports in the French legal order? Third, since the WTO Agreement has been ratified as a mixed agreement, the question arises: would the situation differ if a WTO dispute settlement report would be addressed only to France concerning an issue which falls exclusively within the competence of France?

1.3.3.1 The legal status and effect of WTO dispute settlement reports within the French legal order

As has been discussed above,[127] Article 55 CF provides, in case of a conflict between international agreements and French laws, for the primacy of the former – if the conditions of Article 55 CF are met.[128] However, since Article 55 CF does not mention decisions of IOs, it depends on which view one adopts that determines whether decisions of IOs fall within or outside the scope of that provision.[129] If a narrow view is adopted, then decisions of IOs are excluded from the scope of that provision. Whereas if one adopts a broad interpretation of Article 55 CF, it can be argued that international agreements and decisions of IOs are so closely related that they are also covered by that provision. If one adopts the latter view, thus assuming that WTO dispute settlement reports fall within the scope of Article 55 CF, it must be further examined if the other conditions of Article 55 CF are met. First, Article 55 CF requires that the decision be published in an official gazette of France. Second, Article 55 CF requires reciprocity; that is, all other parties of the treaty must equally fulfil the obligations arising out of the decision of the IO. However, already the first condition is not met since WTO dispute settlement reports are not published in any French official gazette. Thus, even if it is assumed that WTO dispute settlement reports fall within the scope of Article 55 CF, they do not meet one of the

[126] Cour de Cassation, chambre crim., 3.5.2001, (no. 00-81691).

[127] See Chapter 2 on France.

[128] Art. 55. - Les traités ou accords régulièrement ratifiés ou approuvés ont, dès leur publication, une autorité supérieure à celle des lois, sous réserve, pour chaque accord ou traité, de son application par l'autre partie.

[129] See Chapter 3 for a similar discussion with regard to Security Council Resolutions.

essential conditions of Article 55 CF in order to obtain primacy over conflicting French laws. Consequently, the legal status of WTO dispute settlement reports is in any case below French laws.

1.3.3.2 The effect of the ECJ on the legal status and effect of WTO dispute settlement reports within the French legal order

As mentioned before, the fact that WTO law – including WTO dispute settlement reports – is an integral part of the Community legal order upgrades it to the highest norm in the EC Member States. This is also the case in France. Accordingly, by virtue of Community law, WTO dispute settlement reports enjoy the highest legal status within the French legal order. Thus, they enjoy supremacy over all conflicting French law, including constitutional law. Moreover, the case-law of the ECJ and CFI on the legal status and direct effect of WTO law and WTO dispute settlement reports within the Community legal order is also superimposed on French courts – with the exception of those matters that fall within the exclusive competence of France.[130] Hence, the influence of Community law on the legal status and effect of WTO law and, in particular WTO dispute settlement reports, is twofold. First, WTO dispute settlement reports obtain the highest legal status within the French hierarchy of norms, which was previously not the case. Second, WTO dispute settlement reports can be invoked by individuals only if they fulfil in particular the *Nakajima/Fediol*-conditions, whereas without the influence of EC law that was not possible at all under the French law. This conclusion is also supported by the only French case found to deal with the issue of direct effect of WTO law within the French legal order.[131] In that case, a French company was charged and found guilty for the importation of hormone-treated meat from the US thereby violating existing Community legislation. In appeal before the *Cour de Cassation*, the company, relying on the relevant provisions of the SPS agreement and the WTO dispute settlement report in the hormones case, argued that the sentence against the company violated Article 55 CF since the Community measures on the prohibition of hormone-treated meat were held to be inconsistent with WTO law.[132] Accordingly, a *'l'exception d'illégalité'* of Community law existed which should result in the non-application of the relevant EC legislation that was found to be inconsistent with WTO law. The *Cour de Cassation* rejected this line of argument by referring to the case-law of the European courts concerning the lack of direct effect of WTO law. Accordingly, the *Cour de Cassation* concluded that the company could not rely on WTO law and thus affirmed the sentence of the lower court.

---

[130] See discussion above on the Netherlands.

[131] Cour de Cassation, chambre crim., 3.5.2001, (no. 00-81691).

[132] See above.

1.3.3.3 Mixed agreement situation

As regards the mixed agreement situation, what has been said above concerning the Netherlands also applies to France. Hence, in a case in which a WTO dispute settlement report concerns an issue that falls within the exclusive competence of France, French courts would be free to decide on the basis of French (constitutional) law what legal status such a WTO dispute settlement report would have within the French legal order and whether or not it could be invoked by individuals before a court. As mentioned above, WTO dispute settlement reports do not meet the conditions of Article 55 CF and thus do not enjoy primacy over conflicting national laws and cannot be invoked by individuals.

Hence, the 'EC law transformed' legal situation created by the influence of Community law substantially affects the legal status and effect of WTO dispute settlement reports within the French legal order in two ways. First, WTO dispute settlement reports are upgraded to the highest norm within the French legal system, which was previously not the case. Second, if they meet the criteria of the ECJ, WTO dispute settlement reports can be invoked by individuals, while under French law that would not be possible. However, the classic legal situation 'WTO law–French law' remains intact when a WTO dispute settlement report concerns an issue that falls within the exclusive competence of France.

1.4 Summary

In summary, it can be concluded that the 'EC law transformed' legal situation created by the involvement of the EC, in particular the ECJ and CFI, as regards WTO law and WTO dispute settlement reports strongly affects the legal status and effect of them in the European and national legal order of the selected EU Member States.

Regarding the European legal order, the case-law of the ECJ and CFI illustrate that the same principles apply for the WTO agreements and the WTO dispute settlement reports. Thus, WTO law is integral part of the Community legal order and enjoys supremacy over conflicting EC law and all national law of the EC Member States. Moreover, WTO law, including WTO dispute settlement reports, which are integral part of the Community legal order are binding on the EC and the European Courts. As a consequence thereof and in line with its own case-law on the consistency of EC law with international law,[133] in the banana and hormones disputes, the ECJ would have had to either interpret the relevant EC legislation in conformity with the WTO dispute settlement reports or declare the Community legislation invalid.

---

[133] Case C-61/94 *Commission* v. *Germany* [1996] ECR I-3989; see also: Heukels (1997); *ibid.* (1999).

Instead, the ECJ and CFI still do not allow Member States or individuals to invoke provisions of WTO agreements or WTO dispute settlement reports before a court, unless they fulfil the *Nakijima/Fediol*-conditions. Moreover, by not declaring the WTO law-inconsistent EC law acts void the European courts force both the EC as well as its Member States to violate their legal obligations under the WTO. As consequence thereof, the US has been allowed by the DSB to suspend tariff concessions worth $191.4 million US dollars a year,[134] while Ecuador has been allowed to suspend tariff concessions worth $201.6 million US dollars a year for failure of the EC to implement the WTO dispute settlement reports on bananas.[135] Similarly, as regards the hormones dispute, the US has been allowed by the DSB to suspend concessions worth $116.8 million US dollars a year for failure of the EC to implement the WTO dispute settlement report on hormone-treated meat.[136] Moreover, this illustrates that at the end of the day, it was the ECJ that prevailed over the German courts with regard to the interpretation of the WTO consistency of the banana Regulation.

Regarding the national legal orders, it has been shown that in all three selected EU Member States the case-law of the ECJ and CFI on the legal status and effect of WTO dispute settlement reports within the Community legal order is replacing the respective pre-existing classic legal situation in the selected EU Member States. Hence, the 'EC law transformed' WTO dispute settlement reports become – by virtue of Community law – the highest legal norm in the domestic legal orders of the EU Member States. In addition, 'EC law transformed' WTO dispute settlement reports can be invoked before a court only if they meet the *Nakajima/Fediol*-conditions. The only exceptions to that are the policy areas which fall within the exclusively competence of the Member States. In those circumstances, Member States and their courts are able to determine in accordance with their respective law the legal status and effect of WTO dispute settlement reports in their domestic legal order. Indeed, one could say that in these cases the 'EC law transformed' legal situation does not play a role: that is, the classic legal situation 'WTO law–national law' remains intact.

2 ECHR judgments

From the outset it must be emphasized that despite the fact that the EC is not a contracting party to the European Convention of Human Rights (ECHR) and cannot become a party to it as the law currently stands,[137] the ECJ

---

[134] WT/DS27/ARB, Decision of Arbitrators, 9.4.1999.

[135] WT/DS27/ARB/ECU, Decision of Arbitrators, 24.3.2000.

[136] WT/DS26/ARB, Decision of Arbitrators, 12.7.1999.

[137] Opinion 2/94 [1996] ECR I-1759.

has been interpreting the ECHR for many years.[138] In the *ERT* case, the ECJ summed up the importance of the ECHR within the Community legal order as follows:

> '41 With regard to Article 10 of the European Convention on Human Rights, referred to in the ninth and tenth questions, it must first be pointed out that, as the Court has consistently held, *fundamental rights form an integral part of the general principles of law, the observance of which it ensures. For that purpose the Court draws inspiration from the constitutional traditions common to the Member States and from the guidelines supplied by international treaties for the protection of human rights on which the Member States have collaborated or of which they are signatories* (see, in particular, the judgment in Case C-4/73 *Nold* v *Commission* [1974] ECR 491, paragraph 13). *The European Convention on Human Rights has special significance in that respect* (see in particular Case C-222/84 *Johnston* v *Chief Constable of the Royal Ulster Constabulary* [1986] ECR 1651, paragraph 18). It follows that, as the Court held in its judgment in Case C-5/88 *Wachauf* v *Federal Republic of Germany* [1989] ECR 2609, paragraph 19, *the Community cannot accept measures which are incompatible with observance of the human rights thus recognized and guaranteed.*'[139]

In the most recent case-law of the ECJ, a new development can be identified since the ECJ no longer uses the reference 'source of inspiration' but rather applies the ECHR directly as if it were an integral part of the Community legal order.[140] As a consequence thereof, the ECHR and the case-law of the ECrtHR enjoy primacy over conflicting secondary Community law and all national law of the EU Member States.[141]

The following analysis examines whether the application of the ECHR and the judgments of the ECrtHR by the ECJ and CFI affect the classic legal situation which exists between the ECHR law and the domestic law of the Member States. In particular, the question arises whether the involvement of the European courts affects the legal status of judgments of the ECrtHR, their binding effect and supremacy in the domestic legal orders of the selected EU Member States.

---

[138] It should be noted that draft Article 7 (2) of the European Constitutional Treaty states that 'the Union shall seek accession to the European Convention for the Protection of Human Rights and Fundamental Freedoms.', CONV 850/03, 18.7.2003. See for details: Jacobs (2001); Oliver (2000); Ress (1999); Callewaert (2001); Rodriguez Iglesias (1995).

[139] Case C-260/89 *ERT* [1991] ECR I-2925, emphasis added.

[140] See: Case C-117/01 *K.B.*, judgment of 7.1.2004; Case C-109/01 *Akrich*, judgment of 23.9.2003; Case C-60/00 *Carpenter* [2002] ECR I-6279; Case C-413/99 *Baumbast* [2002] ECR I-7091. See case-note on Baumbast by: Sewandono (2003); case-note on Carpenter by: Acierno (2003); Staples (2003a); *ibid.*, (2003b); van Ooik/ Staples (2002).

[141] See also: Hilf (1995).

2.1 International law level

The central issue that needs to be addressed in this section is the question of whether judgments of the ECrtHR can be qualified as binding decisions of an organ of an IO.

2.1.1 The ECrtHR as an organ of an IO

As to the question whether the ECrtHR can be qualified as an organ of an IO, two different views can be advanced.

First, the 'incorporation' model can be advanced which argues that the ECrtHR and its judgments are 'part' of the ECHR provision which is at issue in the specific case and therefore does not constitute a decision of an organ of an IO but rather is an incorporated part of the ECHR. That is so because the ECrtHR is merely interpreting the already existing legal obligations which arise out of the ECHR, rather than creating new legal obligations for the contracting parties. This theory is moreover supported by the fact that the ECrtHR is not mentioned in Article 10 of the Statutes of the Council of Europe as an organ of the Council of Europe.[142]

Second, whilst it is admitted that the incorporation theory is generally accepted and carries with it some advantages also for the qualification of ECrtHR judgments in the national legal order[143], the present author considers another view also defendable. In this context, the definition of an organ of an IO as defined in the introduction should be recalled here.[144] Accordingly, an IO is defined as forms of co-operation founded on an international agreement or other instrument governed by public international law creating at one organ which exercizes in its own capacity governmental functions and which may include other entities than states. While it is true that the ECrtHR is not mentioned as an organ of the Council of Europe in Article 10 of the Statutes of the Council of Europe, the incorporation theory fails to explain what the ECrtHR is other than an organ established by an international treaty. Moreover, the argument that the ECrtHR is not mentioned in Article 10 of the Statute of the Council of Europe can be seriously questioned if one considers the fact that the ECrtHR is fully integrated in the system of the Council of Europe and the high importance of the ECHR and the ECrtHR in the Council of Europe system.[145] Moreover, since the 11th Protocol to the ECHR entered into force, the ECrtHR has become a permanent organ in Strasbourg. In addition, the website of the ECrtHR which includes its case-law is fully integrated into the website of

[142] Van Dijk (1995) at 69-70.

[143] See below the section on the Netherlands.

[144] See Chapter 1.

[145] Boer-Buquicchio (2003) at 561-562.

the Council of Europe. Therefore, it could reasonably be argued that *de facto* the ECrtHR has over time become an organ of the Council of Europe – without that this would affect its independence – and thus Article 10 of the Statutes of the Council of Europe should nowadays be read as to include the Strasbourg court.

Besides, one could consider the ECrtHR itself to be an IO, being the only organ of it. In line with the broad definition applied in this research, it is sufficient that contracting parties have established on the basis of a treaty an organ that can exercize in its own capacity governmental functions. Article 19 ECHR establishes the ECrtHR in order to 'ensure the observance of the engagements undertaken by the High Contracting Parties in the Convention and the Protocols thereto'. According to Article 32 ECHR the jurisdiction of the ECrtHR 'shall extend to all matters covering the interpretation and application of the Convention and Protocols thereto'. Finally, according to Article 46 (1) ECHR the judgments of the ECrtHR 'shall be final and the High Contracting Parties undertake to abide by the final judgment of the ECrtHR in any case to which they are parties'. Thus, the ECrtHR must be qualified as an organ established by an international treaty endowed with the competence to adopt final and binding decisions independently from the contracting parties.[146] Thus, if one follows this line of argument, the ECrtHR meets the criteria of being an IO and at the same time being its only organ.

In summary, for the purpose of this research the ECrtHR is qualified as an organ established by an international agreement endowed with the task of adopting final decisions on the interpretation and application of the ECHR.

2.1.2 The binding effect of ECrtHR judgments

As mentioned above, judgments of the ECrtHR are formally binding only on the contracting parties involved in a certain case (Article 46 (1) ECHR).[147]

However, in my view, a more teleological and *effet utile* orientated approach, which aims at ensuring that the ECHR is properly applied in all contracting parties, is to be preferred. Accordingly, it is submitted that the relevant observations of the ECrtHR regarding a specific ECHR provision made in a judgment, i.e. the operative parts, are generally applicable to similar situations in all other contracting parties.[148] In other words, ECrtHR judgments *de facto* exert a binding effect beyond the individual case.

---

[146] Ress (1996) at 353.

[147] See: Ress (1981) in particular 726 ff.

[148] See: Bernhardt (2000) at 153-154; Lawson (1999a) at 92-93; *ibid.* (1999b) at 106-111.

2.2 European law level

Due to the fact that the EC and EU Treaties so far do not contain a catalogue of fundamental rights, the ECJ was forced to look around for other sources and found them in particular in the ECHR.[149] Since the beginning of the 1970s, the ECJ has used the ECHR as a 'source of inspiration' to review Community law acts[150] and Member States acts falling within the scope of Community law.[151] In its most recent case-law, the ECJ does not use the detour of the concept of 'source of inspiration' but it is actually doing nothing less than the ECrtHR, namely, interpreting and applying the ECHR directly.[152] Hence, the ECHR must be considered to be an integral part of the Community legal order. This is in effect also enshrined in Articles 6 (2) in conjunction with 46 (d) TEU.

However, at the same time, the ECJ has explicitly limited its jurisdiction to measures falling within the 'field of application of Community law' when it stated:

> '42 As the Court has held (see the judgment in Joined Cases C-60 and C-61/84 *Cinéthèque* v *Fédération Nationale des Cinémas Français* [1985] ECR 2605, paragraph 25, and the judgment in Case C-12/86 *Demirel* v *Stadt Schwaebisch Gmund* [1987] ECR 3719, paragraph 28), it has no power to examine the compatibility with the European Convention on Human Rights of national rules which do not fall within the scope of Community law. On the other hand, where such rules do fall within the scope of Community law, and reference is made to the Court for a preliminary ruling, it must provide all the criteria of interpretation needed by the national court to determine whether those rules are compatible with the fundamental rights the observance of which the Court ensures and which derive in particular from the European Convention on Human Rights.'[153]

Hence, the question arises: what is exactly meant by the term 'field of application of Community law'?[154] The delimitation of what falls within the scope and

---

[149] See: Nicolaysen (2003); Curtin (2000) at 308.

[150] See e.g.: Case 4/73 *Nold* [1974] ECR 491; see for a detailed analysis: Pernice (1979).

[151] See e.g.: Case C-260/89 *ERT* [1991] ECR I-2925; Joined cases C-297/88 and C-197/89 *Dzodzi* [1990] ECR I-3763; Case C-130/95 *Giloy* [1997] ECR I-4291. See also: Zampini (1999); Spielmann (1999) at 763-764.

[152] See e.g.: Case C-368/95 *Familiapress* [1997] ECR I-3689; Case C-174/98 P *Netherlands and Van der Wal* v. *Commission* [2000] ECR I-1; Case C-60/00 *Carpenter* [2002] ECR I-6279; Case C-413/99 *Baumbast* [2002] ECR I-7091. See also: Curtin (2000) at 311-312; Jacobs (1995) at 563 who writes: '[...] it seems legitimate to speak of the Court [ECJ] applying the Convention [...].'; Toth (1997); Lawson (1995) at 224-227.

[153] Case C-260/89 *ERT* [1991] ECR I-2925.

[154] See for a detailed analysis: De Witte (1999a).

what falls outside the scope of the 'field of application of Community law' is essential, since this in turn determines the scope of the 'EC law transformed' legal situation caused by the application of the ECHR by the ECJ and CFI. Three groups of measures that fall within the 'field of application of Community law' can be distinguished.[155]

First, national measures implementing EC law.[156] Second, national measures adopted under an exception contained in the EC Treaty or in the case-law of the ECJ.[157] Third, national measures reproducing EC law for domestic purposes, that is, measures which voluntarily extend EC rules to purely internal situations in cases which fall outside the scope of application of Community law.[158]

In subsequent cases, the ECJ further defined the conditions for national measures in order to fall within the 'field of application of Community law'.[159] Essentially, there must be a sufficient link between the national measure and Community law, in the sense that the national measure must intend to implement Community law or else affect the effective application of Community law.[160]

However, the case-law of the ECJ has not yet determined whether this also applies to national measures implementing Directives. The ECJ only stated that the duties imposed by Directives on Member States should be read 'in the light of' the general principles of Community law, which also include the ECHR.[161] Similarly, it is not clear whether this applies to the application by Member States of external agreements concluded by the EC or binding decisions adopted by organs established by such agreements. De Witte, who refers only to agreements, argues that this would be logical in view of the case-law of the ECJ.[162] In my view, there are no compelling reasons why this should not equally apply to decisions of IOs, in particular since the ECJ treats decisions that are directly linked with a treaty in the same way as the treaty itself.[163]

As to the substance, the ECJ has considered the most important fundamental rights, such as the principle of equality, freedom of expression, freedom

---

155 *Ibid.*, at 869.

156 See e.g.: Case 230/78 *Eridania-Zuccherifici nazionali* [1979] ECR 2749; Joined cases 201-202/85 *Klensch* [1986] ECR 3477; Case 5/88 *Wachauf* [1989] ECR 2609.

157 See e.g.: Case C-260/89 *ERT* [1991] ECR I-2925; Case C-368/95 *Familiapress* [1997] ECR I-3689.

158 See e.g.: Case 12/86 *Demirel* [1987] ECR 3719; Joined cases C-297/88 and 197/89 *Dzodzi* [1990] ECR I-3763; Case C-231/89 *Gmurzynska-Bscher* [1990] ECR I- 4003; Case C-130/95 *Giloy* [1997] ECR I-4291.

159 Case C-299/95 *Kremzow* [1997] ECR I-2629; Case C-309/96 *Annibaldi* [1997] ECR I-7493; Case C-368/95 *Familiapress* [1997] ECR I-3689.

160 De Witte (1999a) at 872.

161 See e.g.: Case 36/75 *Rutili* [1975] ECR 1219; Case 222/84 *Johnston* [1986] ECR 1651.

162 De Witte (1999a) at 873.

163 See above the section on WTO dispute settlement reports and Chapter 3 on Association Council Decisions.

of religion, freedom of association, right to privacy, right to property, etc. to be included in the 'field of application of Community law'.[164] Thus, it can be summarized that the ECJ applies the ECHR, as interpreted by the ECrtHR, whenever national measures of the Member States that intend to implement Community law also affect the rights protected by the ECHR. This covers in particular the rights connected with the exercise of the four freedoms of the internal market and thus covers the core parts of the EC Treaty. In all these cases, the classic legal situation 'ECHR–national law' is potentially modified by an 'EC law transformed' legal situation 'ECHR–EC law–national law'. In this context, it is also interesting to note that the same limitation is applied to the Charter of Fundamental Rights vis-à-vis the EU institutions and the EU Member States 'implementing Union law' (Article II-51 draft text of a new European Constitution).[165]

2.2.1 Interaction between the ECJ and the ECrtHR

The *Baustahlgewerbe* case is an illustrative example of how the ECJ applies the ECHR. In that case, the ECJ accepted the claim of the appellant – who relied on Article 6 ECHR – that the Court of First Instance failed to conclude the case within a reasonable time.[166] Also the *Krombach* case, in which the ECJ held that Article 6 ECHR is violated if a court of one EU Member State executed a judgment of another EU Member State in which the defendant has no right to defend himself before the court of origin, is a good example of how the ECJ applies the ECHR.[167] More recently, the ECJ accepted that the freedom of expression and of assembly as protected by Articles 10, 11 ECHR could justify a restriction of the free movement of goods as protected by Articles 28, 30, 34 read together with Article 5 EC Treaty.[168] Thus, when the ECJ applies the ECHR and the rulings of the ECrtHR, they are brought into the 'orbit' of EU law. As a result, the ECHR and the case-law of the ECrtHR obtain Community law features such as supremacy over all domestic law of the EU Member States. In other words, all national measures of the Member States that fall within the 'field of application of Community law' are subject to the European courts' interpretation and application of the ECHR. Consequently, the ECJ has seized jurisdiction to interpret and apply the ECHR – in all cases in which a measure

[164] De Witte (1999a) at 868.

[165] CONV 850/03 of 18.7.2003; see also: Final Report of Working Group II 'Incorporation of the Charter/accession to the ECHR', 22.10.2002, CONV 354/02.

[166] Case C-185/95 P *Baustahlgewerbe* v. *Commission* [1998] ECR I-8417.

[167] Case C-7/98 *Krombach* [2000] ECR I-1935.

[168] Case C-112/00 *Schmidberger* [2003] ECR I-5659; see case-note by: Kadelbach/Petersen (2003); Brown (2003).

falls within the 'field of application of Community law', whereas formally, the ECrtHR is the only competent organ to interpret the ECHR.

In the meantime, the ECrtHR has reasserted its competence by also reviewing measures of the Contracting Parties that implement EC law, which is essentially an indirect review of Community law acts.[169] In the *Cantoni* case, the ECrtHR explicitly stated that the fact that a national provision is based almost literally on an EC Directive 'does not remove it from the ambit of Article 7 ECHR', thus enabling the ECrtHR to review such a measure.[170] In the *Matthews* case, the ECrtHR held the UK responsible for failing to allow elections to the EP to be held in Gibraltar.[171] While the Strasbourg Court observed that EC acts as such cannot be challenged before the ECrtHR because the EC is not a Contracting Party of the ECHR, it nevertheless emphasized that, even though the ECHR does not prevent the transfer of competences to international organizations, the Contracting Parties continue to be responsible that the rights provided by the ECHR are secured after such a transfer.[172]

In another case,[173] which has been admitted by the ECrtHR but is still pending, the ECrtHR will examine whether UN sanctions implemented by the EC through EC Regulations and executed by Ireland by national measures violate Article 1 of Protocol No. 1 of the ECHR which protects the right of peaceful enjoyment of possessions. Since Ireland did nothing else than give effect to the EC Regulations implementing the Security Council Resolutions, the ECrtHR will essentially review the conformity of the EC Regulations and the Security Council Resolutions with the ECHR. More interestingly, the ECrtHR will also review the ruling of the ECJ in the same case rendered a few years ago in which it rejected all claims of the applicant by simply referring to the necessity to give full effect to UN Security Council Resolutions.[174]

Another example of the interaction between the ECJ and the ECrtHR is the *Senator Lines* case. Senator Lines and several other maritime transport companies were fined by the Commission for infringing the competition rules of the EC Treaty. In its decision the Commission indicated that in case the companies would appeal against the decision of the Commission, the Commission would not enforce its decision the period in which the proceedings take place if the companies provide bank guarantees that cover the amount of the fines plus interest rates. Due to the high amount of the fines and their bad financial situation Senator Lines and the other companies were unable to secure appropriate bank guarantees. Consequently, in an interim procedure the maritime compa-

---

169 See generally: Canor (2000); Ress (1999).

170 ECrtHR *Cantoni* v. *France*, judgment of 15.11.1996, para. 30.

171 ECrtHR *Matthews* v. *UK*, judgment of 18.2.1999.

172 *Ibid.*

173 ECrtHR *Bosphorus Hava* v. *Ireland*, decision on the admissibility, 13.9.2001.

174 Case C-84/95 *Bosphorus Hava* [1996] ECR I-3953.

nies appealed against the requirement of having to provide bank guarantees in order to avoid having to pay the fine before a final decision in substance has been rendered by the European courts. However, the appeal was rejected by the President of the CFI.[175] The companies again appealed against that decision but this was also rejected by the President of the ECJ.[176] At the same time Senator Lines started a procedure before the ECrtHR against all 15 Member States claiming that Article 6 ECHR (access to court) has been violated by the Commission because it has been required to pay the fine before a decision in substance has been taken by the European courts.[177] In the meantime, the CFI ruled in the substance of the case that the fines have not to be paid by the companies.[178] In turn, the President of the ECrtHR cancelled the hearing in the *Senator Lines* case by apparently assuming that the case has been decided *in fine*.[179] However, it seems to the present author, that the decision of the President of the ECHR might have been taken prematurely since the ruling of the CFI in substance could still be appealed by the parties before the ECJ. Accordingly, it is possible that the ECJ overturns the ruling of the CFI which means that the companies would still have to pay the fines. Whatever the outcome will be, this case illustrates how the decisions of the ECJ and CFI on the one hand and the ECrtHR on the other hand interact with each other and thus influence the outcome of the various proceedings.

Moreover, and in contrast to the *Cantoni* and *Matthews* cases in which the proper implementation of EC law caused a violation of the ECHR, the ECrtHR also ensures that Contracting Parties of the ECHR which are members of the EU fulfil their obligations under Community law as far as the provisions of the ECHR are concerned. Accordingly, in a case against Greece the ECrtHR ruled that:

> '45. By refraining for more than five years from taking the necessary measures to comply with a final, enforceable judicial decision [ECJ judgement C-147/86 (*Commission* v *Greece*), ECR 1988, p. 1637] in the present case the Greek authorities deprived the provisions of Article 6 para. 1 of the Convention (art. 6-1) of all useful effect.'[180]

---

[175] Case T-191/98 R *DSR- Senator Lines* [1999] ECR II-2531.

[176] Case C-364/99 P (R) *DSR-Senator Lines* [1999] ECR I-8733.

[177] ECrtHR *Senator Lines* v. *15 Member States of the EU* (application no. 56672/00); see for the full text of the application: HRLJ 2000, 112-128.

[178] Case T-191/98 and T-212/98–T-214/98 *Senator Lines et. al.*, judgment of 30.9.2003.

[179] Press release issued by the Registrar, 16.10.2003; available at: http://www.echr.coe.int/Eng/Press/2003/oct/SenatorLinescancelled.htm.

[180] ECrtHR *Hornsby* v. *Greece*, judgment of 19.3.1997.

More recently, in the *Dangeville* case, the ECrtHR considered the failure of France to properly implement an EC tax Directive as a violation of the right to property as enshrined in the 1st Protocol to the ECHR.[181] Thus, there is an interaction between the ECrtHR and the ECJ that can enhance the overall protection level of the ECHR, but can also lead to divergent interpretations of the ECHR, especially since both courts are not bound by each other's interpretation.[182]

2.2.2 Divergent interpretations of the ECHR

In a few cases, a divergent interpretation between the ECJ and the ECrtHR exists.[183] However, the most recent case-law suggests that the existing differences are being reduced by a slow convergence of the case-law of both European courts.

For instance, there is the interpretation adopted by the ECJ in the *Hoechst*[184] case as compared with the position of the ECrtHR in the *Niemietz*[185] case regarding the question of whether or not business premises that have been searched are protected by Article 8 ECHR. Whereas the ECJ determined that the scope of Article 8 ECHR could not be extended to business premises, the ECrtHR adopted a much broader view by ruling that Article 8 ECrtHR covers professional offices. Although, it must be admitted that there is a difference between business premises and premises of professionals such as lawyers, it is interesting to note that the ECJ did not take this development into account in its case-law. Be that as it may, more recently, the ECrtHR explicitly stated in the *Colas Est* case that 'under certain circumstances' Article 8 ECHR is applicable to business premises and indeed a Chamber of seven judges unanimously ruled that in this case France violated Article 8 ECHR by ordering the search of business premises without a prior authorization of a judge.[186] A few months later, the ECJ – while repeating its position adopted in the *Hoechst* case – took note in a preliminary consideration of the *Cola Est* ruling without making clear whether or not the extension of the scope of Article 8 ECHR is also applicable to measures that fall within the 'field of application of Community law'.[187] Thus, it must be concluded that, while it is clear that the ECJ did not ignore the importance of the *Colas Est* ruling of the ECrtHR, it failed to indicate whether it

---

181 ECrtHR *S.A. Dangeville* v. *France*, judgment of 16.4.2002; see also: Geursen (2002).

182 See in particular the very useful extensive analysis of the interaction between both courts by: Burgorgue-Larsen (2000); *ibid.*, (2001); Spielmann (1999) at 761-762; Toth (1997) at 492; Lawson (1994).

183 See: Toth (1997) at 499-500; Lawson (1994).

184 Joined cases 46/87 and 227/88 *Hoechst* [1989] ECR 2859.

185 ECrtHR *Niemietz* v. *Germany*, judgment of 16.12.1992.

186 ECrtHR *Colas Est e.a.* v. *France*, judgment of 16.4.2002.

187 Case C-94/00 *Roquette Frères* [2002] ECR I-9011; see case note by: Lienenmayer/Waelbroeck (2003).

follows the ECrtHR and thus establishes a convergence between the case-law of both courts.[188]

In the *Orkem*[189] case, the ECJ adopted a more restricted approach regarding the right not to give evidence against oneself by denying the application of Article 6 ECHR to undertakings, while in the *Funke*[190] case, the ECrtHR could not find a justification for denying that right to undertakings.

More recently, the issue of the position of Advocate Generals, *Commissaire du Gouvernement* and comparable advisory functions concerning their role and influence on the decision-making process of a court has been judged upon in the context of Article 6 ECHR by the ECrtHR and the ECJ. In a series of cases, the ECrtHR has clearly established that the impossibility for the parties to respond to the opinion of Advocate Generals, *Commissaire du Gouvernement*, etc. and the fact that, in some cases, they participate in the deliberations of the court (even without having the right to vote), violates the right of adversarial proceedings as enshrined in Article 6 ECHR.[191] This case-law of the ECrtHR covers penal, civil, social and administrative law procedures.[192]

In contrast and despite the fact that parties are prohibited to respond to the opinion of the AG during a procedure before the ECJ, the ECJ ruled in the *Emesa Sugar*[193] case that:

> '16 Having regard to both the organic and the functional link between the Advocate General and the Court, referred to in paragraphs 10 to 15 of this order, the aforesaid case-law of the European Court of Human Rights does not appear to be transposable to the Opinion of the Court's Advocates General.'

Although it is admitted that the situation of the European AG is not entirely the same compared to national AGs, in principle they perform the same task, namely, to submit an independent opinion that advises and accordingly influences the court.[194] That is also underlined by the fact that in a large majority of cases the ECJ follows the opinion of the AGs. Thus, there are no funda-

---

188 See: Kranenborg (2003); Van der Wal (2002).

189 Case 374/87 *Orkem* [1989] ECR 3283.

190 ECrtHR *Funke* v. *France*, judgment of 25.2.1993.

191 See e.g.: ECrtHR *Borgers* v. *Belgium*, judgment of 30.10.1991; ECrtHR *Lobo Machado* v. *Portugal*, judgment of 20.2.1996; ECrtHR *Vermeulen* v. *Belgium*, judgment of 20.2.1996; ECrtHR *Bulut* v. *Austria*, judgment of 22.2.1996; ECrtHR *Van Orshoven* v. *Belgium*, judgment of 25.6.1997; ECrtHR *J.J.* and *K.D.B.* v. *Netherlands*, judgment of 27.3.1998; ECrtHR *Reinhardt & Slimane-Kaïd* v. *France*, judgment of 31.3.1998; ECrtHR *Quadrelli* v. *Italy*, judgment of 11.1.2000; ECrtHR *Voisine* v. *France*, judgment of 8.2.2000; ECrtHR *Kress* v. *France*, judgment of 7.6.2001.

192 See for a detailed discussion: Benoît-Rohmer (2001a).

193 Order of the ECJ in Case C-17/98 *Emesa Sugar* [2000] ECR I-665; see case-note by: Lawson (2000).

194 *Ibid.*, at 986-988.

mental differences between the system of the European AG and national AGs that would convincingly justify the deviating approach of the ECJ. The divergence between the case-law of both courts has only been partly reduced by the *Kress* judgment of the ECrtHR.[195] In this case, which concerned the role of the *Commissaire du Gouvernement* before the French *Conseil d'Etat*, the ECrtHR found a violation of Article 6 ECHR only insofar as the *Commissaire du Gouvernement* is often present at the deliberations of the *Conseil d'Etat*, while it considered the existing possibility to reply to the submissions of the *Commissaire du Gouvernement* by means of a memorandum to the *Conseil d'Etat* to be compatible with Article 6 ECHR. Whereas the incompatibly of the European system with Article 6 ECHR lies in the fact that – as the ECJ repeated again – parties to a procedure before the ECJ are prohibited from responding to the opinion delivered by the AG.[196] In this context, it should be noted that the AG never participates in the deliberations of the ECJ.[197]

Nevertheless, in some cases the ECJ has adopted a more liberal approach than the ECrtHR. That is, for example, the case concerning the application of fair trial principles as contained in Article 6 ECHR in staff cases. While in the *Dufay*[198] and *Johnston*[199] cases, the ECJ applied them to staff members, the ECrtHR did not apply them in the *Neigel*[200], *Lombardo*[201], *Massa*[202] and *Pellegrin*[203] cases. More recently, in the *Carpenter* case, the ECJ interpreted several elements of Article 8 ECHR more dynamically than the ECrtHR.[204] For instance, the ECJ accepted that the element 'family life' exists even though Mrs. Carpenter was raising the children of Mr. Carpenter that are children of his first marriage. Apparently, only in one (unpublished) case before the European Commission of Human Rights was this situation considered as meeting the condition of 'family life'.[205] Moreover, the ECJ also adopted a more dynamic approach when it accepted the denial of a residence permit as an interference with the 'family life', whereas in the case-law of the Strasbourg court that is not

---

[195] ECrtHR *Kress* v. *France*, judgment of 7.6.2001; see case-note by: Bok (2002).

[196] Case C-466/00 *Kaba* [2003] ECR I-2219.

[197] It is interesting to note that the ECrtHR justifies its ruling on the point of participation of the *Commissaire du Gouvernement* at the deliberations by explicitly referring to the European AG who does not attend the deliberations of the ECJ, ECrtHR *Kress* v. *France* judgment of 7.6.2001, para. 86.

[198] Case 257/85 *Dufay* v. *EP* [1987] ECR 1561.

[199] Case 222/84 *Johnston* [1986] ECR 1651.

[200] ECrtHR *Neigel* v. *France*, judgment of 17.3.1997.

[201] ECrtHR *Lombardo* v. *Italy*, judgment of 26.11.1992.

[202] ECrtHR *Massa* v. *Italy*, judgment of 24.8.1993.

[203] ECrtHR *Pellegrin* v. *France*, 8.12.1999; see also: Prétot (2000b).

[204] Case C-60/00 *Carpenter* [2002] ECR I-6279; see case-note by: Forder (2002).

[205] *Ibid.*

the case.[206] Finally, the ECJ accepted the right of the Carpenters to choose their residence, whereas the ECrtHR stated that Article 8 ECHR does not oblige the Contracting Parties of the ECHR to respect the choice of married couples of the country of their matrimonial residence nor to accept the non-national spouses for settlement in that country.[207]

Consequently, when the ECJ interprets and applies the ECHR and thus the judgments of the ECrtHR, it attaches Community law features such as supremacy and binding effect on all Member States and their courts[208] to them, thereby adding legal weight. So, while the possibility for divergent interpretations of the ECHR cannot be excluded, it must be emphasized that due to the fact that the ECJ mostly applies the ECHR in accordance with the case-law of the ECrtHR, the ECHR obtains a higher status in the domestic legal order of the Member States and the interpretation given to the ECHR by the ECJ are binding on all Member States courts.

Hence, it can be concluded that – insofar as a measure falls within the 'field of application of Community law' – the previously existing classic legal situation (ECHR–national law) is modified into an 'EC law transformed' legal situation (ECHR–EC law–national law) whenever the ECJ applies the ECHR and the case-law of the ECrtHR. However, if the EU would indeed accede to the ECHR as draft Article-7 (2) of the European Constitution provides for, then the ECJ would be formally bound by the interpretations of the ECrtHR and thus would not be free anymore to chose whether or not to follow the ECrtHR case-law – at least as far as they concern issues that fall within the competence of the EU.

2.3 National law level

2.3.1 Germany

In Germany, the ECHR has been incorporated in the German legal order by a federal statute of 1952.[209] Accordingly, the ECHR enjoys the same legal rank as the federal statute, i.e. similar to other federal statutes and below the *Grundgesetz*. As mentioned above, Ress considers it possible to qualify the ECrtHR as an organ of an IO.[210] Accordingly, the ECrtHR could be considered a *'zwischenstaatliche Einrichtung'* within the scope of Article 24 GG. If this conclusion would be accepted then the ECHR would enjoy primacy over conflict-

---

206 ECrtHR *Abdulaziz, Cabales and Balkandali* v. *UK*, judgment of 28.5.1985.

207 ECrtHR *Abdulaziz, Cabales and Balkandali* v. *UK*, judgment of 28.5.1985, para. 68; ECrtHR *Ahmut* v. *the Netherlands*, judgment of 28.11.1996; but see a more dynamic approach adopted by the ECrtHR in *Sen* v. *the Netherlands*, judgment of 21.12.2001.

208 See for a detailed analysis: Toth (1984).

209 BGBl. II, 7.8.1952, 685.

210 Ress (1996) at 353.

ing German statutes. Bleckmann comes to the similar result of granting the ECHR primacy over conflicting German statutes, but argues that the ECHR is part of customary international law and thus falls within the scope of Article 25 GG, which provides for supremacy of customary international law over conflicting statutes.[211] While the present author agrees with the approach of Ress, it must be admitted that this opinion has not been generally accepted yet.

The incorporation of the ECHR says nothing as regards the legal effect of the judgments of the ECrtHR in the German legal order. Neither the ECHR nor the *Zustimmungsgesetz* (the federal statute implementing the ECHR) contain any explicit provisions concerning the domestic legal effect of ECrtHR rulings. Accordingly, the German legislature did not endow a competence to the ECrtHR to bind German courts.[212] Thus, from a formal legal point of view, German courts are not bound by the judgments of the ECrtHR. However, most German courts[213] do use the judgments of the ECrtHR as a tool to interpret German laws in order to ensure their conformity with the ECHR. Also the *BVerfG* takes the ECHR provisions as an interpretative tool into account[214] and has emphasized that German laws must be interpreted and applied as far as possible in conformity with international obligations.[215]

In contrast to that, ECJ judgments enjoy primacy over all national law and are binding on all German courts by virtue of Community law. Consequently, the domestic legal status of ECrtHR judgments in the German legal order is lower than ECJ judgments.

Hence, at first sight, in case of a divergent interpretation between the ECJ and the ECrtHR concerning the ECHR with regard to measure that falls within the 'field of application of Community law', German courts would be obliged by virtue of Community law to give preference to the ECJ interpretation. However, Article 307 (ex 234) EC Treaty, that reads as follows:

> **'Article 307 (ex Article 234)**
> The rights and obligations arising from agreements concluded before 1 January 1958 or, for acceding States, before the date of their accession, between one or more Member States on the one hand, and one or more third countries on the other, shall not be affected by the provisions of this Treaty.
> To the extent that such agreements are not compatible with this Treaty, the Member State or States concerned shall take all appropriate steps to eliminate the incompatibilities established. Member States shall, where necessary, assist each other to this end and shall, where appropriate, adopt a common attitude [...]'.

---

[211] Bleckmann (1994).

[212] Fiedler (2000) at 17; Uerpmann (1993) at 187-214.

[213] Uerpmann mentions a few examples in which several German courts did not follow the ECrtHR.

[214] Uerpmann (1993) at 96-108.

[215] BVerfGE 74, 358 (370).

gives the EU Member States the possibility to set aside the EC Treaty and Community law obligations in order to fulfil conflicting obligations arising out of a treaty ratified prior to the EC Treaty. In a recent case, the ECJ summed up its case-law on Article 307 EC Treaty as follows:

> '23. Article 234 of the Treaty is of general scope and applies to any international agreement, irrespective of subject-matter, which is capable of affecting application of the Treaty (Case 812/79 *Attorney General* v *Burgoa* [1980] ECR 2787, paragraph 6; Case C-158/91 *Levy* [1993] ECR I-4287, paragraph 11; Case C-62/98 *Commission* v *Portugal* [2000] ECR I-5171, paragraph 43).
>
> 24. As is clear from paragraph 8 of the judgment in *Burgoa*, the purpose of the first paragraph of Article 234 of the Treaty is to make it clear, in accordance with the principles of international law [see, in that connection, Article 30(4)(b) of the Convention on the Law of Treaties signed in Vienna on 23 May 1969] that application of the Treaty does not affect the duty of the Member State concerned to respect the rights of non-member countries under a prior agreement and to perform its obligations there under.'[216]

Article 307 EC Treaty is applicable to any international treaty, also to the ECHR. Since Germany ratified the ECHR before the EC Treaty, Germany and thus German courts would be able to give preference to an ECrtHR instead of a conflicting ECJ interpretation of the ECHR.[217] Indeed, Lawson unequivocally concludes on this point that:

> 'De lidstaten – Frankrijk mogelijk daargelaten – blijven onverminderd gebonden aan de verplichtingen die zij onder het EVRM zijn aangegaan; het Gemeenschapsrecht mag daaraan geen afbreuk doen.'[218]

Thus, the EC Treaty contains an explicit 'rule of conflict' that enables the EU Member States to set aside the 'EC law transformed' legal situation created by the involvement of the ECJ, and thus restore the previously existing classic legal situation. However, at the same time, the second paragraph of Article 307 EC Treaty clearly indicates that this is only a temporary 'escape route' for the Member States because they are required to do everything in order to resolve the conflicting situation so as to ensure that EC law is again fully applied as the highest norm.[219]

---

[216] Case C-466/98 *Commission* v. *UK* [2002] ECR I-9427.

[217] Ress (1999) at 475-476.

[218] Lawson (1999b) at 78.

[219] See: Petersmann (1997c).

In summary, it can be concluded that, due to the fact that the ECJ applies and interprets the ECHR and the judgments of the ECrtHR (as far as it concerns a measures that falls within the scope of application of Community law), the ECHR becomes an integral part of EC law. Moreover, as a consequence thereof, the legal rank of the ECHR and the judgments of the ECrtHR in the German legal order are upgraded from being equal to statutes to being the 'supreme law of the land', i.e. higher than the *Grundgesetz*. At the same, it should be noted that in a conflict between ECrtHR case-law and EC law German courts would be able to invoke Article 307 EC Treaty, thus enabling them to give preference to the ECrtHR and thereby fully comply with the obligations arising out of the ECHR.

2.3.2 The Netherlands

In the Netherlands, the domestic legal effect of ECrtHR judgments has been discussed in the context of whether they can be qualified as 'decisions of an IO' within the scope of Articles 93, 94 Gw. The *Hoge Raad* has defined the term *'besluit'* (decision) in the sense that the decision of an IO must be taken on the basis of a treaty in which the competence to take binding decisions for the Netherlands has been transferred to the IO.[220] Essentially, two different theories have been developed as regards to ECrtHR judgments.[221]

The first theory qualifies judgments of the ECrtHR as *'besluiten'* (decisions) of an IO. Accordingly, the ECrtHR is seen as an organ established by the contracting parties on the basis of the ECHR with the purpose of adopting binding decisions regarding the interpretation and application of the ECHR.[222] The second theory uses an 'incorporation' model by arguing that a judgment of the ECrtHR is 'part' of the ECHR provision which is at issue in the specific case and therefore does not constitute a decision of an IO. The reason for advancing this construction by classifying judgments of the ECrtHR as part of the ECHR rather than as decisions of an IO lies in the constitutional difficulties related to the binding effect of decisions of IO.[223] According to Dutch constitutional law, the following conditions must be met before a decision of an IO can be considered to be binding on anyone: (i) it must be a decision of an IO, (ii) the decision

[220] This definition refers to the question whether the Universal Declaration must be qualified as a decision of an IO. The Hoge Raad stated '[...] omdat de Universele verklaring niet kan worden aangemerkt als een besluit bedoeld in art. 93 Gr.w., nu de onderhavige resolutie niet berust op een bij of krachtens verdrag opgedragen bevoegdheid om voor Nederland bindende besluiten te nemen [...]', Hoge Raad 23.11.1984, NJ 1985/604.

[221] Lawson (1999a) at 99.

[222] Alkema (1985) at 30.

[223] Van der Velde (1990).

must be published in the Netherlands and (iii) the decision must be binding on anyone.

As to the first condition, it has been established above that the ECrtHR fulfils the criteria to be qualified as an organ of an IO. As to the second condition, the judgments of the ECrtHR are not officially published in the Netherlands. Also, the Act concerning the ratification and publication of treaties (*Rijkswet goedkeuring en bekendmaking verdragen*) does not contain a specific obligation to do so. Finally, as to the third condition, it is doubtful whether rulings of the ECrtHR are 'binding on anyone' within the meaning of the Dutch constitution. In principle, according to Article 46 ECHR, a judgment is only binding on the Contracting Parties involved in a specific case. Therefore, it is doubtful whether a judgment in which the Netherlands is *not* involved is binding on the Netherlands as a Contracting Party or on individuals within the scope of Articles 93, 94 Gw. Similarly, it is doubtful whether a judgment in a case in which the Netherlands *is* involved could be binding on anyone. Hence, two of the three conditions are problematic and presumably not met. In order to avoid these difficulties, the incorporation theory opens up the possibility to treat the ECrtHR judgments as part of the Convention itself. Then one would not have to decide whether the judgments of the ECrtHR are decisions of an IO. Instead, one could simply refer to the fact that the ECHR is a treaty published in the Netherlands and therefore also all judgments of the ECrtHR are binding on the Netherlands. The question of whether a specific ECHR provision as interpreted by the ECrtHR is binding on anyone within the meaning of Articles 93, 94 Gw. is then left to the domestic courts to decide on case-by-case basis.

The *Hoge Raad* seems to apply the 'incorporation' model.[224] Accordingly, if one follows that approach, ECrtHR judgments as part of the ECHR enjoy primacy over all conflicting Dutch law –including the *Grondwet*. Similarly, Community law and ECJ judgments also enjoy primacy over all conflicting Dutch law (including the *Grondwet*), but with the difference that EC law always enjoys primacy over all conflicting Dutch law without having to fulfil the criteria of Articles 93, 94 Gw. So, at first sight, Dutch courts might be inclined, in a case of divergent interpretation of the ECHR, to give preference to the ECJ judgment. However, just as in the case of Germany, the Netherlands acceded to the ECHR before it acceded to the EC. Consequently, Article 307 EC Treaty is also applicable in the case of the Netherlands. Thus, in a case of diverging case-law between both European courts concerning a measure that falls within the 'field of application of Community law', Dutch courts would be able to give preference to a judgment of the ECrtHR by virtue of Article 307 EC Treaty.

An interesting practical example of the divergent case-law between the ECJ and the ECrtHR is the issue of the role of the Advocate General (AG) discussed

---

[224] See e.g.: Hoge Raad, judgment of 10.11.1989, NJ 1990, nr. 628; Hoge Raad, judgment of 10.5.1996, NJ 1996, nr. 578; Hoge Raad, judgment of 12.9.1997, RvdW 1997, nr. 168.

above. The ECrtHR ruled in the *J.J. v. the Netherlands* case that the impossibility of the parties to respond to the opinion of the Advocate General submitted in a case before the *Hoge Raad* is violating the right of adversarial proceedings as enshrined in Article 6 ECHR.[225] In contrast, as mentioned above, the ECJ does not consider the impossibility to respond to the opinion of the AG submitted before the ECJ to be comparable with the situation in the Member States and therefore does not regard this to be in violation of the ECHR.[226]

However, in this way a system of two different procedures is created. On the one hand, the parties in Dutch cases that are judged by the *Hoge Raad* have – by virtue of the ECrtHR case-law – the right to respond to the opinion of the AG (the Rules of Procedure of the *Hoge Raad* have been changed in the meantime).[227] On the other hand, in Dutch cases that come before the ECJ, for instance, within a preliminary ruling procedure, parties do not have a right to respond to the opinion delivered by the AG before the ECJ – although the preliminary ruling of the ECJ essentially determines the final judgment of the national court. Even more striking is the difference if one compares the domestic situation with the cases in which legal or natural individuals come as parties directly before the CFI or ECJ, such as in competition cases. In Dutch domestic competition cases, private parties have the right to respond to the opinion of the AG, while in competition cases that come before the CFI (where the role of the AG is taken over by a *judge-rapporteur*) or the ECJ, parties do not have such a right. In my opinion, there is no reason that would justify the difference in the procedural rights, therefore, the ECJ should change its Rules of Procedure so as to allow a right to respond to the opinion of the AG, thereby bringing EC law in line with ECHR law.[228]

2.3.3 France

According to Article 55 CF, international treaties enjoy primacy over conflicting national law (but not over the constitution) if they fulfil two conditions: first, the agreements must be properly ratified and published, and second, they must comply with the reciprocity principle, i.e. the application of the agreement by the other contracting parties.[229] Since the ECHR was duly ratified[230] and published[231] and since it is generally accepted that the reciprocity condition does not apply to the ECHR as it is the task of the ECrtHR to deter-

---

225 ECrtHR *J.J.* v. *the Netherlands*, judgment of 27.3.1998.

226 Case C-94/00 *Roquette Frères* [2002] ECR I-9011; C-466/00 *Kaba* [2003] ECR I-2219.

227 See case-note on the ECrtHR *J.J.* v. *the Netherlands* judgment by: Viering (1998); Ilsink (1998).

228 Benoît-Rohmer (2001b).

229 See generally: Labayle (1998).

230 Loi no. 73-1227, 31.12.1973 autorisant la raification.

231 Décret de publication no. 74-360, 3.5.1974, J.O., 4.5.1974.

mine whether the other contracting parties implement the ECHR properly,[232] all of the conditions of Article 55 CF are met. Accordingly, the ECHR falls within the scope of Article 55 CF and enjoys primacy over conflicting French statutes.

However, the question arises whether judgments of the ECrtHR also fall within the scope of Article 55 CF, as this provision only refers to international agreements. Assuming that is the case, if one applies a broad interpretation of Article 55 CF, the problem remains that there is no general obligation in French law to publish all international treaties and decisions of IOs.[233] Since ECrtHR judgments are not published in a French official gazette, one of the conditions of Article 55 CF is not met. Another way to bring judgments of the ECrtHR within the scope of Article 55 CF is to apply the 'incorporation' model, by arguing that the judgments are part of the ECHR itself. In fact, the *Cour de Cassation* seems to follow this model when it used the phrase:

> 'si l'article 6, alinéa 1er, de la Convention Européenne de sauvegarde des droits de l'homme et des libertés fondamentales, tel qu'interprété par un arrêt de la Cour Européenne des droits de l'homme [...]'.[234]

In a more recent judgment the *Cour de Cassation* used the phrase:

> 'attendu qu'en se déterminant ainsi, alors qu'il résulte des textes susvisés, tel qu'interprétés par la Cour européenne des droits de l'homme [...]'[235]

or the phrase

> 'attendu que la Cour Européenne des droits de l'homme a retenu que la violation de l'article 6 de la Convention [...]'.[236]

Thus, the *Cour de Cassation* applies the provisions of the ECHR as interpreted by the ECrtHR, thereby incorporating the case-law of the ECrtHR into the ECHR.[237] In addition, the *Conseil d'Etat* also appears to apply this approach although in a much more cautious and less explicit way.[238] Consequently, the French courts consider judgments of the ECrtHR as being part of the ECHR,

---

[232] Cassia/Saulnier (1997a) at 412.

[233] Alland (1998) at 1664.

[234] Cour de Cassation, 10.12.1985 (no. 84-16033); Cour de Cassation, 22.1.1985 (no. 84-10160).

[235] Cour de Cassation, 31.1.2002 (no. 00-18365).

[236] Cour de Cassation, 30.5.2002 (no. 01-99010).

[237] See e.g.: Cour de Cassation, 6.5.1997, Rec., 223; Cour de Cassation, 5.10.1999, Bull. civ. 1999, I, 167; Conseil d'Etat, 27.3.1998, RFDA 1998, 645; Conseil d'Etat, 14.2.1996, Rev.trim.dr.h. 1998, 397-410. See generally: Andriantsimbazovina/Sermet (1999); Lachaume (1998); Wachsmann (1998).

[238] Conseil d'Etat, 24.11.1997 (no. 171929); Conseil d'Etat, 13.10.2000 (no. 210942).

thus falling within the scope of Article 55 CF. Accordingly, ECrtHR judgments enjoy primacy over conflicting French statutes.

Moreover, it must be kept in mind that formally speaking, French courts are not bound by the judgments of the ECrtHR. In contrast, French courts (just as all EU Member States' courts) are bound by ECJ rulings, which enjoy primacy over all French law, including constitutional law. Accordingly, if a French court were faced with a diverging interpretation between the ECrtHR and the ECJ, it would be obliged by virtue of Community law to follow the ECJ judgment, so that any conflict would be solved in the advantage of the ECJ. This result is not modified by Article 307 EC Treaty because France, in contrast to Germany and the Netherlands, ratified the ECHR only in 1974, thus Article 307 EC Treaty cannot be applied as regards the ECHR.

As to the practical importance of such a divergence in case-law, the same problem concerning the role of Advocate General (AG) and *Commissaire du Gouvernement* as discussed in the case of the Netherlands can be identified also in France. As mentioned above, the ECrtHR determined in the *Reinhardt and Slimane-Kaïd*[239] case and the *Kress*[240] case that the impossibility to respond to the opinion of the AG submitted before the *Cour de Cassation* and the *Commissaire du Gouvernement* submitted before the *Conseil d'Etat,* is incompatible with Article 6 ECHR. In contrast, the ECJ does not consider the impossibility to respond to the opinion of AG delivered before the ECJ to be problematic with regard to Article 6 ECHR.[241] In this context, it should be noted that the case-law of the ECrtHR, which essentially amounts to determining minimum uniform procedural standards for all contracting parties of the Council of Europe, has been heavily criticized by French legal authors.[242] Be that as it may, the divergence between the ECJ and the ECrtHR on this point results in the creation of two different systems. On the national level, private parties involved in the cases before the *Conseil d'Etat* and the *Cour de Cassation* have recently obtained – by virtue of the case-law of the ECrtHR – the formal right to respond to the opinions of the AG and *Commissaire du Gouvernement* (and in addition, they are no longer allowed to participate in the deliberations of the courts).[243] While on the European level, private parties do not have such a right. Again, in my view, the

---

[239] ECrtHR *Reinhardt and Slimane-Kaïd* v. *France*, judgment of 31.3.1998.

[240] ECrtHR *Kress* v. *France*, judgment of 7.6.2001; see case-notes by: Serment (2002); Sudre (2001); Rolin, (2001).

[241] Case C-94/00 *Roquette Frères* [2002] ECR I-9011; C-466/00 *Kaba* [2003] ECR I-2219.

[242] See for details: Guinchard (2003); Maubernard (2001); Prétot (2001); case-note by: Benoît-Rohmer (1997).

[243] It should be noted that the Conseil d'Etat decided as late as 29.7.1998 that a right to respond to the opinion of the *Commissair du Gouvernement* does not exist on the basis of Article 6 ECHR, Conseil d'Etat (Esclatine), 29.7.1998 (no. 179635 180208).

only solution is to bring the rules of procedures of the CFI and ECJ in line with the case-law of the ECrtHR.[244]

In summary, it can be concluded that also in France the judgments of the ECrtHR are incorporated into the ECHR in order to bring them within the scope of Article 55 CF, which enables French courts to review the conformity of national statutes with the ECHR as interpreted by the ECrtHR. However, since France cannot rely on Article 307 EC Treaty, preference must be given to the ECJ and its interpretation of the ECHR – at least in all cases that concern measures that fall within the 'field of application of Community law'. Thus, in those cases the classic legal relationship 'ECHR law– national law' is modified into an 'EC law transformed' legal relationship 'ECHR law–EC law–national law'.

2.4 Summary

In the Netherlands and in France, the incorporation theory is applied to judgments of the ECrtHR, thus considering them part of the ECHR rather than qualifying them as decisions of an organ of an IO. In Germany, this issue does not play a role since the ECHR and the judgments of the ECrtHR first must be transposed by a domestic legal act before having any legal effect in Germany. While this narrow definition of the term 'decision of IO' is perfectly acceptable, it is submitted that, for the purpose of this research, judgments of the ECrtHR should be considered as binding decisions of an organ of an IO.

The EC is not a contracting party to the ECHR and thus is legally not bound by the binding judgments of the ECrtHR. Nevertheless, the European courts actively refer and apply the ECHR and the case-law of the ECrtHR. In this way, the ECHR and the case-law of the ECrtHR are integrated into the Community legal order, thereby obtaining Community law features such as supremacy over all national law and binding effect on all organs of the Member States. This transformation through EC law in turn upgrades the ECHR as interpreted by the ECrtHR in the domestic legal order from the level of statutes (Germany) and below the constitution (France) to the highest level, even above the constitution (as is already the case in the Netherlands). Consequently, while the EC and the European courts are not bound by the ECHR, the ECJ and CFI are able, by virtue of their jurisprudence and supremacy of Community law, to attach substantially more weight to the ECHR as interpreted by the ECrtHR in the domestic legal order of all Member States – at least as far as measures are concerned that fall within the 'field of application of Community law'.

Due to the fact that two European courts interpret and apply the ECHR, the possibility of a diverging interpretation of the ECHR cannot be excluded. This in turn could bring the national courts of the EU Member States into a difficult position where they would be faced with two divergent interpretations. However,

---

[244] See: Benoît-Rohmer (2001b).

in practice it appears that in most cases the ECJ and CFI follow the line of the ECrtHR and indeed sometimes go even further than the ECrtHR. Moreover, Article 307 EC Treaty enables the national courts in Germany and the Netherlands to give preference to the interpretation of the ECrtHR, while French courts cannot use Article 307 EC Treaty as regards the ECHR since France ratified the ECHR after the EC Treaty.

Thus, it can be concluded that as far as measures fall within the 'field of application of Community law', an 'EC law transformed' legal situation (ECHR–EC law–national law) is created by virtue of the ECJ and CFI jurisprudence and the supremacy of EC law – despite the fact that the EC is not party to the ECHR.

3 Concluding remarks

The case-studies examined in this Chapter illustrated the practical importance of the transformation judicial and quasi-judicial decisions through Community law and its impact on the national legal orders of the EC Member States. They show that judicial and quasi-judicial decisions are transformed in the same way as executive decisions of IOs discussed in Chapter 3. Moreover, the case-studies illustrated the interaction between on the one hand the Appellate Body, Panels and the ECrtHR and on the other hand, the ECJ and CFI. Indeed, the central role played by the ECJ and CFI in this interaction cannot be emphasized enough. This becomes particularly clear if one compares the opposing consequences of the ECJ jurisprudence on the legal effect of WTO dispute settlement reports vis-à-vis judgments of ECrtHR. Whereas in the case of the WTO dispute settlement reports, the jurisprudence of the ECJ and CFI certifies and thus prolongs the application of EC law that has been judged to be inconsistent with WTO law and thus forcing Member States to violate their international legal obligations, the ECJ actively communitarizes the ECHR and the case-law of the ECrtHR and thereby upgrades them to the highest norm in the domestic legal order of the EU Member States. Indeed, the contrast between them cannot be greater when it comes to the protection and effective exercise of the fundamental rights contained in the ECHR. On the one hand, the ECJ and CFI have repeatedly stated that access to justice as enshrined in Articles 6 and 13 ECHR and the existence of a complete system of legal remedies is of fundamental importance in the Community legal order. On the other hand, the jurisprudence of the ECJ and CFI regarding WTO law, especially WTO dispute settlement reports, makes it extremely difficult to exercise effectively this right. Finally, it can be observed that the residual competence of the EU Member States and of their courts, i.e. the existence of a classic legal relationship 'Decisions of IO–national law', has been substantially reduced by virtue of Community law. As regards WTO law, the classic legal situation exists only for GATS and TRIPs matters that have not yet been covered by EC legislation. As regards

ECHR law, the classic legal situation still exists for measures that fall outside the 'field of application of Community law'. Although, that might appear to be still quite a broad area of competence for the EU Member States, the *Carpenter* and *Baumbast* cases of the ECJ indicate that the existence of a very weak link between the national measure and Community law can be sufficient to bring it within the 'field of application of Community law' and thus create an 'EC law transformed' legal situation involving ECHR law. In this context the draft text of the European Constitution should be recalled. Article I-7 provides for the possibility of accession of the Union to the ECHR. As regards the relationship between the Union and the ECHR, Article II-52 (3) draft European Constitution states that insofar as the Charter contains rights which correspond to rights guaranteed by the ECHR, the meaning and scope of those rights shall be the same as those laid down by the ECHR, whilst this does not prevent the Union law providing more extensive protection. Moreover, Article II-53 draft European Constitution states that the Charter shall not restrict or adversely affect human rights protected *inter alia* by the ECHR. Thus, if the Union would accede to the ECHR, the case-law of the ECrtHR would become formally binding on the ECJ and CFI as far as it concerns the field of application of Union law (Article II-51). This in turn would modify the 'EC law transformed' legal situation (ECHR law–EC law–national law) into a classic legal situation (ECHR law–Union law).

In summary, it can be concluded that the involvement of European law, in particular in the form of the ECJ and CFI jurisprudence, does affect the legal status and effect of judicial and quasi-judicial decisions but with very different results.

CHAPTER 5

Decisions Adopted by the EU within the II. and III. Pillars

The purpose of this Chapter is to assess whether, and if so, to what extent Community law principles such as supremacy and direct effect can be applied to decisions adopted by the EU within the so-called II. pillar (Common Foreign and Security Policy) and III. pillar (Justice and Home Affairs, renamed Police and Judicial Co-operation in Criminal Matters). Whereas the previous Chapters dealt with decisions adopted by IOs and thus outside the framework of the EC, this Chapter will examine decisions adopted within the framework of the EU. Since the legal situation of the EU differs in many ways from the one of the EC, the decisions of the EU can to a certain extent be compared with decisions adopted by other IOs. Hence, whereas the EU adopts various binding decisions which impose legal obligations on the EU Member States, the EU allows Member States – to a varying degree – to decide how to implement them. Accordingly, at first sight the legal relationship between the EU acting within the II. and III. pillars vis-à-vis its Member States appears to be a classic one 'EU law–national law'. However, for the following reasons it is quite possible that Community law principles such as supremacy and direct effect influence the classic legal situation in such a way that it can be compared with the 'EC law transformed' legal relationship discussed in the previous Chapters.

In the first place, there is the example of a formal link between a II. pillar decision and a I. pillar instrument in the case of the implementation of Security Council Resolutions. As has been discussed above, the EU implements a Security Council Resolution imposing a trade embargo by first adopting a Common Position in the II. pillar and then issuing an EC Regulation. In this way the classic legal relationship 'EU law–national law' is modified into an 'EC law influenced EU law–national law' legal relationship.

In the second place, there is the functional double-role of the same institutions involved in the decision-making process in all three pillars (*Doppelorganschaft*).[1] While the European Council is the only formal body established by the TEU responsible for the – mainly political – development of the EU,[2] it is in particular the Council and to a much lesser extent the Commission and European Parliament that adopts most legally binding decisions within the II. and III. pillars. In other words, the institutions of the Community are also involved in the decision-making process – albeit under different terms – in the II. and III. pillars.

In the third place, while there are still differences in many respects between the three pillars, it is submitted that the European legal order is considered to be one unified legal order, that is, EC law and EU law belong to the same legal order emanating from the same International Organization (the EU).[3] Consequently, it is possible that Community law features, such as supremacy and direct effect,

---

1 See: Trüe (1997); *ibid.*, (2000).

2 See: Pernice (2003); De Jonghe/Burens (2003); van Grinsven/Melissen (2002).

3 See: Wessel (2003); V. Bogdandy (1999); Pernice (1999); Curtin/Dekker (1999).

are also applicable – possibly to a varying degree – in the II. and III. pillars. This line of argument is also supported by the current discussions in the European Convention that illustrate that the differences between the various pillars will probably be substantially reduced concerning many aspects, for instance, the replacement of III. pillar decisions by EC instruments, the full extension of ECJ jurisdiction to the III. pillar, the reorganization and simplification of the Treaties, replacing all II. pillar instruments by Council decisions, maximum use of QVM in II. Pillar, etc.[4]

Accordingly, the following issues must be discussed. First, can the EU be qualified as an IO when acting within the II. and III. pillars? Second, are the decisions adopted within the II. and III. pillars legally binding on the Member States? Third, are Community law features such as supremacy and direct effect also applicable to II. and III. pillar decisions? Based on the analysis of those questions, it remains to be discussed to what extent can the 'EC law influenced' legal relationship be compared to the 'EC law transformed' legal relationship discussed in the previous Chapters?

1 The EU as an IO when acting within the II. and III. pillars

Recalling the broad definition of an IO as discussed in the introduction, it must be determined whether the EU has been established by an international agreement and endowed with at least one organ that can adopt binding decisions independently from the contracting parties.

Since the Member States of the EU established the EU by virtue of the Maastricht Treaty that entered into force in 1993, the EU has been established by an international agreement.[5] Hence, it must now be determined whether the EU is endowed with organs that have the competence to adopt binding decisions independently from the Member States.

First, the TEU created the European Council as a new organ of the EU (Articles 4, 13 TEU).[6] The European Council is first and foremost responsible to 'provide the Union with the necessary impetus for its development and shall define the general political guidelines' (Article 4 TEU). Considering its very 'heavy' composition of the Heads of State or Government, the President of the Commission, assisted by the Ministers of Foreign Affairs and a member of the Commission, the European Council is of crucial importance for the main future

4 See: Final Report of Working X 'Freedom, Security and Justice', 2.12.2002, CONV 426/02; Final Report of Working Group VII – 'External Action', 16.12.2002, CONV 459/02; Final Report of Working Group IX on Simplification, 29.11.2002, CONV 424/02. See on the last report: De Witte (2002); Von Bogdandy/Bast/Arndt (2002).

5 See: Pernice (1999) in particular at 711-715.

6 De Witte (1998) at 60.

development of the EU.[7] Second, the European Council is also responsible to 'define the principles of and general guidelines for the CFSP, including matters of defence implications' (Article 13 (1) TEU). Third, in addition to these political functions, the European Council has also a legal function since it is competent within the framework of the CFSP to adopt legally binding acts in the form of common strategies (Article 13 (2) TEU).[8] The common strategies 'shall set out their objectives, duration and the means to be made available by the Union and the Member States' and are implemented by the Council, in particular by adopting joint actions and common positions (Article 13 (3) TEU). Thus, the European Council is an organ established by the TEU endowed with the competence to adopt legally binding decisions, although it is interesting to note that, according to the General Secretariat of the EU Council, so far the legal value of common strategies has been limited.[9]

Besides, as mentioned above, also the Community institutions are involved in the decision-making process within the II. and III. pillars. According to Article 3 TEU, the 'EU is served by a single institutional framework'. Article 5 TEU explains what is meant by the term 'single institutional framework':

> 'The European Parliament, the Council, the Commission, the Court of Justice and the Court of Auditors shall exercise their powers under the conditions and for the purposes provided for, on the one hand by [the EC Treaty] ... and on other hand, by the provisions of this Treaty [the TEU]'.

In other words, the same organs that act within the EC are also exercising their powers conferred to them by the TEU within the II. pillar and III. pillar of the EU (*Doppelorganschaft*).[10] Thus, these institutions must in fact be considered as institutions of the Union.[11]

However, establishing the existence of organs acting for the EU is not sufficient. In addition, they must also be able to act independently from the Member States. As will be discussed below, it is the Council of the EU and not the Member States that adopts the various decisions in the II. and III. pillars. Therefore, all essential conditions for qualifying the EU as an IO are fulfilled.[12] This conclusion is also confirmed by draft Article I-6 of the European Constitutional Treaty[13] that provides for a single legal personality, thereby explicitly extending

7 Pernice (2003); De Jonghe/Burens (2003); van Grinsven/Melissen (2002).

8 See e.g.: 1999/414/CFSP: Common Strategy of the European Union of 4 June 1999 on Russia, OJ 1999 L 157/1-10; see also: Trüe (1997) at 14-16; *ibid.*, (2000) at 140-143; Hillion (2000).

9 Common Strategies: Report by the Secretary-General/High Representative, 14871/00 of 21.12.2000; similar observation by Final Report of Working Group VII – 'External Relations', at 25.

10 See: Trüe (1997) at 16-20, and more explicitly in (2000) at 144-147.

11 Wessel (1999) at 74-75.

12 See: Klabbers (1998) at 242; De Witte (1998); Devroe/Wouters (1996) at 65-66.

13 CONV 850/03, 18.7.2003.

the EC's legal personality (Article 281 EC Treaty) to the EU. Moreover, since the EC undoubtedly meets the criteria of an IO, the single legal personality of the Union will support the conclusion that the whole Union must be considered to meet the criteria of an IO.[14]

2 The legal effect of II. and III. pillar decisions

In this section, the various instruments of the II. and III. pillars are discussed separately, in particular with regard to the question of whether and, if so, to what extent are they legally binding on the Member States?

2.1 The II. pillar decisions

The EU Treaty enumerates Common Positions (Article 15 TEU) and Joint Actions (Article 14 TEU) as the two legal instruments to be used in order to implement the CFSP of the EU.[15]

2.1.1 Common Positions

Article 15 [Common Positions]

> The Council shall adopt Common Positions. Common Positions shall define the approach of the Union to a particular matter of a geographical or thematic nature. Member States shall ensure that their national policies conform to the Common Positions.

The scope of Common Positions is broadly defined. According to Wessel, Common Positions basically cover three main areas.[16]

Firstly, Common Positions are used to implement sanctions imposed by the UN Security Council under Chapter VII against a certain state. Common Positions falling under this category make up the bulk of Common Positions issued by the EU. This is mainly due to the fact that Articles 301, 60 EC Treaty require the adoption of either a Common Position or Joint Action before an EC Regulation implementing economic sanctions can be issued. However, the EU also uses Common Positions when it imposes sanctions independently from the UN Security Council.[17]

---

[14] See: Wessel (2003).

[15] See extensively: Wessel (1999).

[16] *Ibid.* at 175.

[17] 98/725/CFSP: Common Position of 14.12.1998 defined by the Council on the basis of Article J.2 of the Treaty on European Union on restrictive measures to be taken against persons in the Federal Republic of Yugoslavia acting against the independent media, OJ 1998 L 345/1-2.

An example for the implementation of UN sanctions by the EU is the Common Position against Usama bin Laden and the Al-Qaida organization.[18]

'THE COUNCIL OF THE EUROPEAN UNION,

Having regard to the Treaty on European Union, and in particular Article 15 thereof,

Whereas:

[...]

(2) On 16 January 2002 the United Nations Security Council adopted Resolution 1390 (2002), hereinafter referred to as 'UNSCR 1390 (2002)', setting out measures to be imposed against Usama bin Laden, members of the Al-Qaida organisation and the Taliban and other individuals, groups, undertakings and entities associated with them.

(3) UNSCR 1390 (2002) adjusts the scope of the sanctions concerning the freezing of funds, the visa ban and the embargo on supply, sale or transfer of arms as well as on technical advice, assistance or training related to military activities imposed by UNSCR 1267 (1999) and 1333 (2000).

[...]

(8) For the sake of clarity and transparency, those European Union restrictive measures as referred to in the relevant Council Common Positions should be compiled in one legal instrument and therefore Common Positions 96/746/CFSP (1), 1999/727/CFSP (2), 2001/154/CFSP (3) and 2001/771/CFSP (4) should be repealed.

(9) Action by the Community is needed in order to implement certain measures,

HAS ADOPTED THIS COMMON POSITION:

Article 1

This Common Position applies to Usama bin Laden, members of the Al-Qaida organisation and the Taliban and other individuals, groups, undertakings and entities associated with them, as referred to in the list drawn up pursuant to UNSCR 1267 (1999) and 1333 (2000) to be updated regularly by the Committee established pursuant to UNSCR 1267 (1999).

---

[18] Council Common Position 2002/402/CFSP of 27.5.2002, concerning restrictive measures against Usama bin Laden, members of the Al-Qaida organization and the Taliban and other individuals, groups, undertakings and entities associated with them and repealing Common Positions 96/746/CFSP, 1999/727/CFSP, 2001/154/CFSP and 2001/771/CFSP, OJ 2002 L 139/4.

Article 2

1.The direct or indirect supply, sale and transfer to the individuals, groups, undertakings and entities referred to in Article 1 of arms and related materiel of all types including weapons and ammunition, military vehicles and equipment, paramilitary equipment, and spare parts for the aforementioned, from the territories of the Member States, or using their flag vessels or aircraft, or by nationals of Member States outside their territories, under the conditions set out in UNSCR 1390(2002), shall be prohibited. [...]'

Secondly, Common Positions are used by the EU to develop its policy regarding third states. As Wessel writes, Common Positions are often used to express the EU's concern about developments in a certain state or to formulate in general terms objectives of the EU regarding a third state.[19] An example for a Common Position in this category is the following one concerning Rwanda.[20]

'THE COUNCIL OF THE EUROPEAN UNION,

[...]

HAS ADOPTED THIS COMMON POSITION:

Article 1

The objectives and priorities of the European Union in its relations with Rwanda are to encourage, stimulate and support the ongoing process of:

(a) recovery from genocide and the promotion of national reconciliation,

(b) reconstruction and development,

(c) protection and promotion of human rights and fundamental freedoms,

(d) transition to democracy.

Insofar as regional instability may jeopardise the achievement of these goals, the European Union shall encourage the Government of Rwanda to work, in particular through its foreign policy, towards the achievement of regional stability, as it does with all other parties to conflicts in the region.

Article 2

The European Union affirms that progress in the areas referred to in Article 1 is primarily the responsibility of the Government of Rwanda. In order to support and encourage its efforts, the European Union shall pursue a constructive and critical dialogue with the Government of Rwanda, including through the offices of its Special Envoy to the African Great Lakes Region, on the basis of the following provisions. [...]'

---

19 Wessel (1999) at 178.

20 Council Common Position of 18 September 2000 on Rwanda, OJ 2000 L 236/1-3.

Thirdly, Common Positions are used to develop the EU's policy on specific issues. For instance, Common Positions are used to coordinate and establish a common position in the framework of negotiations leading towards an international agreement.[21] An example for a Common Position on a specific issue is the following supporting the OAU in the peace process between Ethiopia and Eritrea.[22]

> 'THE COUNCIL OF THE EUROPEAN UNION,
> [...]
> HAS ADOPTED THIS COMMON POSITION:
>
> **Article 1**
> The objective of this Common Position is to support the OAU peace process between Ethiopia and Eritrea.
>
> **Article 2**
> The European Union shall in coordinated manner support action taken by the Organisation of African Unity and the United Nations for the implementation of the OAU peace settlement, including the cessation of hostilities agreement signed by the two countries concerned on 18 June 2000. The European Union shall support in particular the deployment of international observers, the delimitation and demarcation of borders, mine-clearance and efforts to assist refugees and displaced persons.
>
> **Article 3**
> The Council notes that the Commission may direct its action towards achieving the objectives of this Common Position, where appropriate, by relevant Community measures.
>
> **Article 4**
> The European Union and its Member States reserve the right to modify or cancel any activities in support of the implementation of the OAU peace package if the parties do not abide by the terms thereof. [...]'

As to the legal effect of Common Positions, especially regarding a possible binding effect on the EU Member States, the second sentence of Article 15 TEU simply states that the national policies of the Member States shall be in conformity with the Common Positions. The question is: what does this mean?

---

21 Wessel (1999) at 181.

22 Council Common Position of 29 June 2000 concerning EU support for the OAU peace process between Ethiopia and Eritrea, OJ 2000 L 161/1.

Essentially one could distinguish between a general and a concrete legal effect of Common Positions. As to the general legal effect, Article 15 TEU requires *in abstracto* a minimum of loyalty from the Member States comparable to Article 10 EC Treaty. Thus, Member States are in general terms required to act in a way that does not undermine the achievement of the aims of Common Positions.[23]

The concrete legal effect of Common Positions for the Member States depends on the specific contents of each Common Position. This is particularly the case because Common Positions are used for a variety of purposes, ranging from adopting political programs to implementing sanctions. But as the above-mentioned examples and the research of Wessel indicate, most Common Positions set out the *Union's* policy – at least in the first place.[24] Thus, the legal obligation of the Member States is more of a passive nature in the sense of not acting contrary to Common Positions. Nevertheless, it should be emphasized that there are Common Positions that are clearly addressed to the Member States. For instance, in the case of sanctions, Common Positions require the EU Member States to prohibit the trade between them and the targeted country and freeze all assets.[25] Another example is the Common Position on combating terrorism that specifically directs the Member States to adopt the required measures.[26]

2.1.2 Joint Actions

Article 14 [Joint Actions]

1. The Council shall adopt Joint Actions. Joint Actions shall address specific situations where operational action by the Union is deemed to be required. They shall lay down their objectives, scope, means to be made available to the Union, if necessary their duration, and the conditions for their implementation.
2. (...)
3. Joint Actions shall commit the Member States in the positions they adopt and in the conduct of their activity.

---

[23] Trüe (2000) at 157; even Koenig/Pechstein(1998) acknowledge 'eine indirekte Rechtsbindung' at 127, no. 233.

[24] Wessel (1999) at 180.

[25] See for instance: 1999/318/CFSP: Common Position of 10.5.1999 adopted by the Council on the basis of Article 15 of the Treaty on European Union concerning additional restrictive measures against the Federal Republic of Yugoslavia, OJ 1999 L 123/1-2.

[26] 2001/931/CFSP: Council Common Position of 27.12.2001 on the application of specific measures to combat terrorism, OJ 2001 L 344/93.

In contrast to Common Positions, the wording of Article 14 TEU implies that Joint Actions come into play when 'operational action' is required. Indeed, it is only very recently that the EU has adopted its first Joint Actions that involve under its supervision 'operational action' in the form of police and military tasks in the Balkans.[27]

'THE COUNCIL OF THE EUROPEAN UNION,

Having regard to the Treaty on European Union and, in particular, Article 14, Article 25, third subparagraph, Article 26 and Article 28(3) thereof,

[...]

HAS ADOPTED THIS JOINT ACTION:

Article 1

Mission

1. Based on arrangements with NATO and subject to a further decision by the Council, as specified in Article 3, the European Union shall conduct a European Union military operation in the Former Yugoslav Republic of Macedonia, at the request of the FYROM government, in order to ensure the follow-on to the NATO operation "Allied Harmony".

2. The forces deployed to that effect shall operate in accordance with the objectives set out in the general concept approved by the Council.

3. The operation shall be carried out with recourse to NATO assets and capabilities, on the basis agreed with NATO.

[...]

THE COUNCIL OF THE EUROPEAN UNION,

Having regard to the Treaty on European Union and, in particular, Article 14 thereof,

[..]

Article 1

Mission

1. The European Union hereby establishes a European Union Police Mission (EUPM) in order to ensure the follow-on to the United Nations International Police Task Force (IPTF) in Bosnia and Herzegovina (BiH) as from 1 January 2003. Before that date and in order to prepare the EUPM a Planning Team shall be established not later than 1 April 2002 and shall be operational until 31 December 2002.

2. The EUPM shall operate in accordance with the objectives and other provisions as contained in the mission statement set out in the Annex hereto.'

---

27 Council Joint Action 2003/92/CFSP of 27.1.2003 on the European Union military operation in the Former Yugoslav Republic of Macedonia, OJ 2003 L 34/26; Council Joint Action of 11.3.2002 on the European Union Police Mission, OJ 2002 L 70/1.

Prior to that, Joint Actions were mainly used to cover two broad areas.[28]

First, many Joint Actions dealt with 'support activities in third countries'. These are not always directed to the Member States but rather to the Union/ Council or the Presidency of the Council (that is to the EU itself). These Joint Actions contain obligations to adopt certain measures by the EU or its organs. For instance, the Joint Action to support the Georgian authorities concerning an OSCE mission contains obligations specifically directed towards the EU as a whole as well as towards several EU institutions.[29]

> **'Article 1**
>
> 1. The European Union shall provide assistance to reinforce the capacity of the Georgian authorities to provide, through their Border Guards, support and protection for the OSCE Observer Mission on the border of Georgia with the Chechen Republic of the Russian Federation.
>
> 2. For this purpose, the European Union shall provide aid to the Government of Georgia by 15 September 2000 in the form of equipment which shall be transported to the Shatili border post by 30 September 2000.
>
> **Article 2**
>
> 1. The Council shall entrust the Commission with the implementation of this Joint Action with a view to meeting the objective specified in Article 1(2).
>
> 2. The Commission shall monitor and evaluate the effective delivery of the equipment to the Georgian Border Guards, its further use and the successful implementation of this Joint Action.
>
> 3. The Commission shall report to the Council under the authority of the Presidency assisted by the Secretary-General of the Council, High Representative for the CFSP.
>
> 4. In carrying out its activities, the Commission will cooperate, as appropriate, with local missions of Member States.'

Second, Joint Actions are used to shape the general international policies of the EU. For example, a Joint Action was used to lay down the actions to be taken by the EU with regard to the problem of anti-personnel landmines.[30]

---

[28] Wessel (1999) at 163-167.

[29] Council Joint Action of 20.7.2000 regarding a contribution of the European Union towards reinforcing the capacity of the Georgian authorities to support and protect the OSCE Observer Mission on the border of the Republic of Georgia with the Chechen Republic of the Russian Federation, OJ 2000 L 183/3.

[30] Joint Action 97/817/CFSP of 28.11.1997 adopted by the Council on the basis of Article J.3 of the Treaty on European Union, on anti-personnel landmines, OJ 1997 L 338/1-4.

> 'THE COUNCIL OF THE EUROPEAN UNION,
> [...]
> HAS ADOPTED THIS JOINT ACTION:
>
> **Article 1**
>
> The Union is committed to the goal of total elimination of anti-personnel landmines worldwide as well as to contributing to solving the problems already caused by these weapons. The aim of this Joint Action is to reinforce the extensive political and practical actions already taken by the Union in pursuit of these objectives.
>
> To this end, this Joint Action entails three elements, as set out in Titles I, II and III:
>
> - continued political efforts by the Union in pursuit of these objectives,
> - a common moratorium on transfers and a common moratorium on production of anti-personnel landmines,
> - a multi-faceted contribution by the Union to mine-clearance and related activities.
>
> **Article 2**
>
> The Union is committed to the goal of total elimination of anti-personnel landmines worldwide and welcomes in this connection the Convention on the prohibition of the use, stockpiling, production and transfer of anti-personnel mines and on their destruction. [...]'

Besides the above, Joint Actions are also used for the establishment of institutions and appointments of special envoys.[31]

Also in the case of Joint Actions, one can distinguish between a general and a possible specific legal obligation of the Member States. The general legal obligation is expressed by the words 'shall commit the Member States in the positions they adopt and in the conduct of their activity' used in Article 14 (3) TEU. This general obligation can – to a certain extent – be compared to the general obligation imposed by Article 25 UN Charter on the UN member states regarding binding Security Council Resolutions.[32] In both cases, the addressees are the member states of the IO and, in both cases, they are legally required to act in such a way as to give full effect to the binding decision taken by the organ of the IO.

---

[31] See e.g.: Council Joint Action of 14.12.2000 appointing the Special Representative of the European Union for the African Great Lakes Region and repealing Joint Action 96/250/CFSP; Council Joint Action of 14.12.2000 appointing the Special Representative of the European Union to act as Coordinator of the Stability Pact for South-Eastern Europe and repealing Joint Action 1999/523/CFSP; Council Joint Action of 14.12.2000 appointing the European Union Special Representative for the Middle East peace process and repealing Joint Action 96/676/CFSP. All published in: OJ 2000 L 318/1-5.

[32] Wessel (1999) at 156.

The specific legal obligation of Joint Actions for the Member States depends on the contents of each Joint Action and thus must be determined on a case-by-case basis. As mentioned above, a Joint Action may only oblige the Union and/or its organs to act in a particular way as the above-mentioned Joint Action on Georgia shows, but a Joint Action[33] may also request the EU Member States to adopt the following measures:

> **'Article 3**
> Member States shall consider the application of such controls also in cases where the technical assistance relates to military end-uses other than those referred to in Article 2 and is provided in countries of destination subject to an arms embargo decided by a common position or joint action adopted by the Council or a decision of the OSCE or an arms embargo imposed by a binding resolution of the Security Council of the United Nations. [...]
>
> **Article 5**
> Each Member State which has not yet included in its national legislation or practices control provisions which implement this Joint Action or determined the sanctions to be taken shall bring forward appropriate proposals to:
> (a) implement this Joint Action through laying down control provisions;
> (b) determine the sanctions to be taken at national level. [...]'

This Joint Action is clearly directed towards the Member States and contains specific legal obligations imposed on them by the EU. In other words, in this case the Council of the EU has taken a legally binding decision vis-à-vis its Member States.[34]

2.1.3 The choice between Common Position and Joint Action

Formally speaking, the difference in language between Articles 14 and 15 TEU suggests a legal distinction between situations where 'operational action is deemed to be required' and where a decision relates to 'the approach of the Union to a particular matter'. This seems to imply that Joint Actions are used for more important or 'heavy' decisions requiring specific implementation acts by the Member States, while Common Positions would be used more for political and diplomatic purposes as a tool to co-ordinate the position of the EU and the Member States. However, practice shows that the Council is not always

---

33 Council Joint Action of 22.6.2000 concerning the control of technical assistance related to certain military end-uses, OJ 2000 L 159/216-217.

34 Another example of a Council Joint Action imposing legally binding obligations on the Member States is: 97/817/CFSP: Joint Action of 28.11.1997 adopted by the Council on the basis of Article J.3 of the Treaty on European Union, on anti-personnel landmines, OJ 1997 L 338/1-4.

consistent in the application of these two instruments. According to Wessel, two indicators exist that determine in many cases the choice between Joint Actions and Common Positions.[35] The first indicator concerns the imposition of sanctions. Although, Article 301 EC Treaty states 'where it is provided, in a Common Position or Joint Action', and thus implying that both instruments can be used, the Council has always been using Common Positions for the imposition of sanctions. The second indicator refers to the fact that most Joint Actions are explicitly based on general guidelines of the European Council, which is not the case for Common Positions. Moreover, as mentioned above, the most recent practice of the EU indicates that Joint Actions have finally been used for their primary purpose, namely, for 'heavy' operational actions.

2.2 The III. pillar decisions

Article 34 TEU identifies the instruments to be used in the III. pillar in order to achieve the aim set out in Article 29 TEU, i.e., to create an area of freedom, security and justice with a high level of safety for the European citizens.

Whereas Article 34 (1) TEU calls upon the Member States to inform and consult one another within the Council in order to co-ordinate their actions, Article 34 (2) TEU enumerates a number of legal instruments that can be used by the Council. Article 34 (2) TEU reads as follows:

> **'Article 34 (2) TEU**
> [...] acting unanimously on the initiative of any MS or the Commission, the Council may:
> a) adopt *Common Positions* defining the approach of the Union to a particular matter;
> b) adopt *Framework Decisions* for the purpose of approximation of the laws of and regulations of the MS. Framework Decisions shall be binding upon the Member States as to the result to be achieved but shall leave to the national authorities the choice of form and methods. They shall not entail direct effect;
> c) adopt *Decisions* of any other purpose consistent with the objectives of this Title, excluding any approximation of laws and regulations of the MS. These decisions shall be binding and shall not entail direct effect; the Council, acting by a QMV, shall adopt measures necessary to implement those decisions at the level of the Union, [...]'

Moreover, the Council has been using also other instruments not mentioned in Article 34 TEU such as Council Resolutions, Conclusions and Recommendations.[36] However, it is submitted that these instruments must be considered as

---

[35] Wessel (1999) at 129-130.

[36] Zott (1999) at 214 and at 287; Peers (2000) at 29-30.

legally non-binding acts and therefore will not be discussed. Finally, it should be noted that this section will focus only on the binding legal instruments available within the III. pillar, leaving out the whole issue of the transfer of the Schengen *aquis*.[37]

2.2.1 Common Positions

As a preliminary remark, it should be recalled that Common Positions were introduced by the Amsterdam Treaty. Prior to the entry into force of the Amsterdam Treaty, the Maastricht Treaty provided for Joint Positions, which were to be used in order 'to promote, using the appropriate form and procedures, any co-operation contributing to the pursuit of the objectives of the Union'.

Accordingly, a pre-Amsterdam Joint Position was used to harmonize the application of the term 'refugee' in the EU Member States when processing applications for refugee status.[38] In addition, a pre-Amsterdam Joint Position was used for more practical purposes such as setting up training assistance in third countries in order to assist local police officers at third country airports when checking Member States' travel and visa-documents.[39] Finally, pre-Amsterdam Joint Positions were used to coordinate the position of the Member States in ongoing negotiations in international fora.[40]

Instead, Common Positions are currently used only for the coordination of negotiation positions of the Member States within the framework of negotiations concerning international treaties. For example, a Common Position was used to coordinate the negotiation position of the Member States regarding the Council of Europe Convention on Cyber Crime.[41] Similarly, a Common Position was used to co-ordinate the position of the Member States in the negotiations in

---

[37] See for a detailed analysis: Hailbronner (2000).

[38] 96/196/JHA: Joint Position of 4.3.1996 defined by the Council on the basis of Article K.3 of the Treaty on European Union on the harmonized application of the definition of the term 'refugee' in Article 1 of the Geneva Convention of 28.7.1951 relating to the status of refugees, OJ 1996 L 063/2-7.

[39] 96/622/JHA: Joint Position of 25.10.1996 defined by the Council on the basis of Article K.3 (2) (a) of the Treaty on European Union, on pre-frontier assistance and training assignments, OJ 1996 L 281/1-2.

[40] 97/783/JHA: Second Joint Position of 13.11.1997 defined by the Council on the basis of Article K.3 of the Treaty on European Union on negotiations held in the Council of Europe and the OECD on the fight against corruption, OJ 1997 L 320/1-2; 1999/235/JHA: Joint Position of 29.3.1999 defined by the Council on the basis of Article K.3 of the Treaty on European Union, on the proposed United Nations convention against organised crime, OJ 1999 L 087/1-2.

[41] 1999/364/JHA: Common Position of 27.5.1999 adopted by the Council on the basis of Article 34 of the Treaty on European Union, on negotiations relating to the Draft Convention on Cyber Crime held in the Council of Europe, OJ 1999 L 142/1.

the OECD and the Council of Europe concerning the fight against corruption.[42] Finally, a Common Position was also used with regard to the Protocol against illicit manufacturing of and trafficking in firearms supplementing the UN Convention against transnational organised crime.[43]

Neither Article 34 (2) TEU nor any other provision of the TEU give any indication as to the legal effect of Common Positions of the III. Pillar. According to Degen, they cannot be qualified as legally binding decisions under public international law, but rather simply constitute '*politische* gentlemen's agreements'.[44] Similarly, Monar also assumes that 'a Common Position is a decision on political strategy rather than a binding legal act.'[45] However, in my view, the fact that Article 37 TEU explicitly calls upon the Member States to 'defend adopted Common Positions' in international fora, indicates that Common Positions require at the very least *in abstracto* a minimum of loyalty from the EU Member States – otherwise it would make no sense to require Member States to 'defend them' on the international level. In addition, depending on the contents, Common Positions may contain specific obligations requiring the EU institutions and/or the EU Member States to act in certain way or to achieve a certain result. Such Common Positions must be considered to be legally binding.

2.2.2 Framework Decisions

In the first place, it should be noted that Framework Decisions were introduced by the Amsterdam Treaty as new instruments for the III. pillar. Framework Decisions and the newly introduced Decisions[46] have replaced the Joint Actions within the III. pillar. Prior to the Amsterdam Treaty, Article K.3 (2) (b) TEU provided for the adoption of

> 'Joint Actions in so far as the objectives of the Union can be attained better by joint action than by the Member States acting individually on account of the scale or effects of the action envisaged [...]'.

Instead, as Article 34 (2) (b) TEU explicitly states, Framework Decisions shall be used for the approximation of laws and regulations of the Member States. This

---

[42] 97/661/JHA: Common Position of 6.10.1997 defined by the Council on the basis of Article K.3 of the Treaty on European Union on negotiations in the Council of Europe and the OECD relating to corruption, OJ 1997 L 279/1.

[43] 2000/130/JHA: Council Common Position of 31.1.2000 on the proposed protocol against the illicit manufacturing of and trafficking in firearms, their parts and components and ammunition, supplementing the United Nations Convention against transnational organised crime, OJ 2000 L 37/1.

[44] Degen (1997) at 1058.

[45] Monar (1998) at 327.

[46] See below.

formulation goes much further than the previous one because it now explicitly allows the Council to approximate the laws of the Member States in policy areas that previously were clearly outside the competence of the EU. In fact, this formulation ('approximate the laws of the Member States') is comparable to Article 95 EC Treaty, which allows for the approximation of laws of the Member States through Directives and Regulations to create a functioning internal market.[47]

The pre-Amsterdam Joint Actions were used for different purposes, ranging from co-ordinating the policies of Member States to requiring Member States to change their national laws. An example of a pre-Amsterdam Joint Action is the one on 'good practice in mutual legal assistance in criminal matters' in which Member States were required to deposit within 12 months a statement of good practice indicating the procedures for handling requests of assistance in criminal matters.[48] A Joint Action was also used to create a new 'European Judicial Network' between the Member States, which shall enhance the contacts and the exchange of experience between members of the judicial authorities of the Member States.[49] A more far-reaching example of a pre-Amsterdam Joint Action is the one on making the participation in a criminal organization a criminal offence in all EU Member States.[50] This Joint Action defines in detail the legal requirements that all Member States are obliged to implement in order to make participation in a criminal organizations punishable under their criminal codes.

However, the full legal impact of the transformation of Joint Actions into Framework Decisions is only now becoming visible with the first Framework Decisions that have recently been adopted. For example, the Council adopted a Framework Decision on combating terrorism.[51] This Framework Decision defines in detail those offences uniformly considered to be terrorist offences in all EU Member States and also prescribes the minimum penalties that must be applied for those offences. In other words, this measure essentially harmonizes the criminal law of the EU Member States – at least as regards those offences.

---

47 See: Monar (1998) at 326.

48 98/427/JHA: Joint Action of 29.6.1998 adopted by the Council on the basis of Article K.3 of the Treaty on European Union, on good practice in mutual legal assistance in criminal matters, OJ 1998 L 191/1-3.

49 98/428/JHA: Joint Action of 29.6.1998 adopted by the Council on the basis of Article K.3 of the Treaty on European Union, on the creation of a European Judicial Network, OJ 1998 L 191/4-7.

50 98/733/JHA: Joint action of 21.12.1998 adopted by the Council on the basis of Article K.3 of the Treaty on European Union, on making it a criminal offence to participate in a criminal organisation in the Member States of the European Union, OJ 1998 L 351/1-3.

51 Council Framework Decision of 13.6.2002 on combating terrorism, OJ 2002 L 164/3-7.

'Article 1

Terrorist offences and fundamental rights and principles

1. Each Member State shall take the necessary measures to ensure that the intentional acts referred to below in points (a) to (i), as defined as offences under national law, which, given their nature or context, may seriously damage a country or an international organisation where committed with the aim of:

- seriously intimidating a population, or

- unduly compelling a Government or international organisation to perform or abstain from performing any act, or

- seriously destabilising or destroying the fundamental political, constitutional, economic or social structures of a country or an international organisation, shall be deemed to be terrorist offences:

(a) attacks upon a person's life which may cause death;

(b) attacks upon the physical integrity of a person;

(c) kidnapping or hostage taking;

(d) causing extensive destruction to a Government or public facility, a transport system, an infrastructure facility, including an information system, a fixed platform located on the continental shelf, a public place or private property likely to endanger human life or result in major economic loss;

(e) seizure of aircraft, ships or other means of public or goods transport;

(f) manufacture, possession, acquisition, transport, supply or use of weapons, explosives or of nuclear, biological or chemical weapons, as well as research into, and development of, biological and chemical weapons;

(g) release of dangerous substances, or causing fires, floods or explosions the effect of which is to endanger human life;

(h) interfering with or disrupting the supply of water, power or any other fundamental natural resource the effect of which is to endanger human life;

(i) threatening to commit any of the acts listed in (a) to (h).

2. This Framework Decision shall not have the effect of altering the obligation to respect fundamental rights and fundamental legal principles as enshrined in Article 6 of the Treaty on European Union. [...]

Article 5 Penalties

1. Each Member State shall take the necessary measures to ensure that the offences referred to in Articles 1 to 4 are punishable by effective, proportionate and dissuasive criminal penalties, which may entail extradition.

2. Each Member State shall take the necessary measures to ensure that the terrorist offences referred to in Article 1(1) and offences referred to in Article 4, inasmuch as they relate to terrorist offences, are punishable by custodial sentences heavier than those imposable under national law for such offences in the absence of the special intent required pursuant to Article 1(1), save where the sentences imposable are already the maximum possible sentences under national law.

> 3. Each Member State shall take the necessary measures to ensure that offences listed in Article 2 are punishable by custodial sentences, with a maximum sentence of not less than fifteen years for the offence referred to in Article 2(2)(a), and for the offences listed in Article 2(2)(b) a maximum sentence of not less than eight years. In so far as the offence referred to in Article 2(2)(a) refers only to the act in Article 1(1)(i), the maximum sentence shall not be less than eight years. [...]'

Similarly, a Framework Decision has been used on the protection of the environment through criminal law.[52] Moreover, the Council has adopted a Framework Decision on joint investigation teams[53] as well as on the European arrest warrant and the surrender procedure between Member States.[54] In addition, a Framework Decision was used to harmonize the standing of victims in criminal proceedings in the Member States.[55] Also, a number of Framework Decisions have been adopted to fight against fraud and counterfeiting of the euro and non-cash payments[56] as well as on money laundering.[57] Finally, Framework Decisions have been adopted on various matters such as strengthening the penal framework to prevent the facilitation of unauthorised entry, transit and residence[58] and combating trafficking in human beings.[59] Moreover, a number of far-reaching Framework Decisions have been proposed and are currently discussed.[60]

---

52 Council Framework Decision 2003/80/JHA of 27.1.2003 on the protection of the environment through criminal law, OJ 2003 L 029/55-58.

53 Council Framework Decision 2002/465/JHA on joint investigation teams, OJ 2002 L 162/1-3.

54 Council Framework Decision 2002/584/JHA of 13.6.2002 on the European arrest warrant and the surrender procedures between Member States, OJ 2002 L 190/1.

55 Council Framework Decision 2001/220/JHA of 15.3.2001 on the standing of victims in criminal proceedings, OJ 2001 L 082/1-4.

56 Council Framework Decision 2001/888/JHA amending Framework Decision 2000/383/JHA on increasing protection by criminal penalties and other sanctions against counterfeiting in connection with the introduction of the euro, OJ 2001 L 329/3; Council Framework Decision 2001/413/JHA of 28.5.2001 combating fraud and counterfeiting of non-cash means of payment, OJ 2001 L 149/1-4.

57 Council Framework Decision 2001/500/JHA of 26.6.2001 on money laundering, the identification, tracing, freezing, seizing and confiscation of instrumentalities and the proceeds of crime, OJ 2001 L 182/1-2.

58 Council Framework Decision 2002/946/JHA on the strengthening of the penal framework to prevent the facilitation of unauthorised entry, transit and residence, OJ 2002 L 328/1-3.

59 Council Framework Decision 2002/629/JHA on combating trafficking in human beings, OJ 2002 L 203/1-4.

60 See e.g: Proposal for a Council Framework Decision on attacks against information, 6671/1/03 REV 1; Proposal for a Council Framework Decision on combating racism and xenophobia, 6658/03 ADD 1; Draft Framework Decision on the application of the principle of mutual recognition to financial penalties, 6685/01/03, REV 1; Draft Framework Decision on combating corruption in the private sector, 5282/03.

Thus, Framework Decisions are now mainly used to approximate the laws and regulations of the EU Member States in the highly sensitive areas of justice and home affairs. Indeed, Framework Decisions penetrate the codes of criminal law and procedures of the EU Member States, thereby starting a process of legal harmonization – at least for certain offences.

As to the legal effect of Framework Decisions, one cannot fail to notice the similarities with EC Directives.[61] Article 34 (2) (b) TEU expressly stipulates that Framework Decisions are binding as to the result and the period of time in which the result must be achieved, while at the same time allowing Member States to choose the means to achieve those results in a given period of time. Despite the similarity with EC Directives, there is one important difference, namely the explicit exclusion of any direct effect for Framework Decisions.

Hence, it seems as if the EU Member States intentionally wanted to prevent the ECJ from developing a similar case-law regarding a possible direct effect of Framework Decisions as it did for EC Directives.[62]

2.2.3 Decisions

Article 34 (2) (c) states that the Council may:

> 'adopt Decisions of any other purpose consistent with the objectives of this Title, excluding any approximation of laws and regulations of the MS. These decisions shall be binding and shall not entail direct effect; the Council, acting by a QMV, shall adopt measures necessary to implement those decisions at the level of the Union'.

In the first place, it should be noted that the instrument of 'Decision' was newly introduced by the Amsterdam Treaty. As Article 34 (2) (c) TEU states, Decisions shall be used if no harmonization of the laws of the EU Member States is intended. The acts adopted under this provision are called 'Council Decisions'. Council Decisions are used for a wide variety of different purposes, for example, a Council Decision to establish a new European Police College (CEPOL).[63] But a Council Decision was also used to combat child pornography on the Internet by laying down general guidelines for the Member States linked with a request to follow them.[64] This Council Decision could also be seen as preparing the ground for subsequent legal acts that entail the approximation of laws on child pornography as the Framework Decision indicates.[65] Finally, a Euro-

---

[61] Monar (1998) at 326.

[62] See: Fennelly (2000).

[63] Council Decision of 22.12.2000 establishing a European Police College (CEPOL), OJ 2000 L 336/1.

[64] Council Decision of 29.5.2000 to combat child pornography on the Internet, OJ 2000 L 138/1.

[65] Council Framework Decision 2004/68/JHA on combating the sexual exploitation of children and child pornography, OJ 2004 L 13/44.

pean network of contact points in respect of persons responsible for genocide and other crimes was established by a Council Decision in order to increase the effectiveness of investigations within the framework of the International Criminal Court.[66] Thus, the instrument of 'Decision' is chosen when approximation of the laws of the Member States is to be excluded or if it is not required under the specific circumstances. Similar to the other instruments mentioned in Article 34 TEU, Decisions are also declared to be legally binding, i.e. the EU Member States are legally required to take the necessary steps in order to implement the Decisions, but any direct effect is excluded. The difference with Framework Decisions is essentially the exclusion of any legally binding harmonizing or approximating effect of the Member States' laws.

2.3 Summary

From the previous analysis it can be concluded that the Council is able to adopt independently from the Member States legally binding decisions with regard to the II. and III. pillar policy areas. However, at the same time it should be noted that the examined II. and III. pillar decisions are to a varying degree legally binding on the EU Member States. Moreover, the following differentiations must be kept in mind.

In the first place, it must be recalled that the exact extent of the legal binding effect of each instrument must be determined on the specific contents of the respective decision, thus the title used for a certain decision is not necessarily indicative of the extent of its binding effect.

In the second place, a clear contrast between the II. and III. pillar decisions can be identified as to the explicit description used in the EU Treaty provisions regarding their intended binding effect. Whereas Article 34 TEU clearly spells out that the instruments mentioned are binding on the Member States and at the same time explicitly excludes direct effect for Decisions and Framework Decisions, Articles 14, 15 TEU are silent on these issues.

In the third place, one has to keep the differences between Common Foreign and Security Policy (CFSP) and Justice and Home Affairs (JHA) in mind. Whereas the CFSP is principally externally orientated involving very sensitive high politics, diplomacy and defence issues, JHA is more internally orientated, in fact closely related to the internal market, and concerns more the rights of EU citizens.

---

66 Council Decision 2002/494/JHA setting up a European Network of contact points in respect of persons responsible for genocide, crimes against humanity and war crimes, OJ 2002 L 167/1-2.

3 The application of Community law principles (supremacy and direct effect) to II. and III. pillar decisions

After determining that the II. and III. pillar decisions are – to a varying degree – legally binding on the EU Member States and that a sufficient legal and institutional link exists between those decisions and EC law, the question arises whether and, if so, to what extent Community law principles such as supremacy and direct effect are also applicable to them. In other words, how closely are II. and III. pillar decisions linked to the Community legal order? In order to answer this question, it is first appropriate to recall the reasons for establishing the specific Community law features of supremacy and direct effect.[67]

3.1 Reasons for developing supremacy and direct effect of Community law

De Witte defines direct effect and supremacy as follows:

> 'Direct effect can be provisionally defined as the capacity of a norm of Community law to be applied in domestic court proceedings; whereas supremacy (or primacy) denotes the capacity of that norm of Community law to overrule inconsistent norms of national law in domestic court proceedings.'[68]

From the outset, it should be recalled that historically speaking both principles were developed within a very short time in 1963-1964 and are closely related.[69] Accordingly, in the *Van Gend & Loos* case the ECJ not only developed the direct effect principle but also prepared the ground for the supremacy principle, which was worked out in detail in the *Costa/ENEL* ruling.

3.1.1 Direct effect

In *Van Gend & Loos*,[70] the ECJ developed the direct effect principle in the following way.

> 'The objective of the EEC Treaty, which is to establish a Common Market, the functioning of which is of direct concern to interested parties in the Community, implies that this Treaty is more than an agreement which merely creates mutual

---

67 See for details: Barents (2000).

68 De Witte (1999a) at 177.

69 See in particular for the historic evolution: *Ibid.*

70 Case 26/62 *van Gend & Loos* [1963] ECR 95.

> obligations between the contracting states. This view is confirmed by the Preamble to the Treaty which refers not only to governments but to peoples. It is also confirmed more specifically by the establishment of institutions endowed with sovereign rights, the exercise of which affects Member States and also their citizens. Furthermore, it must be noted that nationals of the states brought together the Community are called upon to cooperate in the functioning of this Community through the intermediary of the European Parliament and the Economic and Social Committee.
>
> In addition the task assigned to the Court of Justice under Article 177, the object of which is to secure uniform interpretation of the Treaty by national courts and tribunals, confirms that the states have acknowledged that Community law has an authority which can be invoked by their nationals before those courts and tribunals. The conclusion to be drawn from this is that the Community constitutes a new legal order of international law for the benefit of which the states have limited their sovereign rights, albeit within limited fields, and the subjects of which compromise not only Member State but also their nationals. Independently of the legislation of Member States, Community law therefore not only imposes obligations on individuals but is also intended to confer upon them rights which become part of their legal heritage. These rights arise not only where they are expressly granted by the treaty, but also by reason of obligations which the Treaty imposes in a clearly defined way upon individuals as well as upon Member States and upon the institutions of the Community.'

The ECJ started its reasoning by pointing to the special nature of the EC Treaty compared to usual international agreements. According to the ECJ, the EC Treaty created 'more' than just obligations between states since it also refers to the people. This is especially illustrated by the existence of the EC institutions endowed with sovereign rights and the possibility for the people to participate in the establishment of the Common Market through the EC institutions. The central role of the individual is particularly visible in the possibility for the citizens to enforce Community law against their states before their domestic courts (and through Article 234 ECT in cooperation with the ECJ).[71] It is for these reasons that the ECJ came to the crucial conclusion that Community law must be qualified as *a new legal order of international law* that also benefits the EC citizens. Consequently, Community law not only imposes obligations but also grants rights to the people of the Member States.

3.1.2 Supremacy

In its seminal *Costa/ENEL*[72] ruling, the ECJ used the following reasons for developing and justifying the principle of supremacy.

---

71 See on this point: De Witte (1999a) at 205-206.

72 Case 6/64 *Costa* v. *ENEL* [1964] ECR 585.

'By contrast with ordinary international treaties, the EEC Treaty has created its own legal system which on the entry into force of the Treaty, became an integral part of the legal systems of the Member States and which their courts are bound to apply.

By creating a Community of unlimited duration, having its own institutions, its own personality, its own legal capacity and capacity of representation on the international plane and, more particularly, real powers stemming from a limitation of sovereignty or a transfer of powers from the states to the Community, the Member States have limited their sovereign rights, albeit within limited fields, and have thus created a body of law which binds both their nationals and themselves.

The integration into the laws of each Member State of provisions which derive from the Community, and more generally the terms and the spirit of the treaty, make it impossible for the states, as a corollary, to accord precedence to a unilateral and subsequent measure over a legal system accepted by them on a basis of reciprocity. Such a measure cannot therefore be inconsistent with that legal system. The executive force of Community law cannot vary from one state to another. In deference to subsequent domestic laws, without jeopardizing the attainment of the objectives of the Treaty set out in Article 5 (2) and giving rise to this discrimination prohibited by Article 7.

The obligations undertaken under the Treaty establishing the Community would not be unconditional, but merely contingent, if they could be called in question by subsequent legislative acts of the signatories.

Wherever the Treaty grants the states the right to act unilaterally, it does this by clear and precise provisions [...].

The precedence of Community law is confirmed by Article 189, whereby a Regulation "shall be binding" and "directly applicable in all Member States". This provision, which is subject to no reservation, would be quite meaningless if a state could unilaterally nullify its effect by means of a legislative measure which could prevail over Community law.

It follows from all these observations that the law stemming from the Treaty, an independent source of law, could not, because of its special and original nature, be overridden by domestic legal provisions, however framed, without being derived of its character as Community law and without the legal basis of the Community itself being called into question.

The transfer by the states from their domestic legal system to the Community legal system of the rights and obligations arising under the Treaty carries with it a permanent limitation of their sovereign rights, against which a subsequent unilateral act incompatible with the concept of Community cannot prevail.'

The ECJ started its analysis by picking up its definition of the legal nature of Community law given in the *Van Gend & Loos* case. Instead of defining Community law as a new legal order of public international law, the ECJ defined Community law in the *Costa/ENEL* case as *'its own legal system'* and as *'an independent source of law'*. It seems that with this definition the Court took EC law definitely out of the domain of public international law and placed it within a completely new domain of law (*sui generis*).[73]

Based on that, the Court focuses extensively on the special institutional features of the EC. Because the EC has its own institutions, own legal capacity and real powers (i.e. issuing binding decisions such as Regulations and Directives), Member States limited their sovereignty in certain policy areas. As a consequence thereof, the ECJ concluded that uniformity of Community law is a prerequisite for the proper functioning of the EC. Bearing in mind the great differences in the legal systems of the Member States, the ECJ found in the supremacy principle an easy and effective method to overcome possible obstructions by the legislative activities of the Member States.

To sum up, the ECJ used the special institutional characteristics of the EC to justify the supremacy and direct effect principles. In particular, the possibility of the citizens enforcing Community law with the help of national courts and the ECJ played a major role in justifying the development of the supremacy and direct effect principles independent of national constitutions.

3.2 Supremacy and direct effect applicable to II. pillar decisions?

From the outset, it should be recalled that neither the EC Treaty nor the EU Treaty contain clear answers as to the legal nature of CFSP decisions. In addition, the ECJ's lack of jurisdiction in the II. pillar (Article 46 TEU) has prevented the Court from pronouncing itself on this issue. An illustrative example of the existing legal insecurity can be found in the attempt of Oppermann to define CFSP decisions. He describes Common Positions and Joint Actions as follows:

> 'Beide Handlungsformen, die im Kern gemeinschaftsnahe völkerrechtliche Beschlüsse im Unionsbereich darstellen, sind für die Mitgliedstaaten bindend gemeint.'[74]

Further on, Oppermann argues that CFSP decisions do not have direct effect, and as to the legal nature states that:

> 'das GASP-Recht (noch) kein Gemeinschaftsrecht ieS [im engeren Sinne], sondern im Kern Völkerrecht ist.[75]

---

[73] See generally: De Witte (1984).

[74] Oppermann (1999) at 127, no. 307.

[75] *Ibid.*

This definition is quite interesting because it reveals the dual character of secondary CFSP law. Apparently, Oppermann considers them to be placed within the domain of public international law, but with some degree of 'closeness' to Community law (*gemeinschaftsnah*), though clearly not yet part of it. The term *'gemeinschaftsnah'* is apparently deliberately used by Oppermann to indicate that somehow CFSP decisions are 'more' than simply international decisions adopted by a usual IO. Indeed, the term *'gemeinschaftsnah'* indicates that there must be an institutional and legal interaction between EU law and EC law, which justifies Oppermann's claim of *Gemeinschaftsnähe*.

The institutional interaction is most visible in the *'Doppelorganschaft'* of the Council, i.e. the double-function of the Council as the major decision-making body in both the EC and in the EU. This is especially evident in the everyday practice of the Council. The same Council adopts decisions in both pillars without a difference being apparent from the outside. In fact, CFSP decisions are published in the *L-Series of the Official Journal of the European Union* next to EC Regulations and EC Directives.

The legal interaction is, in particular, visible in the context of the imposition of (economic) sanctions against third states, either as implementation of UN Security Council Resolutions or imposed by the EU on the basis of its own initiative. As discussed above, Articles 301, 60 EC Treaty explicitly require the prior adoption of a Common Position or Joint Action before an EC Regulation can be adopted.

A further legal interaction between I. and II. pillars exists as regards the financing of II. pillar activities.[76] According to Articles 28 EU Treaty, 268 EC Treaty, the administrative and operational expenditures for the II. pillar are charged to the EC budget. The only exceptions are CFSP actions that involve military or defence implications or when the Council decides unanimously to charge operational expenditures to the EU Member States.[77] This budgetary linkage between EU law and EC law also results into an institutional linkage concerning the powers of the European Parliament.[78] Generally speaking, the European Parliament is not involved in the decision-making process within the II. pillar, since the European Parliament is merely consulted and kept informed by the Council Presidency (Article 21 TEU). In addition, the European Parliament may ask questions of the Council and make recommendations (Article 21 TEU). However, due to the strong position of the EP within the budgetary domain of the EC, i.e. the EP needs to approve the EC budget according to Article 272 EC Treaty, it can and does exercise (in particular supervisory) powers within the II. pillar which it formally would not have under the TEU.

---

[76] See: Wessel (1999) at 220-223.

[77] *Ibid.*, at 223.

[78] De Zwaan (1998).

Similarly, the existing legal linkage between the I. and the II. pillars regarding sanctions allows the ECJ to undermine the general exclusion of its jurisdiction within the II. pillar. The lack of jurisdiction of the ECJ within the II. pillar leaves its full jurisdiction over the I. pillar unaffected. Thus, the ECJ and CFI are able to review Community law acts adopted on the basis of Articles 301, 60 EC Treaty. In the framework of this review, the ECJ can also review indirectly the compatibility of Joint Actions or Common Positions with Community law.[79]

Thus, there is some legal and institutional 'closeness' between II. pillar decisions and Community law. However, the question arises: is this sufficient in order to apply direct effect and supremacy to II. pillar decisions?

As to direct effect, it must be recalled that Articles 14, 15 TEU do not explicitly exclude a direct effect of binding Common Positions and Joint Actions, which means that in principle the application of it is possible.

It could be conceived that Common Positions and Joint Actions can impose obligations, which do not only affect the EU Member States but also individuals, particularly in the case of sanctions. However, due to the nature and contents of Joint Actions and Common Positions that are adopted in the political and diplomatic sphere concerning related issues outside the EU, the language used in those instruments is very general in order to accommodate the divergent interests of all EU Member States. Accordingly, it is difficult to conceive that CFSP decisions could meet the conditions of direct effect, i.e., sufficiently clear, precise and unconditional, thereby conferring rights on individuals which could be enforced by them before their domestic courts. Moreover, the absence of the jurisdiction of the ECJ makes it unlikely that a possible direct effect of II. pillar decisions is recognized and imposed uniformly on all EU Member States. So, while direct effect for Common Positions and Joint Actions is – formally speaking – possible, in practice it seems very unlikely to me.

Also, supremacy is not explicitly excluded by Articles 14, 15 TEU and therefore could be applicable to binding CFSP decisions. However, in order to apply the supremacy principle to CFSP decisions, the special characteristics of Community law would have to be found in the II. pillar. In particular, the unique preliminary ruling system as well as the involvement of the European Parliament in the decision-making process within the II. pillar would have to exist. As the law stands now, Article 46 TEU excludes the jurisdiction of the ECJ within the II. pillar. Consequently, the ECJ is neither able to ensure uniform application of CFSP decisions in the Member States, nor are the domestic courts allowed to request preliminary rulings. Equally, the European Parliament (EP) is absent in the decision-making process within the II. pillar. The only involvement of the EP in the II. pillar is contained in Article 21 TEU which provides that the European Council and the Commission keep the EP informed. Thus,

79 Wessel (1999) at 223-229. See: Case T-306/01 R *Aden* [2002] ECR II-2387; Case T-47/03 R *Sison*, order of 15.5.2003.

the reasons for developing the specific Community law characteristics of supremacy and direct effect are so far absent in the II. pillar.

In sum, it appears that – despite the existence of some legal and institutional links – the differences between the I. and II. pillars are so extensive that an analogous application of the Community law principles, in particular supremacy, must be rejected. Indeed, von Bogdandy/Bast/Arndt conclude that:

> 'Allgemein kann für den Bereich der GASP ein hinter dem Gemeinschaftsrecht, aber auch hinter der PJZ erheblich zurückbleibender Grad an Verrechtlichung diagnostiziert werden. [...] Ohne eine Zuständigkeit des EuGH zur Wahrung des Rechts auch in der Aussen- und Sicherheitspolitik der Union ist auch die Übertragung von Erkenntnissen zu den gemeinschaftsrechtlichen Handlungsformen auf Art. 12 EU praktisch ausgeschlossen.'[80]

This conclusion is also supported by the current discussion within the European Convention. The Final Report of the Working Group on External Action neither recommends a stronger involvement of the EP nor a jurisdiction of the ECJ in the II. pillar.[81] Indeed, the present draft text of the European Constitution[82] only prescribes in Article I-39 (6) that the EP shall be regularly informed without being involved in the decision-making process. Moreover, Article III-282 excludes the jurisdiction of the ECJ concerning CFSP acts. Finally, European decisions are to be adopted in the field of CFSP (Article I-39 (7)) as opposed to European laws and European Framework laws (Article I-32). However, at the same time it must be noted that the draft Article 10 (1) of the proposed European Constitutional Treaty (currently) states that:

> 'The Constitution, and *law adopted by the Union's Institutions* in exercising competences conferred on it, shall have *primacy over the law of the Member States*.'[83]

This provision, which belongs to 'Title I Definitions and Objectives of the Union' is intended – since there is no limitation in the wording – to apply generally to all Union law including legally binding acts adopted in the II. pillar. Consequently, if this provision were to become law then this would clarify the currently existing insecurity over the legal status of II. pillar decisions in the national legal orders of the Member States, in the sense that despite the absence of Community law features, the supremacy principle would apply to II. pillar decisions.

---

80 Von Bogdandy/Bast/Arndt (2002) at 114.

81 CONV 459/02.

82 CONV 850/03, 18.7.2003.

83 *Ibid.*, emphasis added.

3.3 Supremacy and direct effect applicable to III. pillar decisions?

Similarly to the previous section, the main question to be addressed is whether and, if so, to what extent similarities exist between decisions adopted within the III. pillar and I. pillar, which could justify the analogous application of Community law principles (supremacy and direct effect) to them. This would be the case if the special characteristics of Community law as discussed above also exist in the III. pillar.

3.3.1 Institutional aspects

From the outset, it should be noted that the institutional architecture of the III. pillar is much more supranational than the II. pillar. First, the Commission shares the right to make proposals for legislation in the III. pillar with the Member States (Article 34 (2) TEU). This puts the Commission in a much more powerful position as compared to the II. pillar in which the Commission is completely excluded from the decision-making process. Second, also the EP is more greatly involved in the III. pillar as compared to the II. pillar. According to Article 39 (1) TEU, the Council shall consult the EP before adopting Framework Decisions, Decisions or Conventions. The EP has three months time to deliver its opinion. Although the opinion of the EP is not binding on the Council, it is an important tool for the EP to have a good overview of the future JHA legislation. In addition, the EP is regularly informed by the Presidency and the Commission (Article 39 (2) TEU) and may also ask questions to the Council (Article 39 (3) TEU) concerning the III. pillar. Moreover, the cost of the activities of the III. pillar are covered by the Community budget. Accordingly, the EP has the possibility of influencing the JHA policy through its budgetary powers given to it under the EC Treaty (Article 41 (2)-(4) TEU). In summary, the institutional architecture of the III. pillar is noticeably more supranational and thus differs substantially from the practically intergovernmental structure of the II. pillar.

However, the most important difference between the II. and the III. pillars is to be found in the jurisdiction of the ECJ. Whereas the jurisdiction of the ECJ is excluded in the II. pillar, the ECJ is able to review III. pillar decisions, albeit in more limited way than in the I. pillar.[84]

According to Article 35 (1) TEU the ECJ has jurisdiction to give preliminary rulings on the validity and interpretation of Framework Decisions and Decisions as well as on the interpretation of Conventions and the validity of measures implementing them. But, it should be noted that Common Positions (and all other 'soft law' instruments which are used by the Council) are not mentioned in this enumeration and therefore are presumably not covered by the

---

[84] See for details: Zott (1999) at 277-283; Fennelly (2000) at 8-12; Monar (1998) at 330-332; Peers (2000) at 46-48.

jurisdiction. Besides, the jurisdiction of the ECJ is further limited by Article 35 (5) TEU that, in order to maintain law and order and ensure internal security, excludes the jurisdiction to review the proportionality of operations carried out by the police or other law enforcement services of a Member State. Moreover, in contrast to the I. pillar, the jurisdiction of the ECJ is neither compulsory nor automatic. According to Article 35 (2) TEU, Member States wishing to accept the jurisdiction of the ECJ within the III. pillar must make a special declaration to that effect. More specifically, Member States are able to choose whether they want to limit the possibility of domestic courts to request preliminary rulings to the highest courts against whose decisions there is no judicial remedy available under national law (Article 35 (2) (a) TEU), or to extend it to any court that considers a preliminary ruling of the ECJ as necessary in order to render a judgment (Article 35 (2) (b) TEU). In addition, Member States can choose to make it either obligatory or not for the highest courts to request a preliminary ruling. Cases involving the review of Framework Decisions and other Decisions can be brought before the ECJ by a Member State or the Commission within a period of two months (Article 35 (6) TEU). The grounds for such a review are very similar to the ones applicable in Community law (Article 230 (2) EC Treaty), i.e. lack of competence, infringement of an essential procedural requirement, infringement of the EU Treaty or any rule of law relating to its application or misuse of power. Furthermore, Article 35 (7) TEU differentiates between the parties involved in a dispute. First, the ECJ has jurisdiction to rule on any dispute between the Member States regarding the interpretation or the application of acts adopted under Article 34 (2) TEU whenever such a dispute cannot be solved within six months in the Council. Apparently, the formulation 'acts adopted under Article 34 (2) TEU' is more broadly formulated than for preliminary rulings, since Common Positions and possibly all other 'soft law' acts are covered by the jurisdiction of the ECJ. Second, the ECJ also has jurisdiction to rule on any dispute between the Member States and the Commission regarding the interpretation or application of conventions established under Article 34 (2) (d) TEU.

Obviously, comparing the jurisdiction of the ECJ in the III. pillar with its jurisdiction in the I. pillar shows some important differences.

First, the possibility for Member States to choose from a number of options or even to refuse the jurisdiction of the ECJ altogether is in contrast with the general and compulsory jurisdiction of the ECJ for the I. pillar. However, it must be mentioned that also within the I. Pillar, the jurisdiction of the ECJ is differentiated, for instance, in the new title IV of the EC Treaty on visas, asylum, immigration or as regards the EMU.

Second, as to the *locus standi* before the ECJ, the fact that the EP cannot bring any actions indicates its still weak position in the III. pillar.

Third, due to the fact that the jurisdiction of the ECJ within the III. pillar is not compulsory, differences remain in the Member States regarding the right of domestic courts to ask the ECJ for preliminary rulings within the III. pillar.[85]

---

[85] See: OJ 1999 C 120/24.

The situation is as follows: Spain accepted the possibility of requesting preliminary rulings but has limited it to the highest court against whose decision there is no judicial remedy. In contrast to that, the following Member States, Belgium, German, Greece, Italy, Luxembourg, the Netherlands,[86] Austria, Portugal, Finland, Sweden and France,[87] allow any of their courts to request a preliminary ruling from the ECJ. Moreover, Belgium, Germany, Spain, Italy, Luxembourg, the Netherlands, Austria and France have reserved the right to introduce in their domestic laws the provision that the highest court against whose decision there is no judicial remedy is required to ask a preliminary ruling from the ECJ, if the domestic court considers it necessary for deciding the case before it. Indeed, Germany has chosen this option by adopting a new formal law to that effect.[88] Thus, only the UK, Ireland and Denmark have so far not accepted the jurisdiction of the ECJ for the III. pillar. Accordingly, the large majority of the Member States allow their domestic courts to request preliminary rulings from the ECJ concerning III. pillar issues. Indeed, recently, the ECJ rendered its first preliminary ruling within the procedure of Article 35 TEU.[89]

Finally, it should be remembered that the ECJ is also able and willing to indirectly review JHA decisions if they are connected with Community law, as it pointed out in the *Transit visa*[90] case:

> '17. It follows that the Court has jurisdiction to review the content of the Act [Joint Action] in the light of Article 100c of the EC Treaty in order to ascertain whether the Act affects the powers of the Community under that provision and to annul the Act if it appears that it should have been based on Article 100c of the EC Treaty.'

Thus, institutionally speaking, there is a considerable closeness between the III. pillar and the I. pillar, in particular as regards the powers of the Commission and the jurisdiction of the ECJ. One important difference remaining, however, is the still very limited powers of the European Parliament in the decision-making process of the III. pillar. Nevertheless, sufficient Community law features exist

---

86 Rijkswet van 24.12.1998, houdende de goedkeuring van het Verdrag van Amsterdam, Staatsblad 1998, 737 as corrected by Tractatenblad 2002, no. 153.

87 See: Décret no. 2000-668 du 10 juillet 2000 portant publication de la déclaration de la France pour la mise en oeuvre de l'article 35 du traité sur l'Union européenne, 14.3.2000, J.O. No. 165, 19.7.2000, 11073.

88 Gesetz betreffend die Anrufung des Gerichtshofes der EG im Wege des Vorabentscheidungsverfahrens auf dem Gebiet der polizeilichen Zusammenarbeit und der justitiellen Zusammenarbeit in Strafsachen nach Artikel 35 des EU Vertrages (EuGH-Gesetz- EuGHG), 6.8.1998, BGBl. I, 1998, Nr. 50, 13.8.1998, 2035.

89 Joined cases C-187/01 and C-385/01 *Gözütok and Brügge* [2003] ECR I-1345.

90 Case C-170/96 *Commission* v. *Council* [1998] ECR I-2763.

within the III. pillar which justify the assumption that supremacy and direct effect are also applicable to the binding III. pillar decisions.

Indeed, this conclusion is strongly supported by the current developments in the European Convention. For instance, the Working Group on 'Freedom, Security and Justice' recommended that the III. pillar instruments (Framework Decisions, Decisions and Common Positions) should be

> 'replaced by Regulations, Directives and Decisions (as currently foreseen in the EC Treat) [...]. The normal rules governing these instruments should in the future apply, even if this may require adaptation of legal systems in some Member States. This should include the possibility of direct effect of such directives conferring rights to individuals.'[91]

Moreover, the same Working Group recommended extending the system of full jurisdiction of the ECJ as it exists within the I. pillar to the III. pillar, thereby abolishing the currently limited jurisdiction of the ECJ in the III. pillar.[92] In addition, it is recommended that the Commission should play its role fully as the guardian of the Treaty by extending the infringement procedure of Article 226 EC Treaty to the III. pillar.[93] Similarly, the Working Group IX on Simplification recommended that there should be only three main legislative instruments of the Union (European laws, European framework laws) that should be applied to what is currently the I. and II. pillars, while decisions should be used for the II. pillar.[94] In fact, Article I-32 draft text of the European Constitution provides for one set of acts (European law, European framework law and European regulation) which are also applicable in the policy areas of the III. pillar (Article I-41).[95] Besides, the draft text of the European Constitution does not contain an explicit exclusion of direct effect of Union acts adopted in the policy areas of the III. pillar. Moreover, Article III-283 extends the jurisdiction of the ECJ to all III. pillar measures except concerning the review of the validity or proportionality of operations carried out by police or other law-enforcement services of Member State. Finally, it should be emphasized that Article 10 of the draft text of the European Constitution also applies to III. pillar decisions. Accordingly, III. pillar decisions would also enjoy primacy over the national law of the Member States – irrespective of the issue of whether those III. pillar decisions enjoy direct effect or not. Thus, from a formal point view, the legal situation in the areas of the III. pillar will resemble very much the legal situation in the I. pillar.

---

91 Final Report of Working Group X on 'Freedom, Security and Justice', CONV 426/02 of 2.12.2002 at 7.

92 *Ibid.*, at 24-25.

93 *Ibid.*, at 21.

94 Final Report of Working Group IX on Simplification, CONV 424/02 of 29.11.2002.

95 CONV 850/03, 18.7.2003.

3.3.2 Substantive aspects

Before starting the analysis, it is appropriate to briefly recall the reasons why the ECJ developed the supremacy and direct effect principles for Community law. As regards supremacy, De Witte summarizes the main reason as follows:

> 'The only decisive argument for supremacy, in my view, is the *effet utile* argument: if states accept legal duties at the international level, they should be prepared to allow for the translation of those duties into daily practice, by means of judicial and other instruments. [...] But the special feature of the EEC Treaty is that it, unlike other treaties, provided for the ingenious judicial mechanism which allowed the Court of Justice to state its supremacy doctrine and to request national courts to follow suit.'[96]

As regards direct effect, Craig/De Búrca refer to essentially the same two reasons:

> 'The policies which first prompted the Court to develop the idea of the direct effect of Treaty provisions were equally strong here [regarding direct effect of Directives]: those of legal integration and effectiveness. [...] If States are failing or refusing to implement such measures, those Community policies will suffer. Thus the Court's inclination has been to encourage national courts, especially at the suit of aggrieved individuals who have become aware of the provisions of a directive in their favour, to enforce the provisions of the directive directly, even in the absence of its domestic legislative implementation.'[97]

Accordingly, it is the concern for the legal effectiveness of Community law in all Member States and the ability of the national courts, in co-operation with the ECJ through the preliminary ruling procedure, to ensure that Member States fulfil their legal obligations of Community law, which were the main reasons for the ECJ developing supremacy and direct effect. Thus, in order to be able to apply the supremacy and direct effect principles to binding JHA decisions, the main reasons for their development should also be found in the III. pillar.

As to direct effect, Article 34 (2) TEU explicitly excludes direct effect for Framework Decisions and Decisions, while direct effect is neither excluded for Common Positions nor for provisions of Conventions concluded on the basis of Article 34 (2) (e) TEU. Hence, a direct effect for Common Positions and provisions of Conventions is possible if they meet the general requirements of direct effect as established by the case-law of the ECJ.[98]

---

96 De Witte (1999a) at 183.

97 Craig/De Búrca (1998) at 186.

98 See for detailed analysis: Craig/De Búrca (1998); De Witte (1999a).

However, as regards Framework Decisions, the similarities between Framework Decisions and EC Directives justify the analogous application of the 'indirect effect' principle. As Peers rightly points out:

> 'It is therefore strongly arguable that at least the weaker *Von Colson* version of the same principle [indirect effect principle] applies under the EU Treaty, and it may even be arguable that the stronger *Marleasing* version [...] applies.'[99]

The ECJ developed the indirect effect principle for EC Directives in the *Von Colson*[100] case by arguing in the following way:

> '1. Although the third paragraph of Article 189 of the Treaty leaves Member States free to choose the ways and means of ensuring that the Directive is implemented, that freedom does not affect the obligation, imposed on all the Members States to which the Directive is addressed, to adopt, within the framework of their national legal systems, all the measures necessary to ensure that the Directive is fully effective, in accordance with the objective which it pursues.
>
> The Member States' obligation arising from a Directive to achieve the result envisaged by the Directive and their duty under Article 5 of the Treaty to take all appropriate measures, whether general or particular, to ensure the fulfilment of that obligation, is binding on all the authorities of Member States including, for matters within their jurisdiction, the courts. It follows, that in applying national law and in particular the provisions of a national law specifically introduced in order to implement a Directive, the national court is required to interpret its national law in the light of the wording and the purpose of the Directive in order to achieve the result referred to in the third paragraph of Article 189.'

In my opinion, the same reasoning is applicable *mutatis mutandis* to Framework Decisions, since Member States are legally obliged to achieve the objectives of Framework Decisions. They have to do this by implementing Framework Decisions into their national legal order similar to the case of EC Directives. Accordingly, when national courts are faced with the interpretation of national law they are required to interpret it in the light of the Framework Decision in question. And if the national court is unsure how to interpret the Framework Decision, it can request a preliminary ruling from the ECJ – if that Member State has accepted the jurisdiction of the ECJ within the III. pillar. The legal situation of EC Directives and Framework Decisions are so similar that it can be expected that the ECJ would reason in the same way as it did in *Von Colson*.

---

99 Peers (2000) at 49.

100 Case 14/83 *Von Colson and Kamann* [1984] ECR 1891.

In *Marleasing*[101], the ECJ confirmed the indirect effect principle and went further by extending it even to national law adopted prior to the Directive. The ECJ simply stated:

> '1. The Member States' obligation arising from a directive to achieve the result envisaged by the directive and their duty under Article 5 of the Treaty to take all appropriate measures, whether general or particular, to ensure the fulfilment of that obligation, is binding on all the authorities of Member States including, for matters within their jurisdiction, the courts. It follows that, in applying national law, whether the provisions in question were adopted before or after the directive, the national court called upon to interpret it is required to do so, as far as possible, in the light of the wording and the purpose of the directive in order to achieve the result pursued by it and thereby comply with the third paragraph of Article 189 of the Treaty.'

Again, there is no reason why the *Marleasing* version of the indirect principle should not be applicable to Framework Decisions. This is, in particular, the case because Framework Decisions concern the approximation of the laws of the Member States, especially in the area of criminal law, criminal procedural law, administrative law and administrative procedural law that usually have been adopted prior to the Framework Decision in question. However, one must be careful not to interpret the quoted paragraph of the *Marleasing* case too extensively.[102] In particular, the phrase 'as far as possible' indicates that the duty to interpret national law in the light of the Directive is not unlimited.[103] Similarly, in the case of Framework Decisions, national courts would only have to interpret national law 'as far as possible' in the light of the Framework Decision. Nonetheless, the acceptance of the indirect effect principle for binding III. pillar decisions would be a powerful principle to ensure that Member States bring their existing, as well as future, domestic legislation in line with the Framework Decisions.

Another way to apply Framework Decisions directly could be based on the constitutional law of the EU Member States. As discussed above, Framework Decisions must be considered as binding decisions of an IO. Accordingly, in the case of the Netherlands, Articles 93, 94 of the Dutch *Grondwet* could be applied to Framework Decisions. Hence, a Dutch judge could set aside conflicting national law if he thinks that a provision of a Framework Decision meets the conditions of Articles 93, 94 Gw. However, this would mean that the Dutch judge would have to interpret Article 34 TEU in clear contrast to the express will of the contracting parties of the TEU. This is very unlikely since Dutch courts

---

[101] Case C-106/89 *Marleasing* [1990] ECR I-4135.

[102] Craig/De Búrca (1998) at 202-206.

[103] See: Arnull (1999) at 126-131.

place significant weight on the will and intention of the contracting parties concerning the issue of whether or not a provision should have direct effect.[104] Thus, it would be very unlikely that a direct effect of a Framework Decision would be accepted against the explicit intention of the contracting parties as expressed in Article 34 TEU.

As to supremacy, we do not find any explicit exclusion of it in the EU Treaty. This opens up the possibility of examining whether supremacy as a Community law principle could be applied in an analogous way to binding III. pillar decisions, such as Decisions and Framework Decisions. In particular, the strong resemblance of Framework Decisions with EC Directives could justify the application of the supremacy principle to Framework Decisions. Since the ECJ is to a large extent involved in the III. pillar through the possibility of giving preliminary rulings, the aspect of uniform interpretation and application of III. pillar decisions is of particular importance. More specifically, since the ECJ is able to review the validity of Framework Decisions and Decisions, the development of uniform criteria applicable in all the Member States that have accepted the jurisdiction seems indispensable. However, the most important reason for considering supremacy, as applicable in this context, is the fact that Framework Decisions aim at approximating the laws of the EU Member States. As the experience with the approximation of laws through EC Directives shows, Member States often fail to take any action at all or fail to implement them correctly. The establishment of the supremacy principle (and the possibility of direct effect of EC Directives) was instrumental in forcing Member States to improve their implementation record. Along the same lines, the *effet utile* principle calls for the acceptance of supremacy for binding III. pillar decisions since it is the only tool of the ECJ that ensures that Member States implement Framework Decisions and Decisions correctly.

However, it could be argued that, due to the close relationship between the direct effect and supremacy principles, the explicit exclusion of direct effect for Framework Decisions and Decisions would also exclude the supremacy principle. Although it is acknowledged that both principles are closely connected, one nevertheless must distinguish them in the following way.

Direct effect within the Community legal order always presupposes supremacy, whereas supremacy does not depend on direct effect. To put it differently: all Community law (primary and secondary EC law) enjoys supremacy above all national law, while at the same time clearly not all Community law is directly applicable. The seminal *Francovich* case[105] is a very illustrative example in which

---

[104] See e.g.: Hoge Raad, judgment of 30.5.1986 (NS), NJ 1986/688, 'Of de verdragsluitende Staten al dan niet hebben beoogd aan art. 6 lid 4 ESH directe werking toe te kennen, is niet van belang nu noch uit de tekst, noch uit de geschiedenis van de totstandkoming van het verdrag valt af te leiden dat zij zijn overeengekomen dat aan art. 6 lid 4 die werking niet mag worden toegekend.'

[105] Joined cases C-6/90 and C-9/90 *Francovich* [1991] ECR I-5357.

the supremacy of the EC Directive in question was used by the ECJ in order to rule that Italy failed to fulfil its Community law obligations even though *Francovich et. al.* could not rely directly on the relevant provisions of the Directive. Similarly, III. pillar decisions can enjoy supremacy over conflicting national law, even if direct effect has been explicitly excluded by the EU Treaty. For example, Article 5 (1) of the Framework Decision on combating corruption in the private sector[106] states that:

> '1. Each Member State shall take the necessary measures to ensure that legal persons can be held liable for offences referred to in Articles 2 and 3 committed for their benefit by any person, acting either individually or as part of an organ of the legal person, who has a leading position within the legal person, based on:
> (a) a power of representation of the legal person, or
> (b) an authority to take decisions on behalf of the legal person, or
> (c) an authority to exercise control within the legal person.'

For example, in a tender for a contract to build a bridge in one Member State, a company got the contract awarded because of corruptive activities while the other competing companies suffered financial losses. The competing companies could not rely directly on that provision against the corruptive company because of the general wording of this provision and because it involves two private parties. However, if a Member State where the company is located has failed to implement Article 5 of the Framework Decision so that such actions are not punishable and thereby preventing the competing companies to held the corruptive company responsible for their financial losses, the competing companies should be able to hold the Member State responsible for its failure to make such activities punishable by requesting compensation for the damages suffered. In other words, the Framework Decision could enjoy supremacy over national law irrespective of the fact whether it is directly applicable or not. Consequently, the explicit exclusion of direct effect for Framework Decisions and Decisions does not affect the proposed supremacy of binding III. pillar decisions over national law of the Member States.

3.4 Summary

First, it has become clear that the various II. and III. pillar decisions are legally binding decisions on the Member States adopted by the EU acting as an IO.

Second, as the law currently stands, a distinction must be made between the II. and III. pillar decisions regarding the possibility of applying the Community

[106] Council Framework Decision 2003/568/JHA on combating corruption in the private sector, OJ 2003 L 192/54.

law principles of supremacy and direct effect to them. The difference is caused by the fact that the II. pillar is lacking most of the important features of the I. pillar, such as a jurisdiction of the ECJ or the participation of Commission and EP in the decision-making process. While supremacy and direct effect can in principle be applied to II. pillar decisions, the lack of Community law features in the II. pillar as well as the vague terminology used in most II. pillar decisions, make their application in practice unlikely. In contrast, while direct effect is explicitly excluded for Framework Decisions and Decisions, the application of the supremacy principle on them is not affected by it. Moreover, nothing stands in the way for the application of the 'indirect effect' principle as applied in the Community legal order to III. pillar decisions.

Finally, the current developments within the European Convention indicate that it is quite possible that the differences between the three pillars will be substantially reduced in many respects. In particular, the explicit general acceptance of the supremacy of all acts of the EU over national law of the Member States will end any doubts as to the legal effect of II. and III. pillar decisions within the domestic legal order. Moreover, the replacement of the III. pillar instruments by Community law instruments as well as the creation of a full jurisdiction of the ECJ will essentially make III. pillar law comparable to I. pillar law, thus leaving only the II. pillar law as a field of Union law that is not fully governed by Community law principles.

4 The 'EC law influenced' legal status and effect of II. and III. pillars decisions

Based on the discussion so far, it is now time to examine whether and, if so, to what extent the 'EC law influenced EU law–national law' legal relationship can be identified in the case of II. and III. pillar decisions.

4.1 The II. pillar decisions

Despite the fact that the II. pillar is lacking most of the Community law features, thus excluding in principle supremacy and direct effect, there is at least one case in which the 'EC law influenced' legal interplay – based on a formal legal relationship – can be identified. This case concerns the implementation of UN Security Council Resolutions that impose sanctions against a state. As has been discussed above, Security Council Resolutions are implemented on the basis of a two-step procedure. First, the Council must adopt a Common Position (or Joint Action) on the basis of Articles 14, 15 TEU, before an EC Regulation is adopted on the basis of Article 301 EC Treaty. This basically is a case of a formalized example of an 'EC law influenced' legal interaction between a Common Position adopted within the II. pillar lacking supremacy and an

EC Regulation enjoying supremacy over all national law of the Member States. In this way, a binding decision of public international law (Security Council Resolution) is first implemented by a II. pillar decision (Common Position) which leaves, to a large extent, its public international character intact before it is communitarized into EC law (EC Regulation), thereby obtaining supremacy over all national law of the Member States. In addition, this communitarization also results into the creation of a jurisdiction of the ECJ to decide on the proper implementation of Security Council Resolutions by the EC and/or the Member States that otherwise would not be the case.

Another example that can be mentioned is the legal interplay that takes place with regard to the budget of II. pillar activities of the EU which are covered by the EC budget. For instance, the aforementioned EU Police mission is, according to Article 9 of the Joint Action, financed out of the EC budget.[107] In this way, the provisions of the EC budget are extended to a II. pillar activity which brings, for instance, the European Parliament indirectly into the arena of the II. pillar. This is an important aspect since, without a budget, no mission is possible. Thus, the budgetary issues of a II. pillar activity is brought into the Community legal order, thereby attaching Community law features to it. In sum, an 'EC law influenced' legal interplay that can to a certain extent be compared to the 'EC law transformed' legal relationship can be identified with regard to II. pillar decisions – albeit only in limited cases.

4.2 The III. pillar decisions

As discussed above, supremacy is clearly existent with regard to III. pillar decisions, in particular, Framework Decisions. Accordingly, while formally speaking Framework Decisions are adopted outside the EC Treaty, they in fact have a similar impact on the domestic legal order of the Member States as, for instance, EC Directives. The only important difference is the exclusion of any direct effect of Framework Decisions and Decisions. Besides, the jurisdiction of the ECJ is more limited than within the I. pillar. Nonetheless, the jurisdiction of the ECJ is a good example of an 'EC law influenced' legal interaction. Whereas the ECJ is an organ of the EC, it can be called upon by domestic courts of most Member States to render judgments concerning III. pillar decisions. In this way, the ECJ is able to impose on the Member States a uniformed interpretation concerning III. pillar law comparable to the impact the ECJ has on the uniform interpretation of Community law. A legal interplay between III. pillar decisions and I. pillar decisions can also be identified in policy areas that can or must be dealt with by measures from both pillars. An example for this is the Framework Decision on the protection of the environment through criminal law. Originally, the Commission proposed, on the basis of Article 175(1) EC Treaty, an

[107] Council Joint Action 2002/210/CFSP on the European Union Police Mission, OJ 2002 L 070/1-6.

EC Directive that intended to enforce with the help of criminal penalties the effective implementation of the environmental legislation of the EC. However, the Council considered that this would go beyond the competence of the EC. Instead, the Council decided to simply 'convert' the proposal for an EC Directive into a Framework Decision.[108] The result is, to a large extent, the same, except that direct effect is excluded and the jurisdiction of the ECJ is more limited, in particular, with regard to the Member States that have not accepted the jurisdiction at all. Another example of such legislative interplay concerns the Schengen Information System, i.e. the database used for screening visa and asylum applications. Whereas the Schengen *aquis* is to a large part incorporated in Title IV of the EC Treaty and thus governed also by Community legislation,[109] some measures must still be adopted within the III. pillar. For instance, in the case of the development of the second generation Schengen Information System (SIS II), a III. pillar Council Decision as well as an EC Regulation had to be adopted in order to cover both III. pillar and I. pillar usage of the system.[110] Accordingly, due to their institutional interaction and resemblance to Community law acts, Framework Decisions and Decisions are from the point of view of the Member States a very special source of law, that comes very close to secondary EC law. Thus, with regard to III. pillar decisions, an 'EC law influenced' legal relationship be observed that is to a large extent comparable to the 'EC law transformed' legal relationship.

5 Concluding remarks

From the analysis above, it can be concluded that the EU is acting as an IO vis-à-vis its Member States when it adopts binding decisions in the II. and III. pillars. In general, it can be said that the legal effect of the various instruments depends on the specific contents of each measure. However, III. pillar decisions, in particular in the form of Framework Decisions, impose more far-reaching legal obligations compared to II. pillar decisions which seem to contain more of a loyalty obligation in the sense that the EU Member States should not undermine the decisions of the EU.[111] Moreover, the lack of jurisdiction of the ECJ and the absence of the Commission and the European

---

[108] It should be noted that the Commission has started legal proceedings against the Council before the ECJ because of the legal basis chosen by the Council. The case is listed under C-176/03, OJ 2003 C 135/21.

[109] See: Wagner (1998); Kuijper (2000).

[110] 2001/886/JHA: Council Decision of 6.12.2001 on the development of the second generation Schengen Information System (SIS II), OJ 2001 L 328/1-3; Council Regulation (EC) No 2424/2001 of 6.12.2001 on the development of the second generation Schengen Information System (SIS II), OJ 2001 L 328/4-6.

[111] See also: Blokker (1999) at 28-35.

Parliament in the decision-making process within the II. pillar reduces the applicability of the supremacy and direct effect principles. In contrast, the closeness of Framework Decisions with EC Directives allows for the analogous application of Community law principles supremacy and 'indirect' effect. Nevertheless, despite the existing differences between II. and III. pillars, in both cases an 'EC law influenced' legal relationship, that is to a large extent comparable with the 'EC law transformed' legal relationship, can be identified which applies to a legislative and an institutional one. This close relationship between the various pillars is also confirmed by the current developments within the European Convention which clearly illustrate that the differences between the three pillars will most likely be substantially reduced – if not completely eliminated. At least the III. pillar will resemble Community law to a very large extent, which means that there will probably be only two pillars left, that is, the I. and II. pillars with distinctive features. Accordingly, the 'EC law influenced' legal relationship will probably disappear for III. pillar decisions as they will have essentially the same legal characteristics as Community law acts.

CHAPTER 6

General Conclusions

As has been shown in the preceding Chapters the transformation of binding decisions of IOs by Community law significantly modifies their legal status and effect before they enter the domestic legal order of the selected EU Member States. In this Chapter the main research results are presented.

Before doing so, it is appropriate to recall the central research question. The central research question of this contribution has been to assess the impact of Community law on the transformation of the legal status and effect of decisions of IOs in the domestic legal orders of the selected EU Member States (G, NL, F). In other words, is and, if so, to what extent the classic legal situation 'law of IOs–national law' modified by the influence of European law into an 'EC law transformed' legal situation 'law of IOs–European law–national law'?

The main presumption underlying the research question has been that, due to the extensive participation of the EU in many IOs and the growing activity of IOs in adopting binding decisions, the EU is increasingly involved in the implementation and application of those decisions. As a consequence thereof, the binding decisions are – to a varying degree – communitarized, thereby obtaining Community law features, such as supremacy over conflicting secondary EC law and all national law of the EU Member States and possible direct effect. This communitarization, it has been presumed, takes place in two ways: first, through European legislation and second, through the jurisprudence of the ECJ and CFI. In this way, the legal status and effect of the binding decisions of IOs is transformed into Community law before they enter the domestic legal orders of the EU Member States.

Similarly, it has been assumed as regards binding II. and III. pillar decisions that, because of their close legal and functional relationship with the I. pillar, those decisions can obtain Community law features, thereby modifying the existing legal relationship 'EU law–national law' into an 'EC law influenced EU law–national law' relationship. The similarity with the 'EC law transformed' legal situation lies in the modification of the legal characteristics of II. or III. pillar decisions by infusing Community law features into them. As a consequence thereof, II. and III. pillar decisions also obtain – to varying degree – supremacy and (in)direct effect.

1 International law level

As regards the law of IOs, three research results merit attention. First, the currently accepted definition of an organ of an IO could be insufficiently broad in order to cover other structures in which bodies can adopt binding decisions having a similar domestic effect without them fulfilling the formal criteria of being an organ of an IO. Second, the special characteristics of decisions of IOs and their impact on the domestic legal order justify a more general recognition of them as a distinct source of public international law.

Third, the application of non-consensual voting procedures for the adoption of binding decisions in many organs of IOs is significant because it undermines the general rule of public international law which provides that a state cannot be legally bound against its will.[1]

1.1 The definition of an organ of an IO

In the course of this research, one recurring issue has been the question of whether or not the body that adopts a decision can be considered to be an organ of an IO acting independently from the member states. This point is relevant because it determines whether or not a certain organ that adopts binding decisions falls within the scope of the main research question.

This issue played a role in the case of the Association Council, the ECrtHR and in particular the COPs/MOPs established by multilateral environmental agreements (MEAs). While the definition of Schermers/Blokker is already broad,[2] recent practice within the law of IOs illustrates that many bodies have been established with the competence to adopt binding decisions which do not meet all the criteria of an organ of an IO. This is for instance the case with regard to the decisions adopted by the COPs/MOPs. Indeed, the discussion within the ILC concerning the draft articles regarding the responsibilities of IOs indicates that a broader definition might be useful and necessary.[3] In my view, this research shows that the discussion concerning a broader definition of IOs is of general importance and should not be confined to the question of the responsibility of IOs. This would help to adequately recognize on a general level the full impact of binding decisions of organs of IOs or comparable structures.

1.2 Binding decisions of IOs

Despite the legal importance of binding decisions of international organizations, the research results indicate that only very few states – at least within the EU – explicitly recognize or deal with the legal status and effect of binding decisions of IOs in their domestic legal order. Similarly, and probably connected with the preceding remark, there is only a small amount of legal literature and case-law that deal with decisions of IOs. However, as this study has shown, this *lacuna* is in most cases circumvented by treating decisions of IOs in a similar way as international treaties. That is, for instance, the case with regard to the EC, Germany and to a lesser extent in France. Only the Dutch *Grondwet* explicitly mentions decisions of IOs, whereas in the other cases, the assimila-

1 Article 34 Vienna Convention on the Law of the Treaties, 1969 states: 'A treaty does not create either obligations or rights for a third State without its consent.'

2 See Chapter 1.

3 *Ibid.*

tion of decisions with treaties has been developed on the basis of jurisprudence. Nevertheless, it should be emphasized that, while binding decisions of IOs share some similarities with treaties, they also have some characteristics that are clearly distinctive from treaties.[4] Moreover, one should also note that within the group of decisions of IOs there are some differences.

(Quasi)judicial decisions settle a specific case between certain parties and formally do not bind other parties which were not involved in the dispute. Non-judicial decisions usually are generally applicable and bind all contracting parties – unless opted out. Even so, the fact remains that all of those decisions belong to the field of public international law and are all adopted by bodies that have been established by international treaties endowed with the competence to adopt binding decisions. In fact, the essential aspect of the communitarization of decisions which in turn affects their domestic legal effect is an issue that plays a role in all decisions – whether (quasi)judicial or non-judicial. Accordingly, the significance of decisions of IOs as a special source of the law of IOs and thus of public international law should be kept in mind when analyzing them.

1.3 Non-consensual decision-making process within organs of IOs

The third interesting result of this research relates to the method of adoption of decisions of IOs as compared to international treaties.

The inclusion of Chapter 2 within this research was justified *inter alia* because of the close relationship between international treaties and decisions of IOs. However, two important differences remain and therefore should be emphasized in this context. First, in contrast to international treaties, decisions of IOs (including those of institutionalized international agreements) generally do not require ratification by the contracting parties in order to enter into force. Second, the requirement of expressing its will to be bound by an international agreement as a precondition for being legally bound by a treaty is undermined by the non-consensual voting procedures in several organs of IOs. Thus, while a state cannot be legally bound by an agreement without its consent, this can very well be the case with regard to certain decisions of IOs. For example, whereas the requirement of consensus can still be found in several organs of IOs, i.e. Regional Fisheries Organizations, Association Council, there are other organs of IOs which adopt binding decisions on the basis of some sort of majority voting, that is, a state can be bound by a decision even against its will (Security Council).[5] However, at the same time, it must be mentioned that in many of these cases, states that do not wish to be bound by a decision still have the possibility

---

4 See below section 1.3.

5 See generally: Tomuschat (1993).

to opt out, thereby preventing the decision from becoming legally binding on them (ICAO Council, most COPs/MOPs). Nevertheless, there are also examples in which a small minority of contracting parties can bind the majority of contracting parties – sometimes even without a possibility of opting out and thus against their explicit will. This is, for instance, the case with amendments to the Montreal Protocol in which parties can only avoid to be bound by a MOP decision by revoking the whole protocol. Similarly, the 15 members of the Security Council can adopt sanctions under Chapter VII UN Charter that bind all other 176 member states. An interesting example of non-consensual voting procedures is the voting requirement for the adoption of Panel and Appellate Body reports within the Dispute Settlement Body (DSB) of the WTO. In this case, a report becomes legally binding when it is adopted by the Dispute Settlement Body in which all contracting parties are represented unless all parties agree not to adopt the report. This kind of 'reversed' consensus prevents on the one hand that the 'losing' party can block the adoption of the report (which used to be the case under the GATT 1947), while at the same time it ensures that the report becomes *de facto* automatically binding when it is circulated in the DSB – since it is most unlikely that a 'winning' party would agree that the report should not be adopted.

Finally, decisions of IOs can under certain circumstances become legally binding even on non-members of an IO or non-contracting parties of an international treaty. That is, for example, the case with the EC in regard to Security Council Resolutions imposing sanctions and used to be the case with binding Panel reports under the old GATT 1947. In both cases, the EC is/was not member of them but was bound by their binding decisions by virtue of its exclusive competence in trade matters (Article 133 EC Treaty). Thus, the research results illustrate that in all those cases in which binding decisions of IOs are not adopted by unanimity but rather by some sort of majority or even minority voting, states cannot control any longer the future scope of their legal obligations when they ratify a treaty that establishes a body that is empowered to adopt binding decisions. In summary, these conclusions underline the legal significance of binding decisions of IOs in the domestic legal orders of the states.

2 European law level

As the previous Chapters have shown the influence of European law is the central factor responsible for the transformation of the legal status and effect of decisions of IOs. As will be discussed in more detail below, this transformation takes place through Community legislation as well as through the jurisprudence of the ECJ and CFI. Moreover, the influence of Community law principles such as supremacy and direct effect can also to a certain extend be detected regarding II. and III. pillar decisions. As there are differences between the EC legal order (I. pillar) and the EU legal order (II. and III. pillar), they are discussed in the following sections separately.

2.1 EC legal order

As regards the EC legal order, the following three research results appear to be particularly relevant and therefore will be discussed in more detail below: first, the legal status and effect of decisions of IOs in the Community legal order; second, the communitarization of decisions of IOs through EC legislation and third, the communitarization of decisions of IOs through the jurisprudence of the ECJ and CFI.

2.1.1 Legal status and effect of decisions of IOs in the EC legal order

The EC Treaty does not either determine the legal status of decisions of IOs in the Community legal order or of international treaties. Article 300 EC Treaty merely stipulates that international agreements concluded by the EC are binding on the EC and its Member States. One has to look at the jurisprudence of the ECJ and CFI in order to extract the relevant points concerning the legal status and effect of binding decisions within the Community legal order.

First, the ECJ determined that from the moment the EC ratifies an international agreement, either alone or together with the Member States through the adoption of a Council act, the complete treaty becomes an integral part of the Community legal order. Similarly, when the EC obtains exclusive external competence in a certain policy area, a treaty concluded by the Member States that falls within this exclusive competence also becomes an integral part of the Community legal order even without membership of the EC (GATT 1947).[6] Consequently, international agreements that have (also) been concluded by the EC and thus have become an integral part of the Community legal order and are ranked between primary and secondary EC law, enjoy primacy over secondary Community law but not over the EC Treaty.[7]

Second, when a decision of an organ of IO becomes legally binding and falls within the competence of the EC, it similarly becomes an integral part of the Community legal order. Moreover, the ECJ and CFI treat decisions of IOs that are directly linked with the international treaty in the same way as the treaty itself.[8] Accordingly, decisions of IOs enjoy the same legal status

6 See e.g.: Case 12/86 *Demirel* v. *Stadt Schwäbisch Gmünd* [1987] ECR 3719; Case 21-24/72 *International Fruit Company* v. *Produktschap voor Groenten en Fruit* [1972] ECR 1219.

7 See generally: Klabbers (2001); Hartley (2001).

8 See e.g.: Case C-192/89 *Sevince* [1990] ECR I-3461; Case T-18/99 *Cordis* [2001] ECR II-913.

within the Community legal order as treaties, i.e. lower than the EC Treaty but higher than conflicting secondary Community law. In addition, the decisions obtain Community law features such as supremacy over all domestic law of the Member States and direct effect if they meet the criteria as established by the ECJ and CFI.

However, the research results show that this general rule is not always consistently applied. In particular, the example of the treatment of WTO dispute settlement reports regarding the banana and hormones disputes by the ECJ and CFI indicate that they were not willing to effectuate the WTO dispute settlement reports despite the fact the DSB unequivocally found that the EC measures were inconsistent with WTO law. Nonetheless, leaving the WTO dispute settlement reports aside, it can be concluded that other decisions of IOs are treated by the ECJ and CFI in accordance with their own case-law. Hence, they obtain Community law features such as supremacy and possible direct effect – features that they previously did not necessarily possess. This modification of the legal characteristics of decisions of IOs is described as their communitarization.

2.1.2 Communitarization of decisions of IOs through EC legislation

As has been discussed in Chapter 2, the participation of the EC in international treaties and IOs depends on the scope of its competence. Similarly, the communitarization of decisions of IOs by way of EC legislation depends on the scope of that competence. Accordingly, decisions of IOs are communitarized by way of legislation as far as the EC is competent in the respective policy areas. Moreover, as the research results indicate, there are also instances in which decisions of IOs are communitarized by legislation despite the fact that the EC is not member of that IO (ICAO).

Accordingly, in the cases in which the EC is exclusively competent and thus alone member of the IO, i.e. regional fisheries organizations, the decisions of the regional fisheries organizations are implemented by the EC through the adoption of Community legislation. Consequently, from the point of view of the domestic legal order of the EU Member States, those decisions have the legal character of pure EC legislation, even though they originated as rules of public international law. Moreover, it is also possible that the EC is exclusively competent in a certain policy area but is nevertheless not a member of the IO. This was the case regarding the GATT 1947 prior to the entry into force of the WTO Agreement and is still the case regarding the UN, in particular, concerning Security Council Resolutions imposing economic sanctions. In those cases, due to the exclusive competence of the EC in external trade matters (Article 133 EC Treaty), the EC is solely competent to implement the decisions adopted by the organs of those IOs (the GATT 1947 being considered a *de facto* IO), despite the fact that the EC is not member of those IOs.[9] Accordingly, these decisions are first implemented by Community legislation and thus are treated as EC law by the domestic legal orders of the EU Member States.

Then there are the cases in which the EC is not exclusively competent, i.e. the competence is shared between the EC and the Member States, and not a member of the IO as is the case with the ICAO. In this situation, the EU Member States remain in principle competent so that the classic legal situation 'law of IOs–national law' remains intact – as long as there is no 'interference' by the EC. For example, whenever the EC exercises its internal competence to legislate, for instance, on noise limits of aeroplanes applicable within the EC, it can copy into its legislation the relevant decisions adopted by the ICAO Council. If that occurs, the legal situation is modified into an 'EC law transformed' legal situation, thereby converting the previously public international law decision into a Community law measure. Thus, while the Member States continue to be bound by the decisions of the ICAO Council, they are, after the communitarization of ICAO decisions, also bound to implement them by virtue of Community law.

Finally, we find the cases of mixed agreements, which touch upon both the competence of the EC and its Member States and thus require a mixed participation of both the EC and its Member States as in the case of the Association Agreement EC-Turkey, WTO Agreement and some MEAs. In those cases, the extent of the 'EC law transformed' legal situation runs parallel to the extent of the competence of the EC. In other words, the classic legal situation 'law of IOs-national law' remains intact only as far as the EC has not legislated on a certain issue or as far as it concerns issues that fall clearly within the exclusive competence of the Member States. The problem here is that the ECJ often avoids making a clear delineation of the competences and instead prefers to apply an expansive definition of the Community's competence. That is, for instance, the case with various provisions of Association Council Decision 1/80 and Article 50 (6) of the TRIPS. Nonetheless, it has become clear that the scope of the competence of the EC to legislate determines at the same time the scope of communitarization of binding decisions of organs of IOs.

Moreover, the research results indicate that a correlation exists between the instruments used for implementing decisions of IOs and the scope of competence of the EC. In the case of exclusive competence of the EC (Fisheries, SC, GATT), the EC uses Regulations as the main instrument, whereas in the cases of concurrent competence, the EC appears to prefer Directives as the main instrument for implementation of decisions of IOs – although sometimes also Regulations or Council Decisions are used. Also in the case where the EC is not

9 In the meantime SC Resolutions are implemented on the basis of a two-step procedure on the basis of Art. 15 TEU and Art. 301, 60 ECT and not anymore on the basis of Art. 133 ECT. Also, since the entry into force of the WTO Agreement, the situation changed as the EC has become Member of the WTO.

member of the IO (ICAO), the EC uses Directives when it implements Annexes adopted by the ICAO Council. Thus, there appears to be a correlation between the extent of the competence of the EC and the choice of instruments used for implementing decisions of IOs – at least as far as the decisions examined in this research are concerned. This correlation can be explained by the fact that in cases in which the EC has exclusive competence, the EC can enforce its exclusive competence the best by using Regulations as the main instrument since this ensures quick and uniform application and severely limits the room of manoeuvre of the Member States. Whereas in the case of concurrent competences the influence of the Member States is greater which is also reflected in the choice of Directives as the main implementing instrument because the Directive gives Member States a certain period of time and allows them to choose how to implement the Directive. However, it should be noted that not all decisions of IOs are implemented as the example of the Association Council Decisions indicate.

An interesting aspect in this context is the effect of the communitarization of decisions of IOs on the consent of the Member States concerning the decision of the IO and the Community measure implementing it.

On the one hand, the situation can arise that an EC Member State did not consent on the international level to be bound by a certain decision whereas the very same decision is communitarized by the EC, for instance, by a Directive adopted in the Council with qualified majority voting (i.e. against the explicit will of that Member State). The main difference between the explicit denial to be bound by a decision on the international and European level is that the Member State cannot avoid being bound by the communitarized decision by virtue of EC law, whereas in most cases it can avoid being bound by the decision adopted on the international law level. Moreover, the communitarized decision enjoys supremacy over all national law and possible direct effect by virtue of Community law – irrespective of the constitutional situation in the EC Member States.

On the other hand, the situation can arise that a Member State wants to implement a binding decision of an IO but is prevented from doing so by virtue of Community law. That was, for instance, the case with Germany in the banana dispute in which it wanted to implement the binding WTO dispute settlement report but was prevented from doing so because it had to apply the WTO law-inconsistent EC Regulation. Thus, the communitarization of decisions of IOs through legislation can have different legal effects for the EU Member States.

2.1.3 Communitarization of decisions of IOs through the jurisprudence of ECJ and CFI

Besides the communitarization of decisions of IOs by legislation, this research clearly demonstrated the important role of the ECJ and CFI in the communitarization process by way of their case-law. Indeed, it is the cases that come before the European courts, in which the conflicts within the 'EC law transformed' legal interplay, that highlight the actual relevance of the communitarization of decisions of IOs.

The research results show that not all decisions of IOs that have been examined feature equally prominently in the jurisprudence. It appears that so far the legal conflicts focus on the WTO dispute settlement reports, the Association Council Decisions and the ECHR as interpreted by the ECrtHR, whereas they are less apparent in the case of Security Council Resolutions, decisions of Regional Fisheries Organizations and decisions of the COPs/MOPs.

Within the group of cases in which the 'EC law transformed' legal interplay is highlighted, the various conflicts can be distinguished in terms of which legal orders are involved. For example, the conflict regarding the WTO dispute settlement report concerning bananas involved a conflict between, on the one hand EC law, and on the other hand, WTO law and presumably German constitutional law. In the case of the various provisions of Association Council Decisions 1/80 and 3/80, the conflict concerned the national laws of various EC Members States that repeatedly were applied in violation of the Association Council Decisions. In the case of ECHR, the divergent case-law of the ECJ and the ECrtHR creates tensions on the national law level between the legal obligations of the Member States arising out of Community law versus those arising out of the ECHR.

In addition, the research results reveal that the effect of the communitarization of decisions of IOs through the application of the European courts can be very different regarding the various decisions examined. For instance in the case of the WTO dispute settlement report on bananas, the ECJ and CFI case-law has been instrumental in creating and sustaining a legal conflict between WTO law and fundamental rights protected by the German constitution. So, in this case, the 'EC law transformed' legal situation prevented the proper implementation of the WTO dispute settlement reports, thereby undermining its legal force and the credibility of the WTO dispute settlement system. In contrast, the dynamic case-law of the ECJ regarding the Association Council Decisions strengthened their legal force in the domestic law of the Member States and ensured that the Member States grant the rights to the Turkish workers and their family members as prescribed by the Association Council Decisions.

Another research result that illustrates a distinction between the different decisions of IOs is the treatment by the ECJ and CFI regarding their direct effect in the Community legal order. The ECJ and CFI make a distinction between WTO dispute settlement reports and the rest of the other decisions examined in this research. Whereas the same criteria (unconditional, clear, precise, nature and purpose of the decision) are applied to all decisions, the WTO dispute settlement reports must additionally fulfil the *Nakajima/Fediol*-conditions. The *Nakajima/Fediol*-conditions mean that Community law will only be reviewed with regard to WTO law, including WTO dispute settlement reports, if the EC measure intends to implement WTO law or explicitly refers to WTO law.

Similarly, private parties can only rely on WTO law, including WTO dispute settlement reports, if the *Nakajima/Fediol*-conditions are met. However, the recent Opinion of AG Alber in the *Biret* case provided convincing arguments for significantly narrowing down the separate status of WTO dispute settlement reports in the Community legal order.[10] In his Opinion, AG Alber concluded that adopted WTO dispute settlement reports against the EC are binding on the EC and require the EC to implement them within the prescribed deadline. More importantly, the AG concluded that if the EC fails to implement the WTO dispute settlement report within the deadline, it violates Community law principles. In order to protect the principle of legality, private parties that have suffered from the failure of the EC to implement the WTO dispute settlement report must be able to start a procedure against the EC on the basis of Article 228 EC Treaty to claim compensation for the damages. Since, according to the case-law of the ECJ, the decision must be directly applicable in order to be able to claim damages on the basis of Article 228 EC Treaty, the AG concluded that a direct effect of binding WTO dispute settlement reports must – exceptionally – be accepted for the period starting after the end of the implementation deadline. However, as discussed before, in its judgment in the *Biret* case the ECJ did not deal with this issue, but rather left it open whether in a case with different factual circumstances it would follow the reasoning of the AG.[11] In summary, the research results illustrate that the effect of the communitarization of binding decisions of IOs through European jurisprudence is very significant.

2.2 EU legal order

Despite the still existing differences between, on the one hand, the I. pillar and, on the other hand, the II. and III. pillars, the research results have shown that Community law features penetrate the legal relationship 'EU law–national law' in such a way which modifies it into an 'EC law influenced EU law–national law' legal relationship.

This 'EC law influenced' legal interplay exists by virtue of two reasons: first, because of formal cross-references in the provisions as is the case with the implementation of Security Council Resolutions; and second, because of the functional double-role of the institutions, such as the Council as the central decision-making body in the II. and III. pillars and the (partial) involvement of the ECJ and the Commission in the III. pillar.[12] Moreover, the EP is also indirectly involved due to the fact that most of the activities of the II. and III. pillars are paid out of the EC budget, thus extending the budgetary powers of the EP to the other pillars.

[10] Opinion AG Alber in Case C-93/02 P *Biret* of 15.5.2003; see also case-note by: Lavranos (2004).

[11] Case C-93/02 P *Biret*, judgment of 30.9.2003.

[12] See on the functional double role in the II. pillar: Pernice/Thym (2002).

However, a distinction must be made between the II. and III. pillars with regard to the intensity of the Community law infusion.

Regarding the II. pillar, it can be stated that the 'EC law influenced' legal interplay remains limited. With the exception of the formal cross-reference between II. and I. pillars, in the case of the implementation of Security Council Resolutions (Article 15 EU Treaty and Article 301 EC Treaty), the application of the Community law features supremacy and direct effect, while formally possible, are very limited. In this context, it should be noted that only 'European Decisions' and not 'European laws' or 'European framework laws' are mentioned as legal instruments to be used for the CFSP policy area (Articles III-196 ff. Draft Constitutional Treaty).[13] Also, the jurisdiction of the Court within the CFSP remains excluded with the exception of Article III-209 Draft Constitutional Treaty that states that the implementation of the CFSP shall not affect the other competences of the Union.[14]

In contrast, the 'EC law influenced' legal interplay is much stronger in the III. pillar, not only because of the existing jurisdiction of the ECJ and the shared right of initiative to propose legislation by the Commission, but also because of the similarity between Framework Decisions and EC Directives. Although, the TEU explicitly excludes a direct effect for Framework Decisions and Decisions, this does not prevent the application of the supremacy principle or the application of the 'indirect effect' principle that has been developed by the ECJ in regard to EC Directives.[15]

This observation is furthermore supported by the ongoing developments in the European Convention. If the current draft text of the European Constitutional Treaty[16] would become law, then this would assimilate the III. pillar to the I. pillar. In this case, direct effect would become applicable in this policy area, the jurisdiction of the ECJ would become compulsory and almost as complete as in the I. pillar (Article III-283), and the Commission and the EP would become fully involved in the decision-making process. Moreover, binding Union legislation in the areas of the III. pillar will enjoy primacy over the law of Member States. Whereas the jurisdiction of the ECJ will still remain excluded, also the involvement of the Commission and the EP will remain very limited and supremacy is not explicitly provided for CFSP decisions.

In summary, the still-existing intergovernmental elements within the III. pillar would disappear and thus also the 'EC law influenced' legal interplay would be replaced by the normal legal interplay 'EC law–national law'. Thus, the 'EC law influenced' legal interplay would then remain noticeable only in the II. pillar.

---

[13] *Ibid.*

[14] *Ibid.*

[15] See: Timmermans (2001) in particular at 9-10.

[16] CONV 850/03, 18.7.2003.

3 National law level

The research results illustrate that – despite the constitutional differences in the three selected EU Member States – decisions of IOs are treated in the same way as international treaties. This approach is laid down in Articles 93, 94 of the Dutch *Grondwet* which explicitly mention both international treaties and decisions of IOs and prescribe their primacy over all conflicting Dutch law if they are 'binding on anyone' (*iederen verbindend*), i.e. sufficiently precise, clear and unconditional.

In contrast to the Netherlands, the German *Grundgesetz* does not mention decisions of IOs. However, the requirement of a domestic transformation act for the implementation of international treaties (Article 59 (2) GG) is also applied for decisions of IOs – with the difference that decisions of IOs do not have to be implemented by a federal statute but can also be transposed by executive regulations, while treaties need to be implemented by a federal statute. Indeed, as this research illustrates decisions of IOs are often implemented by executive regulations. Accordingly, these decisions enjoy the same legal rank as executive regulations, i.e. below the *Grundgesetz* and below federal statutes.

Finally, also the *Constitution Française* only mentions international agreements (Article 55 CF) that enjoy primacy over conflicting French laws (if they meet the requirements of Article 55 CF) – but not over the constitution or other constitutional norms. Nevertheless, in the case of ECrtHR judgments and Security Council Resolutions, they are assimilated with the founding treaties. Thus, the existing constitutional differences between Germany, the Netherlands and France, as regards the legal status of international treaties within their domestic legal orders, is similarly applied to the legal status of decisions of IOs. However, these differences are eliminated when Community law is involved in the implementation of binding decisions of IOs. In those cases, the decisions of IOs are transformed into Community law measures which means that they enjoy the same legal status in all EU Member States. In other words, regardless of the constitutional differences in the Member States, all decisions of IOs which are communitarized enjoy the highest status in the legal hierarchy in the respective domestic legal orders and enjoy supremacy over all conflicting law. This conclusion can indeed be generalized for all Member States as Community law enjoys the same legal status in all Member States.

In the following sections, two aspects of the research results concerning the implementation of communitarized decisions of IOs through national legislation and through the application by national courts will be discussed in more detail.

3.1 Implementation of communitarized decisions of IOs through national legislation

In the first place, the research results indicate that in all three selected EU Member States, decisions of IOs are – whether communitarized or not – essentially implemented in the same way, namely, through the adoption of executive regulations, i.e. *Rechtsverordnung, ministeriële regeling* or *AMvB, décret* or *arrêté*. So, the difference in the origin of the decisions, i.e. public international law or Community law, apparently does not matter for the implementation on the national level. In other words, the 'EC law transformed' legal situation is treated in the same way as the classic legal situation 'law of IOs-national law'. In the second place, the research results indicate that in general the national provisions that provide for the legal basis for the implementation of international obligations are formulated very broadly, in the sense that they cover the execution of obligations arising out of international treaties/IOs and EC law. Accordingly, in some cases the national provisions simply refer to the implementation of 'international obligations', while in many other examples, the provision refers to obligations arising out of both the EC and international treaties/IOs. In other words, the implementation of binding decisions of IOs is often treated in the same way as the implementation of decisions adopted by the EC, thus making no formal distinction between decisions that derive from public international law and those that originate from Community law. In this way, the Member States are able to implement decisions of IOs as quickly and effectively as Community law decisions. Thus, whether a decision of an IO is communitarized or not does not affect the way it is implemented in the selected EU Member States. The only interesting exception to that refers to the penalties applicable for the violation of Security Council Resolutions in Germany. Paragraph 34 (4) of the *Außenwirtschaftsgesetz* prescribes a higher penalty if an EC Regulation which implements a Security Council Resolution adopted on the basis of Chapter VII is violated than would be the case if no Community legislation would have been involved.

In summary, while in most cases the legislation of the EU Member States does not make a formal distinction between the implementation of communitarized and non-communitarized decisions of IOs, this does not change the fact that communitarized decisions of IOs have the status of Community law within the domestic legal order of the Member States, which is not necessarily the case for non-communitarized decisions of IOs.

3.2 Application of communitarized decisions of IOs by national courts

The research results illustrate that the application and interpretation of communitarized decisions of IOs are particularly visible in the case of the Association Council Decisions and WTO dispute settlement reports. While, as regards the decisions of the other IOs examined, the research results indicate that they raise only very few conflicting issues before the national courts of the selected Member States.

Concerning the EC-Turkey Association Council Decisions, the impact of the ECJ jurisprudence forced the domestic courts of the selected Member States to grant rights to Turkish workers and their family members, in particular to accept the linkage of working and residence permits, which otherwise they would not have been granted on the basis of the national rules applicable to non-EU foreigners. Accordingly, German, Dutch and French courts were forced to grant direct effect to provisions of Association Council Decisions, interpret national provisions more favourably and annul decisions that were based on domestic laws because of their incompatibility with the Association Council Decisions as interpreted by the ECJ. In other words, the transformation of decisions of IOs through the involvement of the ECJ case-law forced the domestic courts of the Member States to apply the Association Council Decisions and the relevant national provisions in a way which they probably would not have done without the involvement of the ECJ jurisprudence. So, in this case, one could say that the 'EC law transformed' legal interplay ensured that the national courts of the Member States would properly apply the Association Council Decisions, thereby strengthening the legal force of those decisions.

The same cannot be said with regard to the implementation of the WTO dispute settlement reports in the banana and hormones disputes. Despite the fact that the DSB found the EC Regulation organizing the common banana market (and its revised version) to be in conflict with WTO rules, the ECJ still denies Member States as well as individuals to rely on the WTO dispute settlement report in order to challenge the EC Regulation. As a consequence thereof, the WTO law-inconsistent EC Regulation remains applicable, thereby enabling the EC to continue to violate WTO law, despite the fact that the EC is obliged to implement WTO dispute settlement reports. The same essentially applies to the hormones dispute. The approach of the ECJ is also in clear conflict with its own case-law in which it held that Community law must be interpreted as far as possible in the light of international obligations. As a result, German courts were faced with two conflicting binding decisions. On the one hand, the DSB determined that the banana regulation violates WTO rules. On the other hand, the ECJ refuses to review whether the banana regulation is in conformity with WTO rules. However, the German courts were forced by virtue of Community law to follow the case-law of the ECJ, thereby compelling Germany to violate its WTO law obligations (and violating the obligation to ensure that Germany fulfils its international obligations). So, in this case, the 'EC law transformed' legal interplay – in the guise of the ECJ and CFI jurisprudence – formed an insurmountable obstacle for the Member States and their courts that prevented the proper implementation of a binding decision of an organ of an IO.

In summary, the aspect of communitarization of decisions of IOs before national courts is particularly visible when the ECJ and CFI are directly involved in the 'EC law transformed' legal interplay and a difference of opinion between the European courts and national courts exist.

4 Conclusion and outlook

The central research question of this contribution has been to analyse how European law influences the legal status and application of binding decisions of organs of IOs in the three selected Member States.[17]

The answer to this question is that the European law transforms the classic legal relationship 'law of IOs–national law' into an 'EC law transformed' one 'law of IOs–European law–national law'. This process of communitarization modifies the legal nature of decisions of IOs that fall within the competence of the EC from a source of public international law into source of Community law. As a result, they obtain Community law features such as supremacy over all national law – including constitutional law – of the Member States and possible direct effect. They thus enjoy the same legal status in all Member States irrespective of the differences in the constitutional systems. Moreover, the communitarization of decisions of IOs also introduces the European institutions, in particular the European courts, as new actors that are involved in the implementation and application of decisions of IOs. This in turn affects the national courts of the Member States that are bound by the jurisprudence of the European courts. At the same time, this research illustrates that the influence of European law on the various decisions of IOs is not always the same. In most cases, EC law acts as an amplifier strengthening the legal status and effect of decisions of IOs in the domestic legal orders of EC Member States, while in certain cases (WTO) EC law acts as an obstacle reducing the legal force of decisions of IOs. Besides, the influence of Community law is also visible as regards III. pillar decisions and to a lesser extent as regards II. pillar decisions. Indeed, this development of reducing the differences between the various pillars will be intensified when the draft European Constitution enters into force. Hence, it can be concluded that in most cases the influence of Community law on the decisions of IOs is of amplifying or boosting nature in the sense that their legal status and effect in the Member States is substantially strengthened by attaching supremacy and possible direct effect to them. Thus, in the metaphor used in this research, decisions of IOs that fall within the competence of the EC are generally transformed from 12 Volt into 220 Volt before they enter the electric circuit of the Member States. In this way, Community law can help to strengthen the compliance with binding decisions emanating from IOs in the EU Member States. However, the exam-

[17] See Introduction.

ple of WTO dispute settlement reports shows that the current of 12 Volt can be transformed by Community law to 1,5 Volt, thereby weakening the legal force of WTO dispute settlement reports.

On a more general level, the phenomenon of the far-reaching effects of binding decisions of IOs fits into the current trend of globalization and institutionalization of international law.[18] This trend towards concluding more international treaties, establishing IOs, international courts and tribunals etc. is clearly visible. At the same time and as a consequence of the continuing institutionalization of international law, states seem to loose increasingly control over the scope and extent of their international obligations. If these observations are accepted, the question of parliamentary and judicial control of for instance binding decisions of IOs on the national level becomes more and more important. The following two issues seem to be particularly important.

First, as this research illustrates, the decisions of IOs of an executive or legislative nature are adopted by organs without parliamentary control on the international level. In turn, these decisions are implemented by the states often through the adoption of executive regulations issued by the government or the responsible minister again with very limited parliamentary involvement. And even if national parliaments are involved as is usually the case when decisions of IOs are implemented by a law, the influence of the parliament on the contents of the decisions is negligible as the contents of the decisions has been determined already on the international level and cannot be changed anymore by the individual state. This situation is also not changed by the communitarization of decisions of IOs through the involvement of Community law, since also the EP cannot change the contents of a decision of IOs if it is implemented by a Regulation or Directive. In other words, it appears that with regard to the adoption and implementation of decisions of IOs, parliamentary control is insignificant. As a result thereof, national parliaments and the citizens they represent hardly have any possibility of influencing or controlling the decision-making process in IOs, apart from holding their own governmental representatives responsible for their actions in the international fora.

Second, the research results also showed that decisions of IOs affect the rights and obligations of natural and legal persons – as the examples of Association Council Decisions, Security Council Resolutions and WTO dispute settlement reports illustrate. Accordingly, the question of effective judicial review of those decisions, for instance regarding their consistency with national (constitutional) law and fundamental rights, becomes increasingly relevant.

On the international law level, there is generally no possibility of judicial review of decisions of IOs of executive or legislative nature. The only possible exception exists regarding Security Council Resolutions that could potentially be

18 See generally: Coicaud/Heiskanen (2001); Stein (2001); Uerpmann (2001).

reviewed by the ICJ – although this has not happened yet.[19] However, due to the transformation effect of Community law, all binding decisions that fall within the competence of the EC can be reviewed by the ECJ as well as well as III. pillar decisions – albeit to a more limited extent. Whilst this potentially provides for effective judicial review, one must not overlook the existing difficulties such as the strict standards of *locus standi* before the ECJ and CFI[20] and the refusal of the European courts to allow certain decisions of IOs to be invoked, which restrict the possibilities of natural and legal persons to actually invoke or challenge decisions of IOs.

Moreover, another avenue to review Community law – and thus also communitarized decisions of IOs – has been opened up by the jurisprudence of the ECrtHR. Since its judgment in the *Matthews*[21] case, the ECrtHR seems to be prepared to review also a genuine Community law act. Indeed, the judgment in the *Bosphorus*[22] case is still awaited, while in the *Senator Lines*[23] case, the hearing was cancelled by the President of the ECrtHR before a decision of the ECrtHR was taken. This new avenue can provide additional judicial review, although one must remember that the cases brought before the ECrtHR take many years before they are decided by the ECrtHR.

On the national level, the possibilities of the national courts to review binding decisions of IOs has been limited to the extent that all decisions of IOs that fall within the competence of the EC fall within the jurisdiction of the ECJ. Accordingly, national courts are only able to review those decisions of IOs that fall within the exclusive competence of the Member States.[24] Accordingly, it can be concluded that judicial review that encompasses communitarized decisions of IOs is potentially available.

---

19 De Wet (2004). In the preliminary ruling of the dispute between Libya and the USA/UK concerning the Lockerbie bombing and the sanctions imposed by the Security Council against Libya in order to force it to extradite the supposed Libyan suspects, the ICJ asserted its jurisdiction by arguing that it was seized by the case before the Security Council adopted the Resolutions. So the ICJ used the argument of the sequence of events to assert its jurisdiction without deciding whether it would also consider itself competent if the Security Council acted prior to the moment the case is brought before the ICJ; see: ICJ, *Libyan Arab Jamahiriya* v. *UK/USA*, Preliminary objections in case concerning questions of interpretation and application of the 1971 Montreal Convention arising from the aerial incident at Lockerbie, judgment of 27.2.1998, available at: http://www.icj-cij.org/icjwww/idocket/ilus/ilusjudgment/ ilus_ijudgment_980227_frame.htm.

20 Case C-50/00 P *UPA* [2002] ECR I-6677.

21 ECrtHR *Matthews* v. *UK*, judgment of 18.2.1999.

22 ECrtHR *Bosphorus Hava* v. *Ireland*, ruling on admissibility of the case, 13.9.2001.

23 ECrtHR *Senator Lines* v. *15 EU Member States*, application no. 56672/00: see for details Chapter 5.

24 See regading Security Council Resolutions: De Wet/Nollkaemper (2002).

In summary, whereas this research confined itself to examine the formal relationship between decisions of IOs, European law and the domestic legal orders of the EC Member States, it also highlighted implicitly the aspects of democratic and judicial control which become more pressing due to the growing invasiveness of decisions of IOs. These aspects certainly deserve more detailed research in the future.

Bibliography

ABEYRATNE, R. (1992)
"Law making and Decision making powers of the ICAO Council – A critical analysis", (1992) *ZLW*, 387-394

ACIERNO, S. (2003)
"The Carpenter judgment: fundamental rights and the limit of Community legal order", (2003) *E.L. Rev.*, 398-407

ALKEMA, E. (1985)
"Toepassing van de Europese Conventie voor de Rechten van de Mens in Nederland", *Preadvies Vereniging van het Recht van België en Nederland*, Zwolle 1985

ALLAND, D. (1998)
"Le droit international 'sous' la Constitution de la Ve République", (1998) *RDP*, 1649-1670

ALSTON, P. (ED.) (1999)
The EU and Human Rights, Oxford 1999

ALSTON, P. AND WEILER, J.H.H. (1999)
"An 'ever closer union' in need of a human rights policy: The EU and Human Rights", *Harvard Jean Monnet Working Paper 1/99*

AMERANSINGHE, C.F. (1996)
Principles of Institutional Law of International Organizations, Cambridge 1996

ANDRIANTSIMBAZOVINA, J. AND SERMET, L. (1999)
"Jurisprudence administrative et Convention européenne des droits de l'homme", (1999) *RFD adm.*, 799-813

ARNULL, A. (1999)
The EU and its Court of Justice, Oxford 1999

ARTS, K. (2003)
"ACP-EU relations in a new era: The Cotonou Agreement", (2003) *CML Rev.*, 95-116

AUVERT-FINCK, J. (2003)
"Les procédures de sanction internationale en vigueur dans l'ordre interne de l'Union et la défense des droits de l'homme dans le monde", (2003) *RTD eur.*, 1-21

BALFOUR, J. (1995)
European Community Air Law, London 1995

BALFOUR, J. (1997)
"Aviation relations between EC Member States and other states", (1997) *EFA Rev.*, 97-108

BALFOUR, J. (1998)
"Les relations aériennes de la CE avec les pays tiers", (1998) *Rev. du Marché commun et de l'UE*, 172-176

BARENTS, R. (2000)
De Communitaire rechtsorde, Deventer 2000

BARENTS, R. (2003)
"Een midzomernachtsdroom op de Kirchberg", (2003) *SEW*, 2-9

BARKHUYSEN, T. AND EMMERIK, M.L. (1999)
"Improving the implementation of Strasbourg and Geneva decisions in the Dutch legal order: reopening of closed cases or claims of damages against the state", in Barkhuysen/Emmerik/van Kempen (eds.), *The execution of Strasbourg and Geneva Human Rights decisions in the national legal order*, The Hague 1999, 3-27

BARTELT, S. AND ZEITLER, H.E. (2003)
" 'Intelligente Sanktionen' zur Terrorismusbekämpfung in der EU", (2003) *EuZW*, 712-717

BEBR, G. (1983)
"Gemeinschaftsabkommen und ihre mögliche unmittlebare Wirksamkeit", (1983) *EuR*, 129-160

BELL, J. AND BOYRON, S. AND WHITTAKER, S. (1998)
Principles of French Law, Oxford 1998

BENOÎT-ROHMER, F. (1997)
"Case-note on the judgment of the ECrtHR in the Lobo Machado v. Portugal case", (1997) *RTD eur.*, 373-389

BENOÎT-ROHMER, F. (2001A)
"L'affaire Emesa Sugar: L'institution de l'Avocat Général de la Cour de Justice des CE à l'épreuve de la jurisprudence Vermeulen de la Cour Européenne des droits de l'homme", (2001) *Cahier de droit Européen*, 403-426

BENOÎT-ROHMER, F. (2001B)
"Le commissaire du gouvernement auprès du Conseil d'Etat, l'avocat général de la Cour de justice des CE et le droit à un procès équitable", (2001) *RTD eur.*, 727-741

BENTZIEN, J. (1998)
"Die Zuständigkeit der EU für Luftverkehrsabkommen mit Drittstaaten", (1998) *ZLW*, 439-455

BERNHARDT, R. (2000)
"Die Entscheidungen des Europäischen Gerichtshofs für Menschenrechte im deutschen Rechtsraum", in Geiger, R., (hrsg.), *Völkerrechtlicher Vertrag und staatliches Recht vor dem Hintergrund zunehmender Verdichtung der internationalen Beziehungen*, Baden-Baden 2000, 147-155

BERROD, F. (2000)
"La Cour de justice refuse l'invocabilité des accords OMC: essai de régulation de la mondialisation", (2000) *RTD eur.*, 419-450

BESSELINK, B. (1995)
Staatsrecht en buitenlands beleid, Ars Aequi Cahiers (2e ed.), Nijmegen 1995

BETHLEHEM, D. (1998)
"International Law, EC Law, National Law: Three systems in search of a framework", in Koskenniemi, M. (ed.), *International Law aspects of the EU*, The Hague 1998, 169-196

BETHLEHEM, D. (2001)
"Regional Interface between Security Council Decisions and Member States implementation: The example of the EU", in Gowlland-Debbas, V. (ed.), *United Nations Sanctions and International Law*, The Hague 2001, 291-305

BIERNAT, E. (2003)
"The Locus Standi of private applicants under Article 230 (4) EC and the principle of judicial protection in the European Community", (2003) *Jean Monnet Working Paper* 12/03

BINDER, D. (1995)
"The ECJ and the protection of fundamental rights in the EC: new developments and future possibilities in expanding fundamental rights review to Member State action", *Harvard Jean Monnet Working Paper* 4/95

BLANCHARD, D. (2003)
"Les effets des rapports de l'organe de règlement des différends de l'OMC – à la lumière du règlement 1515/2001 du Conseil de l'UE", (2003) *Rev. du Marché commun et de l'UE*, 37-48

BLECKMANN, A. (1975)
Grundgesetz und Völkerrecht, Berlin 1975

BLECKMANN, A. (1983)
"The mixed agreements of the EEC in public international law", in O'Keeffe, D. and Schermers, H. (eds.), *Mixed Agreements*, 1983, 155-165

BLECKMANN, A. (1994)
"Verfassungsrang der Europäischen Menschenrechtskonvention?", (1994) *EuGRZ*, 149-155

BLOKKER, N. (1999)
"Decisions of IOs: The case of the EU", (1999) *NYIL*, 3-44

BLOKKER, N. AND SCHERMERS, H. (EDS.) (2001)
Proliferation of International Organizations, The Hague 2001

BODANSKY, D. (1999)
"The Legitimacy of International Governance: A coming challenge for International Environmental Law?", (1999) *AJIL*, 596-624

BOER-BUQUICCHIO, M. (2003)
"Klarstellung zum Status des Europäischen Gerichtshofs für Menschenrechte und seiner Beziehung zum Europarat", (2003) *EuGRZ*, 561-563

BOHBOT, C. (1999)
"Les battues administratives aux loups mises en échec par la convention de Berne", (1999) *RJE*, 391-415

BOK, A.J. (2002)
"Case-note on Kress judgment of ECrtHR", (2002) *NJCM-Bulletin*, 747-759
BOHR, S. (1993)
"Sanctions by the UN Security Council and the EC", (1993) *EJIL*, 256-268
BOURGEOIS, J. (1984)
"Effects of international agreements in EC law: are the dice cast?", (1984) *Michigan Law Review*, 1250-1273
BOURGEOIS, J. (1995)
"The EC in the WTO and Advisory Opinion 1/94: An Echternach procession", (1995) *CML Rev.*, 763-787
BRANDL, U. (1999)
"Die Umsetzung der Sanktionsresolutionen des Sicherheitsrats im österreichischem Recht", (1999) *Zeitschrift für Öffentliches Recht*, 161-218
BRONCKERS, M. (2001)
"La jurisprudence des juridictions Communautaires relatives à l'OMC demande réparation: Plaidoyer pour les droits des états membres", (2001) *Cahiers de Droit Européen*, 3-14
BRÖLMANN, C. AND VIERDAG, B. (1996)
"National report: the Netherlands", in Eisemann, P., (ed.), *The integration of international and European Community law into the national legal order*, The Hague 1996, 433-459
BROUWER, J. (1992)
Verdragsrecht in Nederland, Zwolle 1992
BROWN, CH. (2003)
"Case-note on C-112/00 Schmidberger", (2003) *CML Rev.*, 1499-1510
BROWNLIE, I. (1990)
Principles of Public International Law, (4th ed.), Oxford 1990
BUERGENTHAL, TH. (1969)
Law-making in the ICAO, New York 1969
BUERGENTHAL, TH. (1992)
"Self-executing and non-self-executing Treaties in national and international law", (1992) IV, *Recueil des Cours*, 303-400
BULTERMAN, M. (1999)
"Van wapenembargo tot luchtvaartverbod: het Europese sanctieregime voor Joegoslavië", (1999) *NTER*, 203-206
BULTERMAN, M. (2002)
"De financiële strijd tegen het terrorism en de mensenrechten", (2002) *NJCM-Bulletin*, 834-848
BURGORGUE-LARSEN, L. (2000) AND (2001)
"Chronique de jurisprudence européen comparée", (2000) *RDP* 1081-1150 and (2001) *RDP*, 693-736

CALLEWAERT, J. (2001)
"Het EVRM en het communautair recht: een Europese globalisering?", (2001) *NTER*, 259-267

CANOR, I. (1998)
" 'Can two walk together, except they be agreed?' The relationship between international law and European law: The incorporation of UN Sanctions against Yugoslavia into European Community law through the perspective of the ECJ", (1998) *CML Rev.*, 137-187

CANOR, I. (2000)
"Primus inter pares. Who is the ultimate guardian of fundamental rights in Europe?", (2000) *E.L. Rev.*, 3-21

CASSIA, P. AND SAULNIER, E. (1997A)
"Le Conseil d'Etat et la Convention européenne des droits de l'homme", (1997) *AJDA*, 411-420

CASSIA, P. AND SAULNIER, E. (1997B)
"L'imbroglio de la banane", (1997) *Rev. du Marché commun et de l'Union européenne*, 527-544

CASTILLO DE LA TORRE, F. (2002)
"Case-note Opinion 1/00", (2002) *CML Rev.*, 1373-193

CHURCHILL, R. (1980)
"Revision of the EEC's Common Fisheries Policy", (1980) *E.L.Rev.*, 95-111

CHURCHILL, R. (1987)
EEC Fisheries Law, Dordrecht 1987

CHURCHILL, R. (1999A)
"The EU as an International Fisheries Actor - Shark or Minnow?", (1999) *EFA Rev.*, 463-483

CHURCHILL, R. (1999B)
"The EC and its Role in some issues of International Fisheries Law", in Hey, E. (ed.), *Developments in International Fisheries Law*, The Hague 1999, 533-573

CHURCHILL, R. AND ULFSTEIN, G. (2000)
"Autonomous Institutional Arrangements in Multilateral Environmental Agreements: A little-noticed Phenomenon in International Law", (2000) *AJIL*, 623-659

CLASSEN, C.-D. (1993)
"Maastricht und die Verfassung; kritische Bemerkungen zum neuen 'Europa-Artikel' 23 GG", (1993) *ZRP*, 57-61

COICAUD, J.-M. AND HEISKANEN, V. (2001)
The legitimacy of International Organizations, Tokyo 2001

COOMANS AND GRÜNFELD AND HARTOGH AND JANSEN (1995)
"Doorwerking en effecten van sanctiemaatregelen van de VN", (1995) *SEW*, 501-513

COSNARD, M. (2000)
"Case note on Cour de Cassation judgment of 15.7.1999", (2000) *JDI*, 45-55
COTTIER, TH. (1998)
"Dispute settlement in the WTO: Characteristics and structural implications for the EU", (1998) *CML Rev.*, 325-378
CRAIG, P. AND DE BÚRCA, G. (1998) AND (2003)
EU Law (2nd ed.), Oxford 1998 and (3rd ed.), Oxford 2003
CREMONA, M. (1999)
"External Relations and External Competence" in Craig, P. and De Búrca, G. (eds.), *The Evolution of EU law*, Oxford 1999, 167-168
CURTIN, D. (2000)
"The "EU Human Rights Charter" and the Union legal order: The 'Banns' before the Marriage?", in O'Keeffe, D., (ed.), *Judicial Review in EU Law - Liber Amicorum Lord Slynn of Hadley*, The Hague 2000, 303-318
CURTIN, D. AND DEKKER, I. (1999)
"The EU as a 'layered' International Organization: Institutional unity in disguise", in Craig, P. and De Búrca, G. (eds.), *The Evolution in EU Law*, Oxford 1999, 83-136
DASHWOOD, A. (2000)
"Preliminary rulings on the interpretation of mixed agreements", O'Keeffe, D. (ed.), *Judicial Review in EU Law - Liber Amicorum Lord Slynn of Hadley*, The Hague 2000, 167-175
DE JONGHE, K. AND BURENS, P. (2003)
"Naar een meer legitiem Europa?", (2003) *Internationale Spectator*, 120-126
DE WET, E. (2004)
The Chapter VII powers of the UN Security Council, Oxford 2004
DE WET, E. AND NOLLKAEMPER, A., (2002)
"Review of Security Council Resolutions by national courts", (2002) *GYIL*, 166-202
DE WITTE, B. (1984)
"Retour à 'Costa' – La primauté du droit communitaire à la lumière du droit international", (1984) *RTD eur.*, 425-454
DE WITTE, B. (1998)
"The pillar structure and the nature of the EU: Greek temple or French gothic cathedral", in Heukels/Blokker/Brus (eds.), *The EU after Amsterdam: A legal analysis*, The Hague 1998, 51-68
DE WITTE, B. (1999A)
"Direct effect, supremacy, and the nature of the legal order", in Craig, P. and De Búrca, G. (eds.), *The evolution of EU law*, Oxford 1999, 177-213

DE WITTE, B. (1999B)
"The past and future role of the ECJ in the protection of Human rights", in Alston, P. (ed.) *The EU and Human Rights*, Oxford 1999, 859-897

DE WITTE, B. (2001)
Internationale verdragen tussen lidstaten van de EU, Preadvies NVIR 123, The Hague 2001, 79-131

DE WITTE, B. (2002)
"Simplification and reorganization of the European Treaties", (2002) *CML Rev.*, 1255-1287

DE ZWAAN, J. (1998)
"Community dimensions of the second pillar", in Heukels/Blokker/Brus (eds.), *The EU after Amsterdam: A legal analysis*, The Hague 1998, 179-214

DECAUX, E. AND EISEMANN, P., GOESEL-LE BIHAN, V., STERN, B. (1996)
"National report: France", in Eisemann, P. (ed.), *The integration of International and European Community law into the national legal order*, The Hague 1996, 241-286

DEGEN, M. (1997)
"Kommentar zu [ex] Art. K", in Groeben/Thiesing/Ehlermann (hrsg.), *Kommentar zum EU-/EG-Vertrag*, Vol. 5, Baden-Baden, (5. Aufl.) 1997, 999-1087

DELBRÜCK, J. (2002)
"Prospects for a 'World (Internal) Law?': Legal developments in a changing international system", (2002) *Indiana Journal of Global Legal Studies*, available at: http://ijgls.indiana.edu/about/delbruck.shtml.

DESMEDT, A. (2000)
"ECJ on the effect of WTO agreements in the EC legal order", (2000) *LIEI*, 93-101

DESMEDT, A. (2001)
"Rechtstreekse werking van WTO-akkoorden via de achterdeur? De bevoegdheid van de nationale rechter tot de interpretatie van het TRIPs-akkoord na de Dior-zaak", (2001) *NTER*, 79-83

DEVROE, W. AND WOUTERS, J. (1996)
De Europese Unie, Leuven 1996

DIEDERICKS-VERSCHOOR, I. (1993)
An introduction to Air Law (5th ed.), Deventer 1993

DUTHEIL DE LA ROCHÈRE, J. (1987)
"France", in Jacobs, .F. and Roberts, S. (eds.), *The effect of treaties in domestic law*, London 1987, 39-61

DUTHEIL DE LA ROCHÈRE, J. (1992)
"National Report on France", in Meessen, K. (ed.), *International Law of Export Control*, London 1992, 79-87

DUTHEIL DE LA ROCHÈRE, J. (1999)
"Environmental law in France", in Koeman, N. (ed.), *Environmental Law in Europe*, The Hague 1999, 217-272
DUVIGNEAU, J. (1998)
"From Advisory Opinion 2/94 to the Amsterdam Treaty: Human rights protection in the EU", (1998) *LIEI*, 61-91
DUYNSTEE, F. (1954)
Grondwetsherziening 1953, Deventer 1954
EBERLE, C. (2001)
Die EG als Partei internationaler Umweltschutzübereinkommen: Fragen des Abschlusses von Übereinkommen und deren Implementierung, Diss., Heidelberg 2001
EECKHOUT, P. (1997)
"The domestic legal status of the WTO Agreement: Interconnecting legal systems", (1997) *CML Rev.*, 11-58
EECKHOUT, P. (2004)
The external relations of the EU, Oxford 2004
ERDMENGER, J. (1997)
"Kommentar zu [ex] Art. 84", in Groeben/Thiesing/Ehlermann (hrsg.), *Kommentar zum EU-/EG-Vertrag*, Vol. 1, Baden-Baden 1997, 1737-1776
ERLER, J. (1967)
Rechtsfragen der ICAO, Köln 1967
EVERLING, U. (1993)
"Überlegungen zur Struktur der EU und zum neuen 'Europa-Artikel' des Grundgesetzes", (1993) *DVBl.*, 936-947
EVERLING, U. (1996)
"Will Europe slip on bananas? The bananas judgment of the Court of Justice and national courts", (1996) *CML Rev.*, 401-437
FENNELLY, N. (2000)
"The Area of Freedom, Security and Justice and the ECJ - A personal view", (2000) *ICLQ*, 1-14
FÉRVRIER, J.-M. (2001)
"Contrôle de Conventionalité – Conseil d'Etat, 8.12.2000", (2001) *AJDA*, 775-780
FIEDLER, P. (2000)
"Quantitative und qualitative Aspekte der Einordnung der BRD in völkerrechtliche Verträge", in Geiger, R., (hrsg.), *Völkerrechtlicher Vertrag und staatliches Recht vor dem Hintergrund zunehmender Verdichtung der internationalen Beziehungen*, Baden-Baden 2000, 11-21
FORDER, C. (2002)
"Case note on Carpenter case", (2002) *European Human Rights Cases*, 739-749

FROWEIN, J.A. (1987)
"Germany", in Jacobs, .F. and Roberts, S. (eds.), *The effect of treaties in domestic law*, London 1987, 63-86
FROWEIN, J.A. AND OELLERS-FRAHM, K. (1996)
"National report: Germany", in Eisemann, P., (ed.), *The integration of International and European Community Law into the national legal order*, The Hague 1996, 69-114
GAJA, G. (2003)
"First report on responsibility of International Organizations", A/CN.4/532, 26.3.2003
GEHRING, TH. (1990)
"International Environmental Regimes: Dynamic Sectoral Legal Systems", (1990) *YIEL*, 35-56
GEHRING, TH. AND OBERTHÜR, S. (EDS.) (1997)
Internationale Umweltregime – Umweltschutz durch Verhandlungen und Verträge, Opladen 1997
GEIGER, R. (1994) AND (2002)
Grundgesetz und Völkerrecht (2. Aufl.) 1994 and (3. Aufl.) München 2002.
GEIGER, R. (1995)
Kommentar zum EG-Vertrag (2. Aufl.) München 1995
GEISLER, M. (1997)
"Die 'Bonusliste' des Bundesministeriun für Verkehr als Grundlage für Nachtflugbeschränkungen auf deutschen Verkehrsflughäfen", (1997) *ZLW*, 307-319
GEURSEN, W. (2002)
"Het arrest Dangeville: EHRM oordeelt over schending van gemeenschapsrecht", (2002) *NTER*, 294-299
GIARDINA, A. (1987)
"International Agreements of the Member States and their construction by the Court of Justice", in Caporti, F., et.al. (eds.), *Du droit international au droit de l'integration – Liber Amicorum Pescatore*, Baden-Baden 1987, 263-273
GIEMULLA, E. (2000)
"Die Grundrechtskonformität von Nachtflugbeschränkungen für den Passagierflugverkehr mit Bonuslistenflugzeugen und für den Frachtverkehr mit besonders scheren Bonuslistenflugzeugen", (2000) *ZLW*, 30-35
GIEMULLA, E. AND SCHMID, R.(2000)
Kommentar zum Luftverkehrsgesetz, Neuwied 2000
GOVAERE, I. (1997)
"Een juridische schets van de Europa Akkoorden", (1997) *SEW*, 42-47

GOWLLAND-DEBBAS, V. (ED.) (2001)
United Nations Sanctions and International Law, Graduate Institute of International Studies, The Hague 2001

GREWE, C. (2001)
"Le 'traité de paix' avec la Cour de Luxembourg: l'arrêt de la Cour constitutionnelle allemande du 7.6.2000 relatif au règlement du marché de la banane", (2001) *RTD eur.*,1-17

GROENENDIJK, K. (1992)
"Europese migratiepolitiek na Maastricht: uitbreiding en beperking van vrijheden", (1992) *MR*, 76-86

GROENENDIJK, K. (1993)
"De betekenis van het arrest-Kus voor Turkse werknemer in de EG en voor de positie van het Hof van Justitie", (1993) *MR*, 76-78

GROENENDIJK, K. (1994)
"Betekenis Associatie EEG-Turkije voor Turkse werknemers in Nederland", (1994) *MR*, 199-208

GUILLAUME, M. (1998)
"L'introduction et l'exécution dans les ordres juridiques des états des Résolutions du Conseil de Sécurité des nations unies prises en vertu du Chapitre VII de la charte", (1998) *RIDC*, 541-549

GUINCHARD, S. (2003)
"Dialogue imaginaire entre un justiciable moyen et un juriste désespéré par l'arrêt Kress", (2003) *Le Dalloz*, 152-154

GUNDEL, J. (1999)
"Der Status des Völkerrechts in der französischen Rechtsordnung nach der neueren Rechtsprechung des Conseil d'Etat: Von der Öffnung zum Rückzug?", (1999) *AVR*, 438-462

GUTMANN, R. (1996)
Die Assoziationsfreizügigkeit türkischer Staatsangehöriger, Baden-Baden 1996

HAAK, W. (1988)
"Experience in the Netherlands regarding the case-law of the Chamber of Appeal of the Central Commission for Navigation on the Rhine", (1988) *NYIL*, 3-52

HAILBRONNER, K. (2000)
Immigration and Asylum Law and Policy of the EU, The Hague 2000

HANCHER, L. (1994)
"Constitutionalism, the Community Court and International Law", (1994) *NYIL*, 259-298

HANDL, G. (1990)
"Environmental Security and Global Change: The Challenge to International Law", (1990) *YIEL*, 3-33

HARTLEY, T. (2001)
"International and the law of the EU – A reassessment", (2001) *BYIL*, 1-35
HELISKOSKI, J. (2000)
"The jurisdiction of the ECJ to give preliminary rulings on the interpretation of mixed agreements", (2000) *Nordic Journal of International Law*, 395-412
HELISKOSKI, J. (2001)
Mixed agreements as a technique for organizing the international relations of the EC and its Member States, The Hague 2001
HERINGA, A.W. (1993)
"Judicial enforcement of Article 26 of the International Covenant on Civil and Political Rights in the Netherlands", (1993) *NYIL*, 139-182
HERINGA, A.W. (1994)
"De toepassing van artikel 26 IVBPR door de Nederlandse rechter", (1994) *NJCM-Bulletin*, 855-864
HERRMANN, CH. (2002)
"Common Commercial Policy after Nice: Sisyphus would have done a better job", (2002) *CML Rev.*, 7-29
HEUKELS, T. (1997)
"Richtlijn- en gemeenschapsrechtconforme interpretatie: nieuwe internationale dimensies", (1997) *NJB*, 1845-1850
HEUKELS, T. (1999)
"Von richtlinienkonformer zur völkerrechtskonformen Auslegung im EG-Recht: Internationale Dimensionen einer normhierarchiegerechten Interpretationsmaxime", (1999) *ZEuS*, 313-333
HILF, M. (1995)
"EU und EMRK", in Beyerlin/Bothe/Hofmann/Petersmann, *Recht zwischen Umbruch und Bewahrung – FS für Bernhardt*, Berlin 1995, 1193-1210
HILLION, C. (2000)
"Institutional aspects of the partnership between the EU and the newly independent states of the former Soviet Union: case studies of Russia and Ukraine", (2000) *CML Rev.*, 1211-1235
ILSINK, J.W. (1998)
"De conclusie na Borgers", (1998) *NJB*, 1108-1110
JANS, J.H. (1987)
Grensoverschrijdend milieurecht, Zwolle 1987.
JANS, J.H. (1999)
"Annotatie C-53/96 Hermès", (1999) *SEW*, 214-221
JANS, J.H. (2000)
European Environmental Law (2nd ed.), Groningen 2000

JACOBS, F. (1994)
"European Community law and the ECHR", in Curtin, D. and Heukels, T. (eds.), *Institutional Dynamics of European Integration – Essays in Honour of Schermers*, Vol. II, Dordrecht 1994, 561-571

JACOBS, F. (2001)
"Human rights in the EU: the role of the Court of Justice", (2001) *E.L. Rev.*, 331-341

KADELBACH, S. AND PETERSEN, N. (2003)
"Anmerkung zum EuGH-Urteil in der Rs. C-112/00 (Schmidberger v. Österreich)", (2003) *EuGRZ*, 693-698

KAPTEYN, P. (2003)
"The role of the ECJ in implementing Security Council Resolutions", in De Wet/Nollkaemper (eds.) *Review of Security Council by Member States*, Antwerp 2003, 57-62

KEARNS, J. AND CHARNOVITZ, S. (2002)
"Adjudicating compliance in the WTO: A Review of DSU Art. 21.5", (2002) *JIEL*, 331-352

KEMPER, G.H. (1995)
"Die neue Rechtsprechung des Bundesverwaltungsgericht zum Ausländer- und Staatsangehörigkeitsrecht", (1995) *NVwZ*, 1073-1082

KEUNEN, F. (2001)
Schets van het Europees sociaalzekerheidsrecht, Lelystad 2001

KLABBERS, J. (1998)
"Presumptive Personality: The EU in International Law", in Koskenniemi, M., (ed.), *International Law Aspects of the EU*, The Hague 1998, 231-253

KLABBERS, J. (2001)
"International law in Community law: The law and politics of direct effect", (2001-2002) *YEL*, 263-298

KOERS, A. (1977)
"The external authority of the EEC in regard to Marine Fisheries", (1977) *CML Rev.*, 269-301

KOERS, A. (1984)
"The EEC and International Fisheries Organisations", (1984/1) *LIEI*, 113-131

KOENIG, CH. AND PECHSTEIN, M. (1998)
Die Europäische Union, Tübingen 1998

KOMURO, N. (2000)
"The EC banana regime and judicial control", (2000) *JWT*, 1-87

KORTMANN, C. (1997)
Constitutioneel Recht, Deventer 1997

KOUTRAKOS, P. (2002)
"The interpretation of mixed-agreements under the preliminary ruling procedure", (2002) *EFA Rev.*, 25-52

KRANENBORG, H. (2003)
"Art. 8 EVRM en de verificatiebevoegdheden van de Commissie – Colas Est en Roquette Frères", (2003) *SEW*, 49-57
KRONENBERGER, V. (2000)
"A new approach to the interpretation of the French constitution in respect to international conventions: From hierarchy of norms to conflict of competence", (2000) *NILR*, 323-358
KRÜCK, H. (1997)
"Kommentar zu Art. [ex] 164", in Groeben/Thiesing/Ehlermann (hrsg.), *Kommentar zum EU-/EG-Vertrag*, Vol. 4, Baden-Baden 1997, 360-390
KUIJPER, P.J. (1979)
The Netherlands and International Organizations, Asser Instituut, Vol. II, The Hague 1979, 4-41
KUIJPER, P.J. (1980)
"De nieuwe Sanctiewet", (1980) *SEW*, 319-342
KUIJPER, P.J. (2000)
"Some legal problems associated with the communitarization of policy on visas, asylum and immigration under the Amsterdam Treaty and incorporation of the Schengen aquis", (2000) *CML Rev.*, 345-366
KUIJPER, P.J. (2003)
"Implementation of Binding Security Council Resolutions by the EU/EC", in De Wet/Nollkaemper (eds.) *Review of Security Council by Member States*, Antwerp 2003, 39-55
KUILWIJK, K.J. (1996)
The ECJ and the GATT dilemma: Public interest versus individual rights?, Beuningen, 1996
KUSCHEL, H.-D. (1996)
"Wie geht es weiter mit der Bananenmarktordnung?", (1996) *EuZW*, 645-650
LABAYLE, H. (1998)
"Droit fondamentaux et droit européen", (1998) *AJDA*, 75-90
LACHAUME, J.-F. (1998)
"Droit fondamentaux et droit administrative", (1998) *AJDA*, 92-105
LANFRANCHI, M.-P. (1997)
"La valeur juridique en France des Résolutions du Conseil de Sécurité", (1997) *Annuaire Français de Droit International*, 31-57
LAVRANOS, N. (1999)
"Die Rechtswirkungen von WTO panel reports im Europäischen Gemeinschaftsrecht sowie im deutschen Verfassungsrecht", (1999) *EuR*, 289-308
LAVRANOS, N. (2002A)
"Multilateral Environmental Agreements: Who makes the binding decisions?", (2002) *EEL Rev.* 44-50

LAVRANOS, N. (2002B)
"Annotatie zaak Schieving-Nijstad", (2002) *SEW*, 192-195
LAVRANOS, N. (2002C)
"Case-note on Schieving-Nijstad", (2002) *LIEI*, 323-333
LAVRANOS, N. (2002D)
"Some proposals for a fundamental DSU reform", (2002) *LIEI*, 73-82
LAVRANOS, N. (2003)
"Case note on open skies judgment", (2003) *LIEI*, 81-91
LAVRANOS, N. (2004)
"Die EG darf WTO-Recht weiterhin ignorieren", to be published in (2004) *EWS*, issue 4
LAWSON, R. (1994)
"Confusion and Conflict? Diverging interpretations of the ECHR in Strasbourg and Luxembourg", in Lawson, R. and de Blois, M. (eds.), *The Dynamics of the Protection of Human Rights in Europe – Essays in Honour of Schermers*, Vol. III, Dordrecht 1994, 219-252
LAWSON, R. (1995)
"Positieve verplichtingen onder het EVRM: Opkomst en ondergang van de 'fair balance' test – Deel I", (1995) *NJCM-Bulletin* 558-573 and Deel II, 727-750
LAWSON, R. (1999A)
"Internationale rechtspraak in de Nederlandse rechtsorde", Preadvies, *Handelingen NJV*, 1999-I, 1-125
LAWSON, R. (1999B)
Het EVRM en de Europese Gemeenschappen, Leiden 1999
LAWSON, R. (2000)
"Case-note on the Emesa Sugar case", (2000) *CML Rev.*, 983-990
LEAL-ARCAS, R. (2003)
"Exclusive or shared competence in the Common Commercial Policy: From Amsterdam to Nice", (2003) *LIEI*, 3-14
LE BIHAN, CH. (2003)
"La réforme de la politique commune de la pêche", (2003) *Rev. du Marché commun et de l'UE*, 80-89
LE CORNEC, E. (1999)
"Protection de la nature – commerce international", (1999) *RJE*, 103-110
LEEFMANS, P.J. (1998)
Externe milieubevoegdheden: communautairrechtelijke grenzen aan externe milieubevoegdheden van de EG-lidstaten, Deventer 1998
LIENENMEYER, M. AND WAELBROECK, D. (2003)
"Case-note on Roquette Frères", (2003) *CML Rev.*, 1481-1497
LIMBACH, J. (2000)
"Die Kooperation der Gerichte in der zukünftigen europäischen

Grundrechtsarchitektur", lecture at the WHI in Berlin, 29.6.2000, FCE 7/00

LOUIS, J.-V. (2000)
"Some reflections on the Implementation of WTO rules in the EC legal order", in Bronckers, M. and Quick, R. (eds.), *New Directions in International Economic Law – Essays in Honour of Jackson*, The Hague 2000, 493-507

MACLEOD, I, AND HENDRY, I.-D. AND HYETT, ST. (1996)
The external relations of the EC, Oxford 1996

MALLMANN, O. (1995)
"Zur aufenthaltsrechtlichen Bedeutung des Assoziationsratsbeschlusses EWG/Türkei", (1995) *JZ*, 916-920

MANIN, P. (1997)
"A propos de l'accord instituant l'Organisation du Commerce et de l'accord sur les marches publics: la question de l'invocabilité des accords internationaux conclus par la Communauté européenne", (1997) *RTD eur.*, 399-428

MARESCEAU, M. (ED.) (1997)
Enlarging the European Union, Relations between the EU and Central and Eastern Europe, London 1997

MARQUARDT, S. (2001)
"The conclusion of international agreements under Article 24 TEU", in Kronenberger, V. (ed.), *The EU and the International Legal Order: Discord or Harmony?*, The Hague 2001, 333-348

MARTENCZUK, B. (2001)
"Decisions of bodies established by international agreements and the Community legal order", in Kronenberger, V. (ed.), *The EU and the International Legal Order: Discord or Harmony?*, The Hague 2001, 141-163

MARTIN MARTINEZ, M. (1996)
National sovereignty and International Organizations, The Hague 1996

MAUBERNARD, CH. (2001)
"L'arrêt Kress c/ France de la Cour européenne des droits de l'homme: le rôle du commissaire du gouvernement près du Conseil d'Etat à la lumière de la théorie des 'apparences'", (2001) *RDP*, 895-911

MAYER, F. (2000)
"Grundrechtsschutz gegen europäische Rechtsakte durch das BVerfG: Zur Verfassungsmässigkeit der Bananenmarktordnung", (2000) *EuZW*, 685-689

MCNELIS, N. (2003)
"What obligations are created by WTO Dispute Settlement Reports?", (2003) *JWT*, 647-672

MENGOZZI, P. (1999)
"Structure et principes de l'OMC à la lumière de la mise en œuvre des

recommandations de l'ORD dans l'affaire Bananes III", (1999) *Rev. Marché Unique Européen*, 11-24

MENGOZZI, P. (2000)
"La Cour de justice et l'applicabilité des règles de l'OMC en droit communautaire à la lumière de l'affaire Portugal c. Conseil", (2000) *Rev. du Droit de l'Union Européen*, 509-522

MIDDELDORP, G. AND VAN OOIK, R. (2003)
"Van verdeelde open skies naar een uniform Europees extern luchtvaartbeleid", (2003) *NTER*, 1-10

MONAR, J. (1998)
"Justice and Home affairs in the Treaty of Amsterdam: Reform at the Price of Fragmentation", (1998) *E.L. Rev.*, 320-335

MORRISON, F. AND WOLFRUM, R. (EDS.) (2000)
International, Regional and National Environmental Law, The Hague 2000

MOSLER, H. (1992)
"Die Übertragung von Hoheitsgewalt", in Isensee, J. and Kirchhof, P. (hrsg.), *Handbuch des Staatsrechts der BRD*, Band VII, Heidelberg 1992

NACHBAUR, A. (1995)
"Türkische Arbeitnehmer in der EU - Drittstaatsangehörige Unionsbürger?", (1995) *NVwZ*, 344-345

NAUD, F. (1997)
"L'embargo: Une valse à trois temps Nations Unies, Union Européenne et états membres", (1997) *Rev. du Marché commun et de l'UE*, 25-33

NEFRAMI, E. (2001)
"La compétence de la Cour de justice pour interpréter l'Accord TRIPs selon l'arrêt 'Parfums Christian Dior'", (2001) *Rev. du Droit de l'UE*, 491-519

NEUWAHL, N. (1991)
"Joint Partnership in International Treaties and the Exercise of Power by the EEC and its Member States: Mixed Agreements", (1991) *CML Rev.*, 717-740

NEUWAHL, N. (1996)
"Shared Powers or Combined Incompetence? More on Mixity", (1996) *CML Rev.*, 667-687

NEUWAHL, N. (1998)
"A partner with a troubled personality: EU Treaty-making in matters of CFSP and JHA after Amsterdam", (1998) *EFA Rev.*, 177-195

NICOLAYSEN, G. (2003)
"Die gemeinschaftliche Begründung von Grundrechten", (2003) EuR, 719-743

NOLLKAEMPER, A. (1987)
"The EC and International Environmental Co-operation: Legal Aspects of External Community Powers", (1987/2) *LIEI*, 61-91

NOLLKAEMPER, A. (1998)
"Judicial application of international environmental law in the Netherlands", (1998) *RECIEL*, 40-46
NOLLKAEMPER, A. (2002)
"International Environmental Law in the courts of the Netherlands", in Anderson, M. and Galizzi, P. (eds.), *International Environmental Law in National Courts*, London 2002, 183-193
NOLTE, G. (1988)
"Case note on the ECJ judgment Case 12/86 (Demirel)", (1988) *CML Rev.*, 403-415
O'KEEFFE, D. (1999)
"Community and Member State Competence in External Relations Agreements of the EU", (1999) *EFA Rev.*, 7-36
OKOWA, P. (1997)
"Legal consequences of EC participation in International Environmental Agreements", in Evans, M. (ed.), *Aspects of Statehood and Institutionalism in Contemporary Europe*, Dartmouth 1997, 301-329
OLIVER, P. (2000)
"Fundamental rights in EU law after the Treaty of Amsterdam", in O'Keeffe (ed.), *Liber Amicorum in Honour of Lord Slynn of Hadley – Judicial Review in EU Law*, The Hague 2000, 319-342
ONDOUA, A. (2000)
"La Cour de Cassation et la place respective de la constitution et des traités dans la hiérarchie des normes", (2000) *RGDIP*, 985-1001
OPPERMANN, TH. (1999)
Europarecht (2nd ed.) München 1999
OTT, A. (2001)
"Thirty years of case-law by the European Court of Justice on international law: A pragmatic approach towards its integration", in Kronenberger, V. (ed.), *The EU and the International Legal Order: Discord or Harmony?*, (2001) The Hague, 95-140
OTT, H.H. (1998)
Umweltregime im Völkerrecht, Baden-Baden 1998
PAVONI, R. (1999)
"UN Sanctions in EU and national law: The Centro-Com case", (1999) *ICLQ*, 582-612
PEERS, S. (2000)
EU Justice and Home affairs Law, Harlow 2000
PEERS, S. (2001)
"WTO dispute settlement and Community law", (2001) *E.L. Rev.*, 605-615
PERNICE, I. (1979)
Grundrechtsgehalte im Europäischen Gemeinschaftsrecht, Baden-Baden 1979

PERNICE, I. (1999)
"Multilevel Constitutionalism and the Treaty of Amsterdam: European constitution-making revisited", (1999) *CML Rev.*, 703-750

PERNICE, I. (2001)
"Les bananes et les droits fondamentaux: La Cour Constitutionnelle Allemande fait le point", (2001) *Cahiers de Droit Européen*, 427-440

PERNICE, I. (2003)
"Democratic leadership in Europe: The European Council and the President of the Union", WHI Paper 1/03, available at: http://www.rewi.hu-berlin.de/WHI/deutsch/index.htm

PERNICE, I. AND THYM, D. (2002)
"A new institutional balance for a European Foreign Policy?", (2002) *EFA Rev.*, 369-400

PESCATORE, P. (1983)
"Die Rechtsprechung des Europäischen Gerichtshofs zur innergemeinschaftlichen Wirkung völkerrechtlicher Abkommen", in Bernhardt/Geck/Jaenicke/Steinberger (hrsg.), *Festschrift für Mosler*, Berlin 1983, 661-689

PESCATORE, P. (1987)
"Treaty-making by the European Communities", in Jacobs, F. and Roberts, S. (eds.), *The effect of treaties in domestic law*, London 1987, 171-195

PESCATORE, P. (1999)
"Opinion 1/94 on 'conclusion' of the WTO Agreement: is there an escape from a programmed disaster?", (1999) *CML Rev.*, 387-405

PETERS, A. (1998)
"Recent developments in the application of international law in domestic and European Community law", (1998) *GYIL*, 9-77

PETERSMANN, E.-U. (1997A)
"Darf die EG das Völkerrecht ignorieren?", (1997) *EuZW*, 325-331

PETERSMANN, E.-U. (1997B)
International Trade Law and the GATT/WTO Dispute Settlement System, The Hague, 1997

PETERSMANN, E.-U. (1997C)
"Kommentar zu Art. [ex] 234", in Groeben/Thiesing/Ehlermann (hrsg.), *Kommentar zum EU-/EG-Vertrag*, Vol. 5, Baden-Baden 1997, 562-588

PITSCHAS, CH. (2003)
"Anmerkung zum EuGH Urteil in der Rs. Biret", (2003) *EuZW*, 758-763

PIEROTH, B. AND GÖRISCH, C. (2000)
"Die Grundrechtskonformität von Nachflugbeschränkungen für den Passagierflugverkehr mit Bonuslistenflugzeugen", (2000) *ZLW*, 17-29

POIRAT, F. (2000)
"Les résolutions du Conseil de Sécurité devant le Conseil d'Etat et la Cour de Cassation: variations sur un même thème", (2000) *RGDIP*, 541-558

PRECHAL, S. AND PARRET, L. (2003)
"Annotatie C-50/00 *UPA*", (2003) *SEW*, 35-39

PRÉTOT, X. (2000A)
"La Cour de Cassation, la Constitution et les traités", (2000) *RDP*, 1037-1049

PRÉTOT, X. (2000B)
"Le contentieux de la fonction publique et la Convention européenne des droits de l'homme", (2000) *RDP*, 617-632

PRÉTOT, X. (2001)
"Le commissaire du gouvernement et le droit au procès: dernier sursis avant exécution?", (2001) *RDP*, 983-1002

PRIEUR, M. (2000)
"Le Code de l'environnement", (2000) *ADJA*, 1030-1038

PRIEUR, M. (2001)
Droit de l'environnement (4th ed.), Paris 2001

PROUTIÈRE-MAULIN, G. (1998A)
"Commentaire de loi No. 97-1051 du 18.11.1997, d'orientation sur la pêche et les cultures marines", (1998) *RJE*, 319-323

PROUTIÈRE-MAULIN, G. (1998B)
"Aperçu des premiers décrets pris en application de la loi d'orientation sur la pêche maritime et les cultures marines du 18.11.1997", (1998) *Le droit maritime français*, 1188-1193

PUISSOCHET, J.-P. (1997)
"The Court of Justice and the international action by the EC: The example of the embargo against the former Yugoslavia", (1997) *Fordham International Law Journal*, 1557-1576

RANDELZHOFER, A. (1992)
"Kommentar zu Art. 24 GG", in Maunz, Th. and Dürig, G., *Grundgesetz Kommentar*, München, Lieferung Dez. 1992

REMY-GRANGER, D. (2001)
"The ambiguities of the state based on the Rule of Law; a Unitary System à la Francaise", in Vandamme, Th. and Reestman, J.-H. (ed.), *Ambiguity in the Rule of Law*, Groningen 2001, 53-62

RESS, G. (1983)
"Die 'Einzelfallbezogenheit' in der Rechtsprechung des Europäischen Gerichtshofs für Menschenrechte", in Bernhardt/Geck/Jaenick/Steinberger (hrsg), *Festschrift für Mosler*, Berlin 1983, 719-744

RESS, G. (1996)
"Wirkung und Beachtung der Urteile und Entscheidungen der Straßburger Konventionsorgane", (1996) *EuGRZ*, 350-353

RESS, G. (1999)
"Die EMRK und das Europäische Gemeinschaftsrecht: Überlegungen zu den Beziehungen zwischen den Europäischen Gemeinschaften und der Europäischen Menschenrechtskonvention", (1999) *ZEuS*, 471-485

REST, A. (1997)
"International Environmental Law in German courts", (1997) *EPL*, 409-420

RICHARDS, C. (2000)
"Sarran et Levacher: ranking legal norms in the French Republic", (2000) *E.L. Rev.*, 192-199

RÖBEN, V. (2000)
"Institutional Developments under Modern Environmental Agreements", (2000) *Max-Planck Yearbook of UN Law*, 363-443

RODRIGUEZ-IGLESIAS, G. (1995)
"Zur Stellung der EMRK im europäischen Gemeinschaftsrecht", in Beyerlin/Bothe/Hofmann/Petersmann, *Recht zwischen Umbruch und Bewahrung – Festschrift für Bernhardt*, Berlin 1995, 1269-1281

ROHDE, B. AND KALTENBORN, M. (1993)
"Neuere Entwicklungen im Assoziationsrecht der EG", in Coen/Hölscheidt/Pieper, *Europa '93 Auf dem Weg zur EU, Festschrift für Bleckmann*, Herne/Berlin 1993, 237-249

ROJAHN, O. (2000)
"Die Auslegung völkerrechtlicher Verträge in der Entscheidungspraxis des Bundesverwaltungsgerichts", in Geiger, R., (hrsg.), *Völkerrechtlicher Vertrag und staatliches Recht vor dem Hintergrund zunehmender Verdichtung der internationalen Beziehungen*, Baden-Baden 2000, 123-140

ROLIN, F. (2001)
"Case note on the Kress judgment of the ECrtHR", (2001) *ADJA*, 675-684

ROSAS, A. (1998)
"Mixed Union - Mixed Agreements", in Koskenniemi, M. (ed.), *International Law aspects of the EU*, The Hague 1998, 125-148

ROSAS, A. (2000A)
"The EU and mixed agreements", in Dashwood, A. and Hillion, C., *The General law of EC external relations*, London 2000, 200-220

ROSAS, A. (2000B)
"Case-note on C-149/96 (Portugal v. Council)", (2000) *CML Rev.*, 797-816

ROSAS, A. (2001)
"Implementation and enforcement of WTO Dispute Settlement Findings: An EU perspective", (2001) *JIEL*, 131-144

ROYLA, P. (2001)
"WTO-Recht–EG-Recht: Kollision, Justiziabilität, Implementation", (2001) *EuR*, 495-521
ROUCOUNAS, E. (1996)
"L'application du droit dérivé des Organisations Internationales dans l'ordre juridique interne", in Eisemann, P. (ed.), *The integration of International and European Community law into the national legal order*, The Hague 1996, 39-49
RUFFERT, M. (2000)
"Zuständigkeitsgrenzen internationaler Organisationen im institutionellen Rahmen der internationalen Gemeinschaft", (2000) *AVR*, 129-168
RUMPF, C. (1995)
"Zur Ausweitung der Freizügigkeit türkischer Arbeitnehmer durch die Rechtsprechung des EuGH", (1995) *RIW*, 764-768
RYDELSKI, M. (1995)
"Die nichtmilitärischen Sanktionen der VN", (1995) *RIW*, 803-807
SACK, J. (2001)
"Die EU in den Internationalen Organisationen", (2001) *ZEuS*, 267-284
SANDS, P. (1991)
"European Community Environmental Law: The Evolution of a Regional Regime of International Environmental Protection", (1991) *YLJ*, 2511-2523
SANDS, P. (1995)
Principles of International Environmental Law, Manchester 1995
SCHÄTZEL, W. AND SCHLOCHAUER, H.-J. (HRSG.) (1956)
Rechtsfragen der Internationalen Organisation – Festschrift für Wehberg zu seinem 70. Geburtstag, Frankfurt am Main 1956
SCHERMERS, H.G. (1987)
"The Netherlands" in Jacobs, F. and Roberts, S. (eds.), *The effect of treaties in domestic law*, London 1987, 109-122
SCHERMERS, H.G. AND BLOKKER, N., (2004)
International Institutional Law (4th ed.), The Hague 2004
SCHMID, CH. (1998)
"Immer wieder Bananen: Der Status des GATT/WTO-Systems im Gemeinschaftsrecht", (1998) *NJW*, 190-196
SCHMIDT, R. (2001) (1999) (1997)
"Neuere höchstrichterliche Rechtsprechung zum Umweltrecht", (2001) *JZ* 1165-1177 and (1999) *JZ*, 1147-1156 and (1997) *JZ*, 1042-1052
SCHNEIDER, H. (1999)
Wirtschaftssanktionen, Berlin 1999

SCHOLENS, H. (2001)
"Luchtvaartwetgeving", in Schuurman and Jordens, *Nederlanse Wetgeving*, Vol. 104-II, 2001
SCHOLZ, R. (1996)
"Kommentar zu Art. 23 GG", in Maunz, Th. and Dürig, G., *GG Kommentar*, München Lieferung Oktober 1996
SCHREUER, CH. (1977)
Die Behandlung internationaler Organakte durch staatliche Gerichte, Berlin 1977
SCHREUER, CH. (1981)
Decisions of International Institutions before domestic courts, London 1981
SCHREUER, CH. (1993)
"The waning of the sovereign state: Towards a new paradigm for international law?", (1993) *EJIL*, 447-471
SCHRÖDER, M. (1997)
"Kommentar zu Art. [ex] 227", in Groeben/Thiesing/Ehlermann (hrsg.), *Kommentar zum EU-/EG-Vertrag*, Vol. 5, Baden-Baden 1997, 442-474
SCHWENK, W. (1995)
Handbuch des Luftverkehrsrechts (2nd ed.), Köln 1995
SEIDL-HOHENVELDERN, I. AND STEIN, T. (2000)
Völkerrecht (10. Aufl.) Köln 2000
SEIDL-HOHENVELDERN, I. AND LOIBL, G. (2000)
Das Recht der Internationalen Organisationen (7. Aufl.) Köln 2000
SERMENT, L. (2002)
"Case note on the Kress judgment of the ECrtHR", (2002) *Rev. trm. dr. h.*, 223-258
SEVINGA, K. (2003)
"Open skies-arresten en wat erop volgde", (2003) *NTER*, 321-325
SEWANDONO, I. (1998A)
"Hebben de Turkse werknemer en zijn gezinsleden en kinderen een tewerkstellingsvergunning nodig?", (1998) *SEW*, 53-59
SEWANDONO, I. (1998B)
"Nachschrift – Besluit 1/80 van de Associatieraad EEG/Turkije is voor Nederland verbindend", (1998) *SEW*, 253-254
SEWANDONO, I. (2003)
"Annotatie Zaak C-413/99 *Baumbast*", (2003) *SEW*, 70-75
SHAW, I. (1997)
International Law (4th ed.), Cambridge 1997
SKUBISZEWSKI, K. (1968)
"A new source of the law of nations: Resolutions of International Organizations", in *En Hommage à Paul Guggenheim*, Genève 1968, 508-520

SNYDER, F. (2003)
"The gatekeepers: The European courts and WTO law", (2003) *CML Rev.*, 313-367

SØRENSEN, M. (1983)
"Autonomous legal orders: Some considerations relating to a systems analysis of IOs in the world legal order", (1983) *ICLQ*, 559-576

SPIELMANN, D. (1999)
"Human Rights case law in the Strasbourg and Luxembourg courts: Conflicts, Inconsistencies, and Complementarities", in Alston, P. (ed.), *The EU and Human Rights*, Oxford, 1999, 757-780

STAPLES, H. (1997)
"Een onbeperkt verblijfsrecht voor Turkse werknemer?", (1997) *NTER*, 269-272

STAPLES, H. (1999A)
"Legaal arbeid en toegang tot de arbeidsmarkt; nogmaals Besluit 1/80", (1999) *NTER*, 71-75

STAPLES, H. (1999B)
"De Associatieovereenkomst EEG-Turkije", (1999) *MR*, 179-187

STAPLES, H. (1999C)
"Toch nog directe werking voor Besluit 3/80", (1999) *NTER*, 243-249

STAPLES, H. (2000A)
"Het begrip openbare orde in de Turkije Associatieovereenkomst", (2000) *NTER*, 124-126

STAPLES, H. (2000B)
"De standstill-bepaling nader beschouwd", (2000) *NTER*, 265-268

STAPLES, H. (2002)
"Gelijke behandeling voor onderdanen van de Midden- en Oost-Europese landen die in een lidstaat arbeid in loondienst verrichten", (2002) *NTER*, 81-85

STAPLES, H. (2003A)
"Het verblijfsrecht van burgers van de Unie en hun familieleden", (2003) *NTER*, 49-54

STAPLES, H. (2003B)
"Annotatie Zaak C-60/00 *Carpenter*", (2003) *SEW*, 31-35

STEIN, E. (2001)
"International Integration and Democracy: No love at first sight", (2001) *AJIL*, 489-534

STEINBERGER, H. (1988)
"Entwicklungslinien in der neueren Rechtsprechung des Bundesverfassungsgerichts zu völkerrechtlichen Fragen", (1988) *ZaöRV*, 1-17

STOLL, P.-T. (1997)
"Freihandel und Verfassung. Einzelstaatliche Gewährleistung und die konstitutionelle Funktion der Welthandelsordnung (GATT/WTO)", (1997) *ZaöRV*, 83-146

STREINZ, R. (2001)
Europarecht (5. Aufl.) Heidelberg 2001
SUDRE, F. (2001)
"Case note on the Kress judgment of the ECrtHR", (2001) *La semain juridique*, 1568-1573
SZÉLL, P. (1996)
"Decision Making under Multilateral Environmental Agreements", (1996) *EPL*, 210-214
TAMMES, A. (1958)
"Decisions of International organs as a source of International Law", (1958) II *Recueil des Cours*, 261-364
TAMMES, A. (1962)
"Een ieder verbindende verdragsbepalingen", (1962) *NJB*, 69-80 and 89-99
TEMPLE LANG, J. (1986)
"The Ozone Layer Convention: A New Solution to the Question of Community participation in 'mixed' International Agreements", (1986) *CML Rev.*, 157-176
THIEME, D. (2001)
"European Community External Relations in the Field of Environment", (2001) *EEL Rev.*, 252-264
TIETJE, CH. (1999)
"The changing legal structure of International Treaties as an aspect of an emerging Global Governance architecture", (1999) *GYIL*, 26-55
TIMMERMANS, J. (2001)
"The constitutionalization of the EU", (2001-2002) *YEL*, 1-11
TOMUSCHAT, CH. (1993)
"Obligations arising for States without or against their will", (1993) IV *Recueil des Cours* 195-374
TOTH, A.G. (1984)
"The Authority of Judgments of the ECJ: Binding Force and Legal Effects", (1984) *YEL*, 1-77
TOTH, A.G. (1997)
"The EU and Human Rights: The way forward", (1997) *CML Rev.*, 491-529
TRÜE, C. (1997)
"Verleihung von Rechtspersönlichkeit an die EU und Verschmelzung zu einer einzigen Organisation-deklaratorisch oder konstitutiv?", *Vortrag, Reden und Berichte aus dem Europa-Institut*, Nr. 357, Saarbücken 1997.
TRÜE, C. (2000)
"Rechtspersönlichkeit der EU nach den Vertragsänderungen von Amsterdam: Wer handelt in GASP und PJZ?", (2000) *ZEuS*, 127-176

UERPMANN, R. (1993)
Die Europäische Menschenrechtskonvention und die deutsche Rechtsprechung, Berlin 1993

UERPMANN, R. (1995)
"Grenzen zentraler Rechtsdurchsetzung im Rahmen der VN", (1995) *AVR*, 107-130

UERPMANN, R. (2001)
"Internationales Verfassungsrecht", (2001) *JZ*, 565-573

UERPMANN, R. (2003)
"International law as an element of European constitutional law: International supplementary constitutions", *Jean Monnet Working Paper* 9/03

VAN BIJSTERVELD, S.C. (1992)
"Artikel 91" and 93", in Akkermans. P.W.C. and Koekkoek, A.K., *De Grondwet*, (2e druk) Zwolle 1992, 838-854 and 863-872

VAN DEN BOSSCHE, P. (1996)
"Een vraag die vragen doet rijzen", (1996) *NTER*, 211-213

VAN DEN BOSSCHE, P. (2004)
The Law of the WTO, Cambridge 2004

VAN DEN BOSSCHE, P. AND MARCEAU, G. (1998)
"Le système de règlement des différends de l'OMC", (1998) *Rev. du Marché Unique Européen*, 29-68

VAN DEN BROEK, N. (2001)
"Legal persuasion, political realism, and legitimacy: The European Court's recent treatment of the effect of WTO agreements in the EC legal order", (2001) *JIEL*, 411-440

VAN DER ESCH, B. (1988)
"Main issues of Community law governing access to air transport and member states control of fares", *Community Report (part I) to the 13th F.I.D.E Conference*, Saloniki, 28.9.-1.10.1988, 39-85

VAN DER VELDE, J. (1990)
"Case-note on the judgment of the Hoge Raad of 10.11.1989", (1990) *NJCM-Bulletin*, 584-588

VAN DER WAL, G. (2002)
"EHRM: het kantoor als woning", (2002) *NTER*, 191-194

VAN DIJK, P. (1995)
"Handelingen", *NJV 1995-II*, 69-70

VAN GRINSVEN, P. AND MELISSEN, J. (2002)
"Europese Raad tussen marginale aanpassing en radicale hervorming", (2002) *Internationale Spectator*, 421-425

VAN OOIK, R. (1997)
"Vrije vestiging van Oost-Europese prostitutie in Nederland", (1997) *NTER*, 245-248

VAN OOIK, R. (2002A)
" 'Een activiteit waarbij onder bezwaarde titel een dienst wordt verricht ten behoeve van de ontvanger, zonder dat materiële goederen worden geproduceerd of overgedragen' – Over de Jany-uitspraak en prostitutie als economische activiteit", (2002) *NTER*, 1-7

VAN OOIK, R. AND STAPLES, H. (2001)
"Het rechtstreekse beroep van Oost Europese zelfstandigen op de Europa Akkoorden", (2001) *NTER*, 313-320

VAN OOIK, R. AND STAPLES, H. (2002)
"Het recht op gezinsvorming en gezinshereniging volgens het Europese Hof van Justitie", (2002) *NTER*, 269-276

VAN PANHUYS, H.F. (1953)
"The Netherlands Constitution and International Law", (1953) *AJIL*, 537-558

VAN RIJN, TH. (1997)
"Kommentar zur Fischereipolitik", in Groeben/Thiesing/Ehlermann (hrsg.) *Kommentar zum EU-/EG-Vertrag*, Vol. 1, Baden-Baden 1997, 1012-1046

VANHAMME, J. (2001)
"Annotatie C-300/98 and C-392/98 Dior and Assco", (2001) *SEW*, 396-399

VEDDER, CH. (1988)
"Ausländerrecht für türkische Arbeitnehmer – Die Demirel-Entscheidung des EuGH, das BVerfG und die Folgen", (1988) *EuR*, 50-66

VEDDER, CH. (1994)
"Rechtswirkungen von Assoziationsratsbeschlüssen – Die Kus-Entscheidung des EuGH", (1994) *EuR*, 202-214

VERBOOM, J.J. (1998)
"De WAV en de Associatie-overeenkomst EEG-Turkije", (1998) *SEW*, 252-253

VERMULST AND MAVROIDIS AND WAER (1999)
"The functioning of the Appellate Body after 4 years", (1999) *JWT*, 1-50

VERSCHUEREN, H. (1997)
"Na het arrest Taflan-Met: is er leven na de dood?", (1997) *MR*, 29-34

VIERDAG, B. (1995)
Het Nederlandse verdragenrecht, Zwolle 1995

VIERING, M. (1998)
"Case note on the judgment of the ECrtHR in J.J. v. The Netherlands", (1998) *NJCM-Bulletin*, 884-895

VON BOGDANDY, A. (1999)
"The legal case for unity: The European Union as a single organization with a single legal system", (1999) *CML Rev.*, 887-910

VON BOGDANDY, A. AND BAST, J. AND ARNDT, F. (2002)
"Handlungsformen im Unionsrecht", (2002) *ZaöRV*, 77-161
VON MÜNCH, I. AND KUNIG, P. (2000)
Grundgesetz Kommentar (5. Aufl.), München 2000
WACHSMANN, P. (1998)
"L'article 55 de la Constitution 1958 et les conventions internationales relatives aux Droits de l'Homme", (1998) *RDP*, 1671-1685
WAGNER, E. (1998)
"The integration of Schengen into the framework of the EU", (1998) *LIEI*, 1-60
WASSENBERGH, H. (2000)
"Common Market, Open Skies and Politics", (2000) *Air & Space Law*, 174-183
WEBER, A. (1997A)
"Die Bananenmarktordnung unter Aufsicht des BVerfG?", (1997) *EuZW*, 165-169
WEBER, A. (1997B)
"Kommentar zu [ex] Art. 238", in Groeben/Thiesing/Ehlermann (hrsg.) *Kommentar zum EU-/EG-Vertrag*, Vol. 5, Baden-Baden, (5. Aufl.) 1997, 744-751
WEBER, A. AND MOOS. F. (1999)
"Rechtswirkungen von WTO-Streitbeilegungsentscheidungen im Gemeinschaftsrecht", (1999) *EuZW*, 229-236
WEBER, L. (1981)
Die Zivilluftfahrt im Europäischen Gemeinschaftsrecht, Berlin 1981
WEBER, C. (1995)
"Die Rechte erwerbsunfähiger türkischer Arbeitnehmer nach dem Assoizationsratsbeschluss EWG-Türkei Nr. 1/80", (1995) *NVwZ*, 1080-1082
WEILER, J.H.H. (1996)
"The jurisprudence of human rights in the EU: integration and disintegration, values and processes", *Harvard Jean Monnet Working Paper 2/96*
WEISS, E.B. (ED.) (1992)
Environmental Change and International Law, Tokyo 1992
WERKSMAN, J. (1996)
"The Conference of Parties to international treaties", in Werksman, J., (ed.), *Greening International Institutions*, London 1996, 55-68
WESSEL, R. (1999)
The EU's Foreign and Security Policy, The Hague 1999
WESSEL, R. (2003)
"The constitutional relationship between the EU and the EC: Consequences for the relationship with the Member States", *Jean Monnet Working Paper 9/03*

WIJMENGA, B. (2002)
"Internationale sanctieregimes en de gewijzigde Sanctiewet 1977", (2002) *SEW*, 42-51
WOUTERS, J. (2002)
"De Europese Unie als internationale actor na het Verdrag van Nice", (2002) *NTER*, 62-69
ZAMPINI, F. (1999)
"La Cour de justice des Communautés européennes gardienne des droits fondamentaux 'dans le cadre du droit communautaire', (1999) *RTD eur.*, 659-707
ZONNEKEYN, G. (1999)
"The legal status of WTO panel reports in the EC legal order", (1999) *JIEL*, 713-722
ZONNEKEYN, G. (2000A)
"The status of adopted panel and Appellate Body reports in the ECJ and CFI", (2000) *JWT*, 93-108
ZONNEKEYN, G. (2000B)
"The status of WTO law in the EC legal order – The final curtain?", (2000) *JWT*, 111-125
ZONNEKEYN, G. (2001)
"The latest on indirect effect of WTO law in the EC legal order the Nakajima case law misjudged?", (2001) JIEL, 597-608.
ZONNEKEYN, G. (2002A)
"Enkele kanttekeningen bij Verordening 1515/2001 inzake de tenuitvoerlegging van besluiten van het Orgaan voor geschillenbeslechting van de WTO", (2002) *SEW*, 97-101
ZONNEKEYN, G. (2002B)
"Annotatie Zaken T-18/99, T-30/99, T-52/99", (2002) *SEW*, 149-152
ZONNEKEYN, G. (2003)
"The ECJ's *Petrotub* judgment: towards a revival of the '*Nakajima* doctrine?'", (2003) *LIEI*, 249-266
ZOTT, R. (1999)
Der rechtliche Rahmen der innen- und justizpolitischen Zusammenarbeit in der EU, Diss., Frankfurt 1999
ZULEEG, M. (1996)
"Annotation of the Eroglu case", (1996) *CML Rev.*, 93-101

Table of Cases

Judgments and Opinions of the European Court of Justice and Opinions of Advocate Generals

Case 26/62 *van Gend & Loos* [1963] ECR 95 [English Edition], [1963] ECR 3 [Dutch Edition] 211, 213
Case 6/64 *Costa* v. *ENEL* [1964] ECR 1141 211, 212, 213
Case 22/70 *AETR* [1971] ECR 263 4
Case 21-24/72 *International Fruit Company* v. *Produktschap voor Groenten en Fruit* [1972] ECR 1219 29, 36, 44, 237
Case 9/73 *Schlüter* v. *Hauptzollamt Lörrach* [1973] ECR 1135 44
Case 167/73 *Commission* v. *France* [1974] ECR 359 114
Case 181/73 *Haegeman* v. *Belgium* [1974] ECR 449 4, 24, 31
Case 4/73 *Nold* v. *Commission* [1974] ECR 491 29, 166, 169
Case 36/75 *Rutili* [1975] ECR 1219 170
Case 87/75 *Bresciani* [1976] ECR 129 42, 44
Joined Cases 3,4, and 6/76 *Officier van Justitie* v. *Kramer* [1976] ECR 1279 55
Case 50/76 *Amsterdam Bulb* [1977] ECR 137 57
Case 230/78 *Eridania-Zuccherifici nazionali* [1979] ECR 2749 170
Case 270/80 *Polydor* v. *Harlequin Record Shops* [1982] ECR 329 41
Case 17/81 *Pabst & Richarz* v. *Hauptzollamt Oldenburg* [1982] ECR 1331 41
Case 104/81 *Hauptzollamt Mainz* v. *Kupferberg* [1982] ECR 3641 4, 31 *ff*, 36, 38 *ff*
Joint cases 267-269/81 *Amministrazione delle finanze dello Stato* v. *SPI and SAMI* [1983] ECR 801 29
Case 14/83 *Von Colson and Kamann* [1984] ECR 1891 223
Joined cases 209-213/84 *Ministère Public* v. *Lucas Asjes* [1986] ECR 1425 114
Case 222/84 *Johnston* [1986] ECR 1651 144, 166, 170, 176
Joined cases 201-202/85 *Klensch* [1986] ECR 3477 170
Case 257/85 *Dufay* v. *EP* [1987] ECR 1561 176
Case 46/86 *Romkes* [1987] ECR 2671 59
Case 12/86 *Demirel* v. *Stadt Schwäbisch Gmünd* [1987] ECR 3719 24, 27, 31 *ff*, 42, 62, 71, 160, 169, 170, 237
Case 314/85 *Foto-Frost* [1987] ECR 4199 153
Case 70/87 *Fediol* [1989] ECR 1781 38
Case 5/88 *Wachauf* [1989] ECR 2609 166, 170
Joined cases 46/87 and 227/88 *Hoechst* [1989] ECR 2859 174
Case 374/87 *Orkem* [1989] ECR 3283 175
Case C-192/89 *Sevince* v. *Staatssecretaris van Justitie* [1990] ECR I-3461 5, 24, 27, 33, 42 *ff*, 53, 63, 71, 139, 237
Joined cases C-297/88 and C-197/89 *Dzodzi* [1990] ECR I-3763 169, 170
Case C-231/89 *Gmurzynska-Bscher* [1990] ECR I-4003 170
Case C-106/89 *Marleasing* [1990] ECR I-4135 224
Case C-18/90 *Kziber* [1991] ECR I-199 41, 42, 44

Case C-69/89 *Nakajima* [1991] ECR I-2069 38, 143
Case C-260/89 *ERT* [1991] ECR I-2925 29, 30, 34, 166, 169, 170
Case C-258/89 *Commission* v. *Spain* [1991] ECR I-3977 55
Joined cases C-6/90 and C-9/90 *Francovich* [1991] ECR I-5357 225
ECJ Opinion 1/91 *EEA* [1991] ECR I-6079 41, 141, 142
Case C-163/90 *Legros* [1992] ECR I-4625 41, 44
Joined cases C-63/90 and 67/90 *Portugal and Spain* v. *Council*
[1992] ECR I-5073 56
Case C-237/91 *Kus* [1992] ECR I-6781 63, 71, 73
Case C-312/91 *Metalsa* [1993] ECR I-3751 41, 42, 44
Case C-58/93 *Yousfi* [1994] ECR I-1353 41-44
Case C-432/92 *Anastasiou* [1994] ECR I-3087 27, 44
Case C-379/92 *Peralta* [1994] ECR I-3453 33
Case C-404/92 *X* v. *Commission* [1994] ECR I-4737 29
Case C-280/93 *Germany* v. *Council* [1994] ECR I-4973 37, 138
Case C-355/93 *Eroglu* v. *Baden-Würtemberg* [1994] ECR I-5113 63, 64, 68, 69
ECJ Opinion 1/94 *WTO Agreement* [1994] ECR I-5267 27, 33, 135, 158, 159
Case C-103/94 *Krid* [1995] ECR I-719 41, 43, 44
Case C-465/93 *Atlanta Fruchthandelsgesellschaft* v. *Bundesamt für*
Ernährung and Fortswirtschaft [1995] ECR I-3761 138, 153
Case C-469/93 *Amministrazione delle finanze dello Stato* v.
Chiquita Italia [1995] ECR I-4533 37
Case C-25/94 *Commission* v. *Council* [1996] ECR I-1469 55
ECJ Opinion 2/94 *Accession of EC to the ECHR* [1996] ECR I-1759 165
Case C-84/95 *Bosphorus Hava* [1996] ECR I-3953 96, 172
Case C-61/94 *Commission* v. *Germany* [1996] ECR I-3989 24, 31, 33, 142, 164
Case C-277/94 *Taflan-Met* [1996] ECR I-4085 62, 64
Case C-126/95 *Hallouzi-Choho* v. *Bestuur van de Sociale*
Verzekeringsbank [1996] ECR I-4807 43, 44
Case C-124/95 *Centro-Com* [1997] ECR I-81 96, 98
Case C-177/95 *Ebony Maritime* [1997] ECR I-1111 98
Case C-299/95 *Kremzow* [1997] ECR I-2629 30, 170
Case C-368/95 *Familiapress* [1997] ECR I-3689 29, 169, 170
Case C-130/95 *Giloy* [1997] ECR I-4291 159, 169, 170
Case C-36/96 *Günaydin* v. *Freistaat Bayern* [1997] ECR I-5143 69
Case C-98/96 *Ertarnir* v. *Land Hessen* [1997] ECR I-5179 69
Case C-309/96 *Annibaldi* [1997] ECR I-7493 170
Case C-4/96 *NIFPO* [1998] ECR I-681 56
Joined cases C-364/95 and 365/95 *T.Port* [1998] ECR I-1023 138, 151
Case C-170/96 *Commission* v. *Council* [1998] ECR I-2763 220
Case C-53/96 *Hermès* [1998] ECR I-3603 33, 155, 158
Case C-389/96 *Aher-Waggon GmbH* v. *Germany* [1998] ECR I-4473 114, 117
Case C-185/95 P *Baustahlgewerbe* v. *Commission* [1998] ECR I-8417 171

Case C-416/96 *El Yassini* [1999] ECR I-1209 41
Case C-262/96 *Sürül* [1999] ECR I-2685 42, 43, 65, 74, 75
Case C-346/97 *Braathens Sverige* [1999] ECR I-3419 117
Case C-206/97 *Sweden* v. *Council* [1999] ECR I-3885 56
Case C-179/95 *Spain* v. *Council* [1999] ECR I-6475 56
Case C-104/97 P *Atlanta* [1999] ECR I-6983 138, 140, 143, 146
Case C-149/96 *Portugal* v. *Council* [1999] ECR I-8395 35*ff*, 82, 138, 143, 160
Case C-364/99 P (R) *DSR-Senator Lines* [1999] ECR I-8733 173
Case C-174/98 P *Netherlands and Van der Wal* v. *Commission*
[2000] ECR I-1 169
Case C-17/98 *Emesa Sugar* [2000] ECR I-665 175
Case C-340/97 *Nazli* [2000] ECR I-957 42, 64, 70
Case C-329/97 *Ergat* [2000] ECR I-1487 42, 64, 69
Case C-7/98 *Krombach* [2000] ECR I-1935 29, 171
Case C-37/98 *Savas* [2000] ECR I-2927 42, 70
Case C-237/98 P *Dorsch Consult* [2000] ECR I-4549 95
Case C-65/98 *Eyüp* [2000] ECR I-4747 42, 64, 70
Joined cases C-300/98 *Dior* and 392/98 *Assco*
[2000] ECR I-11307 33, 153, 155, 160
Case C-274/99 P *Connolly* v. *Commission* [2001] ECR I-1611 29
Case C-89/99 *Schieving-Nijstad* [2001] ECR I-5851 33, 155, 161
Case C-63/99 *Gloszczuk* [2001] ECR I-6369 43
Case C-235/99 *Kondova* [2001] ECR I-6427 43
Case C-257/99 *Barkoci and Malik* [2001] ECR I-6557 43
Case C-377/98 *Netherlands* v. *EP and Council* [2001] ECR I-7079 83
Case C-120/99 *Italy* v. *Council* [2001] ECR I-7997 56
Case C-268/99 *Jany and others* [2001] ECR I-8615 43
ECJ Opinion 2/00 *Biodiversity Convention* [2001] ECR I-9713 82
Case C-162/00 *Pokrzeptowicz-Meyer* [2002] ECR I-1049 35, 43
Joined cases C-27/00 and C-122/00 *Omega Air* [2002] ECR I-2569 117
Case C-13/00 *Commission* v. *Ireland* [2002] ECR I-2943 27
ECJ Opinion 1/00 *ECAA* [2002] ECR I-3493 142
Case C-60/00 *Carpenter* [2002] ECR I-6279 29, 34, 166, 169, 176
Case C-50/00 P *UPA* [2002] ECR I-6677 57, 58, 249
Case C-413/99 *Baumbast* [2002] ECR I-7091 34, 166, 169
Case C-94/00 *Roquette Frères* [2002] ECR I-9011 174, 182, 184
Cases C-466/98, C-467/98, C-468/98, C-469/98, C-471/98, C-472/98,
C-475/95, C-476/98 *Open skies agreements* [2002] ECR I-9427 115, 179
Case C-188/00 *Kurz* [2002] ECR I-10691 64
Case C-76/00 P *Petrotub* [2003] ECR I-79 38
Joined cases C-187/01 and C-385/01 *Gözütok and Brügge*
[2003] ECR I-1345 220
Case C-466/00 *Kaba* [2003] ECR I-2219 176, 182, 184

Case C-171/01 *Wählergruppe Gemeinsam Zajedno/Birlikte Alternative und Grüne GewerkschafterInnen/UG* [2003] ECR I-4301 64, 65
Case C-112/00 *Schmidgerger* [2003] ECR I-5659 30, 34, 171
Case C-109/01 *Akrich*, judgment of 23.9.2003 166
Case C-93/02 P *Biret* v. *Council*, judgment of 30.9.2003 40, 139, 140, 146, 242
Joined cases C-317/01 *Abatay et. al.* and C-369/01 *Sahin*, judgment of 21.10.2003 64
Case C-117/01 *K.B.*, judgment of 7.1.2004 166
Opinion AG Alber in Case C-93/02 P *Biret* v. *Council* of 15.5.2003 5, 24, 39, 53, 137, 140, 142, 145, 242
Opinion of AG Jacobs in Case C-263/02 *Jégo-Quéré* of 10.7.2003 57, 58

Judgements of the Court of First Instance

Case T-115/94 *Opel Austria* [1997] ECR II-39 35
Case T-184/95 *Dorsch Consult* [1998] ECR II-667 95
Case T-191/98 R *DSR- Senator Lines* [1999] ECR II-2531 173
Case T-18/99 *Cordis* [2001] ECR II-913 143, 237
Case T-30/99 *Bocchi Food Trade* [2001] ECR II-943 143
Case T-52/99 *T.Port* [2001] ECR II-981 143
Case T-174/00 *Biret* v. *Council* [2002] ECR II-17 38, 53, 139, 140, 145
Case T-220/96 *EVO* [2002] ECR II-2265 95
Case T-177/01 *Jégo-Quéré* [2002] ECR II-2365 57, 58
Case T-306/01 R *Aden e.a.* [2002] ECR II-2387 99
Case T-377/00 *Philip Morris International* v. *Commission* [2003] ECR II-1 144
Case T-47/03 R *Sison*, Order of the President of the CFI of 15.5.2003 99
Case T-191/98 and T-212/98-T-214/98 *Senator Lines et. al.*, judgment of 30.9.2003 173
[judgements an opinions from mid-1997 on are available at: http: //curia.eu.int/jurisp/cgi-bin/form.pl?lang=en]

Judgments of the European Court of Human Rights

Case of *Abdulaziz, Cabales and Balkandali* v. *UK*, judgment of 28.5.1985 177
Case of *Borgers* v. *Belgium*, judgment of 30.10.1991 175
Case of *Lombardo* v. *Italy*, judgment of 26.11.1992 176
Case of *Niemietz* v. *Germany*, judgment of 16.12.1992 174
Case of *Funke* v. *France*, 1993, judgment of 25.2.1993 175
Case of *Massa* v. *Italy*, 1993, judgment of 24.8.1993 176
Case of *Lobo Machado* v. *Portugal*, judgment of 20.2.1996 175
Case of *Vermeulen* v. *Belgium*, judgment of 20.2.1996 175
Case of *Bulut* v. *Austria*, judgment of 22.2.1996 175
Case of *Cantoni* v. *France*, judgment of 15.11.1996 172, 173
Case of *Ahmut* v. *the Netherlands*, judgment of 28.11.1996 177
Case of *Neigel* v. *France*, judgment of 17.3.1997 176

Case of *Hornsby* v. *Greece*, judgment of 19.3.1997 173
Case of *Van Orshoven* v. *Belgium*, judgment of 25.6.1997 175
Case of *J.J.* and *K.D.B.* v. *Netherlands*, judgment of 27.3.1998 175, 182
Case of *Reinhardt & Slimane-Kaïd* v. *France*, judgment of 31.3.1998 175, 184
Case of *Matthews* v. *UK*, judgment of 18.2.1999 172, 173
Case of *Pellegrin* v. *France*, judgment of 8.12.1999 176
Case of *Quadrelli* v. *Italy*, judgment of 11.1.2000 175
Case of *Voisine* v. *France*, judgment of 8.2.2000 175
Case of *Kress* v. *France*, judgment of 7.6.2001 175, 176, 184
Case of *Bosphorus Hava* v. *Ireland*, decision on the admissibility of 13.9.2001 172, 249
Case of *Sen* v. *the Netherlands*, judgment of 21.12.2001 177
Case of *S.A. Dangeville* v. *France*, judgment of 16.4.2002 174
Case of *Colas Est e.a.* v. *France*, judgment of 16.4.2002 174
Case of *Senator Lines* v. 15 *Member States of the EU* (application no. 56672/00), decision of President of ECrtHR to cancel hearing, http://www.echr.coe.int/Eng/Press/2003/oct/SenatorLinescancelled.htm 173, 249
[all judgments are available at: http://www.echr.coe.int/Eng/Judgments.htm]

WTO Panel and Appellate Body Reports

WT/DS8/AB/R, WT/DS10/AB/R, WT/DS11/AB/R, *Japan – Taxes on Alcoholic Beverages* (Appellate Body report of 8.11.1996) 131
WT/DS27/R, *EC – Regime for the importation, sale and distribution of bananas* (Panel report of 22.5.1997) 138
WT/DS27/AB/R, *EC – Regime for the importation, sale and distribution of bananas* (Appellate Body report of 9.9.1997) 138, 165
WT/DS26/AB/R, *EC – Measures concerning meat and meat products (Hormones)* (Appellate Body report of 16.1.1998) 138, 165
WT/DS27/ARB, EC – *Regime for the importation, sale and distribution of bananas* (Decision of the Arbitrators of 9.4.1999) 138, 165
WT/DS26/ARB, *EC – Measures concerning meat and meat products (Hormones)* (Decision of Arbitrators of 12.7.1999) 165
WT/DS27/ARB/ECU, *EC – Regime for the importation, sale and distribution of bananas* (Decision of Arbitrators of 24.3.2000) 165
WT/DS231/AB/R, *EC – Trade description of Sardines* (Appellate Body report of 26.9.2002) 157
[all reports are available at: http://www.wto.org/english/tratop_e/dispu_e/distab_e.htm]

International Court of Justice

27 February 1998, *Case concerning questions of interpretation and application of the 1971 Montreal Convention arising from the aerial incident at Lockerbie; Libyan Arab Jamahiriya v. United States of America*, Ruling on Preliminary Objections [available at: http://www.icj-cij.org/icjwww/idocket/ilus/ilusjudgment/ilus_ijudgment_980227_frame.htm] 249

The Netherlands

Raad van State (Afdeling Rechtspraak), 9.8.1984, AB 1985, 159 71
Raad van State (Afdeling Rechtspraak), 4.12.1990, AB 1991, 687 59
Raad van State (Afdeling Rechtspraak), 21.8.1993, AB 1994, 15 122
Raad van State (Afdeling bestuursrechtspraak), 26.10.1999, JM 1999, 165 88
Raad van State (Afdeling bestuursrechtspraak), 11.9.2002, JB 2002, 306 122
Raad van State (Afdeling bestuursrechtspraak), 11.6.2003, JM 2003, 95 82
Hoge Raad, 23.11.1984, NJ 1985, 604 155, 180
Hoge Raad, 30.5.1986 (*NS*), NJ 1986, 688 225
Hoge Raad (*Harmonisatiewet*), 14.4.1989, AB 1989, 207 20
Hoge Raad, 23.5.1989, NJ 1989, 759 59
Hoge Raad, 10.11.1989, NJ 1990, 628 181
Hoge Raad, 16.11.1990, NJ 1991, 475 21, 124
Hoge Raad, 1.10.1991, NJ 1992, 266 59
Hoge Raad, 10.5.1996, NJ 1996, 578 181
Hoge Raad, 12.9.1997, RvdW 1997, 168 181
Voorzitter College van Beroep voor het Bedrijfsleven, 11.9.1992, AB 1993, 317 105
College van Beroep voor het Bedrijfsleven, 19.8.1999, AB 1999, 472 106
President Rechtbank Rotterdam, 10.2.1993, AB 1993, 318 105
Rechtbank 's-Gravenhage, 10.6.1999, AWB 97, 13082 71
Rechtbank Rotterdam, 27.6.2000, JB 2000, 240 122

Germany

BVerfGE 58, 1, 23.6.1981 18
BVerfGE 59, 63, 10.11.1981 18
BVerfGE 73, 339, 22.10.1986 18
BVerfGE 74, 358, 26.3.1987 178
BVerfGE 75, 1, 31.3.1987 18
BVerfGE 77, 170, 29.10.1987 18
BVerfGE 89, 155, 12.10.1993 150, 151
BVerfG, 26.4.1995, EuZW 1995, 412-413 149
BVerfGE 102, 147, 7.6.2000 151
BVerwGE 75, 285, 17.12.1986 86

BVerwG, 5.10.1990, NVwZ-RR 1991, 118-129 119
BVerwG, 29.1.1991, NWvZ-RR 1991, 601-623 119
BVerwG, 12.12.1995, NVwZ 1996, 1116-1117 66
BVerwG, 12.6.1998, DVBl. 1998, 1184-1188 120
OVG Münster, 21.12.1994, NVwZ 1995, 820-821 69
VGH Baden-Würtemberg, 14.9.1994, InfoAuslR 1995, 51-53 69
VGH Mannheim, 7.11.1994, NVwZ 1995, 821-822 69
VGH München, 25.2.1998, ZLW 1999, 260-271 120
VG Frankfurt, EuZW 1997, 182 151
BGH, 21.4.1995, NJW 1995, 2174-2176 101
BGH, 28.9.1995, NJW 1996, 602-605 103
BAG, 12.2.1992, ZLW 1993, 199-208 119
BFH, 9.1.1996, EuZW 1996, 126-128 149
FG Hamburg, 19.5.1995, EuZW 1995, 413-416 138, 149

France

Conseil d'Etat, 20.11.1981 (*Syndicat national des officiers mécaniciens de l'aviation civile*), Lebon, 428-429 125
Conseil d'Etat, 20.10.1989, Rec. CE, 190 22
Conseil d'Etat, 8.6.1990 (no. 82146+82147+82154) 90
Conseil d'Etat, 13.4.1992, Lebon, 547 125
Conseil d'Etat, 12.2.1993 (no. 115468) 90
Conseil d'Etat, 30.1.1995 (no. 130238) 90
Conseil d'Etat, 23.10.1995 (*Association Artus et autres*) 91
Conseil d'Etat, 17.11.1995 (*Union juridique Rhône-Méditerranée*) 91
Conseil d'Etat, 14.2.1996, Rev.trim.dr.h. 1998, 397-410 183
Conseil d'Etat, 24.11.1997 (no. 171929) 183
Conseil d'Etat, 6.2.1998 (*Ministre de l'Environnement c/ ASPAS*) 91
Conseil d'Etat, 27.3.1998, RFD adm. 1998, 645 183
Conseil d'Etat, 19.6.1998 (no. 137404) 90
Conseil d'Etat, 28.7.1998 (no. 96PA02797 and 96PPA00484) 125
Conseil d'Etat, 29.7.1998 (*Esclatine*) (no. 179635 180208) 184
Conseil d'Etat, 7.10.1998 (*Larquetoux*), RFD adm. 1999, 362-365 125
Conseil d'Etat, 30.10.1998, RFD adm. 1998, 1081-1090 22
Conseil d'Etat, 6.11.1998 (no. 172563) 90
Conseil d'Etat, 30.12.1998 (*Association Artus*) 91
Conseil d'Etat, 6.1.1999 (no. 161403) 90
Conseil d'Etat, 12.3.1999 (*Société Heli-Union*), RGDIP 2000, 541-542 108
Conseil d'Etat, 14.4.1999 (no. 185954, 197159-197162) 90
Conseil d'Etat, 30.6.2000 (no. 98NT01333) 90, 91
Conseil d'Etat, 13.10.2000 (no. 210942) 183
Conseil d'Etat, 8.12.2000 (no. 204756) 91
Conseil d'Etat, 23.11.2001 (no. 19550) 125

Conseil d'Etat, 21.6.2002 (no. 240239) 22
Conseil d'Etat, 10.10.2003 (no. 245342) 73
Tribunal administratif de Saint-Denis-de-la Réunion, 19.2.1997 (*SOPTOM-Réunion*) 90
Cour administrative d'appel de Marseille statuant au contentieux, 28.12.1998 (no. 97MA00640) 91
Cour de Cassation, ch. crim., 8.11.1963, Bulletin crim. 1963, 315 126
Cour de Cassation, ch. crim., 29.6.1972 (no. 71-91581) 126
Cour de Cassation, ch. crim, 29.6.1972 (no. 71-91821) 126
Cour de Cassation, 27.6.1973 (no. 73-90057) 126
Cour de Cassation, 24.5.1975, RGDIP 1976, 960 22
Cour de Cassation, 10.12.1985 (no. 84-16033) 183
Cour de Cassation, 22.1.1985 (no. 84-10160) 183
Cour de Cassation, 10.3.1993 (no. 91-11310) 22
Cour de Cassation, 6.5.1997, Rec., 223 183
Cour de Cassation, ch. civile, 14.1.1999 (no. 97-14757) 75
Cour de Cassation, ch. civile, 14.1.1999 (no. 97-12487) 74
Cour de Cassation, 15.7.1999, J.D.I. 2000, 45-55 109
Cour de Cassation, 5.10.1999, Bull. civ. 1999, I, 167 183
Cour de Cassation, ch. civile, 21.10.1999 (no. 97-22040) 74
Cour de Cassation, ch. civile, 21.10.1999 (no. 97-22039) 74, 75
Cour de Cassation, ch. civile, 21.10.1999 (no. 98-10030) 75
Cour de Cassation, 9.2.2000 (no. 99-88054) 109
Cour de Cassation, 2.6.2000, RGDIP 2000, 1067-1094 22
Cour de Cassation, ch. civile, 13.7.2000 (no. 99-11358) 74
Cour de Cassation, ch. civile, 31.10.2000 (no. 99-11878) 74
Cour de Cassation, ch. civile, 25.1.2001 (no. 99-16462) 74
Cour de Cassation, ch. crim., 3.5.2001 (no. 00-81691) 162, 163
Cour de Cassation, ch. civile, 4.10.2001 (no. 00-11755) 74, 75
Cour de Cassation, 31.1.2002 (no. 00-18365) 183
Cour de Cassation, 30.5.2002 (no. 01-99010) 183
Cour administrative d'appel de Paris, 10.2.1998 (*Compagnie nationale Air France*), ADJA 1998, 227-228 125
Conseil Constitutionnel, 25.6.1986 (no. 86-207) 52

Abbreviations

Literature

AB	Administratiefrechtelijke Beslissingen – Rechtspraak Bestuursrecht
AJDA	L'Actualité juridique droit administratif
AJIL	American Journal of International Law
AVR	Archiv für Völkerrecht
AWB	Jurisprudentie Algemene Bijstandswet en Rijksgroepregelingen
BYIL	British Yearbook of International Law
CML Rev.	Common Market Law Review
DVBl.	Deutsches Verwaltungsblatt
EEL Rev.	European Environmental Law Review
EFA Rev.	European Foreign Affairs Review
EJIL	European Journal of International Law
E.L. Rev.	European Law Review
EPL	Environmental Policy and Law
EuGRZ	Europäische Grundrechte Zeitschrift
EuR	Europarecht
EuZW	Europäische Zeitschrift für Wirtschaftrecht
EWS	Europäisches Wirtschafts- und Steuerrecht
GYIL	German Yearbook of International Law
HRLJ	Human Rights Law Journal
ICLQ	International Comparative Law Quarterly
JB	Jurisprudentie Bestuursrecht
JM	Jurisprudentie Milieurecht
JDI	Journal du droit international
JIEL	Journal of International Economic Law
JWT	Journal of World Trade
JZ	Juristen Zeitung
InfoAuslR	Informationsbrief Ausländerrecht
LIEI	Legal Issues of Economic Integration
MR	Migratierecht
NILR	Netherlands International Law Review
NJ	Nederlandse Jurisprudentie
NJB	Nederlands Juristenblad
NJCM-Bulletin	Nederlands Juristen Comité voor de Mensenrechten
NJW	Neue Juristische Wochenschrift
NTER	Nederlands Tijdschrift voor Europees Recht
NVwZ	Neue Zeitschrift fürVerwaltungsrecht
NVwZ-RR	NVwZ Rechtsprechungs-Report
NYIL	Netherlands Yearbook of International Law
RDP	Revue du droit public
RFD adm.	Revue française de droit administratif
RECIEL	Review of European Community and International Environmental Law

Rev. trm. dr. h.	Revue trimestrielle des droits de l'homme
RGDIP	Revue générale de droit international public
RIDC	Revue internationale de droit comparé
RIW	Recht der Internationalen Wirtschaft
RJE	Revue Juridique de l'Environnement
RTD eur.	Revue trimestrielle de droit européen
RvdW	Rechtspraak van de week
SEW	Sociaal-Economische Wetgeving
YEL	Yearbook of European Law
YIEL	Yearbook of International Environmental Law
YLJ	Yale Law Journal
ZaöRV	Zeitschrift für ausländisches und öffentliches Recht und Völkerrecht
ZEuS	Zeitschrift für Europarechtliche Studien
ZLW	Zeitschrift für Luft- und Weltraumrecht
ZRP	Zeitschrift für Rechtspolitiek

Other

AB	Appellate Body
AG	Advocate General
BFH	Bundesfinanzhof
BGBl.	Bundesgesetzblatt
BGH	Bundesgerichtshof
BVerfG	Bundesverfassungsgericht
BVerfGE	Entscheidungen des Bundesverfassungsgerichts
BVerwG	Bundesverwaltungsgericht
BVerwGE	Entscheidungen des Bundesverwaltungsgerichts
CF	Constitution Française
CFI	Court of First Instance
CFSP	Common Foreign and Security Policy
COP	Conference of Parties
DSB	WTO Dispute Settlement Body
DSU	WTO Dispute Settlement Understanding
EC	European Community
ECJ	European Court of Justice
ECHR	European Convention on Human Rights
ECrtHR	European Court of Human Rights
ECR	European Court Reports
ECT	EC Treaty
EU	European Union
FH	Finanzhof
FTAs	Free Trade Agreements
GATS	General Agreement on Trade in Services

GATT	General Agreement on Trade in Goods
GG	Grundgesetz
Gw.	Grondwet
ICAO	International Civil Aviation Organization
ICJ	International Court of Justice
ILC	International Law Commission
IOs	International Organizations
JHA	Justice and Home Affairs
J.O.	Journal Officiel de la République Française
MEAs	Multilateral Environmental Agreements
MOP	Meeting of Parties
OJ	Official Journal of the European Union
OVG	Oberverwaltungsgericht
SC	Security Council
TACs	Total allowable catches
TEU	Treaty on European Union
TRIPS	Agreement on Trade-Related Aspects of Intellectual Property Rights
UN	United Nations
VG	Verwaltungsgericht
VGH	Verwaltungsgerichtshof
WTO	World Trade Organization

Index

Association Agreement
EC-Turkey *31 ff, 42, 53, 61 ff, 70 ff*
Association Council Decisions *61 ff, 128, 139 ff*
-direct effect *42, 43, 63 ff*
-Dutch legal order *72, 73*
-European legal order *63, 64*
-French legal order *74, 75*
-German legal order *68 ff*
-supremacy *76*
Ausbrechender Gemeinschaftsakt *150 ff*
—
Common Foreign and Security Policy (II. pillar) *191 ff*
-Common Position *193 ff*
-direct effect *214 ff*
-Joint Action *198 ff*
-supremacy *214 ff*
Common Commercial Policy *98, 111, 136, 137*
Communitarization *60, 70, 110, 127, 148, 228 ff*
Conference of Parties/Meeting of Parties (COP/MOP) *76, 77*
-decision-making process *78*
-structure *77, 78*
—
Decisions of COPs/MOPs *76 ff*
-Dutch legal order *87*
-European legal order *81 ff*
-French legal order *89 ff*
-German legal order *84 ff*
Decisions of International Organizations (IOs) *7 ff, 13*
-Dutch legal order *50*
-European legal order *52*
-French legal order *51*
-German legal order *49*
Direct effect
-decisions of IOs *53, 56, 63 ff, 82 ff, 101 ff, 122 ff, 143 ff*
-treaties *35, 36, 41*
—
EC law *211 ff*
-direct effect *211, 212*
-supremacy *212-214*
Effet utile *62, 68, 222, 225*
European Constitution (draft) *26, 32, 57, 136, 137, 171, 177, 187, 193, 217, 217, 221, 243, 247*
European Convention on Human Rights *29, 30, 34, 131 ff, 165 ff*
-Dutch legal order *180*
-European legal order *168 ff*
-French legal order *182*
-German legal order *177 ff*
European Council *191 ff, 203, 216*
—
General Agreement on Trade and Tariffs (GATT) *27 ff*
-direct effect *35 ff, 135, 138, 140, 148 ff*
—
General Agreement on Trade in Services (GATS) *27, 37, 134, 135, 152, 186*
—
International Civil Aviation Organizatiion (ICAO) *111 ff*
-decision-making process *113, 114*
-ICAO Council *112 ff*
-structure *111 ff*
ICAO Annex *112 ff*
-Dutch legal order *120*
-European legal order *114 ff*
-French legal order *124*
-German legal order *118 ff*
Ieder verbindende bepaling *50, 89, 155, 244*
Interaction between ECJ and EcrtHR *171 ff*
International Organizations *11 ff*
-decisions *13, 14*
-definition *11 ff*
International Treaties
-direct effect *35 ff*
-Dutch legal order *19 ff*
-European legal order *23 ff*

- -French legal order 21 *ff*
- -German legal order 17 *ff*
- -jurisdiction of ECJ 31 *ff*, 169 *ff*, 192, 216 *ff*
- -mixed agreements 158 *ff*
- -supremacy 18 *ff*

—

Judgments of the European Court of Human Rights 132, 133, 165 *ff*
- -direct application 166
- -divergent interpretation 174 *ff*
- -Dutch legal order 180 *ff*
- -European legal order 166 *ff*
- -field of application of EC law 169, 170
- -French legal order 182 *ff*
- -German legal order 177 *ff*
- -incorporation model 167, 178, 180 *ff*
- -jurisdiction of ECJ 169 *ff*
- -source of inspiration 166, 169

Jurisdiction European Court of Justice
- -decisions of IOs 63 *ff*, 139 *ff*
- -EC law 31, 169 *ff*, 218
- -EU law 217 *ff*
- -international treaties 31 *ff*, 158 *ff*, 169 *ff*

Justice and Home Affairs (III. pillar) 203 *ff*
- -Common Position 204, 205
- -Decision 209, 210
- -direct effect 218 *ff*
- -Framework Decision 205-209
- -supremacy 218 *ff*

—

Multilateral Environmental Agreements (MEAs) 76 *ff*

—

Regional Fisheries Organizations 53 *ff*
- -decision-making process 54, 55
- -Dutch legal order 58
- -European legal order 55 *ff*
- -French legal order 59
- -German legal order 57
- -structure 54, 55
- -Total Allowable Catches (TACs) 53, 54

—

SARPS 112, 118, 119, 126

Security Council 94 *ff*

Security Council Resolutions 94 *ff*
- -Dutch legal order 104 *ff*
- -European legal order 94 *ff*
- -French legal order 107 *ff*
- -German legal order 100 *ff*
- -Sanctions 94 *ff*

—

(Agreement on) Trade-related Aspects of Intellectual Property Rights (TRIPS) 134, 135, 152 *ff*

Transformation 27, 33, 37

—

World Trade Organisation 134 *ff*

WTO Agreement 27, 37 *ff*, 134

WTO Dispute Settlement Body
- -Appellate Body 131, 134, 140, 141, 156
- -Panel 131, 134, 148, 150, 156
- -reversed consensus 134, 236

WTO Dispute Settlement reports
- -banana dispute 137 *ff*, 149 *ff*
- -direct effect 137 *ff*, 148 *ff*
- -Dutch legal order 155 *ff*
- -European legal order 135 *ff*
- -French legal order 162 *ff*
- -German legal order 148 *ff*
- -hormones dispute 138, 139, 163, 165
- -*Nakajima/Fediol* rule 38, 138, 144 *ff*, 163 *ff*, 241 *ff*
- -supremacy 139 *ff*, 147 *ff*

WTO Dispute Settlement Understanding 38, 39, 131 *ff*, 140 *ff*, 152 *ff*

—

UN Charter 94 *ff*, 201

—

Völkerrechtsfreundlichkeit 18, 153, 154

—

Zustimmungsgesetz 148, 178

Samenvatting

Besluiten van Internationale Organisaties in de Europese en nationale rechtsorde van geselecteerde EU lidstaten

De centrale vraag die ten grondslag ligt aan dit onderzoek is de invloed van het Gemeenschapsrecht op de status en de werking van besluiten van Internationale Organisaties (IOs) in de nationale rechtsorde van drie geselecteerde EG lidstaten (Duitsland, Nederland, Frankrijk).

Omdat de EG in toenemende mate bevoegdheden op steeds meer beleidsterreinen krijgt, wordt de EG steeds vaker lid van IOs en partij bij verdragen – al dan niet samen met de lidstaten. Hierdoor moet de EG regelmatig besluiten van IOs uitvoeren – veelal in plaats van de EG lidstaten. De uitvoering geschiedt ten dele op basis van Europese wetgeving en ten dele op basis van algemene beginselen, die door de jurisprudentie van het Hof van Justitie toegepast worden. Als gevolg hiervan worden besluiten van IOs eerst door Gemeenschapsrecht 'getransformeerd', d.w.z. ze worden deel van het EG recht. Dit heeft als consequentie dat de besluiten gemeenschapsrechtelijke trekken krijgen, zoals voorrang op het nationale recht en directe werking indien aan bepaalde voorwaarden wordt voldaan. Deze transformatie heeft gevolgen voor de nationale rechtsorde van de EG lidstaten.

Vanwege het feit dat IOs meestal op basis van een verdrag worden opgericht, bestaat er een nauwe relatie tussen besluiten van IOs en verdragen. Dit verband wordt door de praktijk in Duitsland, Nederland, Frankrijk en de EG bevestigd. In de praktijk worden verdragen en besluiten van IOs in het algemeen gelijk behandeld en hebben zij derhalve dezelfde status en werking in het interne recht. Om deze reden is in hoofdstuk 2 eerst onderzocht, wat de status en de werking van verdragen in de drie geselecteerde lidstaten en de EG is. Het blijkt dat vanwege de constitutionele verschillen tussen de drie onderzochte lidstaten de status van verdragen verschilt. In Duitsland worden verdragen door het aannemen van een wet (*Zustimmungsgesetz*) in de Duitse rechtsorde ingevoerd. Pas daarna worden ze deel van de rechtsorde (Art. 59 (2) *Grundgesetz*). De status van de verdragen in de Duitse rechtsorde wordt gekoppeld aan de status van het *Zustimmungsgesetz*. De verdragen hebben een lagere status dan het *Grundgesetz* en zijn gelijk aan andere wetten. In Nederland daarentegen zijn verdragen na ondertekening en ratificatie automatisch deel van de Nederlandse rechtsorde zonder dat wetgeving nodig is. Bovendien genieten verdragen op grond van Art. 94 *Grondwet* voorrang en directe werking op tegenstrijdig Nederlands recht – inclusief het constitutionele recht – als het 'een ieder verbindende bepaling' betreft. Wanneer een bepaling 'ieder verbindend' is, wordt per geval door de rechter besloten. In Frankrijk genieten verdragen op grond van Art. 55 *Constitution Française* voorrang op wetten maar niet op de constitutie en andere constitutionele bepalingen.

De hierboven geschetste situatie is *grosso modo* ook op besluiten van IOs van toepassing. Er bestaan echter wezenlijke verschillen tussen verdragen en besluiten van IOs. Zo behoeven in tegenstelling tot verdragen besluiten van IOs normaliter geen ratificatie, zodat het aannemen van een besluit door de IO voldoende is om verplichtingen aan de leden op te leggen. Ook voorzien steeds meer IOs in een besluitvormingsprocedure waarbij een meerderheid van stemmen volstaat, terwijl staten formeel alleen aan een verdrag gebonden zijn als zij dat ondertekend en geratificeerd hebben (Art. 34 Verdrag van Wenen inzake het verdragsrecht, 1969). Dit betekent dat besluiten van IOs vaak ook tegen de wil van leden genomen kunnen worden en bindend kunnen zijn – tenzij er een *opt-out* clausule van toepassing is. In de rechtsorde van de EG tenslotte worden – volgens de jurisprudentie van het Hof van Justitie – verdragen die door de EG (mede)gesloten zijn integraal deel van de gemeenschapsrechtsorde. Hierdoor genieten zij voorrang op conflicterend secundair EG recht (bijv. richtlijnen, verordeningen) en kunnen zij directe werking hebben als zij voldoen aan de door de jurisprudentie van het Hof van Justitie gestelde eisen. Bovendien genieten de zodanig 'getransformeerde' verdragen voorrang op het gehele nationale recht van EG lidstaten.

In hoofdstuk 3 is de transformatie door het EG recht van een aantal besluiten van IOs nader onderzocht. De keuze van de onderzochte besluiten is gebaseerd op de verschillende verdeling van bevoegdheden. Er is onderscheid gemaakt tussen situaties van exclusieve bevoegdheid en exclusief lidmaatschap van de EG in IOs. Ook is onderscheid gemaakt tussen situtaties van gezamenlijke bevoegdheden en gezamenlijk lidmaatschap van EG en lidstaten in de IO. Tenslotte is er een onderscheid gemaakt tussen situaties zonder bevoegdheid en lidmaatschap van de EG en exclusieve bevoegdheid en lidmaatschap van de lidstaten.

Als voorbeeld van een exclusieve bevoegdheid van de EG gecombineerd met exclusief lidmaatschap van de EG zijn besluiten van verschillende regionale visserijorganisaties onderzocht. Op grond van de exclusieve bevoegdheid van de EG op het gebied van visserij is alleen de EG lid van de verschillende visserijorganisaties. In dit geval is de transformatie van de besluiten van de visserijorganisaties door het EG recht volledig, dat wil zeggen, de besluiten worden geheel door de EG in verordeningen omgezet, die als Gemeenschapsrecht in de EG lidstaten gelding hebben. Dit betekent dat uit de optiek van de lidstaten de besluiten van de visserijorganisaties als 'normaal' EG recht worden gezien.

Als voorbeeld van een gemengd akkoord waarbij de EG en de lidstaten gezamenlijk partij zijn, zijn besluiten van de Associatieraad opgericht door het Associatieverdrag tussen de EG, de EG lidstaten en Turkije onderzocht. De besluiten van de Associatieraad kunnen zowel binnen de bevoegdheid van de EG als die van de lidstaten vallen. De Associatieraad heeft drie belangrijke besluiten (1/80, 2/80, 3/80) genomen om de rechtspositie van Turkse werknemers en hun familieleden die in de EG lidstaten werken en verblijven te regelen.

Het Hof van Justitie heeft aan een aantal bepalingen van deze Associatieraadsbesluiten directe werking toegekend. Haar dynamische uitleg, die de rechtspositie van Turkse werknemers in de EG lidstaten verbeterd heeft, stuitte op veel verzet met name in Duitsland en Nederland. Vanwege de transformatie van de Associatieraadsbesluiten middels de jurisprudentie van het Hof van Justitie, zijn deze besluiten integraal deel van het EG recht geworden en genieten zij daardoor voorrang op het nationaal recht en kunnen zij directe werking in de EG lidstaten hebben. Nationale rechtbanken moesten derhalve de uitleg van het Hof van Justitie volgen. Dit is een goed voorbeeld van het versterkende karakter dat het EG recht op de transformatie van de status en het effect van besluiten van IOs kan hebben.

Als tweede voorbeeld van gemengd lidmaatschaap en gezamenlijke bevoegdheden van de EG en de lidstaten zijn de besluiten van Conference/Meeting of Parties (COPs/MOPs) die door verschillende milieuverdragen opgericht zijn onderzocht. De transformatie van COP/MOP besluiten illustreert dat de transformatie al naar gelang het onderwerp binnen of buiten de bevoegdheid van de EG kan liggen. De transformatie van COP/MOP besluiten die binnen de bevoegdheid van de EG vallen vindt plaats zowel door Europese wetgeving als ook door de jurisprudentie van het Hof van Justitie. In deze gevallen worden de besluiten dus eerst in EG recht getransformeerd voordat zij in de rechtsorde van de EG lidstaten komen. De andere besluiten die binnen de bevoegdheid van de lidstaten blijven, worden daarentegen gewoon volgens het respectievelijke nationaal recht omgezet.

In het derde voorbeeld is de omzetting van bindende Resoluties van de VN Veiligheidsraad onderzocht. Hoewel de EG geen lid van de VN is, zet zij, als gevolg van haar exclusieve bevoegdheid met betrekking tot de handelspolitiek toch de Veiligheidsraadresoluties die economische sancties tegen een staat opleggen om. Veiligheidsraadsancties worden eerst door de EU (Gemeenschappelijke standpunten) en dan door een EG (verordening) omgezet. De EG-lidstaten worden dus door het Europees recht gebonden om de Veiligheidsraadsancties uit te voeren. Tegelijkertijd blijven de EG lidstaten als leden van de VN verplicht om de Veiligheidsraadsancties om te zetten. Hier is dus sprake van een dubbele verplichting voor de EG lidstaten om Veiligheidsraadresoluties om te zetten.

Het laatste onderzochte voorbeeld betreft besluiten van de Internationale Burgerluchtvaartorganisatie (ICAO). Hoewel de EG geen lid van de ICAO is zet zij soms toch besluiten van de ICAO Council (Annex) in Gemeenschapsrecht om. Dit gebeurt met name als een ICAO Annex een onderwerp regelt (bijvoorbeeld geluidsnormen van vliegtuigen) dat binnen de bevoegdheid van de EG valt. Tengevolge hiervan leggen de door het EG recht 'getransformeerde' ICAO Annexen gemeenschapsrechtelijke verplichtingen aan de EG lidstaten op. Hierdoor krijgen zij voorrang op het nationale recht en kunnen zij directe werking hebben.

In hoofdstuk 4 wordt de transformatie door het EG recht van rechterlijke en quasi-rechterlijke besluiten onderzocht. Deze besluiten hebben in beginsel alleen geldigheid voor de betrokken partijen in een specifiek geschil.

Het eerste voorbeeld betreft de rapporten van panels en van de Beroepsinstantie van de Wereld Handelsorganisatie (WTO). In geval van een geschil tussen de leden van de WTO kunnen de leden het geschil aan een panel voorleggen en laten beslechten. Zij kunnen tegen een rapport van een panel in hoger beroep gaan bij de Beroepsinstantie, die als hoogste instantie het geschil door het uitbrengen van een rapport beslecht. Omdat de panels en de Beroepsinstantie onafhankelijk van de WTO leden hun rapporten uitbrengen, kan men deze als quasi-rechterlijke besluiten van de WTO kwalificeren. De EG en de EG lidstaten zijn leden van de WTO en zijn derhalve beiden voor de omzetting van de WTO verplichtingen, inclusief WTO rapporten, verantwoordelijk. Volgens de rechtspraak van het Hof van Justitie maken zowel het WTO verdrag als ook de WTO rapporten, die binnen de bevoegdheid van de EG vallen, integraal deel uit van de Gemeenschapsrechtsorde. Voorbeelden van WTO rapporten waarbij problemen zijn opgetreden, zijn de rapporten van de bananen en met hormonen behandeld vlees. De WTO heeft vastgesteld dat de bananen-verordening van de EG niet conform WTO recht is. Ook in Duitsland achten enkele rechtbanken de bananen-verordening niet conform het WTO recht. Desondanks heeft het Duitse *Bundesverfassungsgericht* als hoogste rechter besloten dat de bananenverordening in Duitsland van toepassing blijft, zonder inhoudelijk te beslissen of deze strijdig is met het WTO recht of met het Duitse *Grundgesetz*. Het Hof van Justitie en het Gerecht van eerste aanleg weigeren om de verordening aan het WTO recht te toetsen. Als gevolg hiervan is het noch voor Duitsland noch voor particuliere importeurs van bananen mogelijk om zich op het WTO rapport te beroepen om de verordening aan te vechten. Omdat ook de nationale rechtbanken aan de jurisprudentie van het Hof van Justitie gebonden zijn en deze jurisprudentie voorrang op het nationale recht geniet, blijft de verordening van kracht zodat de EG en de lidstaten verhoogde invoerrechten voor de invoer van producten naar de VS betalen. Deze situatie herhaalt zich min of meer bij het geschil met betrekking tot met hormonen behandeld vlees. Dit is een voorbeeld waar de invloed van EG recht de werking van besluiten van IOs niet versterkt maar juist afzwakt.

In het tweede voorbeeld van hoofdstuk 4 wordt de interactie tussen het EG recht en arresten van het Europees Hof voor de Rechten van de Mens en het Europese Verdrag voor de Rechten van de Mens (EVRM) onderzocht. Hoewel de EG geen partij bij het EVRM is en formeel dus niet aan het EVRM en de arresten van het EVRM Hof gebonden is, verwijst het Hof van Justitie sinds de jaren 1990 steeds vaker naar het EVRM en de jurisprudentie van het EVRM Hof. Hierdoor is het EVRM recht geleidelijk onderdeel van het EG recht geworden. Recentelijk is het Hof van Justitie nog een stap verder gegaan door het EVRM direct toe te passen. Hierdoor krijgt het EVRM en de jurisprudentie van het

EVRM Hof net zoals EG recht voorrang op het hele nationale recht van de EG lidstaten. Tegelijkertijd blijven de EG lidstaten partij van het EVRM en zijn zij dus ook aan de uitspraken van het EVRM Hof gebonden. Dit betekent dat twee hoven het EVRM interpreteren en toepassen. Hoewel dit meestal in harmonie gebeurt zijn er ook voorbeelden te vinden waar een divergentie van de jurisprudentie voorkomt.

In hoofdstuk 5 wordt de invloed van het Gemeenschapsrecht op de besluiten van de EU in de Tweede pijler (Gemeenschappelijk Buitenlands en Veiligheidsbeleid) en Derde pijler (Politiële en Justitiële Samenwerking) onderzocht. In tegenstelling tot de Eerste pijler (EG verdrag) die door de gemeenschapsrechtelijke principes (voorrang en directe werking) en door de betrokkenheid van Commissie, Europees Parlement en Hof van Justitie wordt gekenmerkt (supranationaal), zijn de Tweede en Derde pijler door de centrale rol van de Raad en van de lidstaten en de beperkte rol van de andere EG instellingen meer intergouvernementeel van aard. Uit die optiek zijn de besluiten die door de EU op het gebied van de Tweede en Derde pijler vis-à-vis de lidstaten worden genomen, enigszins vergelijkbaar met besluiten van andere IOs vis-à-vis de lidstaten. Het is niet zonder meer duidelijk of het recht van de Tweede en Derde pijler voorrang en directe werking geniet zoals het EG recht. De directe werking is voor Derde pijler kaderbesluiten uitdrukkelijk uitgesloten. Desalniettemin wordt de stelling verdedigd dat ondanks de bestaande verschillen tussen enerzijds de Eerste pijler en anderzijds de Tweede en Derde pijler, deze verschillen niet zo groot zijn dat de invloed van EG recht uitgesloten is. Hiervoor kan op de volgende aspecten gewezen worden. Ten eerste moet het gehele Europees recht als eenheid worden beschouwd omdat het door dezelfde IO uitgevaardigd wordt. Ten tweede bestaan er wel degelijk verbanden – zowel institutioneel als ook materieel – tussen de verschillende pijlers. Het zijn immers dezelfde organen die in alle pijlers volgens hun bevoegdheden bij de totstandkoming van het Europees recht betrokken zijn (Art. 3, 5 EU verdrag). Daarnaast bestaan er materiële verbanden tussen de Tweede en Eerste pijler bij de omzetting van Veiligheidsraadsancties, die zowel een Tweede pijler als ook een Eerste pijler besluit vereisen. Bovendien zijn er veel minder verschillen tussen de Derde en Eerste pijler dan tussen de Tweede en Eerste pijler. Als gevolg hiervan is dus ook wat betreft de Tweede en meer nog Derde pijler besluiten het EG recht wel van invloed. Dat betekent dat Tweede en Derde pijler besluiten ook voorrang op het nationale recht hebben en dat directe werking indien aan de eisen van het Hof voldaan is wel mogelijk is – tenzij het uitdrukkelijk uitgesloten is. Deze ontwikkeling wordt door de voorgestelde nieuwe Europese constitutie voortgezet. In de constitutie wordt inderdaad voorrang aan het gehele Europese recht op het nationale recht vastgelegd. Ook worden de verschillen tussen de Eerste en Derde pijler verwijderd. Alleen de Tweede pijler, waar het intergouvernementele regime van toepassing blijft, blijft gehandhaafd. Men kan dus concluderen dat hoewel minder dan bij besluiten van andere IOs een zekere invloed van het EG recht op Tweede en Derde pijler besluiten vast te stellen is.

Samenvattend kan worden gesteld dat de transformatie van besluiten van IOs door Gemeenschapsrecht grote gevolgen heeft voor de nationale rechtsorde van de EG lidstaten. 'Getransformeerde' besluiten van IOs worden integraal deel van het EG recht en genieten uit dien hoofde voorrang op tegenstrijdig secundair Gemeenschapsrecht als ook op het gehele nationale recht van de EG lidstaten. Bovendien kunnen deze besluiten directe werking hebben indien zij aan de eisen, die door het Hof van Justitie en het Gerecht van Eerste Aanleg gesteld worden, voldoen. Uit de onderzochte praktijk blijkt dat de transformatie van besluiten van IOs door Europese wetgeving in de lidstaten weinig problemen oplevert. De transformatie van besluiten van IOs door Europese jurisprudentie daarentegen levert wel een aantal goede voorbeelden op die de interactie tussen besluiten van IOs, Europees recht en nationaal recht illustreren. Omdat de EG – straks de Unie – haar bevoegdheden zal blijven uitbreiden, zal interactie tussen het Europees en het internationaal recht – zij het verdragen of besluiten van IOs – die binnen de reikwijdte van het EG recht (straks Unie recht) vallen – alleen maar blijven toenemen. Deze conclusie doet vragen rijzen, zoals over de democratische en rechterlijke controle van IOs en hun besluiten, die hier uitdrukkelijk niet aan de orde waren, maar waar in toekomst nader onderzoek naar gedaan dient te worden.

Curriculum Vitae

Curriculum Vitae

N. Lavranos, geboren 13.3.1971 in Frankfurt, studeerde van 1990-1996/97 rechten aan de J.W. Goethe Universität Frankfurt (1. Staatsexamen). In het studiejaar 1992-1993 was hij ERASMUS uitwisselingsstudent aan de Universiteit Maastricht. In het studiejaar 1996-1997 heeft hij een Masters of Law (L.L.M.) (*cum laude*) in Europees en Internationaal Recht aan de Universiteit Maastricht behaald. In 1998 heeft hij het Diploma in EU Law van de Academy of European Law, EUI, Florence ontvangen. Tussen 1997 en eind 2001 was hij als AIO, later onderzoeker, verbonden aan de Universiteit Maastricht, waar ook dit onderzoek grotendeels plaatsgevonden heeft.

Sinds eind 2001 is hij als Universitair Docent Europees Recht en Senior Onderzoeker Internationaal Recht verbonden aan de Universiteit van Amsterdam, Faculteit der Rechtsgeleerdheid.

List of Publications 1994 – 2004

1) DNA-Profiling and information technology – A new weapon for crime detection and prevention?, in: *European Journal of Crime, Criminal Law and Criminal Justice* 1994, issue 4, pp. 359-378.
2) Nouveaux développements dans le secteur de l'energie dans l'Union européenne à la lumière de l'affaire Almelo, in: *Tendances actuelles et évolution de la jurisprudence de la Cour de justiceet du Tribunal de première instance des Communautés européennes: suivi annuel, Volume 2, Sous la direction de Spyros A. Pappas*, EIPA Maastricht 1995, pp. 137-150.
3) Burundi: A way out of the dilemma?, in: *International Peacekeeping*, Vol. 3, No. 1 (December 1995/January 1996), pp. 8-11 (samen met Ch.Mayer and Th.Kurzidem).
4) Datenschutz in Europa – Am Beispiel der Datenschutzrichtlinie, des Schengen Information System (SIS) und Europol, in: *Datenschutz und Datensicherheit*, July 1996, pp. 400-408.
5) Helms-Burton en de EU, in: *Internationale Spectator*, Jaargang 51, nr.10, Oktober 1997, pp. 563-566 (samen met Prof. Cees Flinterman).
6) Bookreview: European ambitions of the national judiciary, in: *Maastricht Journal of European and Comparative Law*, Vol. 5, No. 2, 1998, pp. 210-216.
7) Die Rechtswirkungen von WTO panel reports im Europäischen Gemeinschaftsrecht sowie im deutschen Verfassungsrecht, in: *Europarecht*, Vol. 34, No. 3, May-June 1999, pp. 289-308.
8) Besteht wirklich ein Demokratie-Defizit in der EG? – Anmerkungen zu Christine Lemkes Beitrag "Europa als politischer Raum", in: *Kritische Justiz*, Vol. 31, No.3, 1999, pp. 426-429.

9) Bookreview: The EU and its European Court of Justice, in: *Maastricht Journal of European and Comparative Law,* Vol. 7, No. 3, 2000, pp. 326-330.
10) An Introduction into the Regional Economic Integration process of the Americas, in: *Zeitschrift für Europarechtliche Studien* (ZEuS), Vol. 4, No. 1, 2001, pp. 127-164.
11) Annotatie: Gevoegde zaken T-186/97 (Kaufring e.a.v. Commission), in: *SEW* 2002, pp. 62-63.
12) Multilateral Environmental Agreements: Who makes the binding decisions?, in: *European Environmental Law Review* 2002, pp. 44-50.
13) Some Proposals for a Fundamental DSU reform, in: *Legal Issues of Economic Integration,* 2002, pp. 79-87.
14) Annotatie: Zaak C-89/99 (Schieving-Nijstad v. Groeneveld), in: *SEW* 2002, pp. 192-195.
15) Case-note: C-89/99 (Schieving-Nijstad v. Groeneveld), in: *Legal Issues of Economic Integration* 2002, pp. 323-333.
16) Case-note: C-466/98 et. al. (open skies agreements), in: *Legal Issues of Economic Integration,* 2003, pp. 81-91.
17) Europol and the fight against terrorism, in: *European Foreign Affairs Review* 2003, pp. 259-275.
18) Europol en de oorlog tegen terrorisme – een eerste analyse, in: *Veiligheid' en het recht van de EU,* pp. 123-131, 32. zitting Asser Instituut Colloquium Europees Recht, T.M.C. Asser Press, The Hague 2003.
19) Die begrenzte, funktionelle Unabhängigkeit der Europäischen Zentralbank – Anmerkung zum Urteil des EuGH vom 10.7.2003, Rs. C-11/00 (Kommission gegen EZB), in: *Europarecht* 2003, pp. 878-887.
20) The limited, functional independence of the ECB, in: *European Law Review* 2004, pp. 115-123.
21) Die EG darf WTO-Recht weiterhin ignorieren, to be published in: *EWS* 2004, issue 4.